MYTHMAKER

Also by John Baxter

The Cinema of Josef von Sternberg

The Gangster Film

Science Fiction in the Cinema

Hollywood in the Thirties

Hollywood in the Sixties

Sixty Years of Hollywood

Stunt:
The Great Movie Stuntmen

The Hollywood Exiles

Ken Russell:
An Appalling Talent

Buñuel

Fellini

Steven Spielberg:
The Unauthorized Biography

Stanley Kubrick:
A Biography

Woody Allen:
A Biography

MYTHMAKER

The Life and Work of GEORGE LUCAS

JOHN BAXTER

SPIKE
AN AVON BOOK

AVON BOOKS, INC.
1350 Avenue of the Americas
New York, New York 10019

Copyright © 1999 by John Baxter
Published by arrangement with HarperCollins*Publishers,* UK
ISBN: 0-380-97833-4

Library of Congress Cataloging in Publication Data:

Baxter, John, 1939–
   Mythmaker : the life and work of George Lucas / John Baxter.—1st ed.
      p.   cm.
"An Avon book."
Filmography: p.
Includes bibliographical references and index.
1. Lucas, George. 2. Motion picture producers and directors—United States Biography. I. Title.
PN1998.3.L835B39   1999   99-37051
791.43'0233'092—dc21   CIP

First Spike Printing: October 1999

SPIKE TRADEMARK REG. U.S. PAT. OFF. AND IN OTHER COUNTRIES, MARCA REGISTRADA, HECHO EN U.S.A.

Printed in the U.S.A.

FIRST EDITION

QPM 10 9 8 7 6 5 4 3 2 1

www.spikebooks.com

To Marie-Dominique
Moveable feast

CONTENTS

ILLUSTRATIONS

Marcia Lucas, *née* Griffin. *(© Peter C. Bosari/People in Pictures)*

Michael Eisner as head of Paramount gave the green light for *Raiders of the Lost Ark* (1981). *(© London Features International)*

Harrison Ford's Indiana Jones. *(© The Ronald Grant Archive)*

Lucas with Steven Spielberg, director of the *Indiana Jones* films; collaborators but also long-time rivals.

The three directors of the *Star Wars* cycle: Irvin Kershner, Lucas, and Richard Marquand.

Kershner, Gary Kurtz, Lucas, and Lawrence Kasdan on the set of *The Empire Strikes Back* (1980). *(© The Ronald Grant Archive)*

Between pages 338 and 339

Richard Marquand and Lucas on location in the redwoods of Northern California with the stars of *Return of the Jedi*. *(© The Ronald Grant Archive)*

Line producer Howard Kazanjian with Lucas and Marquand on the set of *Return of the Jedi*.

Bill Norton, who wrote and directed *More American Graffiti* (1979).

Lucas and Ron Howard on location for *Willow* (1988).

Aubree Miller as Cindel, held hostage by the giant King Terak (Carel Struycken) in *Ewoks: The Battle for Endor* (1983).

Stuntmen doubling as Tim Robbins and the eponymous hero in the climactic chase of *Howard the Duck* (1986).

Lucas on the set of *The Young Indiana Jones Chronicles* (1992). *(© Corbis/Everett)*

For the 'Special Edition' of 1997, Lucas reshoots a scene in *Return of the Jedi*. *(© Corbis/Everett)*

Lucas in the archive at Skywalker Ranch. *(© Corbis/Everett)*

ACKNOWLEDGMENTS

Many people were kind enough to share their memories of George Lucas, notable among them his long-time collaborator, producer, and friend Gary Kurtz, who also made available his unique personal archive of production stills from *Star Wars*. Without his insights, this book would be far less revealing of the man with whom he worked so closely for so many years.

In Hollywood, John Milius was customarily generous with his time and hospitality – a contact which I owe to Adrian Turner, who, with this project as with so many others, has been eminently supportive. Marjorie van Ackeren introduced me to Randy Thom, who gave many fascinating insights into the sound landscape of Lucasfilm. Patrick McGilligan allowed me to use sections of the conversations I had with Lawrence Kasdan for a forthcoming edition of his *Backstory* anthology series, while I'm grateful to Mr Kasdan and to his assistant Jamie Dinsmore for arranging the meeting.

Lucas's friends from the USC days were unfailingly open and generous with their reminiscences. I'm particularly grateful to Charley Lippincott, and his many hours of detailed recollection, as well as access to his personal files. Don Glut gave a vivid account of the USC years, and introduced me to Randy Epstein, whose memories and photographs of that period were invaluable. Richard Walter found time in a busy schedule at UCLA to evoke the mood of USC and describe writing the first version of *American Graffiti*.

In Modesto, I had the great good fortune to be introduced by Alex Kresge to Dot and Cullen Bearden, who offered me their hospitality, as well as their detailed memories of Modesto. This was augmented by Ed Bearden who, with his wife Roberta, was more than generous in locating yearbooks, clippings and other documentary evidence of Lucas's *Graffiti* years, and in giving a flavor of life in Modesto at that time. I am also grateful to editor Mark Varche and picture researcher Katie Roberts of the *Modesto Bee* for access to their files.

In Los Angeles, the generosity and hospitality of old friends Kelvin

Jones, Bill Warren, Tom Rudolph, and Julie Ansell never faltered at even the most demanding request. At this stage of my research, I was extremely fortunate to have the input of Jon Davison, as well as Bruce Bozarth, who gave me access to his encyclopedic knowledge of the world of Edgar Rice Burroughs, and Mark Evanier and John Morrow, who know all there is to know about Jack Kirby and *The New Gods*. Jim Carroll described Marin County in the sixties in a way which brought the period and the place to life. At the University of Southern California, Valarie Schwan screened all of Lucas's student films. During preliminary research, Charles Silver and Ron Magliozzi of the Museum of Modern Art Film Center in New York were customarily helpful.

In London, Harley Cokeliss and Jean Marsh shared memories of working with Lucas. I also took advantage of earlier interviews conducted with Paul Freeman, Bill Hootkins, Julian Glover, Denholm Elliott, and Tom Stoppard for my biography of Steven Spielberg to illustrate the chapters on *Raiders of the Lost Ark*. David Thompson of the BBC and Bill McClure of CBS were generous in the access they offered to TV material about Lucas. John Brosnan lent to me from his collection of documents and magazines covering the world of science fiction cinema. Mary Troath acted as the most assiduous and indefatigable of researchers.

Bill Warren was lavish in his advice and assistance, and kindly read the manuscript, correcting numerous errors and misconceptions. Through Bill, I also had access to a wide circle of experts on all phases of science fiction film. In a no less friendly gesture, Patrick McGilligan also read the book in its final stages, bringing to it his considerable skill both as film scholar and editor. Finally, it was read a third time by Robert Lacey at HarperCollins, the kind of copy editor every author hopes for, but seldom finds. My editorial director Richard Johnson was, as usual, unfailing supportive, informative and good-humored. My warmest thanks to all.

John Baxter
Paris, 1999

There are times when reality becomes too complex for oral communication. But legend gives it a form by which it pervades the whole world.

The computer Alpha 60 in *Alphaville,* by Jean-Luc Godard

The Emperor of the West

The Man in the Panama Hat (years older now) removes
the Cross of Coronado from Indy's belt.
PANAMA HAT: This is the second time I've had to
reclaim my property from you.
INDY: That belongs in a museum.
PANAMA HAT: So do you.

From *Indiana Jones and the Last Crusade.* Screenplay by
Jeffrey Boam, from a story by Menno Meyjes and George Lucas

As he neared his sixtieth year, George Lucas sat in the shade on the
red-brick patio of his home at Skywalker Ranch in Northern California
and thought about destiny.

Almost without realizing it, he had become a legend – a man larger
than life, magnified by his achievements, but dwarfed by them too.
Over forty years, head down, brow furrowed, working every day and
most of every night, ignoring discomfort and ill-health, banishing
every distraction to the edge of his vision, he had created something
remarkable. An empire. A fortune. A myth.

He was not a myth to himself. Only a megalomaniac takes his legend
at face value. A sense of his ordinariness was part of the reason he'd
succeeded. At first, the awe of his acolytes had puzzled him. Then
he'd been amused, but irritated too; he'd been brought up to scorn
self-advertisement and conceit.

But as one ages, adulation rests more comfortably on the shoulders.
Occasionally, these days, he surrendered to the belief that perhaps he
could really achieve anything on which he fixed his energy and instinct.

Other men, less able, less driven than he, paused before embarking
on a project, and sometimes wondered, 'Why am I doing this? What

will be its effects, on me and on others?' They pondered, worried, took advice.

In the beginning, Lucas had sometimes done that, but not lately. Myths don't hesitate.

There was something presidential, even a touch imperial, in his certainty. Though it wasn't something he confided to many people, he knew history. He'd read of Julius Caesar looking out on his empire and proclaiming, 'I came, I saw, I conquered.' He knew of Napoleon as a young officer surveying a world disordered by revolution and being seized by a vision of mankind united under a single rational mind. Above all, he understood Alexander the Great pausing at the end of his last campaign and weeping because there were no new worlds to conquer.

Yet he, a man less favored in his birth, less wealthy, less powerful, less educated, had achieved more than any of these men. He'd conquered not only this world, but other worlds besides. He was, in his way, master of the universe.

Or so his admirers said.

Was it true? He looked around for somebody to ask, and found only the smiling, alert faces of people anxious to do whatever he ordered, agree with whatever he said, set to work on anything he planned.

A legend is always alone.

On 4 July 1980, while Skywalker Ranch was still scrub and pasture, Lucas hosted his first cook-out on the site. There had been nothing much here in those days: just scrub, some cows, and a few deer which had become over the years the main reason for any stranger venturing this far north in Marin County. The spot where the grills were set up had once been occupied by banks of refrigerators to preserve the carcasses of game slaughtered by hunters.

Twenty-five years of construction and landscaping had transformed the old Bulltail Ranch. Anybody driving up from San Francisco along Route 101 and turning onto Lucas Valley Road at the exit marked 'Nicasio' found themselves passing through an expensive housing development, then twisting through an idyllic landscape of rivers and waterfalls. Discreetly, a shining wire fence paralleled the road, just out of sight in the woods. Signs every few yards warned that the fence was electrified – to keep in the deer and other livestock that roamed the estate, explained the custodians of the ranch, though everyone knew of George's nervousness about strangers, and his fears of kidnap.

After eight miles, a sign so undemonstrative that you might well miss it unless you were looking led to a side road that wound through tall redwoods to a guardhouse. Security staff checked the visitors' credentials against a list of people deemed *persona non grata* – ungrateful executives, sceptical critics, invasive journalists, technicians insufficiently respectful of Lucas or his managers. In one famous case, two special-effects technicians had been discovered after a cook-out, 'drunk as skunks,' according to one report, in that holy-of-holies, George's private office. They joined the list of people 'banned from the ranch' – a phrase so much in currency within the effects community that one Los Angeles group took it as its business name.

Those who passed inspection were directed down the hill into the huge underground parking station, where their cars' presence wouldn't intrude on the rural calm. Any who remembered the ranch from the first cook-out didn't recognise it now. A three-storied *fin de siècle* mansion clad in white clinker-built planks like a whaling ship, topped with shingled gables and fringed with wide verandahs, stared west across a wide artificial lake and landscaped grounds to a cluster of equally antique-looking buildings on the far side of the valley.

For centuries, European landowners had built 'follies' on their estates. One could have one's own Roman ruins, with carefully shattered pillars, a picturesquely tumbled wall or two, some fragments of sculpture. Or a grotto in the Gothic style, its fountains decorated with old metalwork that might, if you didn't look too closely, have been looted from some Etruscan tomb. Such buildings bought the owner an instant pedigree, an off-the-hook connection between a *nouveau riche* family and the ancient world.

Skywalker Ranch went one better. If anyone asked, staff recounted an invented history as carefully constructed as any screenplay. They were told that the property had been a monastery until a retired sea captain bought it in 1869. He built the Main House, which recalled the 'cottages' constructed on Newport, Rhode Island, by Vanderbilts and Whitneys at the turn of the century as summer retreats. The captain added a gatehouse the following year, and a stable. In 1880, he was supposed to have diversified into wine-making and built the large brick winery, which was given *art moderne* additions by a forward-looking descendant in 1934. In 1915, another innovative son erected a house spanning a brook on the estate, using the then-fashionable Arts and Crafts style pioneered by William Morris in the late nineteenth century. Later additions included the two-story library in polished redwood under a dome of *art nouveau* stained glass, its shelves housing a well-used and comprehensive reference collection.

On the other side of the valley, 'unwanted relatives' of the captain occupied conveniently remote guesthouses – named, in a lapse of historical authenticity, for Lucas's cultural heroes: Orson Welles, John Huston, George Gershwin. After incidents like the encroachment of the drunken effects men, visitors only entered the main house by invitation. To get into the private compound around the Main House, you needed a coded key-card.

The illusion of old money was as meticulous as anything created in Hollywood at the height of its reconstructive powers in the 1940s. The Victorian-style double-hung windows and other fixtures were made in a workshop on the estate, which also maintained a studio for creating stained glass. The library's well-rubbed redwood came from a demolished bridge in California's Newport Beach, the books in its glassed cabinets from Paramount Pictures; they'd once been the studio's reference library. The two thousand mature oaks, bays, and alders spotted around the 235 redeveloped acres of the ranch were trucked in from Oregon.

One visitor who opened a door marked 'Staff Only' found herself staring into a bunker filled with video surveillance equipment. Hidden cameras watched every corner of the estate; conduits snaking under the tranquil meadows carried enough electrical, telephone, and computer cables to feed a small town. The extent of the ranch's electronics could faze even Lucas. In 1997, looking for a socket into which to plug a journalist's tape recorder, he pulled up a corner of the carpet to reveal a tangle of wires. 'So *that's* what's under there,' he murmured.

In 1987, Lucas retained the San Francisco firm of Rudolph and Sletten to build a 'winery.' A red-brick two-story building with two large wings and an imposing central entrance leading to a three-story atrium with wooden galleries and a glass roof resembled other winemaking facilities in the area. In fact the building housed Skywalker Sound, 150,000 square feet of state-of-the-art post-production studios in the form of eight mixing stages. San Francisco's *avant-garde* Kronos Quartet recorded here. So did the Grateful Dead, and singer Linda Ronstadt. The largest facility, Studio A, also known as the Stag

Theater, replicated a high-style pastel *art deco* cinema of the thirties. Its ninety-six-track mixing console was twenty-four feet long, and on a film like Robert Redford's *The Horse Whisperer* demanded eighty-five technicians.

Elsewhere on the ranch, what looked like a two-story barn held the negatives of Lucas's films and the Lucas Archive. From 1983, Lucasfilm's first archivist, David Craig, began photographing, documenting, and collecting the models, art-work – ten thousand items alone – costumes, story-boards and accumulated relics of the Lucas legend: 'objects of artistic, cultural, and historical significance,' according to the authorized catalog. Donald Bies became archivist in 1988, and helped plan the building, which opened in November 1991.

Lucas's own office in the Main House held no hint of how he earned the money to build and maintain this empire. Friends like Steven Spielberg filled their offices with framed posters, awards, and signed photographs from presidents and box-office legends. Lucas displayed no souvenirs at all of his film career – no references to film at all, except for a pair of Disney bookends. Opposite his desk was a large painting of the enmeshed gears of a sixteenth-century clock. The artist, Walter Murch, a minor modernist of the thirties, was the father of Lucas's close friend, also Walter Murch, who edited *American Graffiti* and with whom, rare for Lucas, he had remained close since they met at college. Elsewhere in the house hung originals by illustrator Maxfield Parrish and *Saturday Evening Post* cover artist Norman Rockwell, artist by appointment to those who, like Lucas and Spielberg, another Rockwell collector, yearned for the imagined certainties of American small-town life between the wars.

Downstairs, inside the front door, a few items, battered relics of Captain Lucas's film-faring days, were displayed behind glass. They included Indiana Jones's stained felt hat and whip; an *ewok*, one of the cuddly forest animals from *Return of the Jedi*, whom Lucas modeled on his then-two-year-old daughter Amanda; a heavily nicked light saber from *Star Wars*; and a creature from *Willow*. The case next to it was empty – for trophies of future triumphs? Or because reality has not kept pace with the growth of the illusion? Because, disguised by all this celebration of past triumphs was the puzzling fact that Lucas had not until 1999 actually directed a film in almost twenty years.

The one aspect of Lucas's activities not relocated to Skywalker by the late nineties was Industrial Light and Magic, which still operated out of San Rafael, outside San Francisco. In 1988, Lucasfilm had opened negotiations with Marin County to develop more of the ranch as a production facility, and to move in ILM. When the supervisors bridled, Lucas offered to set aside most of the remaining thousand acres for 'conservation,' while continuing to own and patrol it. Meanwhile, he kept buying surrounding properties, though not without a fight from local farmers and the zoning authorities. By 1996, he owned 2500 acres and was negotiating for more.

The battle with his neighbors was typical of Lucas's tentative hold on his retreat. In a quarter-century, more than the ranch had changed. Lucas was the second-largest employer in the county. Power calls to power; money draws money. Skywalker had become a focus for the hopes, ambitions, and needs of millions. There was magic in this place, but also greed, resentment, and fear.

Around dawn on any fourth of July during the mid-1990s, hundreds of people would have been on the road heading for Skywalker Ranch, and Lucas's annual cook-out.

The first of them had flown up from Los Angeles on the early shuttle and collected rented cars at San Francisco airport – or been collected, if they had that kind of clout, as many did; there are some invitations that even the highest executives disregard at their peril.

Leaning back in their limos, the agents, producers, and stars skimmed *Variety* and *Hollywood Reporter*. It would be a long trip, and the headlines reminded them why they were making it. '*Star Wars*' All-Time Boxoffice Force,' shrilled *Variety*. 'Lucas' Series Paid off in Spades.' The story spelled out the news, happy for their host, that the three *Indiana Jones* films he'd produced and helped write, the *Star Wars* trilogy he'd conceived and the first of which he'd written and directed, the TV series *The Young Indiana Jones Chronicles*, and the animated films in the series *The Land Before Time* were all making money.

So were his other enterprises. LucasArts Licensing was earning millions from franchising toys, clothes, drinks, candy, comic books, and games inspired by his films. One manufacturer alone, Galoob, would sell $120 million-worth of *Star Wars* toys that year, and the original licensee, Kenner, which still owned some rights, could also have survived comfortably on nothing but *Star Wars* light sabers,

Imperial stormtrooper helmets, and models of Han Solo's ship the *Millennium Falcon* and the series' characters. 'Since the first film came out,' noted one report, '*Star Wars* merchandise sales have totaled more than $2.5 billion. It's safe to say, in fact, that *Star Wars* single-handedly created the film-merchandising business.' So expert was LucasArts Licensing that outside enterprises like the TV series *Saturday Night Live* and the environmental Sierra Club had become clients.

Industrial Light and Magic, founded by Lucas in suburban Los Angeles in 1975 to produce the special effects for *Star Wars*, was now worth $350 million, and had become the world's premier provider of movie special effects. It created *Jurassic Park*'s dinosaurs and arranged for Tom Hanks to shake hands with Jack Kennedy in *Forrest Gump*. THX Sound, developed by Lucas engineers, was gaining ground in theaters across the world, and his recording complex, Skywalker Sound, had a reputation as the best in America. LucasArts Games, LucasArts Learning . . . Whatever George Lucas touched turned to gold. And the gold stuck to his fingers. No financial pages listed these companies. Lucas owned every share of stock himself.

That the staid Sierra Club trusted him with its merchandising wasn't surprising. Lucas radiated probity – too much probity, thought some. Though the movie journal *Millimetre* lauded Lucasfilm as 'a profitable multi-departmental corporation that defines the cutting edge of American film-making,' the *Boston Globe* detected an omnipresent fogey-ism in its creations. A Lucas production, it wrote, 'always seems to be about something like pre-war adventurers or pre-Vietnam teenagers or pre-television broadcasting. Even *Star Wars* is set in the far past, not the far future, and its style famously turned American movies back to old-fashioned (critics say old-hat) narrative strategies.'

Few of the people who distributed Lucasfilms' products, worked on them, bought or sold their merchandise or otherwise derived a living from the group, had any such criticisms. True, British actress Jean Marsh, who played Queen Bavmorda in the fantasy *Willow*, did remark tartly that none of its actors relished being merchandised – 'We would all pay *not* to be on the T-shirts and things' – but she was in the minority. Most felt that, as long as it filled the coffers, Lucas could dramatize *Pollyanna*, or film *Aesop's Fables*.

The cars took at least thirty minutes to skirt downtown San Francisco, cross the sweep of the Golden Gate Bridge, with giant tankers creeping out to sea so far below that they looked like models in a special-effects sequence, and climb the curve of the cliff onto Highway 101, the sole autoroute north into Marin County, and another world.

The social misfits and renegades who fled here in the late sixties, seeking to preserve the spirit of the Summer of Love from a San Francisco inhabited by panhandlers, dope addicts, porn-movie producers, and prostitutes, discovered a haven in old and sleepy towns like San Anselmo, San Rafael, Mill Valley, and Bonitas. Locals found themselves patronizing the hardware store along with long-haired, bearded men, ethereal-looking women in ground-brushing muslin, and barefoot babies. Teepees and geodesic domes mushroomed in the woods, fringed by private gardens of organic vegetables, with, just a few yards down the track, a patch of marijuana, exclusively for private use.

To the relief of locals, the newcomers weren't particularly anxious to share their new lifestyle. When the town council of Bonitas, on the Pacific Coast, erected signs saying 'Welcome to Bonitas,' the hippies took them down. Most felt they already had just as many friends and neighbors as they needed. 'The ideal in those days,' said one refugee from the midwest who briefly settled there in the 1970s, 'was a narrow road winding through the woods without any signs, and a little house at the end. I couldn't stand it. That's no way to live – without people. I moved to San Francisco.'

Sausalito, just across the Golden Gate, gave the first clue to Lucas's guests that they'd moved into this new world. Once San Francisco's yacht port, a cluster of boatyards and little dockside bars, its waterside warehouses now belonged to companies making models for movies, or sound designers like Ear Circus, the company of Randy Thom, who'd won an Oscar for the sound recording of Francis Ford Coppola's *Apocalypse Now*, and who'd worked too on Lucas's ill-starred production *Howard the Duck*.

Thom, large, bear-like, and, like most of the people behind the scenes of special-effects films, shy and soft-spoken, was also on the road, heading north to the ranch. He'd had an office there while he was working on *Howard the Duck*, but after that he'd gradually moved away, until now he hardly visited the place. Like a lot of people who'd joined Lucasfilm in the heady days of its crusading energy, he'd made his own way. Except for Dennis Muren, now head of Industrial Light and Magic, none of the people who'd started ILM under John Dykstra still had jobs there. Nor did most of those who worked on *Star Wars* in other capacities.

Lucas's wife Marcia had gone too, divorcing him in 1983. It surprised many people that the marriage had lasted so long. Marcia edited Lucas's early films, and was good enough to be asked by Martin Scorsese to cut *Alice Doesn't Live Here Any More*, *Taxi Driver*, and *New York New York*. In George's conflicts with the studios and with Francis Coppola, she'd remained loyal, even when she didn't share her husband's obsession. Life with George was no picnic. The narrowness of his vision could be overpowering. 'I heard this story,' says Harley Cokeliss, second-unit director on *The Empire Strikes Back*, 'that Marcia wanted a particular painting for her birthday. She dropped hints and dropped hints and dropped hints, until she was sure even George had got the message. On her birthday, he said, "I've got a nice surprise for you." As Marcia looked around for her painting, George said, "I'm going to have the roof fixed."'

John Milius was on the road, and wondering why he bothered. He and George went back longer than almost anyone. Before *Star Wars*, before *American Graffiti* and *THX1138*, back to 1963, when Lucas was a weedy, close-mouthed kid from upstate California, sitting through the same courses at the film school of the University of Southern California. In the famous malapropism of producer Samuel Goldwyn, they had all passed a lot of water since then – and, in Milius's case, put on a lot of weight. Except that his beard was gray, George still looked the same. But then, he would probably look the same when another twenty years had passed.

Milius assumed that their oldest mutual friend Francis Coppola wouldn't be at the cook-out. The excuse would be the standard one – he was on location on some film. But everyone knew that the two men were no longer close, and that, even though Coppola's vineyards were only a twenty-minute drive from the ranch, George and he seldom saw one another. With Lucas, some rivalries never went away: 'I bear grudges,' he has said.

Coppola had led the move away from Los Angeles. His company American Zoetrope in San Francisco was meant to create a new Hollywood in Marin County. For a while after its collapse, Milius and the rest of the group half-believed that Lucas might pick up where Coppola left off. The mansion he and Marcia bought on Parkway in

San Anselmo as headquarters for Lucasfilm might have been the beginning of an *atelier*, a collaborative film enterprise like Laterna, the Swedish studio-in-a-mansion which inspired Francis to found Zoetrope. But once *Star Wars* started earning, George bought the 1700-acre Bulltail Ranch. In 1979, he received planning permission to begin creating Skywalker.

The ranch, Lucas explained, would give him the freedom to make 'my little films,' abstract, experimental films that would 'show emotions.' *Star Wars*, he insisted, was only a means to an end. It would buy his way out of big-time cinema. He envisaged a 'retreat [with] a rich Victorian character, [containing] film-research and special-effects facilities, art/writing rooms, screening rooms, film-editing areas, film libraries, a small guesthouse, and a recreation area complete with handball courts, tennis courts, and a swimming pool.' His scheme would use only 5 percent of the land area, he said; the rest would remain agricultural.

But old friends like Gary Kurtz, Lucas's one-time producer, watched with growing alarm as this vision metamorphosed into something closer to the private empire of Howard Hughes. 'As the bureaucracy got bigger and bigger,' says Kurtz, 'George seemed to vacillate back and forth between wanting to control everything absolutely, make all the decisions himself, and being too busy to be bothered. He was busy working on his writing and other creative things, and he left his managers to deal with all that. Then he would come back in and want to be in control again, and that kept going back and forth a lot. Frustrating for a lot of people.'

That Lucas regarded the ranch as his monument became clear when, at the 1982 cook-out, a time capsule was ritually interred under the Main House, containing relics of what he hoped would become known as the Lucas Era. They included a microfilmed list of every member of the *Star Wars* Fan Club. He also called in Eric Westin, the designer of Disneyland, to manage the estate.

He hired helpers like Jane Bay. Once secretary to Mike Frankovich, head of Columbia pictures, and later assistant to Californian governor Jerry Brown, Bay was just the sort of management professional Lucas might have been expected to avoid. Shortly after, investment banker Charles Weber became president and chief operating officer of Lucasfilm. He imported studio veterans like Sidney Ganis as his deputies, driving out some of those who had been with Lucas through the long and painful gestation of *Star Wars*. Since then, Lucas had taken back control of the company, dispensing with Weber and appointing himself chairman of the board. 'Critical observers feel, however,' commented the *Los Angeles Times* tartly, 'that if Lucas goes too far out of the Hollywood mainstream, he may end up chairman of the bored.'

These days, Lucas spent his days in a small house on the estate with his three adopted children, only visiting the Main House on semi-ceremonial occasions. Security at the ranch had increased. 'The last thing we want,' said Lucas in justification of the fencing and electronic surveillance, 'is people driving up and down the road saying, "They made *Star Wars* here."' He hated being interviewed or photographed. 'I am an ardent subscriber to the belief that people should own their own image,' he said, 'that you shouldn't be allowed to take anybody's picture without their permission. It's not a matter of freedom of the press, because you can still write about people. You can still tell stories. It just means you can't use their image, and if they want you to use their image, then they'll give you permission.'

His public pronouncements had come to have overtones of the messianic. In 1981, breaking ground on the new USC Film School, to which he contributed $4.7 million, he lectured the audience on their moral shortcomings: 'The influence of the Church, which used to be all-powerful, has been usurped by film. Films and television tell us the way we conduct our lives, what is right and wrong. There used to be a Ten Commandments that film had to follow, but now there are only a few remnants, like a hero doesn't shoot anybody in the back. That makes it even more important that film-makers get exposed to the ethics of film.'

By 1 p.m., most of the guests had arrived and were assembled on the lawn in front of the Main House. At his first cook-out, in 1980, Lucas took the opportunity to hand bonuses to everyone who'd worked with him that year, down to the janitors. Actors and collaborators were given percentage points in his films, and he exchanged points with old friends like Steve Spielberg and John Milius. Overnight, actors like Sir Alec Guinness became millionaires.

There was nothing of that informality and generosity in the cook-out today. Replacing it was something closer to a royal garden party, or the rare personal appearance of a guru. Softly-spoken staff chivvied the guests into roped-off areas, leaving wide paths between.

'George will be coming along these lanes,' they explained. 'You'll have a good chance to see him. If you just move behind the ropes, and please stay in your designated area . . .'

Old friends exchanged significant glances; evidently George shunned physical contact as much as ever. Hollywood mythology also enshrines the moment when Marvin Davis, the ursine oilman who bought Twentieth Century-Fox in the eighties, met Lucas and, overcome with appreciation, picked him off his feet and hugged him. Lucas, it's said, 'turned red, white and blue.'

A moment after his acolytes had passed through the crowd, the host emerged onto the verandah of the Main House. Flanked by his trusted inner group, he moved to the top of the steps and stood expressionless just out of the early-afternoon sun.

It *looked* like the old George. Grayer, of course, and plumper, but still in the unvarying uniform of plaid shirt, jeans, and sneakers, draped over the same short body.

John Milius was a connoisseur of excess. He had penned Colonel Kilgore's speech 'I love the smell of napalm in the morning. It smells like . . . victory,' in *Apocalypse Now*; Robert Shaw's reminiscence in *Jaws* of the USS *Philadelphia* going down off Guadalcanal, and the slaughter of its survivors by sharks; the bombast of Arnold Schwarzenegger in *Conan the Barbarian*.

'I remember one time I was with Steven and Harrison Ford,' Milius recalled. 'These people were coming around and saying, "You can be in this line, and you'll be able to see George if you're over here," and moving us around.'

On that occasion, Milius's mind had flashed to other examples of the cult of personality. Preacher Jim Jones in Guyana, for instance, and those shuddering TV images of bloated bodies fanning out from the galvanized washtubs from which they'd dipped up their last drink of sugar water and strychnine. 'If George gets up there and starts offering Kool Aid,' Milius muttered to Ford and Spielberg, 'I'm bailing out.'

They all laughed, but nobody else around them was smiling. They were all staring with an almost hungry intensity as the frail man in the plaid shirt, jeans, and sneakers moved toward them.

2

Modesto

If there is a bright centre to the universe, this is the place
that's furthest from it.

Luke Skywalker, on Tatooine, his home planet, in *Star Wars*

There is no easy way into Modesto – nor, for that matter, any easy
way out.

Most people approach from the south, up Interstate 5, toughing
out the flat emptiness of the San Joaquin, the 'long valley' John
Steinbeck made famous in his stories of rural life in the twenties and
thirties. Then, as now, this was fruit and vegetable country, the kitchen
garden of California. Orchards, geometric patches of dense, dark foli-
age, interlock with fields of low, anonymous greenery which only a
farmer would recognize as hiding potatoes, beets, beans. Occasionally,
some town raises a banner against mediocrity – '*Castroville, Artichoke
Capital of the World!*' – but the norm is self-effacement, reticence,
reserve.

Zigzagging among the fields, a great irrigation canal, wide as a
highway, delivers water from lakes set back in the hills. No boats move
on its surface, no kids fish from the concrete banks, no families picnic
on its gravelled margins. This water, fenced off from the fields and
the highway behind chain link, isn't for leisure but, like everything
else here, for use.

Modesto sits on almost the same parallel of latitude as San Francisco,
but there any similarity ends. Californian or not, this is a Kansas town
set down twelve hundred miles west. Even more than for most places
in California, the people here are relative newcomers, migrants from

the midwest and the south who fled the dust storms of the twenties and the farm foreclosures that followed.

Laid out flat as a rug on a landscape without a hill to its name, Modesto's sprawl of ranch-style homes and flat-roofed single-story business buildings is divided as geometrically as Kansas City by a grid of streets, in turn cut arbitrarily by railway tracks. Splintered wooden trestles spanning gullies choked with weeds and the rusted hulks of Chevies and Buicks indicate the high tide of rail in the forties, but traffic still idles patiently at level crossings while hundred-car freight trains clank by.

A garage or a used-car lot seems to occupy every second corner – in farm country, anyone without a car might as well be naked – but one sees almost none of the Cadillacs, Porsches, even Volkswagens common in San Francisco and Los Angeles. Pick-ups, trucks and four-wheel drive vehicles predominate, many of them old but mostly well-tended. Cars here aren't playthings or success symbols, but farm machinery.

In so flat a landscape, anything resembling a skyscraper looks like insane audacity. The town's one modern hotel, the Red Lion, twenty stories tall and stark as a wheat silo, respects scale as little as a chair-leg planted in a model-train layout. Building the Red Lion broke Allen Grant, the overambitious Modesto businessman who financed it. Defaulting on his loans, he sold out to a chain. Locals recount this cautionary tale with implicit disapproval of his recklessness. In Modesto, it's the horizontal man who's respected, not the vertical one. If he wanted to erect something, why not a mall? When Grant used to race sports cars, his mechanic and co-driver was George Lucas.

Appropriately, Modesto's monument to its most successful son barely lifts its head higher than George Lucas's five feet six inches. At Five Points, where the narrow downtown streets coalesce into McHenry, a ribbon development of shopping malls and parking lots, a small wooded park next to an apartment block shelters two bronze figures. They loiter against the forequarter of a '57 Chevy, they and the car both cast from metal with the color and buttery sheen of fudge sauce. Toffee-colored Jane perches on the fender, ankles crossed, absorbed in mahogany Dick who, earnestly turning towards her, describes his latest triumph on track or field – it's implicit that nothing which happened in class could remotely interest this couple. What they most resemble is an image from the *Star Wars* trilogy: Han Solo, frozen in carbonite to provide a bas relief for the palace of Jabba the Hutt.

A slab of green marble set into the sidewalk and incised in gold footnotes the figures:

GEORGE LUCAS PLAZA

The movie remembrance of Modesto's past, 'American Graffiti,' was created by the noted film-maker, George Lucas, a Modesto native and a member of the Thomas Downey High School Class of 1962. This bronze sculpture, created by Betty Salette, also entitled 'American Graffiti,' celebrates the genius of George Lucas and the youthful innocence and dreams of the 50s and 60s.

The ritual that inspired *American Graffiti* no longer takes place: large signs specifically indicate 'No Cruising.' In Lucas's time, drivers circulated on Tenth and Eleventh Streets downtown, exploiting a one-way traffic system introduced by shopkeepers to facilitate business parking. Later, the Saturday-night *paseo* moved to McHenry, but it wasn't the same. McDonald's didn't provide either telephones or public toilets, so cruisers congregated in the parking lots of shopping malls, fields of naked asphalt lit by towering lamp standards.

Without the sense of community it enjoyed downtown, cruising became a magnet for the area's rowdies, especially on the second Saturday in June – high school graduation night. In 1988, Modesto's city council belatedly caught up with its own bandwagon and formalized the June weekend bash as an *American Graffiti* festival. As many as 100,000 people converged on Modesto to line McHenry and watch the parade of '32 Deuce Coupes and '57 Chevies. Deejay Robert Weston Smith, aka Wolfman Jack, was master of ceremonies, an honor he enjoyed six more times, the last when he was Cruise Parade Marshal for the 1994 Graffiti USA Car Show and Street Festival. By then, night-time cruising had been banned after repeated problems with drinking and violence. The 1994 parade took place in mid-afternoon. Jack didn't approve: 'My favorite thing was the cruising and me being on the radio, and we don't do that anymore,' he said nostalgically. 'Now they do it in the heat of the day with everyone roasting in their convertibles.' He longed for the days 'when the carbon monoxide was so thick you could hardly breathe.'

15

Meanwhile, Reno and Las Vegas, to the irritation of some Modestoans, launched what they called Hot August Nights, encouraging local owners of classic cars to cruise; and Roseburg, Oregon, launched an annual Graffiti Week. In Los Angeles, Wednesday night was Club Night on Van Nuys Boulevard, in the dormitory suburbs of the San Fernando Valley. After he made *American Graffiti*, Lucas enjoyed hanging out there. 'It was just bumper to bumper. There must have been 100,000 kids down there,' he said. 'It was insane. I really loved it. I sat on my car hood all night and watched. The cars are all different now. Vans are the big thing. Everybody's got a van, and you see all these weird decorated cars. Cruising is still a main thread in American culture.' But by the late eighties, the Van Nuys ritual too had disappeared.

One isn't surprised at Modesto banning the Cruise. Cruisers did not plant, nor cultivate, nor harvest. They were a plague, like locusts, and all the more loathed for being locally hatched. Most people in Modesto, if they were honest, would admit they were glad the gleaming cars, the horny guys and giggling girls, the throbbing exhausts and squealing tyres had moved on, taking their creator with them.

Future friends of Lucas like Steven Spielberg who, Angelenos to the heels of their fitted cowboy boots, joked about 'Lucasland,' which they visualized as a place of hot tubs, meditation, and marijuana, couldn't imagine how little his birthplace resembled the satellite communities of San Francisco which furnished this fantasy. 'Southern California ends at Carmel,' any San Franciscan will tell you. 'Once you get to Monterey, you're in Northern California.' And Modesto? 'It's neither. It's the Valley.' Their contempt is obvious, and Lucas shared it. When anyone in Los Angeles asked him where he came from, he said evasively, 'Northern California.'

Nevertheless, the San Joaquin Valley put its stamp firmly on both Lucas and his films. Without the white upper-middle-class Methodist values he absorbed during his upbringing in this most complacent and righteous of regions, the *Star Wars* films, the *Indiana Jones* series, even the more eccentric *THX1138*, let alone *American Graffiti*, would have been very different. Indeed, they might not have existed at all, since Lucas, unlike the directors who joined him in building the New Hollywood in the sixties and seventies, is anything but a natural film-maker. Nothing in his character fits him to make films. The process irritates and bores him, even makes him physically ill.

Actors lament his failure to give them any guidance towards character. Harrison Ford, recalling the making of *American Graffiti* in Modesto, remembers staring for hours out of the windscreen of his car at the camera car towing it. 'The cameraman, the sound man and the director could all sit in the trunk, and every time I looked at George, he was asleep.' Cindy Williams, one of the film's stars, was flattered when Lucas called her performance 'Great! Terrific!', until she found he said exactly the same thing to everyone.

It is easy to forget that Lucas, for all his fame and influence, has only directed four feature films in almost thirty years. Repeatedly he's handed the job to others, supervising from the solitude of his home, controlling the shooting by proxy, as Hollywood studio producers of the forties did. As critic David Thomson remarks, 'Lucas testifies to the principle that American films are produced, not directed.'

Martin Scorsese agrees that Lucas differs radically from both himself and others in New Hollywood, especially Spielberg. 'Lucas became so powerful that he didn't have to direct,' he told *Time* magazine. 'But directing is what Steven *has* to do.' Spielberg agreed. 'I love the work the way Patton loved the stink of battle.'

Lucas has less in common with Scorsese and Spielberg than with a producer like Sam Goldwyn, who fed the public taste for escapist fantasy and noble sentiment forty years before him, with films like *Wuthering Heights*, *The Best Years of Our Lives* and *The Secret Life of Walter Mitty*. As a young critic, the British director Lindsay Anderson met Goldwyn, and was impressed by his conviction that nobody knew better what his public wanted and needed. 'Blessed with that divine confidence in the rightness (moral, aesthetic, commercial) of his own intuition,' Goldwyn was, Anderson decided, one of the 'lucky ones whose great hearts, shallow and commonplace as bedpans, beat in instinctive tune with the great heart of the public, who laugh as it likes to laugh, weep the sweet and easy tears that it likes to weep.' Today, the grandchildren of Goldwyn's audience laugh at Chewbacca the *wookiee*, cry at the love of Princess Leia for Han Solo, feel their hearts throb in tune to John Williams's brassy score for *Star Wars*.

★   ★   ★

'He came from a very practical era,' the supervisor of Stanislaus County said of George Lucas Sr when he died in 1991. 'There was never a day that I didn't see George hailing me over. He'd be gesturing with his hands and pointing, and everyone knew that George was on the warpath with the government.'

The Lucases arrived in central California from Arkansas in 1890, after having left Virginia a century before. Before that, the family history is shadowy. 'Nobody knows where we originally came from,' George Jr said later. 'Obviously some criminal, or somebody who got thrown out of England or France.' The remark wasn't made out of embarrassment. In a sort of reverse snobbery, his father had taught him that it was better to trace your roots to Billy the Kid than to the *Mayflower*.

In 1889, Washington and Montana achieved statehood, and California, with its orchards blossoming, its fishing industry thriving and oil being pumped along its central coast, looked like the place to be. Just before World War I, Walton Lucas, an oilfield worker, settled in Laton, a grim little town south of Fresno, where his son George Walton Lucas was born in 1913. George Walton Sr, the film-maker's father, never lost the wiry look of a frontiersman, nor the sense, reinforced by Methodism, that life and work were two sides of the same coin. 'He was one of those people who, at the dinner table, always had little talks about those kind of things,' his daughter Kate recalled. 'He quoted a lot of Shakespeare. "To thine own self be true." He said a lot of things like that.'

In 1928, when George Sr was fifteen, his father died of diabetes, a disease whose gene would skip a generation and pass to his grandson. His widow Maud moved into Fresno, shuffling her son from school to school while she looked for work, a commodity in short supply as America's economy imploded in the worldwide slump. In 1929 they relocated sixty miles from Fresno, to Modesto, and George enrolled in Modesto High School with the idea of studying law. Already convinced by events that the Lord only helped those who helped themselves, he was a serious student, becoming class president in his senior year. His vice president, who also co-starred with him in the senior-class play, was pretty, dark but frail Dorothy Bomberger, daughter of Paul S. Bomberger, a wealthy local businessman who'd built his father's property interests into a large corporation that also included a seed company and a car dealership. They married in 1933, the year Lucas graduated. He was twenty, Dorothy eighteen.

With a wife to support, Lucas abandoned any thought of a law degree and found work in an old established Modesto stationery store, Lee Brothers. Shortly afterwards, one of the biggest stationery stores in the state, H.S. Crocker in Fresno, offered him a job at $75 a week. The couple moved, but Dorothy missed her family, so they returned to Modesto. With Dorothy's father in real estate and her uncle Amos in loans, there was no problem finding a place to live. Lucas and Dorothy moved into an apartment repossessed from a defaulting borrower.

Lucas went to work for LeRoy Morris, who owned the town's oldest stationery supplier, the L.M. Morris Co. Morris had been in business since 1904, and his shop showed it: school supplies and office materials shared space with books, gifts, and toys. With no children of his own, Morris was on the lookout for someone to whom he could hand on the thriving business. Lucas Sr wasn't backward in making it clear he was a candidate.

'This is the next-to-last move I plan to make,' he told his boss. 'By the time I'm twenty-five, I hope to have my own store.'

'That's a very ambitious goal,' Morris said mildly.

But the young man's directness had impressed Morris. Two years later he sought out Lucas in the basement where he was shifting boxes, and asked, 'Are you satisfied with me?'

When Lucas looked blank, Morris continued, 'If you are, I'm satisfied with you. Do you think we could live together for the rest of our lives? You know, a partnership is like getting married – maybe harder in some ways.'

'But I have no money,' Lucas said.

Morris shrugged this off. 'You'll sign a note you owe me so much. This business is no good if it won't pay it out.'

Lucas switched from earning wages to owning 10 per cent of L.M. Morris. His employer's generosity reinforced his belief in patriarchy. When *he* had a son, he would put him into the family business too, and help him run it until he was ready to take over.

In 1934 the Lucases had their first child, Ann, and two years later Katherine, always called Kate. The pregnancies sapped Dorothy's strength, triggering the ill-health that was to haunt the rest of her life, and looking after her two daughters placed a further strain on her frail constitution. Nevertheless, she encouraged her husband, accepting his decision to spend six days a week at the store, and helping with the book-keeping on Sundays. She even got pregnant again, though two miscarriages had convinced her doctors she should not have any more children. Confident of prosperity, Lucas bought a $500 lot on Ramona Avenue, a wide street on what was then the edge of town. With $5000 borrowed from Paul and Amos Bomberger, he built a single-story house at number 530. It was here that his only son, five-pound nine-ounce George Walton Jr, was brought home after his birth on 14 May 1944 – Mother's Day.

3

An American Boy

I might be a toymaker if I weren't a film-maker.
George Lucas to critic Joseph Gelmis, 1973

Ramona Avenue has changed little since 1944. Only two blocks long, and twice as wide as more modern streets, it illustrates the generosity of space with which town planners could indulge themselves in those days of unrestricted development. By comparison, its homes, all bungalows, appear cheap – though now, as in 1944, this corner of Modesto exudes prosperity. No sagging campers or rusting wrecks litter the front yards. Hedges are trimmed, flowerbeds weeded. There are few fences, and those that do exist are low enough to step over. In most cases, immaculate lawns run from the kerb right up to the front door, interrupted only by mimosas, four times taller than the houses, that turn the street into a permanent avenue of shade.

With a business and a family to run, George Sr didn't go to war. Instead, ever the horizontal man, he deepened and widened his niche in Modesto. In shipbuilding, aircraft production, munitions manufacture, prefabricated housing, petrol and rubber production, food growing and canning, and, not least, film production, California led the rest of the Union. Both those *wunderkinder* of World War II's construction industry, shipbuilding king Henry Kaiser and Howard Hughes, his aeronautical counterpart, operated from the state. 'For tens of millions,' writes social historian William Manchester, 'the war boom was in fact a bonanza, a Depression dream come true.'

In 1945, when George Jr was eight months old, the Lucases' fourth and last child, Wendy, was born. Two pregnancies so close together severely strained Dorothy's health. She was never well again, and for the rest of George's childhood the Lucas house, like Ramona Avenue itself, lived in shadow. Dorothy spent long periods in hospital, suffering from elusive internal disorders. Her doctors diagnosed pancreatitis, but later removed a large stomach tumor. Georgie and his sisters were brought up mostly by Mildred Shelley, known as 'Till,' a businesslike housekeeper who moved from Missouri to look after the family, and who became a fixture of the Lucas household.

George Lucas Sr did just as well in the post-war boom and the expansive business climate under Eisenhower as he had during the war. Like Ike, he became a devoted golfer; and he was a pillar of the local chamber of commerce and the Rotary, for both of which his father-in-law served as long-time president. The most doting of grandfathers, Paul Bomberger was around at Ramona Avenue most weekends with his 16mm camera, recording the progress of his three daughters and his diminutive grandson: watchful, silent, and tiny – only thirty-three pounds and three feet seven inches tall at six years of age – but with a reservoir of nervous energy which most of the family believed he inherited from his mother's brother Robert, who was also short and feisty.

Georgie's inquisitive look was accentuated by the Bombergers' trademark protruding ears. His were so prominent that his father contemplated having the fault corrected surgically. Instead, the family doctor persuaded him to tape back the more protruding ear for a year. With childhood memories of lice infestation, George Sr insisted on having his son's head shaved every summer. 'It didn't matter to us,' says Lucas's childhood friend John Plummer, 'but George was humiliated.' In his first feature, *THX1138*, Lucas would show a future repressive society in which everyone's head is shaved.

When George was nine, the fiancé of his oldest sister Ann died in Korea, a loss which affected George deeply: lacking an older brother, he'd co-opted his future brother-in-law into that role. George also recalled a period of existential anguish when he was six. 'It centered around God,' he recalled. 'What is God? But more than that, what is reality? What is this? It's as if you reach a point and suddenly you say, "Wait a second, what is the world? What are we? What am I? How do I function in this, and what's going on here?" It was very profound to me at the time.' At least one other film-maker went through an almost identical crisis at the same age. Woody Allen's parents recalled that, at age six, their son became 'sour and depressed,' setting the scene for his later films.

In 1949 Leroy Morris sold George Sr the rest of the business, retired, and died three days later. Immediately, Lucas moved the store to new premises on I Street, reopening as The Lucas Company. He began specializing in office machines, becoming the major supplier of calculators, copiers and office furniture to Modesto and nearby Stockton. Later he moved to Kansas Avenue as Lucas Business Systems, district agent for the 3M corporation and its products. In his first year of independence he grossed $30,000, a respectable sum for those days. He had built the sort of business any man would be proud to hand on to his son – if his son was interested.

George Jr was not interested, though for a while his father imagined he'd been born for a life of commerce. Georgie impressed everyone with his practical skills, his creativity, energy, seriousness, and persistence. His sisters remember him at two and a half studying workmen making repairs to the house, then finding a hammer and chisel and attacking a perfectly good wall. By the time he was ten, he showed a talent for construction: 'I had a little shed out back with tools, and I'd build chess sets and dolls' houses.' A childhood friend, Janet Montgomery Deckard, says, 'Georgie made an entire doll house out of a cardboard box for my Madame Alexander doll. The top was missing so you could look down into it. The walls were wallpapered and everything was in proportion to Madame Alexander.' A quart milk carton became a sofa, which Lucas covered in blue-and-white chintz, and an old gold lipstick tube served as a lamp.

Lucas also built cars – 'lots of race cars that we'd push around, like Soap Box Derby.' With his friends John Plummer and George Frankenstein, he seized the opportunity of a new phone line being laid in the area to appropriate the giant wooden spool on which the cable was wound and, with a rickety runway and a home-made car, improvised a rollercoaster. Plummer, whose father knew people in construction, procured lumber and cement. Under George's direction they created miniature fortifications and landscapes on which, using toy soldiers and vehicles from the Lucas Company, battles could be fought and refought.

A Lionel model-train set, the best in town, wound through the elaborately re-landscaped garden – a gift from the doting Dorothy. George always knew where to go for help with an ambitious scheme. 'He never listened to me,' said his father. 'He was his mother's pet. If he wanted a camera, or this or that, he got it.'

With his friend Melvin Cellini, who lived on the next street, George created one of his most complex 'environments.' Atmospheric lighting and careful arrangement of props converted the Cellini garage into a haunted house. Kids paid to see it, and there were queues for the first couple of days. George had the idea of encouraging repeat visits by changing the effects periodically. 'George always was gifted with creative talent and business sense,' says Cellini. Through Cellini, Lucas also made his first film. Melvin had a movie camera, and they did a stop-motion film of plates stacking themselves up, then unstacking themselves – Lucas's first experiment in special effects. He never forgot the wonder of it: 'We were so excited, like a pair of aborigines with some new machine.'

Modesto in general wasn't a reading town, but comic books were ubiquitous, fanned by the momentum of the war years, when color printing and the demand for propaganda had turned them into an international enthusiasm. John Plummer's father had a friend who ran a news-stand. Once a month he returned unsold comic books for a refund, but since wholesalers were satisfied with the torn-off covers, the Lucas gang got the books themselves. Georgie's collection of five hundred comics became the envy of the town, and rather than have drifts of *Captain Marvel* and *Plastic Man* litter the house, his father resignedly added shelves to his backyard shed to accommodate it. His sister rescued the comics when George tired of them. Years later, she re-presented them to him. They became the nucleus of a large and valuable collection.

The first TV sets filtered into Modesto in 1949, and the Plummers immediately bought one. Georgie begged his father to do the same, but Lucas refused to allow such a distraction into his house. The Lucases didn't get their own set until 1954. In their home, as in America in general, radio remained the primary entertainment. Eighty-two per cent of people still tuned in every night. 'We didn't get a television set until I was ten years old,' Lucas recalled. 'So for the first ten years, I was in front of the radio listening to radio dramas. It played an important part in my life. I listened to *Inner Sanctum*,

The Whistler, The Lone Ranger – those were the ones that interested me.'

But TV couldn't be stopped. So many people wanted to see the Plummers' set that Mr Plummer put it in the garage and built bleachers to hold the crowd. George and his friends gathered there to stare at the tiny, bulging, almost circular screen of the old brown bakelite Champion. There was only one station, KRON-TV from San Francisco. It broadcast mostly boxing and wrestling matches, with the occasional cartoon, but the idea of an image piped into one's own home awed them; they would have watched the test pattern. Lucas went round religiously to the Plummers' every night at six for *Adventure Theater* – a twenty-minute episode of an old serial, with a *Crusader Rabbit* cartoon. Among the serials was *Flash Gordon Conquers the Universe*. Lucas never forgot it. Once the Lucases got a set, George sat in front of it for hours, especially during the Saturday-morning cartoon programs, with his black cat Dinky curled round his neck.

Lucas has often cited his early experience of television, but is more reticent about movie-going. 'Movies had extremely little effect on me when I was growing up,' he has said. 'I hardly ever went, and when I did it was to meet girls. Television had a much larger effect.'

In 1955, George made the newspapers for the first time. The *Modesto Bee* reported that he and Melvin Cellini had launched a kids' newspaper, the *Daily Bugle*. Cellini saw the idea on TV and co-opted his friend as star reporter, for reasons not unconnected with the family business: George Sr typed the paper's wax stencils and ran them off on his office duplicator, though he insisted the kids paid for supplies from their profits.

In August 1955 they published their first daily one-sheet issue, printing two hundred copies. 'You will get your paper free for two weeks,' it announced, 'but then it will cost 1 cent. Papers will be given out Monday to Friday. But this Friday it won't be out because the press broke down.' Even with George Lucas as reporter, however, the *Daily Bugle* didn't flourish. Although the paper was padded out with jokes and riddles, they had trouble filling its pages with events around Modesto. George's father had flown the family to Los Angeles to visit Disneyland, which opened in July 1955, and George described a different attraction in each issue, but by the second week even this resource was exhausted. 'The *Daily Bugle* stops,' announced their issue of 10 August. 'The *Weekly Bugle* will be put out on Wednesday only. There is the same news.'

That the *Bugle* went out of business so soon is the oddest thing about it, since everyone who knew Lucas as a child agrees that his persistence and tenacity were prodigious. Once launched on a project, he would follow it through to the end. At eleven, given the job of mowing the lawn once a week to earn his pocket money, he saved his allowance until he had $35, borrowed a further $25 from his mother, and bought a power mower to lighten his task. His father, not recognizing the stringy resilience of his own father and grandfather in his son, was furious. Pushing the old mower round the yard every weekend was a valuable discipline. Getting through the job quickly with a power mower demeaned the lesson.

One could imagine Lucas devoting the same energy to the *Bugle* as to lawnmowing: hiring kids as reporters and vendors, making the paper a paying proposition, and ending up a professional publisher at fifteen. Though a team player, he would often in later life begin working with some charismatic and forceful individual, then gravitate to leadership, and finally supplant his mentor. Some people have suggested that this was his response to the lack of a sympathetic father, but Lucas's explanation is more pragmatic: 'That's one of the ways of learning. You attach yourself to somebody older and wiser than you, learn everything they have to teach, and move on to your own accomplishments.' He needed to be both part of a group and in charge of it; otherwise, he lost interest. In childhood, as in adulthood, Lucas belonged with the entrepreneurs who defined 'teamwork' as 'a lot of people doing what I say.'

Cars

I love things that are fast. That's what moved me toward
editing rather than photography. Pictures that move –
that's what got me where I am.

George Lucas, *Los Angeles Times* magazine, 2 February 1997

George Lucas at fourteen, in 1958, was not much different to George
Lucas forty years later. He had already, at five feet six inches, reached
his full height. High-school class photographers habitually stuck him
in the front row, where even classmates of average height loomed over
him. The clothes his mother bought for him – jeans, sneakers, green
polyester sweaters, open-necked blue-and-red-checked shirts with
pearl buttons – would become a lifelong uniform.

By then, Lucas had discovered rock and roll. That was by no means
typical. In the hit parade of 1958, ballads like 'It's All in the Game,'
'All I Have to do is Dream,' and 'It's Only Make Believe' far out-
numbered Chuck Berry's 'Sweet Little Sixteen' and Jerry Lee Lewis's
'Great Balls of Fire.' But Lucas raced home to spend hours
playing Presley, Buddy Holly, Chuck Berry, the Platters, the Five
Satins. An autographed photo of Elvis adorned his wall. He adopted
the personal style that went with rock. His hair grew longer, but no
amount of Dixie Pomade could plaster its natural curl into the classic
Elvis pompadour. His compromise – undulating waves at front and
side, slicked down on top – only called to mind the *Dick Tracy* villain
Flattop.

Lucas's mood was unsure and often depressed: 'I was very much
aware that growing up wasn't pleasant. It was just . . . frightening. I
remember that I was unhappy a lot of the time. Not really unhappy

27

– I enjoyed my childhood. But I guess all kids, from their point of view, feel depressed and intimidated. Although I had a great time, my strongest impression was that I was always on the lookout for the evil monster that lurked around the corner.' In short, he shared the fears and anxieties of every imaginative child, but did not suffer the traumas associated with the break-up of his family or the loss of a loved one – emotional disturbances experienced by many of the people with who he would later work. Steven Spielberg's parents were divorced; Paul Schrader's Calvinist family forbade most secular diversions, including the cinema.

Thomas Downey High was the more modern of Modesto's two high schools. With its *echt*-Californian frontage in modified fifties *art deco*, set well back from the road in wide playing fields, it was an agreeable place to spend one's time; but Lucas took no pleasure in it. 'I was never very good in school,' he says, 'so I was never very enthusiastic about it. One of the big problems I had, more than anything else, was that I always wanted to learn something other than what I was being taught. I was *bored*. I wanted to *enjoy* school in the worst way and I never could. I would have been much better off if I could have skipped [the standard curriculum]. I would have learned to read eventually – the same with writing. You pick that stuff up because you have to. I think it's a waste of time to spend a lot of energy trying to beat education into somebody's head. They're never going to get it unless they want to get it.'

His sister Wendy would get up at 5 a.m. and go through Lucas's English homework, correcting the spelling, but she couldn't be there to help in the classroom. Another Modestan who graduated from Downey a few years after Lucas remembered the battery of tests inflicted by the teachers:

> Some liked 'big' comprehensive tell-me-everything-you've-learned-this-semester tests, and others preferred exams that covered materials since the previous exam in the class. Some classes had quizzes on a weekly or intermittent basis. Others would have weekly or twice/thrice weekly assignments (essays, math homework, book reviews, stuff for art portfolios, language assignments) that would be more cumulative, requiring fewer exams for the teacher to evaluate your progress. I suspect, if George Lucas had a D average, he was constantly late

on a lot of assignments and papers [. . .] Either that, or he didn't 'buckle down' and learn. Or he had/has an undiagnosed learning disability that made it difficult for him to complete the assignments, irregardless of his intelligence.

Lucas's one aptitude was art. At home, he drew elaborate panoramas, and labored over hand-crafted greeting cards. 'I had a strong interest even in high school in going to art school and becoming an illustrator,' he says, 'but my father was very much against it. Said I could do it if I wanted to, but he wasn't going to pay for it. I could do it on my own.' Teachers were no more encouraging. Schoolmate Wayne Anderson remembers the art teacher snapping, 'Oh, George, get serious,' when she found he'd ignored the subject assigned and had instead sketched a pair of armored space soldiers.

When he was fifteen, George's life underwent a fundamental disturbance. Modesto was spreading as fruit-growers sold their orchards for building lots, and planted less fragile and labor-intensive crops. In 1959, George Sr bought thirteen acres under walnut trees at 821 Sylvan Road, on the outskirts of town, and moved his family into a ranch house on the property. George loathed his new home, which cut him off from all his friends. Until he could get his driver's license and, more important, a car, he was a prisoner. When school ended each afternoon at 3 p.m., he rode his bike or took the school bus home, went straight to his room and spent the hours before dinner reading comics and playing rock'n'roll. Emerging, he'd eat in silence, watching the family's Admiral TV, which, fashionably for the time, sat on a revolving 'Lazy Susan' mount that swivelled through 360 degrees. After that, it was back to his room again. Hoping to revive his son's interest in construction, Lucas Sr designed a large box, with a glass top and front, in which he could continue to create his imaginary battlefields. He gave him a 35mm camera for his birthday, and turned the house's second bathroom into a dark room. But while George fitfully pursued these enthusiasms, his heart was no longer in them. He was fifteen – in America, the age when a young man's fancy lightly turns to thoughts of wheels.

★   ★   ★

When America went to war, the car industry was one of the first to be militarized. The Japanese bombed Pearl Harbor in December 1941. By February 1942, every automotive assembly line in America had been turned over to tanks. The government impounded any cars Detroit had in stock, and doled them out to the military and to people in protected occupations. By 1945, the supply of new cars was down to thirty thousand – three days' worth by 1939 rates of sale. The shortage didn't ease for five years, when the government permitted the importation of a few vehicles from Europe, almost entirely luxury cars like the Rolls-Royce, Jaguar, or Bentley, or, at the other end of the market, the Volkswagen and the Fiat Innocenti and the Autobianchi – the kind of 'toy' cars with which Detroit, still committed to the gas-guzzler, refused to soil its hands. (Curt Henderson in *American Graffiti* drives a clapped-out Citroën *Deux Chevaux*.) The occasional independent, like Preston Tucker, who tried to build and sell cars in competition with Detroit was ruthlessly put down.

'If you didn't have a car back then,' says Modestan Marty Reiss, 'basically you didn't exist.' Lucas agrees: 'In the sixties, the social structure in high school was so strict it didn't really lend itself to meeting new people. You had the football crowd and the government crowd and the society–country-club crowd, and the hoods that hung out over at the hamburger stand. You were in a crowd and that was it. You couldn't go up and you couldn't go down. But on the streets it was everyone for himself, and cars became a way of structuring the situation.'

If a kid couldn't afford a VW or Fiat, he grabbed what he could, and adapted it. Four years of tinkering, repairing and making-do, added to the repair skills expected of kids who often needed to service farm machinery, had turned farm boys into fair auto mechanics. Pre-war Detroit made its cars as simply as possible, to standardize spare parts. Two rusting wrecks might be cobbled together into one vehicle. During the war, undertakers could still buy hearses. Ranchers usually got a station wagon, farmers a pick-up. All were ingeniously adapted in the late forties and early fifties.

Surfers liked the long vehicles, ideal for carrying boards, but kids looking for something hot sought out the 1932 Ford Deuce Coupe and the '47 Chevrolet, which they 'chopped' – lowering the roof as close to the hoodline as possible – and 'channelled' – dropping the body down between the wheels. Playing with the suspension could make the car look nose- or tail-heavy, or simply close to the ground in general: the 'low rider' look that signalled a driver looking for trouble. (In *American Graffiti*, John Milner reassures a cop that his front end is the regulation 12½ inches above the road.) Fitted with an engine souvenired from some much heavier car, with a ground-scraping new suspension, the low roofline giving the divided wind-screen the look of threatening slit eyes, all the chrome stripped off, door handles removed, only the legal minimum of lights retained, and the whole thing repainted yellow, with flames down both sides, Grandpa's 1932 Ford became that most ominous of post-war cultural artefacts, the hot-rod.

One end of the post-war car world was represented by customizers like George Barris, who turned Cadillacs into lavish display vehicles for Hollywood stars, with lashings of chrome, iridescent and multiple-layered lacquer finishes, and whorehouse interiors upholstered in ani-mal skin, velvet or fur. At the other extreme was Junior Johnson, a North Carolina country boy who dominated the dirt-track circuits of the rural South, winning such a reputation that Detroit and the tire and gas companies began investing in the burgeoning worlds of stock cars and hot-rods.

Long, straight country roads offered the perfect laboratory for test-ing and perfecting often bizarrely adapted vehicles. The mythology of cars flourished particularly in predominantly white Northern Cali-fornia. Black musicians seldom sang about cars, but white 'surfer' groups like Jan and Dean and, particularly, the Beach Boys made them a staple. The latter's 'Little Deuce Coupe,' 'Shut Down' and '409' – named for the cubic-inch displacement of a Chevrolet engine – were major hits.

All over Stanislaus County, kids worked on their cars through the week and, on Saturdays, brought them to downtown Modesto, where they took advantage of the one-way system imposed by merchants to make a leisurely *tour d'honneur* along Tenth Street, across one block, down Eleventh and onto Tenth again.

Lucas said later, 'When I was ten years old, I wanted to drive in Le Mans and Monte Carlo and Indianapolis,' but his real interest in cars actually began when he was around fifteen, and became a ruling passion. On any Saturday from 1959 onwards, you could have found him on Tenth Street from around four in the afternoon to well after midnight.

Cruising in Modesto had a lot to do with sex, but, though Lucas claimed he lost his virginity in the back of a car with a girl from Modesto High, the tougher and more sexually active of the town's two high schools, nobody has ever admitted to being his girl. John Plummer recognizes a lot of Lucas in the inept teenager played by Charles Martin Smith in *American Graffiti*: 'There's so much of George in Terry the Toad it's unbelievable. The botching of events in terms of his life, his social ineptness in terms of dealing with women.' His mother said, 'George always wanted to have a blonde girl friend, but he never did quite find her.' In *Graffiti*, Terry, who normally bumbles around on a Vespa scooter, inherits the car of his friend Steve Bolander when Steve goes off to college, and immediately snags Debbie (Candy Clark), the most bubble-headed blonde anyone could desire.

As cruising petered out in the early hours, more aggressive drivers peeled off and headed to the long, straight roads on the edge of town, where they could prove just whose car was the fastest. A mythology grew up around these dawn races, which Lucas celebrated in *American Graffiti*. In the film, they take place on Paradise Road – a real Modesto thoroughfare, but too twisty, locals agree, for racing. Dragsters pre-ferred Mariposa Drive, Blue Gum Avenue, or, best of all, Rose Lane, where painted lines marked out a measured quarter-mile. The film showed drivers gambling their registration papers – 'pink slips' – though this was almost unknown: even a $20 side bet was daring. Most kids didn't own the cars anyway: 'You're racing your daddy's car tonight,' was a favorite gibe – used by Harrison Ford as Bob Falfa in *American Graffiti* when he challenges John Milner. If parents bought a second car for their kids, they normally retained title. Most kids simply cruised in the family Chevy or Ford, the automatic trans-missions of which they wrecked in a few months by intemperate 'peel-ing out' at high speed from the kerb, or by racing.

The bad boys of the car culture were the gangs. Modesto already had a hot-car club, the Century Toppers, which went back to 1947 and was led by Gene Wilder, later a prominent professional customizer. A car modelled on his chopped Mercury, the roof so low that the wind-screen is barely a slit, features in *American Graffiti*, but Lucas preferred to confer immortality on a later and raunchier gang, the Faros, arche-typal juvenile delinquents who hung out at a burger joint called the Round Table.

In *American Graffiti*, the Pharaos (sic) and their slow-talking, gum-chewing leader Joe, played by gangling Bo Hopkins, are every mother's nightmare, in glitzy satin jackets and skin-tight jeans. They kidnap Curt (Richard Dreyfuss) and put him through an initiation rite that involves hooking a chain to a police car and ripping out its back axle.

Surviving Faros reject this characterization, and deny charges that they instigated fist-fights or poured gasoline onto roads and set it afire. 'We never got in trouble,' insists Ted Tedesco, one of three brothers, all foundation members of the Faros when the gang formed in 1959. To hear the Tedescos and other ex-members like Marty Reiss tell it, the Faros were just decent kids high on the car culture. 'I don't think more than five people smoked cigarettes,' says Reiss. 'Nobody was on drugs. Any obscenity, including "Hell" and "Damn," was punished by a swat from the club paddle, as was spinning your tires within two blocks of the clubhouse.' They're silent, however, about Lucas's accusation that though he was never a member, they used him as a stooge, sending him in to enrage other gangs who, when they chased the pint-sized troublemaker down an alley, found themselves facing the Faros armed with bike chains.

Lucas was right, they agree, about initiations, but they deny ever having done anything as drastic as trashing a police prowler. (Lucas insisted 'some friends' did try this trick one Halloween, but without the film's spectacular result: 'The car just sort of went clunk, and it was really very undramatic.') The worst a potential member might endure was being rolled through a supermarket on a trolley, dressed only in a diaper, or being blindfolded and forced to eat dogfood, or a live goldfish – and even then, they insist, the fish was replaced by a piece of peach. 'That was the big, tough club,' says Reiss, now a respectable local businessman, like most other members. The Faros' last president, Marty Jackman, even became the local representative of the Sierra Club.

As a teenager, Lucas wanted to join the Faros, or at least win their acceptance. He let his hair grow even longer, fitted silver toecaps to his pointed boots, and wore black Levi's that remained unwashed for weeks at a time. Nagging his parents finally got him a car, a tiny Autobianchi, nicknamed, when Fiat bought up the company, the Bianchina. It had a two-cylinder engine, hardly more powerful than a motorbike, and with an appalling clatter. Even then, there was a trade-off: George would become the delivery boy of his father's business.

Lucas was grateful and resentful at the same time. He had a car, but it was barely a car. It had 'a sewing machine motor in it. It was a dumb little car. What could I do with that? It was practically a motor scooter.' Some of his humiliation would pass to Terry the Toad in *American Graffiti*, forced to bumble about on a Vespa. The deal with his father to work at the store didn't last long. George was expected to haul large, heavy boxes of paper in the summer heat, then sweep up the store, clean the toilets, and lock up. After a few weeks he had a blazing fight with his father, who fired him and offered the job to George Frankenstein. 'The damn kid won't even work for me,' he told Frankenstein, 'after I've built this business for him.' Privately, he called his son 'a scrawny little devil.' Lucas later said of *American Graffiti*: 'In a way, the film was made so my father won't think those were wasted years. I can say I was doing research, though I didn't know it at the time.'

Still a few months shy of the date on which he could get his license, Lucas could only drive on the family ranch. Once, trying to make the Bianchina behave like a high-powered rod, he swung its back end into a walnut tree. He got his license after one failure, for forgetting traffic rules, but promptly drove the Fiat so fast that he rolled it at seventy miles an hour going round a bend.

Lucas had the car towed forlornly to Modesto's Foreign Car Service. Fortunately, his friend John Plummer worked there. Also into cars, he'd rescued and restored an old MG, and offered to help George fix up his Fiat. For weeks, the two boys worked side by side in the garage, which was also the local Renault dealership. After hours, they turned the Fiat into at least an approximation of a lean, mean machine. They cut away the mashed roof entirely, fitted a new low windscreen, and a rollbar. They souped up the engine and put in a silencer, the ominous growl of which belied the feebleness of the motor. Better shock absorbers improved the suspension and minimized the chance of another roll, and Lucas also installed extra-wide professional seatbelts. The Fiat, never very attractive, now looked ungainly and foreshortened – a 'weird little car,' in the words of one friend – but George loved it. He had wheels at last, and he was ready to roll.

He began to explore the pleasures of driving fast. He and Plummer raced on an old go-kart track behind the garage. Plummer inclined to heftiness, but George was light, like the Fiat. He found he could take turns faster than larger cars and still not spin out, which made up for his lack of speed on the straightaways. The experience was exhilarating: 'The engine, the noise, being able to peel rubber through all four gears with three shifts, the speed. It was the thrill of doing something really well. When you drift through a corner and come up at just the right time, and shift down – there's something special about it. It's like running a very good race. You're all there, and everything is working.'

What wasn't working was everything else. George's camera lay unused, the environment box his father built him was discarded. His schoolwork limped along at a D+ average, barely high enough to graduate. Worst of all from the perspective of George Sr, he showed no inclination to take over the Lucas Company. 'I was a hellraiser,' Lucas conceded. 'My father thought I was going to be an automobile mechanic, and that I wasn't going to amount to anything. My parents – not my mother: mothers never write off their sons – but my father wrote me off.' He overstates the case, but not by much. Even when George began his film career, his father was pessimistic. 'He kept telling me he wanted his son to go into his business,' recalled a friend, Modesto city councilman Frank Muratore, 'and didn't think he would do very well in movies. I recall how sad George [Sr] was about that.' George Sr confessed later, 'Frankly, we just didn't understand George. I'd try to get my point across and he'd just sit there and look at me. I'd just run out of breath. He wouldn't pay any attention.'

At sixteen, the gap between Lucas and his father seemed an abyss, but over the next twenty years George would become more and more recognizable as the son of a small-town Methodist businessman. 'It's sort of ironic,' he muses about his father, 'because I swore when I was a kid I'd never do what he did. At eighteen, we had this big break, when he wanted me to go into the business and I refused, and I told him, "There are two things I know for sure. One is that I will end up doing something with cars . . . and two, that I will never be president of a company." I guess I got outwitted.'

Almost as soon as he won his license, George started getting traffic tickets. For the police, hot-rodders were anathema, and trapping them something between a sacred calling and a sport. Most of the local cops were young themselves, had grown up with the low-riders and hot-rodders, and envied their lawless opposite numbers. In *More*

American Graffiti, Lucas brings back Bob Falfa, the rodder defeated by John Milner in the first film, as a California Highway Patrol cop on a motorcycle, booking the people who used to be his rivals. Called into traffic court, Lucas went with his father, who insisted his son get a haircut and wear a suit – the only time anyone ever saw George in collar and tie. Business clothing became the symbol of everything his generation despised: functionaries of all sorts came to be dismissively called 'suits.'

The car culture thrust Lucas into a new, pragmatic world. All that counted were your skills, your capacity for action. Life wasn't for reflection: it was for use, like the landscape around Modesto. 'George has this idea about a used universe,' says sound engineer Randy Thom. 'He wanted things in his films to look like they've been worn down, rusted, knocked about. He didn't want things to look brand new.'

It's not hard to trace this vision to those days in 1960 and 1961 when Lucas kicked around the world of Northern Californian car racing. Plenty of fairgrounds had installed raceways. They staged demolition derbies on weekends, preceded by auto-cross – racing sports and stock cars against the clock. Like hot-rodding, auto-cross was a first step into the pro world of the National Association for Stock Car Racing (NASCAR), or Class C sports car competition. Detroit was already taking an interest in what happened at circuits in Stockton, Goleta, Willow Springs, Cotati, and Laguna Seca, just out-side Monterey. New tires, new fuels, new engines could be tested to destruction by these rural daredevils, some of whom might make it to the sponsored big time, as had Junior Johnson and Freddie Lorenzen, backed by Chevrolet, Ford, Firestone, and Goodyear. Lucas delved into this world in *More American Graffiti*, where John Milner, having made his reputation as a hot-rodder, tries to break into big-time drag racing, with its professional teams sponsored by big automotive companies.

The Bianchina was a toy in the high-powered world of auto-cross, but even if Lucas had had a better car, Californian law forbade anyone to race until they were twenty-one. Always the team player, he attached himself to a winner and insinuated himself into his group until he made himself indispensable, much as he would do with Francis Coppola a few years later.

The winner in this case was Allen Grant, a coming sports-car driver whom Lucas met at Laguna Seca. Four years older than Lucas, he had graduated from Downey in 1958 with grades almost as poor as Lucas's. Now he drove a dazzling Ford Mustang Cobra and was attracting attention from big sponsors. Good-looking, well connected, successful with women, Grant had already embarked on a business career which would make him, for a while anyway, one of the richest entrepreneurs in Northern California.

Grant offered a potent role model. Lucas became his mechanic, and a conveniently light co-driver. He also joined the Ecurie AWOL Sports Car Competition Club, and began editing its newsletter, *BS*. His drawings of sports cars and caricatures of drivers appeared in *BS*, and he sold or gave the originals to his friends, including Grant. Through Grant, Lucas began to sense that another life existed outside Modesto; but he wasn't sure how to exploit this knowledge. He was well into his last year at high school, but didn't delude himself that his grades would get him into junior college, let alone either of California's two main universities, the University of California at Los Angeles (UCLA), with its main campus in Westwood, a luxury suburb of Los Angeles, or the University of Southern California (USC), situated in a funkier corner of the city, on the edge of the old downtown area. UCLA, the official state college, required no tuition fees, but its academic requirements were high. USC had lower requirements, but demanded fees.

Lucas and John Plummer pored over college prospectuses. 'We wanted a school,' says Plummer, 'that didn't have a lot of requirements in math or anything else, but that would let us go into more of the creative side.' If they didn't find one, they had more or less decided to go to Europe together, though with Dorothy Lucas in hospital again and three other children to put through school, George Sr showed no inclination to fund such a trip. Nor could he countenance his son going to study in Los Angeles, which he ridiculed as 'Sin City.'

George persisted. Of the two universities, USC looked the more promising. It even offered a film course, one of the first in the country. 'In those days, film school wasn't like it is now,' says Willard Huyck, the screenwriter who would graduate from USC and, with his wife and writing partner Gloria Katz, script *American Graffiti*. 'Nobody knew about it, and they sort of stood outside the door of film school and grabbed you as you walked by, and asked if you'd like to become a film major.'

The USC course included animation and photography, and Lucas wondered if he could bluff his way in with a portfolio of drawings and his skill with a 35mm camera. First, however, he had to graduate from Downey – and with a D average, that was anything but assured. School 'commencement,' the end of the academic year, was on a Friday in the middle of June. As the day approached, he still had three 'incompletes,' and unless he delivered the papers necessary to finish the coursework, he could fail to graduate.

These things were on his mind when, on a hot Tuesday, 12 June 1962, he drove the Bianchina out of the gate of the walnut ranch and headed for town. His mother was resting, having just returned from another spell in hospital, weak and emaciated: she and her son now both weighed the same, eighty pounds. He'd tried to persuade his sister Wendy to come to the library with him, as she often had before, to help with his spelling and sentence structure, but she preferred to stay by the pool and keep an eye on her mother.

George spent a few hours at the library, but did little work. He would always hate writing, and on a hot day like this, he hated it more than usual. At around 4.30 p.m. he left, and roared the little Fiat back along the road home. He arrived outside his home at 4.50, and swung the car to the left to enter the dirt track leading to the house. He never saw the Chevrolet Impala driven by seventeen-year-old Frank Ferreira, a classmate from Downey, coming up fast behind him. It tried to overtake just as Lucas swung across the road. The heavier Chevy slammed into the side of the Fiat, level with the driver's seat, and sent it bounding like a toy. On the third roll, Lucas's seatbelt snapped and he was thrown clear, flying high into the air before landing with stunning force on his chest and stomach. The car bounced twice more, showering dust and pebbles of safety glass, crashed into a walnut tree at sixty miles an hour, and stuck there, wrapped around the trunk. So great was the impact that the tree, roots and all, shifted two feet.

5

Where Were You in '62?

I should have been killed, but I wasn't. I'm living on borrowed time. Lucas on his accident

Lucas's survival was miraculous. Had the seatbelt not snapped, had he not been thrown clear, had he landed on his head rather than his chest, he would almost certainly have died in the road in front of his own home.

Nobody inside the Lucas house heard the crash. Their neighbor opposite, Shorty Coleman, bolted out, saw him lying unconscious, face bloody, and rang immediately for an ambulance. With the hospital only five miles away, it arrived quickly. As Lucas was loaded in, he began to turn blue with cyanosis, and on the trip to the hospital he started vomiting blood.

At the hospital, the doctor on duty, Paul Carlsen, gave him a blood transfusion and inserted four needles into his stomach to check for the internal bleeding that would indicate ruptured organs. George Sr was telephoned, and he raced to the hospital, then home to collect Wendy and his wife. When they arrived at George's bedside, they found him connected to oxygen and transfusion tubes, his forehead bandaged, his face ashen. 'Mom, did I do something wrong?' he muttered, half unconscious. Dorothy wept, and had to be led from the room. George Sr prayed. Wendy just stared at her brother, and wondered what would have happened had she gone to the library with him. From the look of the car, she would probably have been dead.

A photographer from the *Modesto Bee* took a spectacular photograph of the mangled Fiat, which the paper used on the front page

39

next day, under the heading 'Youth Survives Crash.' 'Just what part in saving his life the rollbar and a safety belt played is not known but George W. Lucas Jr survived this crash yesterday,' said the *Bee*. Later, the circumstances of the accident would be subtly manipulated by the Lucas machine to shift any blame from him. A 1994 book authorized by Lucasfilm describes Ferreira as 'driving behind him at eighty to ninety miles an hour' – a charge not supported by the record – and 'with his headlights off' – hardly a crime at 4.50 p.m. on a summer afternoon. The local police were in no doubt about who was to blame. While he was still in hospital, they gave Lucas a ticket for making an illegal left turn.

The same book magnifies the extent of Lucas's injuries, describing him as 'without a pulse, his lungs collapsed and numerous bones crushed.' In fact, to the surprise of Carlsen and the other medical staff, they proved less severe than they looked. Despite the gash on his forehead and the bruises on his shoulders, he had only two minor fractures, and his liver, spleen, and kidneys were intact, though bruised. The worst damage was to his chest, which had absorbed most of the force. X-rays revealed hematomas on his lungs, which were hemorrhaging. But that could be dealt with. The doctors injected anti-inflammatory drugs, and George, who was in good health generally, started to recover.

Paradoxically, his accident won him the high-school graduation which had been in doubt. On Friday, the day of commencement, someone from the school brought his diploma to the hospital, his failure to make up his courses conveniently forgotten.

Lucas was too dazed to relish his good fortune. If anyone were to ask him the question posed by the publicity for *American Graffiti*, 'Where Were You in '62?', he would have replied, 'In bed.' Most of his summer was spent convalescing, and the legend has grown up of his Pauline conversion during this period to hard work, ambition, and the life of the mind.

It may even be partly true. A lot was happening in the world, and with leisure to contemplate it, Lucas may have seen his life in a new light. During 1962, John Glenn became the first American to orbit the earth; John Steinbeck won the Nobel Prize for Literature; in October, John Kennedy faced down Nikita Khrushchev over the missiles he'd sneaked into Cuba; America exploded a nuclear device over Johnston Island in the Pacific; Polaroid launched a new one-minute color film; and the first Titan inter-continental ballistic missile was installed in a concrete silo in the American heartland, targeted on Russia.

Lucas couldn't get out to see the summer's biggest movies, some of them destined to be among his favorites, like the first James Bond film, *Dr No*, and David Lean's *Lawrence of Arabia*; but he watched plenty of television, none of it very significant. That year's Emmys chose the thoughtful legal series *The Defenders* as the best show of 1961, but the networks, eyes ever on the ratings, premiered nothing as interesting in 1962, which saw the debut of *The Beverly Hillbillies*, the World War II series *Combat*, animated science fiction from Hanna-Barbera in *The Jetsons*, and the mindless comedy *McHale's Navy*. *The Tonight Show* also got a new host, Johnny Carson.

It was a big year for dance music. The Twist was hot – Chubby Checker seemed to be on every TV pop programme – followed by Joey Dee and the Starliters doing 'Peppermint Twist.' Fads like the Limbo Rock, the Mashed Potato, the Watusi and the Lo-co-motion were sent up in 'The Monster Mash' by the Crypt Kickers, with Bobby 'Boris' Pickett, imitating the sepulchral tones of Karloff.

What caught Lucas's ear, however, was a new presence on the air, from an unexpected source – Mexico.

Robert Weston Smith was born in Brooklyn in 1938. His resonant voice and interest in music made him a natural for radio, and by 1962 he was a disc jockey on KCIJ-AM in Shreveport, Louisiana, where as 'Big Smith with the Records' he gained a following among admirers of rhythm and blues. In Shreveport, Smith began developing a fictional character for himself, one which would exploit a certain furtive quality in his voice, and his flair for the outrageous. He took his idea to XERF-FM in Del Rio, Texas. Most of the station's clients were preachers, who paid generously for the right to broadcast their message all over the US via its massive 250,000-watt transmitter – five times the power allowed for stations within the US – sited just over the Mexican border.

Smith convinced XERF that he could win just as many listeners in the late-night and early-morning hours with rhythm and blues and bluegrass music. His sponsors were the same preachers who dominated the daylight hours. Smith's throaty musical introductions, occasional lycanthropic howls, yelps of 'Mercy!' and exhortations to

'Get yo'self nekkid!' interspersed with commercials for plastic effigies of Jesus, sanctified prayer handkerchiefs, and the collected sermons of his holy-rolling backers, soon became a feature of the American soundscape, and 'Wolfman Jack,' as Smith now called himself, an institution.

Lucas became a fan. Later, he would remark that, 'People have a relationship with a deejay whom they've never seen but to whom they feel very close because they're with him every day. For a lot of kids, he's the only friend they've got.'

While he lay in bed listening to the Wolfman, Lucas contemplated his future.

There were plenty of alternatives. As he recovered, his father pressed the point that if there was a time for his son to go into the family business, this was surely it. George responded with the stubbornness which his father must have recognized, since it reflected his own. Lucas Sr saw that money bought power and freedom. So did his son. He believed in a hard day's work for a fair salary. So did his son. He saw discipline, self-control, and self-reliance as the core of good character. So did his son. Lucas Jr rejected his father's values in adolescence, but spent the next years attaching himself to surrogate fathers who would tell him the same things: work hard, make money, and use it to buy independence.

With his car wrecked and no chance of financing another, Lucas's racing days were at an end, unless he took a job as a mechanic servicing someone else's ride. On the plus side, he had, against the odds, graduated from high school; though this had its negative aspects too, since he now became eligible to be drafted. At the end of *American Graffiti*, Terry the Toad, the character with whom Lucas is most identified, goes to Vietnam, where he is listed as missing in action – a fate explained in ironic detail in *More American Graffiti*.

Vietnam posed a potent threat to teenagers like Lucas in 1962. Many, including his future partner Gary Kurtz, served their stint. Some were judged too unhealthy for the army, as Lucas would be, though he didn't yet know it. Others found a way around it. Steven Spielberg would have been happy to hang out in San Jose, California after his high-school graduation (with grades as poor as Lucas's), seeing movies and making a few of his own on 8mm, but the arrival of his Selective Service Notice in early 1964 – delivered by his father while he waited in line to see Stanley Kubrick's *Dr Strangelove or How I Learned to Stop Worrying and Love the Bomb* – concentrated his mind wonderfully, and he enrolled at California State College at Long Beach, thus gaining a student exemption.

As he convalesced, Lucas decided to continue in school, and enrolled in junior college. These halfway houses between high school and college offered two-year courses, usually vocational. In the fall of 1962, Lucas enrolled in Modesto Junior College, assembling an arts major that even further exasperated his father: astronomy, sociology, speech, and art history – none of them any use in selling office supplies.

Except for speech, which Lucas hoped would improve his limited communication skills and eradicate his warbling croak of a voice (it didn't; he admits he was 'terrible in Speech class'), the other courses were those traditionally chosen by adolescents who, having rejected religion, are looking for a new belief system based in rationalism. Reason and science become the new gods. The new believer finds himself worshipping the Divine Order, the Power of the Mind, the Inevitability of Historical Change.

Already, an ambitious science fiction writer named Lafayette Ron Hubbard had cashed in on this thirst for certainties by inventing his own quasi-scientific religion, Scientology, which, with notable shrewdness, he'd launched via an article in the popular magazine *Astounding Science Fiction*. The same magazine gave generous publicity to the experiences of Dr Joseph Rhine of Duke University in hunting the elusive signs of what he christened 'psi powers': telepathy and telekinesis.

Lucas later read the basic works of sociology and anthropology which traced modern religion and morality back to their roots in tribal rituals and earth magic. But though he has been credited, retrospectively, with a near-lifelong interest in cultural studies and science fiction which blossomed in the *Star Wars* films, nobody can remember him being interested in anything but television and cars until long after he left Modesto.

In 1964 Lucas graduated from Modesto Junior College with an Associate in Arts degree, and an A in astronomy and Bs in speech, sociology, and art history. His grade average hovered around C, but that was enough to get into all but the most demanding colleges. John Plummer urged him to try USC with him. But Lucas decided he didn't want to move that far from home. Instead he enrolled at San Francisco State, which had the added advantage of being free.

He still had no clear idea of what career he might follow. At junior college he'd drifted back to photography, this time with an 8mm movie camera bought by his father. Though he no longer had ambitions to drive competitively, he also spent time around the race circuits, hanging out with Allen Grant and other old friends, but filming rather than tinkering with their cars. 'I wasn't the hot guy any more,' he recalled. 'I was sort of over the hill, though I still knew all the guys.'

Lucas discovered the pleasures of watching, ideally through the lens of a camera. People didn't ask awkward questions when you filmed them; they just let you be. And, seen through the camera, they themselves came into sharper focus. You could observe, comment, categorize, without saying a word.

What Lucas found more interesting than human beings, however, were objects. On occasional visits to Berkeley, he saw films of the new American 'underground' – Stan Brakhage's jittering 8mm diaries, Jonas Mekas's *Guns of the Trees* (1961), the abstractions of Harry Smith, John and James Whitney, Robert Breer, and in particular Jordan Belson, who projected his wobbling psychedelic creations on the walls of the San Francisco Planetarium.

The hot documentary from 1960 was *Jazz on a Summer's Day*, about the Newport Jazz Festival, the first and only film by fashion photographer Bert Stern. Stern didn't bother much with interviews. He preferred to stand back and film faces, or the reflections of yacht hulls on the surface of the water, which he cut to music by Mose Allison. There was no commentary, no point of view except that of the camera, no judgments, no argument, no plot. Lucas must have said to himself with some satisfaction, 'I can do that.' A year later, his student film *Herbie* would be made up entirely of reflections on the hubcaps and polished surface of a car, set to jazz by Herbie Hancock. Lucas's first film, made as a child, had been of plates, not people, and he didn't much change as an adult. His early student films would all be about cars. He shot them from a distance and up close, noticing the reflections on a polished fender or a windscreen; or clipped photographs from magazines and cut between them to create a narrative that bypassed performance. The idea of directing actors was, and would remain, distasteful.

★   ★   ★

No two people agree on how Lucas made the first step in the journey from Sunday cameraman to the most successful film-maker in history, but there's little doubt that cinematographer and documentary film-maker Haskell Wexler came into it.

The early sixties saw the arrival of new lightweight 16mm cameras and the documentary movement they engendered, *cinéma vérité*. The image of the cameraman with a 16mm Arriflex on his shoulder and a Nagra tape recorder close to hand – though not *in* hand; most professional tape machines still weighed twenty pounds – became a potent one, and even more so when Eclair launched its NPR, a sleek, updated version of the hand-held 16mm camera. With such equipment, a film-maker was independent, able to shoot where he liked, and with as little light as fast new film stocks would accept. Albert and David Maysles began turning out films in what they called 'Direct Cinema.' They were soon joined by Richard Leacock, D.A. Pennebaker and Robert Drew, who, as Drew Leacock Pennebaker, set most of the benchmarks with films like *Primary*, *The Chair*, and, as far as Lucas was concerned, the 1960 *Eddie*, about racing driver Eddie Sachs.

Haskell Wexler was thirty-six, and widely respected as a cameraman with a penchant for realism and a strong leftist political commitment. In 1958, Irvin Kershner had persuaded producer Roger Corman to finance *Stakeout on Dope Street*, a low-budget thriller about three boys who find a case full of drugs, and are pursued by the gang who owns it. Kershner co-wrote and directed. Wexler shot part of the film, adapting hand-held, low-light documentary technique to drama. He also lit Kershner's *The Hoodlum Priest* (1961), and *A Face in the Rain* (1963). In between, he worked on low-budget experimental films like *The Savage Eye* (1960), and on documentaries. It was one of these that brought him to Modesto.

How he met George Lucas has long been a subject of rival mythologies. Dale Pollock, in the semi-authorized *Skywalking*, says simply, 'Wexler took a liking to the weird skinny kid whose head was bursting with ideas. He went so far as to telephone some friends of his on USC's film school faculty and advised them to watch out for Lucas. "For God's sake, keep an eye on the kid," Wexler told one faculty member [presumably Gene Peterson, who had been his assistant and who now taught cinematography there]. "He's got the calling." But Wexler did not get Lucas into USC, as legend has it. Lucas had applied to the film school prior to meeting Wexler, and to George's and his father's amazement, he was accepted.'

Other sources make a more direct link, and emphasize Wexler's role. Charley Lippincott, who was at USC with Lucas and who would become his head of publicity and marketing, discounts the later story, encouraged by Lucas, that he had already made up his mind to enter film when he met Wexler: 'Wexler was up there doing a film about cars [probably *The Bus*, a documentary Wexler wrote, shot, and directed], and George helped him out, working on the film as production assistant or something.'

As an aficionado of car racing, Wexler inevitably ran into Allen Grant. As they talked, Wexler complained that he was having trouble with his Citroën-Maserati, notorious for its tricky timing. Grant said he knew someone who could help, a guy who'd been his mechanic and co-driver, and who was interested in movies too. 'George met up with Haskell Wexler,' says Lippincott, 'and told him he didn't know what he wanted to do, but that he was interested in film. And Haskell got him into USC. He's the one who persuaded him. I don't think George really knew that much about film at the time.'

John Plummer also played a part. His grades were better than Lucas's, and he wanted to enter USC in Los Angeles as a business major. He was going to LA to take the admission tests, and asked Lucas to keep him company. In fact, why didn't he take the test too? 'So I said, "All right," ' Lucas recalled, ' "but it's a long shot, 'cause my grades aren't good enough to get into a school like that." So I went and took the test and I passed. I got accepted!'

6

USC

[I want to thank] my teachers from kindergarten through college, their struggle – and it *was* a struggle – to help me learn to grow . . .

George Lucas in his speech to the Academy of Motion Picture Arts and Sciences, accepting the Irving Thalberg Award, 30 March 1992

Lucas enrolled at USC as a film major. His junior college courses counted toward credit, so he could skip his freshman and sophomore years, and enter as a junior.

Even then, his father still opposed the move, and scorned the whole idea of training for cinema. 'You're just going to become a ticket-taker at Disneyland,' he told him. 'You're never going to get a real job.' He also doubted his son's will: 'You'll be back in a few years.' George lost his temper. 'I'm never coming back!' he shouted. 'I'm going to be a millionaire before I'm thirty.'

Persistence wore Lucas Sr down. In an ingenious compromise, he offered to send his son through USC as an employee of the Lucas Company. He'd pay him a salary equal to his tuition fees, plus $200 a month – a substantial amount at a time when one could rent a very basic apartment for half that. If George didn't persevere with the course, he could be fired like any stock-room boy. With little choice in the matter, he took the deal.

In the early summer of 1964, he came down to Los Angeles. John Plummer was sharing an apartment in the beachside suburb of Malibu, and Lucas moved in. To fill in before courses and his $200-a-month payment started, he waited tables and did drawings of surfer girls with

47

the wide and dewy eyes of orphan children, which he hawked on the beach.

He also looked for part-time work in the film business. Ventura Boulevard, which ran along the San Fernando Valley side of the mountains separating the city's sprawling dormitory suburbs from Hollywood and Beverly Hills, was lined with two- and three-story office buildings, most of which harbored at least one film company. Lucas visited scores of them. He was the ten thousandth hopeful to do so, and, like everybody else, he found that the fanciful titles of those companies disguised mostly nickel-and-dime operations: freelance editors, producers of educational documentaries, or distributors of 16mm films. Real producers usually had office space on or near one of the big movie-company lots, walled cities where security guards barred anyone without a pass or an appointment.

Lucas checked into USC for his first semester in fall 1964. The university wasn't anything like he expected. It had a notable reputation for high academic distinction. One writer called it 'a citadel of privilege.' For decades it had supplied Los Angeles with its public officials, doctors, and engineers. But unlike UCLA, set among the lawns and groves of pepper trees in the elegant suburb of Westwood, USC had to content itself with what buildings it could find in its area of east LA, an old residential district through which the campus had metastasized over the years.

The best of USC's buildings shared the twenties *faux*-Spanish architecture of the Shrine Auditorium, the area's most distinctive structure, for many years Hollywood's village hall, and the site of the annual Academy Awards ceremony. The worst were functional at best, and were usually allocated to courses which stood well down the list from medicine, engineering, and law. On that scale, the film school, part of the theater department, ranked lowest of all.

Lucas, like all new arrivals, asked, 'Where's the theater department?'

'Over there.'

'But . . . that's a little *house*.'

'That's it.'

'Where are the theaters?'

'Well, we actually only have one. It's an auditorium, and it was built in 1902.'

Despite the grandiose Spanish-style gate that led to it, the film department consisted of three single-story wooden buildings in an expanse of open ground. They'd been stables for the horses of cavalrymen stationed there during World War I. In the twenties, it was the school of architecture, then, after 1929, the film school. Following World War II, the college erected two more army-surplus wooden barracks buildings to house an audio-visual unit which mainly trained government and military personnel to use educational film materials. On the side, it produced instructional films. That unit became the nucleus of the USC Cinema School.

The school had a bare minimum of facilities. The old stables became a sound stage, with a screening room next door, always called Room 108, with 35mm and 16mm projection. Editing machines – ancient upright Moviolas – were crammed into single large room, next to a storage space for cameras and other movie equipment. Classrooms, each with its own 16mm projector, occupied the barracks. There was nowhere to hang out, so students congregated in an open space in the middle of the buildings.

Students were required to live on campus for the first year. A high-rise dormitory, one of the college's few modern buildings, loomed over the cinema department, but it was reserved for female students. Most males, including Lucas, occupied Touton Hall, an older building across campus. It had no cafeteria, so he either had to trudge to the women's dorm and suffer its famously inedible food, or eat in the neighborhood – not then as dangerous as it became after the 1965 riots in nearby Watts.

To his alarm, he found he wouldn't have a room of his own. The college did make an effort to match up people of like interests, so he found himself sharing with Randy Epstein. A genial Angeleno, Epstein, now a successful Californian property developer, was used to prosperity, and was surprised by Lucas's Spartan possessions – which consisted mostly of a Nikon 35mm camera and some clothes. He didn't even have a stereo, a deficiency which Epstein remedied.

Watching him unpack his wardrobe of plaid shirts, jeans, and a boxy jacket with too-wide lapels, woven from a blanket-like fabric with metallic threads, Epstein wondered where Lucas had got his vision of how people dressed in Los Angeles – from the movies? To another student, Don Glut, who'd come from Chicago trailing a reputation as a motorcycle freak and street-gang member, Lucas was 'very conservative-looking. Those were the days of the hippie look, but he had short hair. He looked like a young businessman. Somebody working his way up to corporate office.' Hal Barwood, also in the film school, thought he resembled Buddy Holly. Lucas's long silences emphasized his air of strangeness. Nervousness increased the tremor in his voice, turning it into a nervous warble. Screenwriter Lawrence Kasdan says, 'He's sort of like a cartoon character. In fact his voice, I think, is like about ten different cartoon characters.' Each morning, Lucas walked to his USC window and said, 'Hello, world.' It sounded, says Epstein, 'just like Kermit the frog from *The Muppets*.'

For every USC student doing a course in the humanities, a dozen were on athletics scholarships, including most of the college's few African-Americans, one of whom, on the 1967 football team, was O.J. Simpson. The majority of these jocks lived as if people like Lucas, Epstein, Glut, and the other arts types didn't exist. Glut says disgustedly, 'We were mostly in the company of beer-guzzling, fraternity-type idiots. Lots of football players, who would do isometric exercises by straining against the side of doors, and screaming. It was like they didn't have heads: their neck and head were the same width, as if the head was just another cervical verterbra, only with hair on it.' USC still kept up its intimate relationship with the military, and the film school routinely enrolled a large contingent of air force and navy personnel each year for training in camera operation and sound recording – an older, more reserved, and decidedly non-hippie group which stuck together, and represented a further damping influence.

Surrounded by an atmosphere somewhere between *Animal House* and *Full Metal Jacket*, the remaining film-school students seldom socialized with anyone else on campus. 'When people would ask, "Are you in a fraternity or something?" ' recalls Randy Epstein, 'I'd say, "No, I'm basically going to a private school within a private school, and we never see the outside of these four walls." ' Had they been more gregarious, or the atmosphere more welcoming, the history of cinema might have been very different; but the sense of isolation encouraged a feeling of them-against-us that grew into a revolution.

The USC students of 1966–68 reads like a roll-call of New Hollywood. They included John Milius, director of *Big Wednesday* and *The Wind and the Lion*, the legendary scriptwriter of *Apocalypse Now*, and 'fixer' on films as various as *Jaws* and *Dirty Harry*; Randal Kleiser, director of *Grease* and *The Blue Lagoon*; Basil Poledouris, composer of scores for *Conan the Barbarian* and *Iron Eagle*; Walter Murch, sound editor on *Apocalypse Now* and *The Conversation*, and director of *Return to Oz*; Howard Kazanjian, line producer on *Raiders of the Lost Ark* and other collaborations between George Lucas and Steven Spielberg; screenwriter Willard Huyck, who, with his wife Gloria Katz, then at UCLA, wrote *American Graffiti*, parts of the *Indiana Jones* series, and *Howard the Duck*, which Huyck also directed; Caleb Deschanel, cinematographer of *The Black Stallion* and *The Right Stuff*; and Hal Barwood and Matthew Robbins, who would co-script *Sugarland Express* for Spielberg – Robbins as a director also made films like **batteries not included*, while Barwood, who began as an animator at USC, became a career writer of video games for Lucasfilm. Also in Lucas's classes were Don Glut, who wrote the novelization of *The Empire Strikes Back* and directed *Dinosaur Valley Girls*; and Charley Lippincott, later Lucas's marketing manager, and a force in the launching of *Star Wars*. Then, and later, women played little part in what was seen as a man's business. 'There were about two women in the whole film program,' says John Milius. ('Three', insists Randy Epstein, 'but we weren't sure about one of them.')

To Lucas, the faculty was no more impressive than the campus. 'Most of the people were "those who can't do, teach"-type people,' says Don Glut. 'The film-history class was mostly watching movies and talking about them. That was Arthur Knight's class. His book *The Liveliest Art* became our textbook – which generated a lot of royalties for Professor Knight. The only person who had ever done anything was Irwin Blacker, who taught screenwriting. He'd written some books and screenplays. Mel Sloan was a professional editor. The animation course was directed by Herb Kossower. There was a guy named Gene Peterson whose big claim to fame was he had been a gaffer on *Stakeout on Dope Street*.' (Glut is actually in error here, though the truth is even more improbable. The one film on which Peterson appears to have received a professional credit, indeed as a gaffer, i.e. electrician's laborer, was *The Brain Eaters*, a 1958 horror film directed by Bruno Ve Sota.)

'These people were staff, not professors,' says Charley Lippincott, who came to USC via its night school, which taught a slimmed-down film course. 'Dave Johnson taught production management. He'd been there forever; went to school there. He was probably the best-liked teacher. Ken Miura taught sound. A lot of these guys came out of the Second World War, and had been there on the GI Plan.'

*   *   *

Neat in his Modesto clothes, Lucas turned up dutifully at film classes, as well as those in astronomy and English, which he had to take as part of his regular course. He had no idea what kind of movies he was going to see, but those which were shown jolted someone whose limited experience of cinema was almost entirely Hollywood. Inflamed by legends of 'the Underground,' the students preferred the films of the French New Wave, which had taken off in 1959 with Truffaut's *Les Quatre Cents Coups* and Godard's 1960 *A Bout de Souffle*. The fashion for hand-held cameras, natural light, real locations, and sound recorded 'live' spread through them like a virus.

Godard's 1965 science fiction film *Alphaville* made a particular impression. It followed a secret agent of the future, called 'Lemmy Caution' after Peter Cheyney's detective hero, whom the film's star Eddie Constantine often played on screen, as he infiltrates, none too subtly, the city of Alphaville, controlled by a computer called Alpha 60, which rigorously suppresses all emotion, keeping the inhabitants numbed by drugs, sex, and violent death. With typical bravado, Godard ignored special effects. Footage of Paris's bleaker suburbs stood in for Alphaville, and Alpha 60 was just the disembodied voice of a man speaking through an artificial larynx. To Lucas in particular, it was a powerful lesson, which he would put into practice in his major student film, *THX1138*.

Many of the teachers, particularly those teaching craft courses like camerawork and sound recording, also embraced the *nouvelle vague.* Its techniques weren't much different from those used in documentary everywhere. 'The faculty was into art films,' says Randy Epstein. 'If it had sprocket-holes showing, or was a little out of focus, they loved it.' Richard Walter said scornfully of their attitude, 'A real film-maker didn't write his or her film. They put a camera on their shoulder, sprayed the environment with a lens; they Did Their Own Thing, Let It All Hang Out, and anything they did was beautiful, because Hey, *you're* beautiful.'

Arthur Knight screened the films praised by his generation of critics: the classics of German expressionism like *Metropolis*, Sergei Eisenstein's *Battleship Potemkin*, *Alexander Nevsky*, and *Ivan the Terrible*, D.W. Griffith, F.W. Murnau, Orson Welles, David Lean. Nobody decreed to be 'commercial' received a second look, including later heroes of New Hollywood like Douglas Sirk and Sam Fuller. Even Alfred Hitchcock was regarded as having 'sold out.'

John Milius adulated B-westerns and the films of directors like Fuller, and Don Glut was a fanatic for serials and old science fiction and horror films. As a boy in Chicago, he had made thirty 16mm films, including a version of *Frankenstein*. Such was his enthusiasm for serials that his mother sewed him a Superman suit and another like that worn by the Martian menace of *The Purple Monster Strikes*, both of which he brought to USC. His devotion won over Randy Epstein and other students, who held popular late-night screenings of serials until Herb Kossower ejected them – not for misuse of the facilities, but for the nature of the films they showed. Marked as troublemakers, students like Glut and Milius had a tough time at USC. The faculty almost flunked Glut because of his enthusiasm for cheap fantasy films and his habit of reading comic books between classes. He finally had to do an extra year to get his degree. Milius, refused a passing grade in a French course by a professor who regarded him as 'a savage,' never graduated at all.

Lucas drove a silver Camaro, and continued to wear his Modesto clothes. The only person in the film classes who looked more square was Randal Kleiser, who moonlighted as a photographic model. In their second year at USC, his beach-boy good looks beamed from billboards all over Los Angeles, advertising Pepsi-Cola. Don Glut, who, despite his raffish background, had some of the same style, formed what he called the Clean-Cut Cinema Club. The members were himself, Kleiser, Randy Epstein, Chris Lewis (the son of film star Loretta Young), and Lucas. The group contrasted starkly with the hippie element of the school, personified by Milius, who wore no shoes, extravagantly praised the then-unfashionable films of John Ford and the almost unknown Akira Kurosawa, lived in a converted bomb-shelter near the beach so he could surf every day, and let it be known that he was only marking time in college until he could enter the Marines, go to Vietnam, and die gloriously in battle. When the Marines turned him down because of his chronic asthma, he directed his frustrated taste for heroics into screenwriting.

USC's formal requirements were lax. The few papers required were mostly book reports, and as long as Lucas turned up and took at least a perfunctory part in class discussions, he was unlikely to fail any course for academic reasons. He'd also found his mechanical skill much in demand. The Moviolas and ancient clockwork Cine Special cameras were always breaking down, and he was usually the only person who knew how to fix them.

Like all the students, he gravitated to the congenial teachers, and away from those who demanded too much. The least popular was Irwin Blacker, who taught a screenwriting course from which students had been known to emerge in tears. Unlike almost everyone else, Blacker flunked those who didn't meet his exacting standards, or share his respect for the Aristotelian model of story structure. Those who survived, including Milius and Richard Walter, emerged with a grasp of screenwriting technique that stood them in good stead in Hollywood. Walter, now head of the screenwriting department at UCLA's film school, called Blacker 'a cantankerous, obstinate, boorish bull of a guy,' but 'my mentor and my inspiration.'

Lucas shunned Blacker's class, but enjoyed that of Arthur Knight. The antithesis of Blacker, cordial, clubbable, and social, Knight had come to a comfortable accommodation with both academe and the film business. Through his journalism for magazines like the *Saturday Review* and the *Hollywood Reporter*, he maintained close contacts with the industry, which he exploited on behalf of USC. He ran a lecture series called 'Thursday Night at the Movies' where directors often presented their new films and discussed them with students. Afterwards, Knight liked to invite the guest and some students back to his home for drinks. David Lean previewed *Doctor Zhivago* at one of Knight's evenings in 1965, and Jean-Luc Godard spoke the following year. In both cases, Lucas attended. The screening room in which Knight held court became the *ad hoc* center of film studies at USC, to the extent that when the school was rebuilt in the nineties – largely with Lucas money – a space was named Room 405 in its honor.

Knight's encouragement of his students went beyond occasional *soirées* in the Hollywood Hills. His student assistant had a valuable inside view of what was going on and coming up. Charley Lippincott held the job for a while, after which it passed to Richard Walter. Knight also occasionally recommended students for part-time jobs in the industry, or scholarships which came his way via the few USC alumni who had gone on to make careers in the industry. This small and not-particularly-distinguished group included James Ivory, who in those days before *A Room with a View* and *Howards End* was living in India and making low-budget features like *Shakespeare Wallah* and *The Guru*; cameraman Conrad Hall, a moving force in the setting up of the National Association of Broadcast Employees and Technicians, NABET, the craft union more sympathetic to low-budget producers and television than the monolithic International Alliance of Theatrical and Stage Employees, IATSE; and Denis Sanders, who with his brother Terry had won an Oscar for their short film *A Time out of War* in 1954, and who had gone on to make low-budget independent features like *War Hunt* (1961).

The most distinguished USC alumnus, however, and the most typical of the generation before Lucas and his friends, was Irvin Kershner. Tall and bearded, with a goatish profile like that of a Biblical patriarch or an Arab chieftain, 'Kersh' had many friends on the faculty of the film school, in particular Mel Sloan and Gene Peterson, and sometimes taught courses there when they went on leave. He had drifted into USC after World War II, following desultory attempts at careers in painting and music. The then-dean of communications asked him to give a course in photography, after which he taught himself cinematography to shoot some of the documentaries the school made as part of a deal to supply instructional material to the US Public Health Service.

Kershner's experience of the professional film business was instructive, and enshrined the received wisdom about getting a job in movies after graduation: you didn't have a chance. 'They wouldn't let me in the Cameraman's Union, the Editing Union, or the Art-Director's Union,' he told the students, 'so I said, "There's only one thing to do – direct." ' He sneaked in the back door, getting jobs as a cameraman on TV documentaries which led to his low-budget and non-union feature *Stakeout on Dope Street*, made for a bare-bones $30,000.

At every turn, students like Lucas were told they might as well forget a career in Hollywood feature-film-making. 'Everybody knew there were only three ways to get into the film business,' says Randy Epstein. 'You could be born the son or nephew of a famous film personality, or you could marry a producer's daughter. I forget the third one.' Even if they got into a union, they faced a tortuous apprenticeship of three to five years before they won their card. Gary Kurtz, later Lucas's producer and partner, went through USC from 1959 to 1962, and graduated as a cameraman. 'It was impossible to break into the industry in any of the guilds or unions,' he says. 'So we were more or less forced to work in the low-budget or exploitation area, really. A lot of film-school graduates just got tired of that process and did other things. They became teachers at other film schools or universities, or they went into educational or documentary films, which weren't so rigidly unionized. They started to work for television stations around the country, which didn't have that problem either.'

The very idea of film school was anathema to Hollywood. Charley Lippincott was warned not to mention that he went to USC if he ever visited a studio lot. 'We were all brainwashed with the notion that none of us would ever get into the business,' says Don Glut. 'We might work in camera shops or as projectionists in theaters, but we were never going to work in the business.'

For the craft classes, film lighting, editing, and animation, the end-of-year examination was a film, culminating, in the senior year, in a graduate exercise in film direction; Course 480 of the curriculum. For the first year, everyone in Herb Kossower's animation class was given one minute of black-and-white 16mm stock and told to use the Oxberry animation camera to make a film. Most of them animated drawings or manipulated objects in stop-action. Lucas decided to make a film that was both serious and professional. *A Look at Life* was a collage of photographs from *Life* magazine. Its zooms, cuts, and pans across contrasting images of girls in bikinis, lovers, babies, politicians, vampires, and civilians being shot in the Congo might have been meant to illustrate the popular slogan 'Make love, not war.' Kossower, impressed, urged him to enter it in student film festivals, where its brevity and pace made it a favorite. It won a number of prizes.

Thereafter, Lucas became Kossower's star pupil, and a faculty favorite, a role he cemented with his second film, *Herbie*. An exercise for the lighting class, Lucas made the film with Paul Golding, another above-average student who, like so many, left the industry after graduation. They edited together abstract close-ups of night-time reflections in the polished surface of a car. The vehicle isn't a Volkswagen, though it is normally described as one, since two years later Disney chose the name 'Herbie' for the sentient VW of its fantasy *The Love Bug*. The Herbie of Lucas's title is jazz pianist Herbie Hancock, whom Lucas approached to supply a few minutes of background music. A voice, presumably Hancock's, is heard on the soundtrack saying, 'What can I do for ya?', then, 'Not like sittin' at home, I can tell ya.' In between, the camera of Lucas and Golding watches light ripple over the car's gleaming fenders and spotless windscreen. The credit reads: 'These moments of reflection have been brought to you by Paul Golding and George Lucas.'

★   ★   ★

Lucas was initially rejected by the film-school fraternity, Delta Kappa Alpha, because of his nerdy image, though once it approved him, he took almost no part in its activities except to grab something from its snack bar when the cafeterias were closed. By day, the editing machines were in almost constant use, but Lucas and others sneaked back at night, missing dinner. A diet of candy and junk food finally undermined his frail constitution and brought him down with mononucleosis.

Even when he wasn't working, Lucas didn't mix much, least of all with women. Flirting was integral to college life, and there was a lot of sex about – much, though not all of it, playful. The film-school patio was a short-cut to other parts of the campus, and girls from the nearby women's dorm passed through constantly, to be hit on by the more aggressive male students. Others borrowed telephoto lenses from the camera store to peek into the dorm windows, at which the girls occasionally staged discreet stripteases, tantalizingly terminated at the last moment, to the chagrin of the watchers.

'George was chasing girls,' says Milius. 'He didn't catch them, but he *was* chasing them.' Richard Walter agrees that Lucas was no Lothario. 'I've read books that claimed George was a ladies' man. It's nonsense. He was very, very reticent.' Randy Epstein's girl 'fixed up' Lucas with a friend of hers, with an unconventional result. 'He spoke to her on the phone for many hours over many days before he got the courage to ask her out,' says Epstein, 'and the fascinating thing is, he asked her to describe herself. Then he did an oil painting of what he thought she would look like. Not a sketch, but an actual oil painting. It was amazingly like her. It was like he'd cheated and got a look at her somehow. The girl was just overwhelmed that he had the talent to do this without even seeing her.'

In his second year, Lucas rented a house off-campus, a rickety wooden building on Portola Drive, in the Hollywood hills. His father grudgingly paid the $80 a month rent. To reach the upper floors of the three-level house, you climbed a ladder, and the furniture was minimal, but Lucas felt secure there. After a few months, Randal Kleiser moved in to share the rent. Both were friendly with another of the Clean-Cut group, Christopher Lewis. Lewis's mother, Loretta Young, after a fairly lurid youth, had found God in middle age and, with her husband Tom Lewis, embarked on the production of a pietistic TV series, *The Loretta Young Show*. Since the show ended in

1961, Tom Lewis's production facilities were often unused, and his son persuaded him to let his USC friends edit and record there. For *Orgy Beach Party*, an unfinished parody, produced by Christopher Lewis and directed by Don Glut, of the then-popular 'beach party' films, Kleiser played the handsome hero and Glut the monster who carries off the girl. Lucas shot stills, and they used the Lewis studio to record the theme song with Glut's garage band, the Hustlers. In between, Lewis's friends, including Lucas, often hung out at the sumptuous home of his parents. In their senior year, Lucas and Lewis even formed a production company, Sunrise Films, but it never made a film.

By the start of his second year at USC, Lucas had found his level. His Modesto wardrobe remained, though he'd ditched the unfortunate jackets. He'd also grown a beard, which gave character to his face, and disguised a weak chin, as well as earning him honorary credentials as a radical. At the same time, he remained shrewdly aware of the advantages of good faculty relations. While students like Glut, Milius, and Epstein drew fire from their teachers for turning out pastiches like *Superman and the Gorilla Gang*, which Glut not only wrote, directed, and edited, but for which he also composed the music, built the models, and did the special effects – which were impressive, given the minuscule budget – Lucas went for solid production values and certified liberal sentiments. For his second-year directing project, *Freiheit* ('freedom' in German), introduced as 'A film by LUCAS,' he persuaded Randal Kleiser to play a young man running away from a battle, suggested by sounds of artillery in the distance. He reaches a frontier, evidently that between East and West Germany, but is shot down by a soldier (Christopher Lewis). As he lies bleeding, voices on the soundtrack discuss the significance of freedom and the need to endure sacrifices to protect it.

Whatever else USC taught Lucas, the key concept he absorbed was the importance of teamwork. With so few resources and so little time, nothing got done unless you enlisted people to help you. Projects risked becoming incestuous. Basil Poledouris's senior film, *Glut*, wove a fictional story around the character of USC's most dissident student. Milius wrote it, Lucas recorded sound, and most other students had walk-on parts. It's an effective and amusing little film from a man who would later become best known as a composer. At the start, Glut, playing himself, tries out for a job as a stuntman with Sam Fuller, who asks him if he can do a back-flip. Glut admits he can't, but says he can fall off the back of a truck like Dave Sharpe in one serial, or do a fight like Dale van Sickel in another. 'You're not a stuntman,' says Fuller dismissively. Disconsolate, Glut goes to a party wearing his Purple Monster costume. Scorned by everyone, he leaves, complaining, 'Men don't feel grandeur any more' – a classic Milius line – only to achieve his moment of glory by rescuing a girl from a purse-snatcher.

The USC students helped one another because their instructors made it clear from the start that only results mattered. Not ignorance, nor sickness, nor acts of God excused failing to deliver an exercise on time. 'A student would show his workshop project,' says Richard Walter, 'and someone would say, "Gee, that doesn't make sense to me . . ." And the film-maker would go into a dissertation of explanations. "Well, that day the sound man didn't show up, and the landlady came in and ran us out, and I just had time to get this one angle . . ." And the instructor would say, "Well, put it on a title card at the head of the film. Say, 'This is why the movie is the way it is – because we had all these problems.' " ' To those in the class really listening, the moral was clear: in the outside world, excuses bought nothing. Later, Lucas would put the lesson into the mouth of Yoda, the Jedi master of *The Empire Strikes Back*. When Luke Skywalker says he'll try to harness the power of the Force, the sage says, '*Try not. Do. Or do not. There is no try.*' What people took for Zen was really USC.

Nobody was more generous with assistance than Lucas. He recorded sound and helped edit Milius's animated film, *Marcello, I'm so Bored*, and there were few USC films of the period in which he didn't take a hand. Some people resented his dismissive manner and impatience with the maladroit. Finding Walter Murch developing film in the lab, Lucas told him he was doing it wrong. A native New Yorker, Murch already had a BA in art history and romance languages from Johns Hopkins before he arrived at USC in 1965 to do his masters in cinema. He'd studied Italian medieval art history in Perugia, and French literature and nineteenth-century art history in Paris. Fluent in French and Italian, tall, solemn, erudite, and irascible, he was, says Gary Kurtz, 'quite control-freakish; perfect for an editor,' and didn't suffer criticism gladly. 'Who's this creep?' he demanded. 'Get out of here! What do *you* know?'

But Murch too became a devoted member of the Lucas team. Like Allen Grant before him and Francis Ford Coppola after, Murch was another elder-brother figure from whom Lucas could learn, and in whom in turn he could inspire the kind of personal loyalty that creates effective teams.

Lucas credits Murch for alerting him to the possibilities of sound. Like the new wave film-makers, most USC students didn't much care about their soundtracks, providing the dialogue was improvised and the background sound recorded 'wild,' i.e. on the spot. But Lucas noticed how a good track could lure audiences: 'The screen for the screening room was positioned against a hallway that led out onto a patio where everyone would congregate,' he said. 'The speakers would echo into the hallway and the sound would funnel out into the open space. You knew that if you had a film with a great soundtrack you could draw an audience into the room.'

While many other USC students goofed off, turned on or dropped out, Lucas continued to create ambitious films, and to win prizes with them in student film festivals all over the country. His enthusiasm for Jean-Luc Godard peaked at about the time Godard made a personal appearance at USC in 1966. His interest then switched to slicker, more professional movies.

Charley Lippincott watched the change at first hand. Lippincott had access to the documentaries of the National Film Board of Canada, then in its heyday, and often screened them. In 1965 the CNFB's hottest cameraman was Jean-Claude Labrecque, who shot and directed a film about the Tour de St Laurent, a 1500-mile bike race. He called it *60 Cycles*. A relentless exercise in style, *60 Cycles* emphasized the bikes rather than the men who rode them. Much of it was shot with telephoto lenses that compressed the riders into an apparently motionless mass of furious pedalling humanity, or from a helicopter, so that they appear a single organism, slithering through a town like a snake. The music was mostly hard-driving rock, typified by the pumping organ riff of 'Green Onions' by Booker-T and the MGs.

'I brought down *60 Cycles*,' says Lippincott. 'I may have shown it in directing class too. People were swept away, and George borrowed it, and flipped out over it. I had a terrible time getting it back. I had it for a week, and finally after a week and a half I pried it out of him.

It got me in trouble with the Canadian consulate. But it fit George perfectly. The technical stuff with the lenses was so "George" that it was unbelievable.' When the college acquired the latest 16mm camera, the Eclair NPR, Lucas seized it as his personal property.

Everyone at USC remembers Lucas's films abandoning *nouvelle vague* casualness. He earned a reputation for high production values. 'I had the feeling he had more money than us,' says Don Glut, 'because he was able to do things that we couldn't do. He could get aerial shots; rent airplanes to get shots of race cars from the sky.' The money for the ambitious touches in Lucas's films came from his father, who had attended a student screening, and had been surprised by the respectful reaction of the laid-back and largely stoned audience to his son's films. When they came on, kids murmured, 'Watch this, it's George's film.' Driving back to Modesto, George Sr conceded to his wife, 'I think we may have put our money on the right horse.'

Already, the students were separating into those with grandiose ambitions and those resigned to taking a back seat, or dropping out altogether. During the summer, Walter Murch and Matthew Robbins had gone to England and, 'in a farmer's field,' according to Lippincott, 'had found an old Rolls-Royce, one of those ones with the open back seat. They brought it back and rebuilt it.' Lucas surprised John Milius by telling him he'd met a man with a restored World War II P51 Mustang fighter. If Milius could think up a story that included one, he'd help him film it. 'The rest of them didn't think big,' says Milius. 'They were thinking about meeting some girl, and she was good-looking so they were going to put her in the film, and get to sleep with her. And if not, maybe she'd wear some revealing outfit in the film. Or they would imitate some French film, some *avant-garde* style. I would try and do it through convincing people. George would do it through nuts and bolts. I'd say, "Join me on this great crusade." But George would know someone who had a race car, and he'd go out and persuade him to let him put the camera on his race car. The guy just thought he was going to have pretty pictures of his race car. George was thinking, "This is a film about a race car. It's going to look good, and have great sound, and be in color." '

Everyone in the senior class was gearing up for their last film, the 480 Project. Instead of the normal five-man crew, Lucas called in favors all over campus, and accumulated a team of fourteen. Getting a camera and sound gear was harder. 'You'd try to steal film from the other guys, steal equipment,' says Milius. 'One thing I did do was steal the camera George loved so much, the Eclair. He was the only one who could use that camera. Everyone else was awed by the technology, but George, being a race-car mechanic and a great great visual guy, understanding light and all this stuff, could very quickly master the technology of anything. He really wanted to use that camera, and I stole it, and hid it in my car, and slept in my car with the camera for a week while we used it.'

Lucas's car-race film was called *1.42:08*, named for the lap time of the yellow sports car which was its subject. His expertise with cars had got him a job as cameraman for Saul Bass, Hollywood's premiere creator of title sequences. Lucas shot some material for the short film *Why Man Creates*, one of the few Bass works not attached to a feature. Bass was doing the credits for John Frankenheimer's epic car-racing movie *Grand Prix*, and Lucas used his background in car racing to infiltrate the second unit shooting with James Garner at the Willow Springs raceway, north of Los Angeles. *Grand Prix* provided the impetus for *1.42:08*, but *60 Cycles* was evident in every frame. Lucas persuaded driver Pete Brook to contribute his car and his time. Edward Johnson, his obliging flyer friend, gave him a single aerial shot looking down on the speeding car. *1.42:08* had no sound except the blare of the car's engine. Repeated tracks over the racer as it's gassed up show the enthusiasm for machinery that would typify most of Lucas's later films, and though we do glimpse Brook as humanly fallible when he spins out in the middle of the practice and grimaces at his error, the film has no character except the car.

7

Electronic Labyrinth

'Down there,' he is inclined to say of Hollywood, 'down there, for every honest true film-maker trying to get his film off the ground, there are a hundred sleazy used-car dealers trying to con you out of your money.'

Lucas in *New York Times*, 13 July 1981

Once he graduated from USC, Lucas, outside the protection of his student exemption, was eligible for the draft. With a few other ex-USC people, he was urged to flee to Canada and get a job at the Canadian National Film Board. However, some classmates from the air force contingent counselled him not only to stay in LA, but actually to volunteer. As a college graduate with impeccable film-making credentials, they told him, he'd be immediately sent to Officer Candidate School, then posted to a film-making unit in the US, where he'd gain valuable professional experience far from the front line.

During the summer of his graduation, Lucas, according to legend, tried to enlist, but was turned down because his teenage driving convictions gave him, technically, a criminal record. One is forced to be skeptical about this story. Such minor offences were only taken into account if the offender compounded them by consistently failing to turn up in court, or evaded bench warrants issued by the judge for his arrest; otherwise anyone could have dodged the draft simply by getting arrested for dangerous driving. Had he been accepted for OCS, Lucas might, in fact, have been dismayed by the result. Gary Kurtz, who went through USC from 1959 to 1962, was drafted into the Marines as a cameraman, and didn't get out until 1969. 'There were so many photographers killed,' he says, 'that we became what they called a Critical MOS, and they kept sending us letters saying, "You have been extended, convenience of the government," and in theory, I found out later, they could have done that forever.' Whether Lucas presented himself for military service voluntarily or when he received his Selective Service Notice, he was almost certainly rejected for the same medical reasons that finally kept him out of the forces permanently. The standard physical examination revealed that the diabetes that had killed his grandfather had jumped a generation and reappeared in him. Rating him 4F, the medical board warned him to seek help for what would be a lifetime problem.

Lucas drove shakily to Modesto, where Roland Nyegaard, the physician who'd married his sister Wendy, confirmed the diagnosis. Nyegaard put him on Orinase, an oral drug that replaced the traditional daily insulin injections of most diabetes sufferers, and warned Lucas to start watching his diet: no drugs, no alcohol, above all no sweets. Farewell to chocolate malts, chocolate chip cookies, and Hershey bars, which he'd consumed in quantity since childhood. It was a rite of passage of sorts. With one of the last great pleasures of adolescence denied him, he had no choice but to grow up.

The discovery of his diabetes freed Lucas to launch his adult career. His first thought was to re-enter USC as a graduate student and get his Master of Fine Arts degree, but he was too late for the 1967 intake. All the same, the faculty was sufficiently impressed with his student work to offer him a part-time job in its night school, running a refresher course for navy and Marine Corps cameramen: 'The whole idea of the class was to teach them they didn't have to go by the rulebook,' Lucas said.

He accepted, then went looking for a day job. Bob Dalva, a USC student who would become one of the moving forces of Francis Coppola's American Zoetrope, and who was already adept at keeping his ear to the ground, had a job with Verna Fields, who was compiling a film for the United States Information Agency called *Journey to the Pacific*, about Lyndon Johnson's seventeen-country tour of Australia, Korea, and points east in pursuit of consensus on Vietnam. Dalva proposed Lucas as assistant editor, and Fields hired him.

Burly and aggressive, Fields had grown hard and cynical in a business that routinely demeaned women. She'd been sound editor for Fritz Lang and worked on big productions like Anthony Mann's epic *El Cid*, but never made it past the eighth or ninth panel of the credits. In between projects, she freelanced from her ranch house in the San Fernando Valley, the garage of which she'd converted into cutting rooms. When Gene Sloan went on sabbatical from USC, she taught his editing class, and got to know Lucas. Early in 1967, shortly after USC confirmed he could enter their 1968 graduate course, Lucas began driving out into the Valley every day to help cut the LBJ documentary.

Also heading there was Marcia Griffin, whom Fields had hired from a private film company, Sandler Films, to find and log the thousands of miles of Johnson footage. Space was tight, so Fields put the two newcomers in the same cutting room. Marcia, even shorter than George, had a clean, pastel prettiness that implied an upbringing in some upper-middle-class San Fernando suburb like Encino or Reseda. In fact, she grew up in air force bases all over America as her father hauled his family wherever he was posted, before finally abandoning them. With maintenance and child support patchy at best, Marcia and her sisters became accustomed to doing without, and to getting what they wanted by their own efforts. During her teens, Marcia went to live in Florida for two years with her father, moved back to Los Angeles, took a clerical job and studied chemistry at night school, then dropped out. Always interested in movies, she fell into a job as an apprentice film librarian at Sandler. After that, she embarked on the eight-year apprenticeship demanded by the Motion Picture Editors' Guild as the price of a union card.

Though she looked archetypally Angeleno, Marcia had been born in Modesto while her father was stationed at nearby Stockton. It took her some days to discover that Lucas was from the same town, since her presence in the cutting room reduced him to a near-paralysis of shyness.

'I used to say, "Well, George, where'ya from?"' she recalled.

'"Hmmm, California."'

'"Oh, OK, where in California?"'

'"Ummm . . . Northern California."'

'"Where in Northern California?"'

'"Just up north, the San Francisco area . . ."'

They found common ground in movies, though most of the time they argued about them. Lucas was ruthless at dismissing Marcia's enthusiasms. 'He was the intellectual,' she said bitterly. 'I was just a

Valley girl.' She responded to Dalva's and Lucas's pose of high seriousness by patronizing them too: they were just film students – she was a professional. Lucas put a softer complexion on their early relationship: 'We were both feisty, and neither one of us would take any shit from the other. I sort of liked that. I didn't like someone who could be run over.' But he would consistently underestimate Marcia's commitment to her craft. 'I love film editing,' she said later. 'I have an innate ability to take good material and make it better, and to take bad material and make it fair. I think I'm even an editor in life.'

The Johnson documentary progressed slowly. Its USIA producer demanded as many flattering shots as possible of the president. Above all, any film showing his thinning hair must be avoided. When Lucas edited footage of LBJ's visit to South Korea to suggest, through scenes of students being brutally pacified by the police, that the Korean administration was fascistic, the producer demanded he recut it. Furious, Lucas swore never again to edit other people's films: 'I realized that I didn't want other people telling me how to cut a film. *I* wanted to decide. *I* really wanted to be responsible for what was being said in a movie.'

His insistence on protecting his films against any interference in the cutting room would become obsessive. Friends would roll their eyes and say, 'Lighten up, George,' but on this he was utterly intransigent. Marcia, whom George was now desultorily dating, never came to terms with his emphasis on the sacrosanct nature of editing decisions. It wasn't her style to walk out on a project. One stuck to it and, little by little, got one's way. Her persistence would make her one of the most sought-after editors of New Hollywood. Producer Julia Phillips even rated her 'the better – certainly the warmer – half of the *American Graffiti* team.'

'She was an absolutely stunning editor,' says John Milius. 'Maybe the best editor I've ever known, in many ways. She'd come in and look at the films we'd made – like *The Wind and the Lion*, for instance – and she'd say, "Take this scene and move it over here," and it worked. And it did what I wanted the film to do, and I would never have thought of it. And she did that to everybody's films: to George's, to Steven [Spielberg]'s, to mine, and Scorsese particularly. He'll attest to the fact that she was a great editor. She was a genuinely talented film-maker. She should have become a director.'

But in 1967 people defined Marcia Griffin, as they defined most women in Hollywood, with reference to their men. She was George's girlfriend and, eventually, wife, and very little beyond that. In general, Lucas shared that perception, as did most of New Hollywood's husbands about their wives. Not surprisingly, divorce became the group's norm. The first marriages of Lucas, Spielberg, Milius, Scorsese and most other newcomers of the sixties ended in divorce, their unwillingness to deal on screen with contemporary human situations replicated in their lives. Many marriages expire in the bedroom, but that of George and Marcia Lucas was rare in coming to grief in the cutting room.

Whatever claims were made later, Lucas had little or no interest in science fiction films until after he graduated from USC in August 1966. He wasn't alone in his indifference. The doyen of Hollywood sf, George Pal, hadn't made a movie since *The Conquest of Space* in 1955. The benchmark of big-budget studio science fiction, MGM's *Forbidden Planet*, was a decade old. In Britain, Stanley Kubrick was preparing *2001: A Space Odyssey*, but that wouldn't be released for two years. Only starvation producer Roger Corman consistently turned out sf films, though he hadn't actually shot one for years. It was cheaper to buy Russian or Japanese movies with lavish special-effect sequences, dump their dialogue scenes, then find some hungry young American film-maker to invent a new framing story.

Almost nobody saw these cheap sf movies in the big cities, though they cleaned up in rural drive-ins, where the twelve-to-twenty-five-year-old audience Lucas and Spielberg would inherit had begun to show its muscle. Raised on comic books and television, teenagers wanted sensational stories and gaudy special effects. When they couldn't find them on screen, they invented them. All over the United States, amateur mask- and model-makers were painstakingly creating their own science fiction and horror films on 8mm. By the time Lucas made *Star Wars*, they had ripened into a generation of special-effects technicians ready to tinker together the technology he needed to realize his fantasy.

The big films of 1966 – *A Man for All Seasons, Who's Afraid of Virginia Woolf?* (shot by Haskell Wexler), *The Group* and *The Sand Pebbles* – served an audience as middle-aged as the men who made them. That year's Oscars honored mainly *The Sound of Music.* An unexpectedly large number of films came from Britain. In *Blow-Up,*

Michelangelo Antonioni anatomized Swinging London, which was also exploited in *Georgy Girl* and *Morgan: A Suitable Case for Treatment. Alfie* introduced Michael Caine to an international audience. With heavy US investment, studios like Shepperton, Pinewood, and Elstree flourished in the outer suburbs of London, fostering teams of technicians who could hold their own against those of Hollywood, without the high salaries and crippling union control that made American films so expensive.

The only science fiction film of any size released in 1966 was *Fantastic Voyage*, an elaborate adventure in which a group of medics, including Raquel Welch, statuesque in skin-tight neoprene, are shrunk to microscopic size and injected into the body of a leading scientist to repair a brain lesion. In the days before computer technology, the effects were achieved with wires, models, and out-of-scale sets, with some very obvious back projection and matte work.

It wasn't in cinema that science fiction was taking its steps onto the international stage, but in television. 1966 saw the debuts not only of the live-action *Batman*, the gadget adventure series *Mission: Impossible* and Britain's *The Avengers*: on 8 September, the world was introduced to a phenomenon, as Captain James Kirk and the crew of the starship *Enterprise* boldly went where no man had gone before.

In the fall of 1966, just after he received his BA from USC, and while he was still working for Verna Fields, Lucas told Walter Murch and Matthew Robbins at a party thrown by Herb Kossower about an idea he'd had for a short science fiction film. As a first step into the fantastic, Lucas's idea was tentative. He wondered if one could make an sf film without elaborate sets and costumes, using Los Angeles as Godard had used Paris in *Alphaville*, and simply suggesting the future by manipulating the image as he had in his animated USC films. If Don Glut could make *Superman* in the Valley, how much better might an *avant-gardiste* do? Lucas and Murch put together a couple of pages about an escapee from an underground civilization who emerges through a manhole into a new world; but nobody could see where it might go. Murch and Robbins developed another idea, called 'Star Dance,' but Lucas persisted, assembling a sort of script for a fifteen-minute film.

At this point he began to immerse himself in science fiction and fantasy. *Willow*, with its midget hero making an epic journey to confront the mountain fortress of an enchanter, suggests more than a nodding acquaintance with Tolkien's *Lord of the Rings*. Lucas told Alan Dean Foster, who novelized *Star Wars*, that Conan Doyle's *The Lost World* was his favorite book. Trying to explain his vision of the *Star Wars* films, Lucas often quoted that book's introduction: 'I have wrought my simple plan/If I give one hour of joy/To the boy who's half a man/Or the man who's half a boy.'

Frank Herbert's *Dune* had a more far-reaching influence on Lucas's future work. From the moment in December 1963 when the science fiction magazine *Analog* published the first of three episodes of *Dune World*, with its cover by John Schoenherr of a stone pinnacle spearing out of a desert landscape against a sky with two moons, the novel caught Lucas's imagination. Once Herbert finished the longer book version and its sequels, *Dune*'s story of a universe based on the 'spice' Melange that conferred near-immortality but which existed on only one planet in the universe, the desert world Arrakis, aka 'Dune,' entered the common experience of his generation. Herbert imagined a universe run by the Padishah Emperor Shaddam IV, ruthlessly defending his declining empire from regional families, in particular that of Duke Leto Atriedes, whose son Paul was destined to overthrow him after acquiring near-godlike powers. Manipulating events from behind the scenes were the quasi-religious Bene Gesserit, an ancient sect of nun-like women with telepathic powers – not unlike Lucas's monkish Jedi knights.

By comparison with the coming excesses of 1968, 1967, when Lucas rejoined USC as a graduate student, was calm. While he continued to teach the navy and Marine camera class, most of his Masters work consisted of two films, both building on the success of *1.42:08*. He made *anyone lived in a pretty little [how] town* with Paul Golding, his collaborator on *Herbie*. The film, in CinemaScope and color, used actors and some sophisticated manipulation of images to tell a fable based on the poem of the same name by e.e. cummings. Life in an idyllic town is destroyed when a photographer arrives, each click of his shutter turning living people into dead monochrome images. Despite its greater technical sophistication, the film recalled *A Look at Life* in its graphic stiffness, its avoidance of character and dialogue, its reliance on flashy editing and photographic effects to disguise a lack of interest in people.

Lucas's second film, *The Emperor*, was a documentary, and one of his best. His first idea had been to make a film about Wolfman Jack, but Smith had done such a good job of maintaining his incognito that nobody knew where he could be found. (In *American Graffiti*, one of the kids would insist that he broadcast from a plane circling over the United States.) Lucas compromised by choosing as his subject Bob Hudson, a deejay at KBLA in Burbank, right in the Valley, who grandiosely christened himself 'The Emperor.'

Introduced by a beautiful girl cooing, 'It's his marvellous majesty,' Hudson, surprisingly middle-aged and incoherent for a deejay with a large teenage following, appears making a triumphal progress through the streets of Burbank in the back of Murch and Robbins's restored Rolls-Royce, accepting the plaudits of adoring fans, most of them eager girls. 'Get off the freeway, peasant,' someone shouts. 'The Emperor is coming!' Filmed in wide screen, intercut with helicopter news-shots of jammed freeways, hippie love-ins and facetious commercials with vox pop interviews, *The Emperor* shows Lucas stretching the limits of the short film and the documentary. The credits appear in the middle, and list the entire staff of the film school as student advisers, superimposed over a close-up of Hudson, pouchy, middle-aged and bored.

Marcia helped Lucas edit *The Emperor*. It was the first time many of the USC gang had met her, and the general reaction was astonishment that such an attractive and intelligent woman could see anything in a nerd like Lucas, however talented. 'Marcia was very bright and upbeat,' said Richard Walter. 'Just the loveliest woman that you ever saw in your life. They seemed such an unlikely couple. She's quite adorable.'

Their favorable impression of her strengthened when they saw her work on *The Emperor*. '*The Emperor* is a superb film,' says Milius, who, with Richard Walter, appears on the soundtrack impersonating a Mexican bandido. 'It still holds up today. When you see something like that, you think that maybe one of the great losses is that Marcia never became a film-maker and continued as an editor. But one of the other great losses is that George stopped making movies, and got interested in the sort of stuff that Lucasfilm puts out. Because he was a really dynamic film-maker.'

★   ★   ★

Lucas drifted back into after-hours campus society with the many old friends who were still at USC, including Milius and Charley Lippincott. Now living with Marcia in the ramshackle Portola Drive house, he had his eyes clearly set on a professional career. With that in mind, he even attended a course on direction taught by the comic Jerry Lewis. 'George *hated* that class,' recalls Charley Lippincott. 'He sat back in the very last row, and sometimes I'd sit with him. Lewis had such an outrageous ego, it drove you crazy.' Richard Walter rated Lewis 'a gigantically talented man, but without taste. It's as if those circuits just don't operate. He was still making movies. He was at Columbia, in the midst of a "multi-picture pact." He would frequently hold the class there, at the old Columbia studios on Gower Street. We'd all meet there on the lot; very exciting. And then he'd ad lib and wing it. It was really rather disorganized. I enjoyed being exposed to this wonderful maniac, but I can't say I thought it was a tremendously valuable class.'

Lucas, like many others, signed up for only one reason, according to Walter: 'Lewis encouraged people to believe he could get them into the [Screen Directors'] Guild, and that's why a bunch of these students were coming. Caleb Deschanel and certainly George and others would come to that class not because they wanted to learn from Lewis. They didn't appreciate his movies, though they thought it quite appropriate that the French appreciated his movies. But George really believed he could get them into the Guild, which was a hoax.'

Lewis surrounded himself with sycophants. 'There was a little group of outsiders, tangential to USC, who used to sit in on the course,' says Lippincott. 'They included the actress Corinne Calvet, who had been in one of Lewis's films, and her husband, who was an agent or something. And it was they who brought down a copy of Steve Spielberg's *Amblin'*.'

While Lucas was working his way through USC, Spielberg, rejected by USC because of his poor grades, enrolled at the less prestigious University of California at Long Beach. Aware that he needed a calling card to attract the attention of studios, he persuaded Dennis Hoffman, who ran a small special-effects company, to back a twenty-four-minute 35mm widescreen color short about a young couple who meet on the road while hitch-hiking and fall in love. He called it *Amblin'*. Even Spielberg dismissed the film as a 'Pepsi commercial,' with as little intellectual weight as a piece of driftwood, but he was relentless in showing it to anyone who might help his career. Lewis liked it enough to include it in his USC class, and to have Spielberg introduce it.

As historic meetings go, that between George Lucas and Steven Spielberg was unimpressive. Presenting his film, Spielberg, with his open-necked flowered shirt and leather jacket, his high-pitched voice and nervy delivery which caused him to stumble over his words, made an unattractive impression. His naked ambition to succeed in Hollywood also offended the elitist USC audience. Lucas didn't like *Amblin'*. He told Lippincott it was 'saccharine.' But over the next few months, Spielberg became a fixture at USC, often turning up at 'Thursday Night at the Movies' screenings. 'He became part of the gang right away,' says Milius. 'That was a pretty tight-knit group. We hated UCLA and people like that. We were special – though we didn't think we were going to conquer the world; we didn't think we had a chance. But that's also what made us so tight-knit. But he got accepted right away, because he had the same kind of enthusiasm.' In particular, Spielberg became friendly with Matthew Robbins and Hal Barwood, who shared his ambition to work in studio films. Finally, in 1968, a friend got a copy of *Amblin'* to production head Sidney Sheinberg at Universal, who signed Spielberg to a seven-year contract. Later, Spielberg named his company Amblin Entertainment in acknowledgment of the film's role in his success. Robbins and Barwood would write his first cinema feature, *Sugarland Express*.

Urged by Milius, Lucas started seeing Japanese films at the Toho cinema on La Brea. He discovered Akira Kurosawa, in particular his period adventures like *Seven Samurai, Sanjuro*, and *Yojimbo*. Kurosawa acknowledged John Ford as his master and model. His films have the spaciousness of westerns, and heroes of mythical proportions, often played, in the words of critic Audie Bock, by 'a filthy, scratching, heavy-drinking Toshiro Mifune who tries to avoid violence but when forced to, enters battle with his breath held.' Eighteenth-century Japan, when Kurosawa set most of his films, was so alien it could well have been Mars: the ankle-length robes and rural settings, the castles and swordplay, the culture of imperial power and privilege opposed by daring and belief – all recalled Edgar Rice Burroughs.

Lucas particularly admired *Kakushi Toride no San Akunin* (1958), released in the West as *The Hidden Fortress*. For the first time, Kurosawa shot in CinemaScope, and the film's panoramas, even in black and white, conferred a new spaciousness and energy. Unusually for a Japanese film, the main character is a girl. When civil war threatens her family castle, the princess loads up its treasure, dresses as a boy and enlists the wiliest of her father's retainers (Mifune) as her guide and protector. On the way, they dragoon a couple of peasant soldiers (Kamatari Fujiwara and Minoru Chiaki) into helping them. As played by Misa Uehara, the princess of *Hidden Fortress* is far from the stereotype of the shrinking, submissive Japanese woman. She's ruthless in exploiting the peasants, and no less tough with Mifune, whom she criticizes for having put duty ahead of family, leaving his own sister to die while he flees with her and the treasure.

Lucas loved the formalized sword-duels of Kurosawa's historical films: combatants inching minutely as they searched for a weakness, then slashing out with razor-sharp blades. No less attractive were his themes: loyalty to a lord; honor; mutual respect among warriors; fidelity to *bushido*, the samurai code. The characters, plot and setting of *Hidden Fortress* all found their way into *Star Wars*, as did those of *Seven Samurai*, the story of seven mercenaries who come together to save a village from a predatory warlord. In this case, Lucas's model was John Sturges's 1960 western version of the film, *The Magnificent Seven*, with Yul Brynner as the group's laconic leader Chris and Steve McQueen as his sidekick Vin. Retrospectively, Lucas claimed nobler models for *Star Wars* – 'the Arthurian Quest for the Knight, the Biblical Renewal of Faith and the classic science fiction conflict of Man versus Machine,' as one writer would put it – but in 1974, *Dune, The Magnificent Seven, The Hidden Fortress* and *Flash Gordon* were most on his mind. In February 1975, while he was still on the second draft of the film, he would describe it to *Esquire* magazine as 'the first multi-million dollar *Flash Gordon* kind of movie – with *The Magnificent Seven* thrown in.'

Lucas's Navy Production Workshop was now well on the way to becoming an efficient film crew. All at least ten years older than him, and mostly resentful of having anyone teach them their business, the sailors were contemptuous of almost all civilians, but particularly of hippie students. Shrewdly, Lucas divided the group, and set each half to compete with the other. The better of the two became his crew for his last student film. Making a virtue of necessity, he told them it would be an exercise in the use of available light: the sole artificial light would be three photo-floods for fill-ins.

The men responded with enormous effort, and complete loyalty to Lucas. 'Within a week, those tough navy guys were licking George's boots,' said Dave Johnson respectfully. 'I don't understand how a low-profile guy like George can do those things. But they were following him around like puppy dogs.' It was a social model that owed a lot to Japan, and Lucas may well have adapted some of the rules he saw being practiced in Kurosawa. Lucas was the navy men's *daimyo*, they his samurai, ready to sacrifice friends, even family, in their loyalty. When Lucas came to make the feature version of *THX1138*, he even suggested shooting in Japan, to capture that sense of alienness and focused will.

Once he had decided to make the science fiction film as his graduate project, Lucas put his team to work. 'The navy crew had all the best equipment,' said Willard Huyck later, 'all the free film, so it was very shrewd of him to make *THX* with a navy crew.' Being on official navy business also won Lucas access to otherwise forbidden locations. Looking for futuristic settings, he persuaded USC's computer department to let him shoot there, and bluffed his way into the parking stations at LAX and Van Nuys Airport.

'That was a brilliant piece of generalship,' says John Milius of *THX1138*. 'Everybody wanted the real artistic guys on their crew – guys like Bob Dalva. George went off and got all these navy guys. They were real competent. They knew how to do stuff, and get things done. They got equipment, and they got short ends of film from the navy, so he had five times as much film as everybody else, five times more equipment. That was brilliant. That was real producing.'

Having such a well-organized crew removed some of the strain of directing. But, whether out of genuine illness or because he was aware for the first time of his diabetes, Lucas felt tired most of the time. Hefting a 16mm camera onto his shoulder became increasingly difficult. Equipment was difficult to obtain. They had no dolly: for travelling shots, cameraman Zip Zimmerman sat with the Arriflex on a rolling platform of the sort used to shift loads in a warehouse, and was towed backward.

Most days, Lucas worked for Verna Fields editing Lyndon Johnson material, and shot *THX* at nights and on weekends. At 4 a.m. most mornings, he could be found slumped over the Moviola. He began to look even more frail, and his nervous voice developed a new crack.

The shooting of what Lucas called *THX1138 4EB* – the letters 'EB' collapsed together so they resembled an ideogram or trademark – was laborious but not complicated. Mostly it consisted of THX1138, played by Dan Natchsheim, a navy man who doubled as the film's editor, fleeing down empty corridors or through bleak subterranean bunkers, or shots of technicians and police staring into the eyepieces of machines. A cipher throughout, THX, explained *Los Angeles Times* film critic Charles Champlin after interviewing Lucas on the set of *Star Wars*, was 'a Huxleyian man inadvertently given free will [who] tries to flee the nightmare world of tomorrow.' Joy Carmichael played his girl, LUH7117.

Lucas finished the fifteen-minute film in twelve weeks. The real creativity came in the cutting room and optical lab. Much of the film consists of fuzzy TV images, half obscured by identification numbers and letters along the foot of the screen, and periodically interrupted by the jagged flash of a lens change. Occasionally, the guards' own eyes look back at them from a similar screen – in this world of total surveillance, someone must also watch the watchers. The characters exist in a susurrus of hissing data that swamps the soundtrack, almost drowning the ominous minor organ chords that signify some residual humanity lurking in this sterile world.

'I remember when I saw the first cut,' says Walter Murch. 'There was this wild mixture of Bach, and skittering around in that were the chatterings of almost undistinguishable voices in air traffic control, or something like that.' As in *Alphaville*, the government is a computer. When THX visits a robotic booth doubling as confessional and psychiatrist's couch, the canned voice monotonously repeats, 'Yes . . . yes . . . .'

Lucas showed the film to Irvin Kershner, who had returned to USC to teach direction. 'It was really quite unusual,' says Kershner, dubiously. 'Very cinematic. It was full of technical gewgaws. It was fun.' Anyone acquainted with the *nouvelle vague* recognized the debts to *Alphaville* and Chris Marker's *La Jetée*, a science fiction film in which memory carries a man between a dystopic future and a past of lost opportunities. But whatever its sources, it was an impressive work to have been produced by a university film school, and Lucas emerged even more strongly as USC's *wunderkind*.

THX1138 4EB – the subtitle *Electronic Labyrinth* was added later – was included in a programme of USC films at the Fairfax Theater in Hollywood. One party who went to see it included Fritz Lang;

Forrest J. Ackerman, editor of *Famous Monsters of Filmland*; George Pal, producer of *When Worlds Collide* and many other science fiction films; and young film journalist Bill Warren. 'Among the films shown that night,' recalls Warren, 'were *Glut, The Resurrection of Broncho Billy*, by John Carpenter, and *THX1138 4EB*. Afterwards, we're all standing on the sidewalk outside the Fairfax, and Fritz says, "All right, which one was the best?"

'Forry and George Pal look at each other, and Forry says, "I think we liked *The Resurrection of Broncho Billy* best.' George Pal agreed with Forry. And Fritz says, "That is why your films all stink, George. The best one . . ." He turned to me and said, "Which one was it?" I said, "It was *THX1138 4EB*." And he said, "Yes! That's the one. If I ever meet that young director, I want to tell him how great that film was."'

Of all the people in Old Hollywood with whom George Lucas might have been expected to become involved next, Carl Foreman was among the least probable.

After writing some earnest Hollywood adaptations in the late forties, like *Champion, Home of the Brave*, and *The Men*, Foreman was named as a Communist in 1950, and placed on the studios' covert blacklist. Unable to work in America, he relocated to Europe, leaving behind a western screenplay that Fred Zinnemann turned into *High Noon*. Retrospectively, the film seems to deal with many issues raised by the blacklist: the herd mentality, the unwillingess of people to live up to professed ideals. In fact, Foreman had no such ambitions for it, but happily basked in his unearned reputation as a socialist ideologue.

'Carl Foreman wasn't a very nice guy,' said Mickey Knox, one of the many scriptwriters he employed during an erratic career as writer, director and producer. The opinion was general. In Paris and London, Foreman produced stodgy money-makers like *Born Free* and *The Virgin Soldiers*, and moonlighted on screenplays. By 1967 the political climate in Hollywood had thawed sufficiently for him to return. In 1968 the Writers' Guild would launch a project to uncover the work of blacklisted writers obscured by the names of 'fronts' or deleted altogether, and to restore their rightful credits to the screen. Foreman's first script after his return was *Mackenna's Gold*, based on a Will Henry western novel about a mismatched party of adventurers seeking buried gold. Hoping to attract even a few teenagers to the film, Columbia's publicity department offered to fund two students each from USC and UCLA to make ten-minute films about the production, to be shot on and around its desert locations in Arizona and Utah.

USC, on the recommendation of Arthur Knight, put forward Charles Braverman and Charley Lippincott. Braverman accepted, but Lippincott had been offered a job he preferred, as assistant to a director at Columbia who was planning a film, eventually unmade, on student film-makers. He suggested Lucas.

Lucas accepted the *Mackenna's Gold* job, but without illusions. 'I thought the whole thing was a ruse to get a bunch of cheap, behind-the-scenes documentary films made,' he said, 'and they were doing it under the guise of a scholarship.' But he wanted to direct, and once he graduated, USC would no longer be picking up the bill.

He and Braverman joined David Wyles and David MacDougal from UCLA, and headed for Kanab, Utah. Lucas had one advantage: the project was being supervised by Saul Bass, for whom he'd worked on the credits of *Grand Prix*. Each student crew got a station wagon, film equipment and $200 a week to live on. Given his ascetic tastes, Lucas thought – rightly – that he could save most of that, and arrived back from the trip $800 richer.

He was appalled by the prodigality of a Hollywood unit on location. Nobody could drive anywhere, not even in their own car, without a Teamster at the wheel; hot meals had to be served three times a day; and a full crew of local technicians was kept on salary doing nothing while the imported Hollywood technicians shot the film. 'We had never been around such opulence,' said Lucas; 'zillions of dollars being spent every five minutes on this huge, unwieldy thing. It was mind-boggling to us because we had been making films for $300, and seeing this incredible waste – that was the worst of Hollywood.'

For his film, Braverman interviewed Foreman; MacDougal covered the director, J. Lee Thompson; Wyles the stunt riders and horse-wranglers. Within two days, Lucas was bored with the film-making process. As nervous as ever around people, he made a film without them: one that stood back and saw the production as it might appear to a god – a ripple in time, as insignificant and evanescent as the movement of clouds over the landscape, unnoticed by the insects and animals that struggled to survive in this wilderness. Sixteen years later, he would recognize the same long view in a film by *avant-garde* documentarist Godfrey Reggio. *Koyaanisqatsi* even had some of the same images, like the speeded-up passage of clouds. Francis Coppola had backed *Koyaanisqatsi*, and Lucas would join him as guarantor of Reggio's second (and less successful) *Powaqqatsi* (1988).

Lucas finished shooting his film on 18 June 1967, and called it just that – *6.18.67*. Foreman detested it. He'd tried to dissuade Lucas from making it, and once it was finished, did his best to see it didn't get shown. But PBS made a program about the project and the four films, and Foreman, interviewed for it, had little choice but to smile and say he loved Lucas's work. He was placed even more on the spot when the third National Student Film Festival showed it, along with *The Emperor* and *THX1138 4EB*. *THX* won the drama category; the other two were honorably mentioned. Milius took the animation prize for *Marcello, I'm so Bored*. *Time* magazine featured the two winners from USC and NYU's Martin Scorsese in an article about young film-makers. The photographer asked Milius to sit on the edge of the Steenbeck editing table in a New York cutting room. There was a double irony in this: Milius had never cut a film in his life, and didn't know how – Lucas always helped him – and the flatbed Steenbeck, soon to be the standard editor's tool, and already so in Europe, was shunned by the Hollywood establishment, fanatically loyal to the upright Moviola. At the time, there wasn't a single Steenbeck in the whole of California.

Big Boy Now

I pattern my life on Hitler. He didn't just take over the country. He worked his way into the existing fabric first.

Francis Ford Coppola, *Newsweek*, March 1967

One of the crumbs from the Hollywood table that occasionally fell into the eager hands of institutions like USC was the Samuel Warner Scholarship. The winner spent six months at the studio on a salary of $80 a week, doing what he wanted, learning what he could. He could even nominate the department in which he interned.

In 1967, the shortlist for this perk comprised Lucas and Walter Murch. On the day the decision was announced, they hung out on the USC patio and discussed what they'd do if they won. Whoever got the job, they agreed, the other would do everything he could to help. That was the trouble with Old Hollywood, Lucas argued: its primary directive was 'divide and rule.' It would never be like that with the next generation, he assured his friends. At USC, everyone worked with everyone else on every project. That's how it would be in New Hollywood too.

Lucas won, and in June 1967 he drove his Camaro to Burbank and checked in at the gate. Traditionally, he has said he wanted to spend his six months with the legendary animator Chuck Jones, creator of Bugs Bunny, Wile E. Coyote, the Road Runner and Speedy Gonzales. Directed to the animation department, he found it reduced to a single office with 'one guy, who was sort of head of the department, and he would just sit in his office and twiddle his thumbs all day.' The department had been closed.

Legend also claims that Lucas arrived on the Warners lot on the very day that Jack, last of the four Warner Brothers, cleared out his office. 'From my point of view, the film industry died in 1965,' says Lucas, amplifying this story. 'It's taken this long for people to realize the body is cold. The day I won my six-month internship and walked onto the Warner Bros. lot was the day Jack Warner left and the studio was taken over by Seven Arts. I walked through the empty lot and thought, "This is the end." The industry had been taken over by people who knew how to make deals and operate offices but had no idea how to make movies. When the six months was over, I never went back.'

The skinny, bearded kid in jeans and running shoes ambling across the lot, passing the dapper, impeccably suited Jack Warner with his hairline mustache and insincere smile, trudging into oblivion, is such a Hollywood moment that one wishes it were true. Unfortunately for myth, when Lucas arrived, Warners' animation department had been closed for five years. Since 1962, Chuck Jones had been attached to MGM, turning out versions of *Tom and Jerry* which even he himself rated as inferior. As for Jack Warner, his departure from the lot was as prolonged as a soprano's farewell performances. He sold his stock to Seven Arts in November 1966, but the company encouraged him to stay on in his old office as an independent producer. Long after Steve Ross's Kinney Services bought out Seven Arts in 1969, Warner remained on the lot. Only when Kinney told him they wanted to convert his private dining room into offices did the last of the Warners move over the hills into Century City, on what had been part of the old Twentieth Century-Fox, and set up Jack L. Warner Productions.

Lucas found the Warners lot a ghost town. Director Joseph L. Mankiewicz commented soberly of that time, 'I couldn't get rid of the feeling that any minute I'd look out and see tumbleweeds come rolling past.' Only one film was shooting: *Finian's Rainbow*. Howard Kazanjian from USC was second assistant director, and got Lucas onto the set. He stood at the back and watched a man with a beard and a loud voice order people about and wave his arms a lot. If this was the legendary Francis Ford Coppola, the first film-school student of their generation to penetrate the Hollywood establishment, Lucas wasn't impressed.

In 1968, Coppola, in the estimation of everyone who knew him, had the bucket in his hand and was headed for the well. Before he'd even finished his postgraduate degree at UCLA film school, this ebullient voluptuary with a thick black beard and a tendency to corpulence had directed two soft-core porn films, *The Peeper* and *The Belt Girls and the Playboy*, written both music and lyrics for a musical, finished a feature screenplay, and worked in Roger Corman's film factory, turning foreign sf films into fodder for the drive-ins.

Producer Ray Stark recognized Coppola as someone he could use, and offered him a job as hired gun and script fixer at Seven Arts, for which he was then head of production. Lured by promises of an eventual directing credit, and Stark's flattering assurances of his genius, Coppola accepted. The day he did so, an anonymous sign went up on the UCLA bulletin board. It said simply, '*Sellout.*'

In between fixing broken-down movies for Stark, Coppola turned out at least three screenplays a year, in the hope that Stark would let him direct one. Each time, however, Seven Arts assigned them to someone else. Grown cold and canny, Coppola optioned a 1963 British novel called *You're a Big Boy Now*, offering author David Benedictus $1000 if the film was ever made. He scripted it as a wise-ass comedy with music about a shy boy who spends his days roller-skating round the stacks of the New York Public Library, replacing returned books, and who falls into the bizarre world that surrounds a febrile young library user.

Half flower-power comedy, half pop-art musical, *You're a Big Boy Now* evolved into an American version of Richard Lester's films with the Beatles, with a mobile camera (critic Rex Reed called Coppola 'the Orson Welles of the hand-held camera'), musical numbers erupting into the action, and characters as much comic-strip as Actors' Studio. Seven Arts was sufficiently impressed to sign a new deal with Coppola. He would write three films for them – two, *The Conversation* and *The Rain People*, from his original stories, and the third, *The Scarlet Letter*, from Nathaniel Hawthorne. In return, he could direct the fourth.

You're a Big Boy Now lost every penny of the $800,000 invested in it. In fact, Seven Arts estimated it lost over $1 million, once they counted advertising and print costs. But by the time it came out, the company's mind was elsewhere. Having just bought a tottering Warner Brothers, it wanted something in production quickly. Dusting off the 1947 E.Y. Harburg/Burton Lane Broadway musical *Finian's Rainbow*, a whimsical tale of an eccentric Irishman wandering the rural Southern

United States looking for a leprechaun's buried pot of gold, Warners-
Seven Arts, as it was now known, exercised an outstanding option on
the services of a tottering Fred Astaire, assembled a low-cost supporting cast led by British unknowns Petula Clark and Tommy Steele, and
assigned the film to their cheapest and hungriest director – Coppola.

In June 1967 he started shooting *Finian's Rainbow* on Warners'
Burbank lot. Distracted, he didn't look around for a few days. When
he did, 'I noticed this skinny kid watching me. I was curious who this
young man was, and I think I went over to him and said, "Hi. See
anything interesting?" and he said, "Not much." That was the first
time I met George Lucas.'

This first encounter between two men who were to become pivotal
not only in each other's careers but in the growth of New Hollywood
typified their relationship. Coppola never ceased to think of Lucas as
that grubby boy watching from the shadows. 'Actually,' said Lucas,
'he calls me a stinky kid. He says, "You're a stinky kid. You do what
you want."'

Each day, Lucas came in and stood about on Coppola's set, a
thin, silent guy, habitually dressed in a white T-shirt, black pants
and sneakers. The crew ignored him, and even Coppola, once he'd
established who he was, only spoke to him in passing. It didn't escape
Lucas's notice, however, that he and Coppola were the only people
on the crew under fifty, and the only ones with beards.

After two weeks, Lucas had had enough. He thought the animation
department might have a 16mm camera he could borrow to shoot a
film. Also, Carl Foreman had suggested that if he wrote a treatment
for a feature version of *THX1138 4EB*, he would see if he could
interest Columbia in it. Either way, he felt he had nothing more to
learn by watching Coppola.

'What do you mean, you're leaving?' Coppola blustered when Lucas
told him. 'Aren't I entertaining enough? Have you learned everything
you're going to learn watching me direct?'

Lucas shrugged.

Coppola found he would be sorry to see the kid go. 'I was like a
fish out of water among all these old studio guys,' he said. With Lucas,
he could talk about movies – something Old Hollywood never did,
except to discuss what they cost and what they earned. To keep him
around, Coppola put him on the payroll as his 'administrative assistant.' On 31 July 1967, Lucas signed a contract for six months' work

at a total salary of $3000. His first job was to shoot Polaroid pictures of the set to check that props and furniture stayed in the same place between set-ups. Once there was footage to edit, he spent his time in the cutting room with the studio's longtime head of editing, Rudy Fehr. The *THX* treatment went into the bottom drawer.

Just before Thanksgiving, 1967, Coppola confided to Lucas that he was starting work on his next film for Seven Arts, and that he had a spot for him in the crew.

The shoot on *Finian's Rainbow* was expiring in a gaudy sunset of mutual congratulation. For $3.5 million, Coppola had delivered a film that looked as if it could well have cost $15 million. But he knew the film would fail. The important thing was to get another one up and running before anyone at Seven Arts realized it too. Fortunately, his stock stood so high with the company that they agreed not only to produce his original screenplay, *The Rain People*, but to let him direct it as well. Armed with their backing, Coppola persuaded IATSE to waive its rules and let him shoot the film his way, with a small crew, moving from location to location as the mood took him. Technically, a unit shooting outside Los Angeles was supposed to hire men from the district branch, or 'Local.' If they insisted on using their own technicians, they still had to pay a local crew, as had happened on *Mackenna's Gold*, even if the men simply sat about playing pinochle.

Coppola told IATSE his film was actually a documentary, and so should be exempt from union rules. The union cautiously agreed to at least discuss giving Coppola special consideration. Taking this for *carte blanche*, he wheedled some money out of Seven Arts and assembled a scratch crew with an old friend, Bart Patton, who became the film's line producer.

Coppola based *The Rain People* on an incident from his childhood when his mother, after a family argument, left home and checked into a motel for two days. His heroine, Natalie Ravenna, is a married woman who, finding she's pregnant, goes on the road to 'discover herself.' She drives across country, picking up hitch-hikers, falling into relationships with people, only to shed them and move on. She discovers something about herself, but only at the expense of others. 'Killer' Kilgannon, a brain-damaged football player she picks up, calls her 'a rain person.' In one of Coppola's more portentous lines, he explains, 'The rain people are made of rain, and when they cry, they disappear, because they cry themselves away.' In the end, after having been unable to help Killer, and watching him cheated and humiliated, Natalie stands by helplessly as he battles with Robert Duvall, a cop with whom she has become involved sexually, and Duvall's daughter shoots him.

Killer was played by James Caan, who'd been at Hofstra University with Coppola, and had gone on to Hollywood stardom in Howard Hawks's *Red Line 7000* and *El Dorado*, and Robert Altman's *Countdown*. Coppola flew Caan to Hofstra to shoot a crucial sequence: the football game in which Killer is injured. The trip delighted Lucas, as did the way Coppola brushed away the problems of guerrilla film-making as if they were fluff on his jacket. They couldn't afford a cinematographer or lights? Why not shoot everything with a 16mm Bell & Howell, hand-held? It would look more authentic anyway. No sound recordist? Didn't matter – George could record sound. George, as it turned out, could also carry the camera equipment, find props for the few staged scenes, act as production manager, and almost everything else.

It was a reminder to Lucas of his student film days, and of his time on the race-car circuit. Nothing could have been more different from the elephantine shoot of *Finian's Rainbow*. This was surely the film-making of the future, an American *nouvelle vague*, distinguished by the qualities that François Truffaut had described as typical of American film-making – 'grace, lightness, modesty, elegance, and speed.' Walter Murch said, 'I think for Francis and George, that film was the proto-type. If they could operate making a film out of a storefront in Ogallala, Nebraska – and do it successfully – then there was no reason why they should live in Hollywood.'

But Coppola almost immediately chilled Lucas's enthusiasm. How was the *THX* treatment going? Lucas confessed he hadn't looked at it in weeks.

'You've gotta learn to write,' Coppola told him sternly. 'Nobody will take you seriously unless you can write.'

Lucas explained that writing exhausted him, both physically and mentally, but Coppola told him he was going about it the wrong way. 'He said, "Look, when you write a script, just go as fast as you can. Just get it done. Don't ever read what you've written. Try to get it done in a week or two, then go back and fix it, and then go back through as fast as you can, and then go back and fix it – you just keep fixing it. But if you try to make each page perfect, you'll never get beyond page ten."' He also suggested Lucas read Shakespeare, his own personal inspiration.

Coppola persuaded Warners to option *THX* for $3000, then told Lucas that that would be his salary for working on *The Rain People*. Throughout the shoot Lucas got up at 4 a.m., laboriously wrote a scene for *THX*, in pencil, in crabbed capitals in the sort of lined 'blue books' he'd used for school exams, then started the day's work. Not all such stories have happy endings, however. 'I finished it,' says Lucas, 'and showed it to him, and he said, "This is terrible. I think we ought to hire a writer."'

Coppola found a playwright with some feature-film credentials prepared to work for very little, and set him to work rewriting the screenplay. Meanwhile, Lucas scrounged a 16mm camera and a Nagra tape recorder, and suggested making a documentary on the production. Coppola, a pushover for self-promotion, skimmed $12,000 from the publicity budget to pay for it.

Spending more and more time in New York while Marcia continued to work on commercials in Los Angeles was placing a strain on their relationship, and Marcia finally flew east in February 1968. One of Lucas's jobs was scouting locations, and on a wet Sunday in February he took Marcia to the next one on his list, in Garden City, Long Island, and proposed to her.

In April 1968 Coppola went back to Hofstra to shoot another football game, and late in the summer the *Rain People* caravan of seven vehicles and twenty people started to roll across America. Lucas was on board, but not Marcia. At the start of filming, Coppola magisterially banned wives and girlfriends from the shoot, ignoring the fact that a VW van trailing the caravan carried his wife Eleanor, their two children and, as babysitter, a teenager named Melissa Mathison, later the screenwriter of *E.T.: The Extraterrestrial* and wife of Harrison Ford.

As well as the cast, the caravan included a recreational vehicle fitted with a Steenbeck so that editor Barry Malkin could cut the film as they went along. The cameraman was Bill Butler, who later shot *Jaws* for Steven Spielberg. Everyone kept in touch via two-way radio. Footage was airlifted to New York every day, and rushes normally caught up with them three days later – too late to reshoot if Coppola had second thoughts. In Ogallala, Nebraska, editor Malkin finally called a halt. He needed time to assemble the mountain of material, so the crew camped at the Lakeway Lodge while Coppola occupied an old shoe store downtown as a production office, where Malkin spent five weeks making a preliminary cut.

Lucas persuaded Coppola to hire Marcia as cutting-room assistant. When Lucas rang to tell her, he sensed some resistance. Haskell Wexler had asked her to work on his feature *Medium Cool*, which he was both directing and shooting against the background of the Democratic National Convention in Chicago. Once the convention became the focus of riots over the war in Vietnam, he'd had the audacious idea of setting a fictional story about a reporter at the heart of the disturbances, and shooting it with lightweight camera and fast stock, just like the *cinéma vérité* directors. Wexler's invitation to work on the film excited and flattered Marcia, but she loved Lucas enough to turn it down and leave for Ogallala. Fortunately, Wexler delayed editing, so she was able to work on both films.

All the time, Lucas was shooting his diary of the production, snatching shots of Coppola which, in retrospect, showed him more revealingly than he had either expected or wanted. This Coppola is a blustering, filibustering dynamo, living on his nerves, inventing both the film and himself as he goes along, and relying on his imposing, near-biblical stature and commanding manner to steamroller any opposition.

The documentary shows him hectoring the Warners head office by phone, yelling, 'The system will fall by its own weight! It can't fail to!' Later, he moans, 'I'm tired of being the anchor when I see my world crumbling.' Lucas also glimpsed the paper-thinness of this persona when Coppola decreed that everyone, himself included, should be short-haired and clean-shaven when they rolled into the midwest. (In *Easy Rider*, roughly contemporary with *The Rain People*, long-haired Peter Fonda and Dennis Hopper are blown away by a redneck with a shotgun.) But Coppola without his patriarchal beard proved a different, less imposing person. Nobody took him seriously, not even the crew he'd dominated for so long. Some didn't even recognize him. So startling was the change that Lucas had to add a line to the commentary of his documentary explaining the radical mass-depilation.

When there was time, Coppola and Lucas kicked around ideas for future projects. One was inspired by *Medium Cool*. Why not make a film about Vietnam the same way, shot like a documentary, on 16mm, in black and white, while battles were actually taking place?

Nobody now remembers who first thought of it – or, more correctly, *everyone* is certain that *they* first proposed basing such a film on Joseph Conrad's short novel *Heart of Darkness*. In Conrad's story, a man goes up the Congo River to investigate reports that Kurtz, the local agent for a Belgian trading company, has gone crazy and set himself up as a sort of god. He finds Kurtz ill and raving, and he dies with the words: 'The horror! The horror.'

No factor of Coppola's working methods complicated the making of *The Rain People* more than sex. It suffused the production. James Caan was a notorious seducer, an habitué of Hugh Hefner's Playboy mansion who boasted he'd slept with seventeen consecutive Playmates of the Month. Coppola was also, in the words of a friend, a 'pussy hound.' He would halt production to fly back to New York, supposedly for conferences but actually to pursue some new mistress.

On one occasion, Coppola abandoned the crew in Blue Ball, Pennsylvania, in a motel with no phone, TV, or restaurant. 'I got a little angry about that,' says Lucas. 'Francis was saying all this "all-for-one" stuff, and he goes off and screws around in New York. He felt he had a right to do that, and I told him it wasn't fair. We got into a big fight over it.' Throughout all this, Coppola's wife Eleanor stood by patiently, bringing up the children and accepting the sympathy of everyone.

Coppola fought too with Shirley Knight, his star. Knight, like her character Natalie, was pregnant, and her nerves were on edge. The semi-nude bedroom scenes, dictated by Coppola's conception of Natalie as a woman looking to experience sex with other men before she settled down to motherhood, disturbed her. They wrangled over interpretation, over the problems of this kind of shooting. In reaction, Coppola trimmed her part and built up that of Robert Duvall. Knight protested, and the situation deteriorated still further, exacerbated by Coppola's evident attraction to her.

The tensions increased as production went on. When Marcia came out to Nebraska to work on the film, Coppola took an obvious interest in her. 'Everybody wanted Marcia,' says John Milius. 'Part of [Lucas's] disagreement with Francis is, I'm sure, because Francis attempted to hit on Marcia, because he attempted to hit on the wives of everybody.

87

But that was Francis. What was it Talleyrand said of Napoleon – "He was as great as a man can be without virtue"? Francis was for Francis – but Francis was great; a truly great man. He's still my Führer.'

The production of *The Rain People* was as close to a honeymoon as Lucas and Coppola ever got. 'George was like a younger brother to me,' said Coppola, 'I loved him. Where I went, he went.' But Lucas was less sanguine. 'My life is a kind of reaction against Francis's life,' he mused. 'I'm his antithesis.'

All this would be grist to the *Star Wars* mill, but for the moment confidence was in the ascendant. Like everyone else on the unit, Lucas struggled to save *The Rain People* and Coppola's reputation. He filmed some of the arguments between Coppola and Knight, but didn't use them in his documentary. Francis had become his Führer too.

9

The March Up-Country

We could leave, and live in the superstructure.
LUH, in *THX1138*. Script by Walter Murch and George Lucas

In Ogallala, the locals had been so flattered to have a film crew in town that they offered to convert a local grain warehouse into a sound stage. Despite his memories of those 'Let's do the show *right here!*' musicals of the late thirties, Coppola declined, but it planted the idea of a decentralized film industry, not tied to Hollywood, in his mind.

Indirectly, Coppola brought the dream a giant step closer to fulfilment when he remembered he'd promised to deliver a speech in San Francisco to a forum of eight hundred high-school English teachers on 'Film in Relation to the Printed Word.' Claiming he was needed in Ogallala to tie up loose ends, Coppola persuaded Lucas to do it.

Speaking in public terrified almost all the New Hollywood directors, and Lucas more than most. When he and Spielberg planted their palmprints in the cement outside Mann's Chinese Theater on Hollywood Boulevard for the premiere of *Indiana Jones and the Temple of Doom* in 1984, Spielberg, urged by owner Ted Mann to make a speech, said awkwardly, 'We had snakes in the last picture and bugs in this picture. But supposedly man's greatest fear is public speaking, and that will be our next picture.'

That his audience would be made up of high-school teachers, of whom he had ambivalent memories at best, increased Lucas's distaste for the chore; but such was Coppola's influence that he flew back ahead of the crew to make the appearance, arranging to meet them in Berkeley the following week.

Another speaker at the convention was John Korty. Eight years older than Lucas, he'd worked his way through film school creating animated TV commercials. In 1964 he moved to Stinson Beach, just south of Bolinas, rented a big gray barn for $100 a month, installed some second-hand film equipment, and began making films. He'd produced and directed two independent features, including *The Crazy Quilt* (1966), for less than $250,000 each. They did well, too, and won festival prizes. After the convention, Lucas visited Korty's operation, then rang Coppola in Nebraska. 'You gotta see this,' he said excitedly.

The *Rain People* caravan rolled into the Bay area on 4 July 1968. Radio and TV were still full of the news that Robert Kennedy had died in Los Angeles from gunshot wounds the previous month, less than two months after the assassination of Martin Luther King in Memphis. The deaths of King and Kennedy drove home to Lucas and Coppola the deteriorating nature of big-city American society. As a character remarked in Alan J. Pakula's *The Parallax View* (1974), 'Every time you turned around, someone just shot one of the best men in the country.'

Coppola and unit manager Ron Colby made a side trip to Stinson Beach to look over Korty's operation, and within a week Coppola was the prophet of decentralization. He had seen the future, it worked, and it was in Northern California. 'We started fantasizing about the notion of going to San Francisco,' he said, 'to be free to produce films as we had done on *Rain People*. It was a beautiful place to live, and had an artistic, bohemian tradition.'

In Korty's simple enterprise, Lucas too glimpsed a movie business shaped precisely to his personality. Korty's films were accessible, but not overtly commercial. He was removed from Hollywood, but still connected to the audience by the independent cinemas which had proliferated since the studios relinquished their hold on exhibition. Above all, this was a cinema without big stars and the problems they brought with them – problems Lucas had seen doing their damage on *The Rain People*.

Coppola, inevitably, was more grandiose. Working in a barn on worn-out Moviolas was bullshit. He had something more baronial in mind. This difference in scale would be another wedge driven between Coppola and Lucas, master and mentor.

★　　★　　★

Finian's Rainbow was due for release on 9 October. Nobody expected it to live up to Warners' inflated expectations. Early in August, Coppola gave a gloomy interview to the *Hollywood Reporter*, which headlined it: 'Francis Coppola to Make Only Own Stories in Future.' Shortly after, he told critic Joseph Gelmis: 'It's come to the point where I just want to get out altogether. I'm thinking of pulling out and making other kinds of films. Cheaper films. Films I can make in 16mm.'

With his salary on *Rain People* at an end, Lucas began editing his documentary about *The Rain People*, christened *Filmmaker* – or rather, *filmmaker* – and subtitled 'a film diary'. He also picked up the strings of his friendships with people from USC. Charley Lippincott was finishing his PhD and running the USC film society, but many others were already working in the industry. Milius had just had his first script filmed. Coppola commissioned him (with Warners' money) to write the adaptation of Conrad's *Heart of Darkness* relocated to Vietnam. Lucas would direct it.

'George and I would talk about the battles,' says Milius, 'and what a great movie it would make. He loved it because of all the technology, the helicopters, air strikes by Phantoms, the night-vision scopes and devices to detect people walking around at night, and I loved the idea of a war being fought that way. Of course, we hadn't lost it then, so it was a little easier to be interested in it. We wanted a scene where the guys are doped out of their minds and they call in an air strike on themselves.' The provisional title was *Apocalypse Now*, inspired by a button Milius had seen worn by a hippie that said 'Nirvana Now:' 'I loved the idea of a guy having a button with a mushroom cloud on it that said, "Apocalypse Now."'

Haskell Wexler had hired Walter Murch to mix TV commercials for a company he partly owned. In the autumn, Lucas suggested to Coppola that Murch, whom he hadn't met, mix *The Rain People*. He got the two men together, and after one meeting Coppola pointed to the piled-up cans and said melodramatically, 'Here's the film. Cut the sound.' Murch started work in a tiny house in Benedict Canyon. The fact that he didn't belong to the union worried Murch more than it did Coppola, though he eventually found it an advantage. Too nervous to order sound effects from a library for fear that someone would demand to see his union card, he invented and improvised. The result was a quantum leap in the quality of movie sound. To cover the union problem, Coppola invented some new terms, 'sound design' and 'sound montage,' which conveniently obscured Murch's activities.

Kinney Services, a conglomerate which made its millions out of parking lots, had bought Warner Brothers. Coppola mulled over a way of getting them to back his move to San Francisco. He found it in the experience of Dennis Hopper and Peter Fonda, who'd made *Easy Rider* on a few joints and a shoestring, and who were now the hottest talents in Hollywood. As the novelist Joan Didion wrote, 'every studio in town was narcotisized on *Easy Rider*'s grosses, and all that was needed to get a picture off the ground was the suggestion of a $750,000 budget, a low-cost NABET or even a non-union crew, and this terrific twenty-two-year-old director.' Under ex-agent Ned Tanen, a close friend of editor Verna Fields, Universal had launched a program of 'youth movies' for under $1 million each. This initiative was to produce most of the worthwhile and commercially successful post-*Easy Rider* films by young directors, including *American Graffiti*.

Coppola was twenty-nine, with one dud to his credit and, if he was any judge, another one waiting to emerge in *The Rain People*, but he was ready to embrace the *Easy Rider* ethos if that's what it took to relocate to San Francisco. He and Ron Colby flew to Cologne in the autumn of 1968 for the Photo-kina exhibition, which showcased the latest in film equipment. Dazzled by high-tech German gear, Coppola impulsively ordered an $80,000 Keller sound-mixing system and some cameras, not knowing where the money would come from to pay for them, nor in what premises he would install them.

In Denmark, they visited a company called Laterna Films. 'I was thrilled to see a beautiful old mansion with gardens and trees that had been turned into a film company,' Coppola said. 'The many bedrooms had been transformed into editing rooms, the garage was a mixing studio; everywhere young people were working on their films, discussing their projects while eating lunch in the garden.' He was particularly charmed by the collection of rare magic lanterns and early motion toys kept in the house. They illuminated a route back to the cinema's earliest days, when movies were still a game, and film-makers took to the road whenever it pleased them, setting up studios in barns and improvising stories from the events of the day. He returned to California even more determined to leave Hollywood.

On 22 February 1969, George and Marcia married at the United

First Methodist Church in Pacific Grove, near Monterey. John Plummer was best man. Coppola came, as did Murch, Hal Barwood and Matthew Robbins, and even Verna Fields. The newlyweds left for a honeymoon in Big Sur in Marin. Driving into Marin County, on the other side of San Francisco Bay, they fell for sleepy Mill Valley, a typical Northern California town, with redwoods and a river, and rented a small hilltop house on Vernal Road for $120 a month. Any thought of a career in Hollywood was forgotten. The future was here. Lucas was sure of it.

America was moving toward a more sensual, self-gratifying society, where sex and drugs were more important than rock'n'roll. 1969 saw the publication of *I'm OK – You're OK*, *The Sensuous Woman*, *Everything You Always Wanted to Know About Sex (But Were Afraid to Ask)* and *Portnoy's Complaint*. The year's top tunes were songs from the show *Hair*. Its theme, sung by the Cowsills, and the 5th Dimension's version of 'Aquarius/Let the Sunshine in', like the Beatles' 'Come Together,' and Blood, Sweat and Tears' 'You've Made Me so Very Happy,' promoted peace, happiness, free love and dope. In August, a six-hundred-acre pasture in upstate New York became the site of the cultural phenomenon called Woodstock. It was a good time to be alive, and there was no place better in which to be alive than Marin County.

The rewritten screenplay of *THX* arrived, and Lucas didn't like it: 'It may have been a good screenplay, but it wasn't at all what I wanted to make into a movie.' He shuffled together the exercise books containing his draft, and had them typed up in a legible form.

The Lucases' Mill Valley house was small, with only one bedroom, but they had plenty of visitors from Los Angeles, curious to see what drew the smartest of their contemporaries to the rural wilderness. Richard Walter and his wife visited. So did Milius: 'I remember going up there with my first wife, and sleeping on the floor, and eating this wonderful San Francisco bread, and the food, and all of us going out together and having a great time. They didn't have any money, but it wasn't a bad life. They didn't suffer.' But not suffering wasn't the same as doing well, and Lucas felt the current was leaving him behind, especially when Marcia began getting work. She would have preferred to have a baby, but he shied away from any such commitment.

To open a production company in San Francisco, Coppola needed a film contract. He persuaded the new administration at Warners that he wasn't to blame for the failure of *Finian's Rainbow*. It was a product, he argued, of the old and outdated system fostered by Jack Warner, now swept away. *The Rain People*, on the other hand, was a movie for the new Warners.

It was a shrewd strategy. Warners-Seven Arts visualized itself as a studio for the decade of *Easy Rider*. Its boss, Steve Ross, was a silver-haired, smooth-tongued operator who had taken Kinney out of the mortician business into car hire by renting out at night the limos used for funerals by day. They moved into parking lots, despite the fact that this was a territory that had been associated with organized crime, and then diversified into movies. The studio head was Ted Ashley, a hot talent agent taking his first turn behind an executive desk. John Calley was his lieutenant. Their department for youth films and products was run by Fred Weintraub, who'd made a fortune selling clothing and entertainment to college audiences and running a chain of campus coffee shops.

Coppola played on Warners' greed to sell them a radical proposal. Once his new company was up and running, he would guarantee them seven feature films, none costing more than a million dollars, the first of which would be the long version of *THX1138*, which he budgeted – seven being his lucky number – at $777,777. This would be followed by *The Conversation*, a Coppola original about surveillance experts, probably starring Marlon Brando as 'the best bugger on the West Coast.' He threw in scripts by Huyck and Katz, and Robbins and Barwood. Scratching for 'go' projects, he also offered Lucas and Milius's Vietnam film *Apocalypse Now*.

For the make-or-break meeting, Coppola flew down to Los Angeles, but, *Easy Rider*-like, rode onto the lot astride a huge Harley Davidson. He was well prepared, with the help of Lucas, who gave Charley Lippincott $100 to create a montage of 'underground' films to show the Warners board. 'We put together this presentation showing that it was going to be futuristic,' said Lucas, 'and outlining how we were going to be shooting it on location and such. And we put in there that we were going to develop this very unusual reality using "rotary-cam photography." Fortunately nobody at the studio asked us what it was, because it was nothing.'

After this, Coppola moved in. He had a new movie ready to go, he told the suits. Here's the script – he slammed down a draft of

THX1138, which he'd barely read. Here's the cast – except for Robert Duvall and Donald Pleasence, all were unknown, and none had yet been asked if they wanted to appear. 'Where is the money?' he asked them rhetorically. He departed in a roar of exhaust, leaving them to chew on his proposal. The next day, when he still hadn't received the green light, he wired them: 'PUT UP OR SHUT UP' – or, in some versions, 'SHAPE UP OR SHIP OUT.'

Warners did put up, but not as whole-heartedly as Coppola had hoped. They offered to lend – not advance or invest – $3.5 million, part of it in the form of $2500 a week seed-money while Coppola was setting up his company. If they liked *THX1138*, this sum could become a down-payment on the package. If they didn't, Coppola would have to refund every penny. Given that he had no other offers, Coppola agreed.

Lucas received the news with delight. The way Coppola described it to him, the strings attached to Warners' offer became thistledown. Immediately, he and Coppola, with Korty's help, began visiting mansions in Marin County, looking for the future headquarters of the company. They made an offer on the Dibble estate in Ross, but while Coppola was raising the money, it went to someone else. The buyer already owned another mansion, and Coppola offered on that too, only to have the zoning commission refuse his application to transform it into a film studio.

Gradually, Coppola turned against the Laterna model. If he couldn't find a mansion, maybe he should look for something in San Francisco itself – where, in addition, staff and services were more readily available. Dismayed, Lucas argued that the whole point had been to abandon city influences. He cited Korty's rural retreat. All he wanted, he said, was 'a nice little house to work in.' But Coppola bulldozed him. The sound equipment would arrive shortly from Germany, and they must have a place to install it. Anyway, their working capital was all his, raised by selling his Los Angeles house and taking out substantial loans on the promise of a Warners deal.

Korty found a recording studio at 827 Folsom Street, in what locals derisively called the 'warehouse and wino' section of San Francisco, and Coppola leased three floors. Once Coppola had persuaded Korty to become the first tenant of their new facility, Lucas threw up his hands. Francis had won again.

Eleanor Coppola conceived and managed the décor of the new facility while Francis toyed with names. His first choice, 'Transamerican Sprocket Works,' traded on the current taste for the Edwardian, which had hippie girls wandering Haight-Ashbury in Pre-Raphaelite braids and gypsy skirts, accompanied by men in crimson pre-World War I military tunics over jeans and sandals. Remembering Laterna's magic lanterns, Coppola finally chose 'American Zoetrope,' after the optical toy of a spinning drum with vertical slits through which one glimpses dancing or running figures.

The Rain People, proudly bearing the American Zoetrope logo, opened on 27 August. Reviews were mixed, but Coppola brushed them aside, consumed by the fulfilment of his dream. The new company's name not only implied that it could do everything from A to Z, but, once it was launched as a public company, would alphabetically give it a spot near the top of the share listings.

For the moment, however, nobody but Coppola owned any shares – not even Lucas, whom he grandly named vice president. Mona Skarger, one of the producers on *The Rain People*, became secretary-treasurer. Christopher Pearce was general manager. Jobs were also found for Bart Patton, Bob Dalva and Dennis Jakob, all cronies of Coppola, some going back to high school and Hofstra. Perhaps thinking of insinuating someone more personally loyal to him than to Coppola, Lucas offered the job of head of intellectual property – basically head of development – to Charley Lippincott, who turned him down. He didn't want to move to San Francisco, nor to give up his ambition to make documentary films.

Being located in San Francisco had one definite advantage for Lucas and Coppola: few films were made there, and the local branch of IATSE, its hands full with mainly theatrical technicians, didn't look too closely at who did what at Zoetrope. Cameramen could record their own sound, and even direct. The union listed Walter Murch as simply a post-production worker, a flexible term that could encompass editing, sound editing, even scriptwriting.

The day they took over the building, Coppola ordered everyone up on the roof and had them photographed: Korty, Carroll Ballard and an unknown guy – already names were being forgotten – each with a hand-held 16mm camera; Milius in sombrero and bandoliers; Warners' liaison man Barry Beckerman; Lucas, almost unrecognisable in heavy beard and wide-brimmed black felt hat, like some middle-

European anarchist; Bob Dalva, also with camera; Larry Sturhahn, later to be the producer of *THX*; Al Locatelli, its eventual production manager, incongruously playing a flute; Dennis Jakob, crouched behind an enormous piece of sound equipment. And of course Francis, dressed in a long double-breasted coat and a felt hat with turned-up brim, and clutching a zoetrope under his arm – the model for an allegorical statue in some Sicilian square of the town's great explorer who had encompassed the world.

The sound equipment arrived, and was installed while carpenters were still sawing in the corridors. Walter Murch arrived on his BMW motorbike to supervise. For him, the chance to work on a state-of-the-art Keller system was more than enough reason to relocate to the Bay area. Able to handle seven separate strips of film in gauges from 8mm to 70mm, and video as well, it was the most advanced piece of equipment of its type in America – so advanced that when it broke down, an engineer had to fly in from Hamburg to fix it.

Word quickly spread of the radical new venture. Stanley Kubrick, cinema's most famous recluse, corresponded with Coppola about special effects from his rural hideout in England. John Schlesinger said he wanted to rent space. Mike Nichols intended to invest. One night, Coppola was making coffee in the conference room when Orson Welles rang. He was thinking of making a film in San Francisco, he said. Awed, Coppola talked with him for half an hour, coffee pot in his hand, while the water overflowed from the sink and flooded the room.

American Zoetrope officially became an entity on 14 November 1969, when Coppola's attorney filed the incorporation papers. The facility, though still far from ready, was opened by San Francisco's Mayor Joseph Alioto on 13 December. Alioto announced that Coppola had already spent $500,000 on equipment, never mind staff. Except for John Korty, who was cutting his feature *Riverrun*, the only person actually working there was Haskell Wexler, who was shooting a huge rock concert being held at nearby Altamont with the Maysles brothers. He offered Lucas a few days' work as a cameraman, and Lucas was there on the day when Hell's Angels employed as security men murdered a member of the audience, Meredith Hunter. John Milius insists that Lucas shot the scenes of the killing which were later used in the documentary *Gimme Shelter*. Lucas says he can't remember.

American Zoetrope became a target of pilgrimage. 'It all looked too good to believe,' said one early visitor, 'terribly chic and terribly sincere, with leggy secretaries in crocheted miniskirts, $50,000 KEM and Steenbeck editing tables, Creative Playthings paraphernalia, bubbly chairs, and blowups of D.W. Griffith on the walls.' The main reception area was dominated by a pool table and a silver espresso machine. Fabrics from the Finnish company Marimekko draped the walls, their purples, oranges and yellows echoed even in the décor of the freight elevator. Every Thursday night, Coppola screened classic movies, with a buffet of Chinese food. A lavish brochure in *faux art-nouveau* style promised films and facilities that combined the best of Europe and America, of Hollywood and the Bay area.

Prospective tenants soon found it *was* too good to believe. Zoetrope could only handle the kind of films Coppola wanted to make: mobile movies shot on location with hand-held cameras. There was no sound stage, and only minimal facilities for wardrobe and props. Coppola had recklessly paid $40,000 for a Mitchell BNCR camera which nobody could afford to rent, and bought a range of the latest lightweight Arriflexes and portable tape recorders. His old mentor Roger Corman came to take a look. As well as being godfather to Coppola's son Gio, he was an executor of his will. Coppola asked him what would happen to all this equipment if he died. Corman said, 'I'll put it all in a truck and take it down to LA, because you're in the wrong city, Francis.'

Instead of presiding over a cinematic renaissance, Coppola found himself trying, without success, to supervise a tribe of vigorous young film-makers, all looking out for themselves. 'Everyone was off in his own little corner, competing,' recalls Carroll Ballard. $40,000 worth of equipment disappeared in the first year, and a number of company cars were cracked up. Desperate to put the facility in profit from the start, Coppola set rental rates that were high for the time: $175 a month for one of the seven cutting rooms, $240 a month for an editing machine to go in it, and correspondingly more for office services, production facilities and time on the Keller console. He was parsimonious when it came to funding the projects which would be Zoetrope's lifeblood. To write and direct *THX*, Lucas would get only $15,000; but even that was not immediately forthcoming.

Lucas, fretting about being able to replicate the clinical emptiness of his student *THX*, wondered if he could shoot in Japan. 'The idea was, it was this weird dictatorial society in the future,' says Gary Kurtz, 'and if it was totally alien as an environment to the audience, and it was in a foreign language, you might be able to believe in the isolation of the main characters. Well, nobody in Hollywood liked that idea.' All the same, Coppola truculently announced Japanese locations as an accomplished fact. 'George is going to direct it in his own way. I'm giving him my strength. I'm saying, "If you want me, you've got to give George Lucas his break."'

Warners weren't sure they wanted either of them, particularly when they got around to reading the script of *THX1138*. It had little real plot, aside from the idea of a man fleeing an overpowering society. There was no motivation. Nobody was characterized. The ending was ambiguous, THX climbing from a manhole into a world of which we see nothing except a huge sun and a solitary bird.

Lucas sulked. 'Of course,' he said, 'at the studio they don't understand scripts; that they should look more like blueprints than novels. They don't even know who [Marshall] McLuhan is over there.' Nevertheless, he asked Walter Murch to help with the script, and they amplified the story where they could. 'We just threw everything up in the air and watched it come down,' said Murch. The setting was narrowed down to the twenty-fifth century. They sketched in some social background. Everyone is tranquillized, and their sex drive numbed by drugs. They wear only white, and their heads are shaved. Most, including THX – pronounced 'Thex' – who works on a production line assembling robots, have been grown parthogenetically, by artificial insemination, but his girlfriend LUH7117 – 'Ler' – is a 'natural born,' and therefore suspect.

A god, OMM, dark-eyed, Semitic, with a sensual mouth and a short black beard – the physical antithesis of his predominantly Caucasian subjects – watches unblinking from every wall. He offers benign moral supervision, urging: 'Work hard, increase production, prevent accidents, and be happy.' Citizens commune with him in electronic booths that also fulfil the function of psychoanalysts. A taped voice – Murch's – welcomes them with 'My time is yours,' and responds to their pleas for help with anodyne recorded comments, and an absolution that ends in the exhortation to get back to work. Anyone who demands more is likely to be arrested and beaten by police, sometimes to death, on television.

Robots, uniformly tall, dressed in the black leathers and white helmets of Californian Highway Patrol motorcycle cops but with blank chrome faces – another gibe by Lucas at the *bêtes noires* of his adolescence – impose law and order. During the film we see one of these robots, malfunctioning, walk repeatedly into a wall. Another, ominously, is seen shepherding a tiny child into an elevator.

In the feature version, LUH seduces THX by reducing the medication that suppresses his sexual instinct. Previously satisfied with telecasts of ritual beatings and callisthenic-like dancing by a bald, naked black woman, THX is persuaded to make love to LUH. 'It manages to have a lot of nudity in it,' says Richard Walter of the film, 'but to be anti-erotic. George's work is extremely non-sexual. He is uncomfortable with sexuality' – a view borne out by close-ups of LUH and THX's pale, hairless bodies pressed together in joyless union.

Typical of Lucas's later work, and of his life, the sexual initiative is taken by the woman. The film also has an undercurrent of homo-eroticism. THX's superior, SEN5241, played by British actor Donald Pleasence, is homosexual. His room-mate has just been 'destroyed' for unspecified reasons, and he reprograms the computer to have THX assigned to his living space.

LUH becomes pregnant, and both she and THX are arrested for drug evasion and sexual perversion. In the original screenplay, LUH is raped, then beaten to death on TV, but Lucas never shot these scenes, and we know no more of her fate than the fact that her name is reassigned to one of the countless embryos growing in ranked bottles in the city's labs.

THX and SEN, convicted of interfering with the computer, are sent to a featureless white prison whose inmates remain out of fear of the surrounding formlessness, expending their energy in aimlessly plotting to escape. Exasperated, THX simply walks out, followed by SEN. In the white emptiness they meet SRT, a large, amiable black man convinced he isn't real at all, but a 'hologram' who couldn't make it on TV. They find their way back to the crowded corridors of the main complex, but SEN loses his nerve. Stumbling into the TV studio which broadcasts OMM's image to the psychoanalysis booths, he humbly confesses his shortcomings to the poster-sized picture of the god stuck on the wall.

Awaiting arrest, he watches a group of children playing. All of them have bottles attached to an arm, from which 'liquid education' drips into a vein. One asks SEN to reconnect his tube, and he reminisces about the much larger containers through which one acquired knowledge when he was a boy. As the children gape in astonishment, the police arrive to take him away.

Meanwhile, THX and SRT steal jet cars, but the maladroit SRT can't get his started, and when he does, promptly drives it into a pillar. THX rockets down a series of tunnels, pursued by the motorcycle police. At the end of the line he abandons the car and continues on foot. Lucas shot a scene in which THX falls into a garbage compactor and is menaced by a rat-like creature, but dropped it as unconvincing, only to recycle it in *Star Wars*. THX has less trouble with some scavenging Shelldwellers – bearded dwarfs, the progenitors of *Star Wars'* Jawas, who live in tunnels – and starts climbing a huge ventilation vent towards what he calls 'the upper positive place.' Two police are close to catching him when, abruptly, Control calls off the pursuit: it's exceeded its budget. THX emerges on the surface, where he faces a presumably hopeful sunrise.

Lucas visualized the film in Panavision format, but that would have meant hiring expensive equipment. He compromised with Techniscope, a format popular with cost-cutting European and Asian producers looking to achieve wide-screen without special lenses. It simply cut the frame in half horizontally, producing an image half the height of conventional 35mm and twice the width, which nevertheless could be blown up to normal 35mm in the lab. Its deficiency was obvious: with half of a 35mm frame filling the same screen area as a full frame, the image risked being dark and grainy. But the Technicolor labs could print Techniscope prints direct from the original by using a dye-transfer matrix, avoiding the need to make a negative, so the quality was excellent, and remained so until they abandoned this method.

Other inventors found equally ingenious ways around the patents on various wide-screen systems. Paramount embraced VistaVision ('Motion Picture High Fidelity!'), in which the film ran horizontally through the camera, offering a larger image than conventional 35mm. The clarity was superb, but the fact that it needed special cameras and projectors limited its use. Special-effects technicians, who loved the system for its large negative size, would rescue and restore VistaVision cameras to shoot the next generation of science fiction films, including *Star Wars*.

★   ★   ★

Lucas was delighted to be directing his first feature film. His budget might not be much in Hollywood terms, but his family was astonished at his achievement at only twenty-five years old. On the other hand, directing was daily torture, a constant process of revision and improvisation, with the ten-week production period ticking off in his brain every instant.

San Francisco's new subway, the Bay Area Rapid Transit system (BART), was under construction, and Lucas persuaded them to let him shoot in the completed tunnels. Other sequences were shot in parking stations, Frank Lloyd Wright's Marin County Civic Centre in San Rafael, and at the Lawrence Livermore atomic energy laboratory. The tiny crew moved between locations in one of the vans in which Coppola had crossed the country during the shooting of *The Rain People*.

Robert Duvall from *The Rain People* played THX, and Maggie McOmie LUH. Veteran Ian Wolfe was one of the prisoners windily discoursing on the nature of freedom. Knowing Lucas's discomfort with actors, Coppola told Ron Colby to choose people who wouldn't need more than a hint from the director, but Lucas still wrangled with them. Using a technique he would continue on *American Graffiti*, he shot most scenes with two cameras simultaneously. 'That captures emotional stunts it's hard to get after the first take,' says Duvall.

Coppola imposed his crony Larry Sturhahn on the film as producer. If Lucas could ever have been comfortable with any supervisor, it was certainly not Sturhahn, who, he charged, spent most of his time on the phone, and hung up only to interfere. Coppola later confessed that he knew the two men wouldn't get on. 'George,' he said, 'needed someone to hate.' As long as he could direct his animosity towards Sturhahn, he wouldn't be blaming Coppola.

The pressure of too little money and not enough time encouraged improvisation, some of it inspired. Lucas tinkered together models and fireworks to create the film's few special effects, like an explosion on the robot assembly line. Nobody was happy to have their head shaved, as was required of the whole cast, and there was a shortage of extras until someone thought to approach the drug rehabilitation centres Synanon and the Delancey Street Foundation. Enrolment required addicts to shave their heads as a sign of commitment, and most were happy to earn a few days' wages as extras in the film.

Working with limited lights and a hand-held camera fitted with a thousand-meter telephoto lens pushed Techniscope to its limits. Warners, who, as the financing company, automatically saw the daily rushes, began muttering about the photographic quality. There was a growing sense that Coppola had sold them a pig in a poke. They held off breaking openly with him for only one reason: *Patton*. Franklin Schaffner's film of Coppola's screenplay opened on 5 February 1970, and, despite reviews which fretted about its jingoism, proceeded to make a fortune. Anyone that good, reasoned some within Warners, was worth cutting a little slack. But only a little. Lucas characterized their attitude as: 'We're the king and you're the serfs.'

The attic at Mill Valley became a cutting room, and Lucas spent most nights there with Marcia, editing. At the same time, Walter Murch cut the sound – 'Not,' Lucas agrees, 'the way things usually were done.' Traditionally, movie mixers aimed for clarity, arguing that most cinemas had such poor sound systems that the audience was lucky to hear anything. Lucas wanted *THX1138* to have a 'musical' quality, which Murch took to mean a sense of continuous ambient sound, sometimes almost inaudible. The layering of sounds had always fascinated Murch, and he'd developed a technique called 'air-balling,' in which one sound envelops but never quite obscures another. Renaissance composers for the unaccompanied voice routinely employed this effect, which may be where Murch got the idea, but nobody had yet applied it to film. Murch's experiments spurred Lucas to pioneer better cinema sound. The new system would be called 'THX Sound,' and its slogan would be, 'The Audience is Listening.'

For the soundtrack of *THX*, Murch created, in his phrase, 'a Dagwood sandwich of sound and music, with no clear split between them.' Recorded music was slowed down, speeded up, played backward, mixed with natural sounds or those of machines. For the prison scenes, he used the bass note of a large room humming with machinery.

The credits of *THX1138* ascend the screen, suggesting a steady descent underground, an idea borrowed from an inter-title in Fritz Lang's *Metropolis*. Before them, Lucas inserted one minute from a trailer for *Flash Gordon Conquers the Universe* (1940). Over scratchy, poorly-copied images of spaceships fizzing like firecrackers and a blond Buster Crabbe straight-arming aliens as if they're the Notre Dame defensive line, the voice-over urges audiences to see how this American football hero copes with the threats of the twenty-fifth century – an implied comment that the future might be very different from the one imagined by Hollywood.

Lucas, probably coaxed by Murch, later justified the elaboration of *THX1138* by calling it 'a Cubist film – the story, the sound and the images were all views of the same thing simultaneously.' He defended its didactic tone: 'Everyone else calls it science fiction,' he said. 'I call it documentary fantasy. The film is the way I see LA right now; maybe a slight exaggeration. Duvall comes off drugs and discovers he's been living in a cage all his life with the door open. It's the idea that we are all living in cages and the doors are wide open and all we have to do is walk out.'

Marcia for one didn't buy these justifications. She found the film cold, humorless, and arrogant – a summary of the negative elements of Lucas's character. Coppola agreed. He would later tell Lucas to 'write something out of his own life; something with warmth and humor that people can relate to.' Even Lucas got the message. When he shot a few pick-up scenes in a Los Angeles studio and Willard Huyck and Gloria Katz came to watch, he told them, 'I have an idea I'd love you guys to do. It's a rock'n'roll movie and it takes place in the fifties and it's about music and cruising and deejays.' He sent them his notes, and over the next month they worked up a five-page outline of what Lucas had first entitled 'Another Quiet Night in Modesto,' but now preferred to call *American Graffiti*.

Preoccupied with the slide of American Zoetrope into anarchy and bankruptcy, Coppola took only a fitful interest in the progress of Lucas's film. The first time Marcia showed him a completed reel, he simply shook his head and murmured, 'Strange. Strange.' After that, he didn't see any more until the whole film was edited.

He was more concerned about extracting a long-term commitment to Zoetrope and its program from Warners, which summoned him to a meeting of the studio management on 21 November 1969. Ever the showman, Coppola created a 'black box' for each executive containing the screenplays for all seven proposed films, bound in black with the emblem of American Zoetrope. These boxes in turn went into a crate, ominously coffin-like, which two men carted into the Warners office.

They carted it out almost as quickly. Warners wanted no part of the projects, or of Coppola. His frantic pitch, handing round cigars and assuring them that he and he alone had the secret of making successful films, only alarmed them more. Even before he had seen any of *THX1138*, Frank Wells, head of business affairs, told Coppola they wouldn't be putting up any more money, and they expected him to refund the $300,000 already spent. 'Warner Brothers not only pulled the rug out from Francis,' said Walter Murch grimly, 'they tried to sell it back to him.'

American Graffiti

There's no message or long speech, but you know that,
when the story ends, America underwent a drastic
change. The early sixties were the end of an era. It hit
us all very hard.

George Lucas

The impact on American Zoetrope of Warners' rejection was immediate. The weekly screenings and Chinese buffets ceased. Nescafé replaced espresso. The mini-skirted secretaries evaporated. Just as rapidly, support for projects drained away. Humiliatingly, Coppola had to tell Orson Welles he couldn't make the film they planned. Stanley Kubrick no longer returned his calls. Without being asked, people packed up their offices and left. When those who stayed, like John Korty, found their rent soaring from $200 a month to $1000, they departed too.

Paradoxically, once Coppola abandoned his ambitious production plans and slashed his overheads, American Zoetrope began to turn a small profit. Film-makers on location in the area hired its cutting rooms, equipment, and vehicles. An advertising division made TV commercials for cooking oil and instant paella, and another department, Tri-Media, produced educational films; but none of these enterprises showed enough profit to eat into the mountain of personal debt.

When Coppola did occasionally make one of his grand gestures, it had a rueful overtone. He held a reception to coincide with the 1970 San Francisco Film Festival, but when the Lucases received their lavish invitation, Coppola had attached a note: 'This letter cost $3 to print, type and send to you.' Such comments were motivated less from self-pity than an amused truculence, a gambler's wonder at the ways of chance, but they exasperated the people who'd believed in him and his dream of San Francisco as a new movie capital. Lucas and Milius were particularly incensed, since in the break with Warners the studio kept the rights to *Apocalypse Now*.

Though more than inclined to bear grudges, Lucas didn't immediately vent his frustrations on Coppola, whom he still regarded as a surrogate elder brother. *San Francisco* magazine published a full-page composite photographic portrait, one side Lucas, the other Coppola. The spectacles, the watchful eyes behind them, the pursed lips, the black beard, the open-necked shirt were identical.

To some extent, Lucas felt responsible for Coppola. 'He was constantly jumping off cliffs,' said Lucas, 'and I was always shouting, "Don't do it, you'll get yourself killed!"' John Milius too found Coppola even more operatic and admirable in defeat. He and Coppola agreed to give each other a gun when they directed their first movie: 'Paper is not honorable,' decreed Milius. 'The exchange of weapons is honorable.' They decided to do the same for Lucas after *THX*, and chose a .22 rifle at Abercrombie & Fitch. 'Francis went to charge it,' says Milius, 'and of course they had cut him off. We went back to Zoetrope, and they were trying to turn the lights off, because he had no money. Francis said, "That doesn't matter." Nothing ever changed Francis. He was in debt. He had no money. He had all these people running around, all these hippies, working for him, and all of us, but he was chasing girls ... Nothing slowed Francis down. It was no different than when he had money, except there was more of it.'

Lucas kept working on the script of *American Graffiti*, fumbling through different approaches and combinations of characters. Radio was at the heart of it: 'Graffiti is an Italian word,' he explained, 'meaning a drawing or inscription on walls, glib, funny, immediate. Everybody has a different way of checking out a culture. Some look at clothing, others at cars. My way is to examine rock radio, which is an American graffiti.' Occasionally he veered off into other aspects of radio, like the old suspense programs such as *Inner Sanctum* and *I Love a Mystery* he'd listened to as a boy. Lucas made notes for a possible mystery story set in a radio station. He called it 'The Radioland Murders'.

★   ★   ★

In May 1970, the Warners brass demanded to see *THX1138*. The day before Coppola was to take the first rough copy to Hollywood, Walter Murch screened it for him. 'Well, it's either a masterpiece or masturbation,' Coppola sighed. That night, he called Murch, Matthew Robbins, and cameraman Caleb Deschanel to an emergency meeting. He'd decided the screening would be a disaster, and briefed them accordingly.

In Warners' Theater 'A' next morning were president Ted Ashley, production head John Calley, Richard Lederer, head of marketing, Frank Wells from business affairs, and the studio's day-to-day liaison man with Zoetrope, Barry Beckerman. As expected, they loathed the film. 'This isn't the screenplay we said we were going to do,' complained one. 'This isn't a commercial movie.' Coppola feigned ignorance: 'I don't know *what* the fuck this is.' As they walked out of the theater, talk was only of taking the film away from Lucas and recutting it.

Outside, Murch, Robbins, and Deschanel, as ordered by Coppola, were waiting near the foot of Warners' landmark watertower. As the executives and Coppola emerged from the front door, they burst into the projection box, claiming to be from the studio editorial department, grabbed the film, loaded it into the back of Robbins's van, and drove away.

Kidnapping the work print only delayed the inevitable. Warners put Fred Weintraub, its 'youth' expert, in charge of cutting *THX1138*, and Frank Wells dictated what should be done. Weintraub was convinced that the Shelldwellers, as the film's only 'creatures,' must appear in the first reel. 'If you hook the audience in the first ten minutes,' he told Lucas, 'they'll forgive anything. You gotta put your best stuff up front . . . Put the freaks up front.'

In the midst of these discussions, the original *THX1138 4EB*, now with the added subtitle *Electronic Labyrinth*, was included in *Take One*, three programs of student films, half of them from USC, shown in New York, a fact which gave Lucas a melancholy satisfaction. If the feature version never saw the light of day, at least his first draft would survive.

Lucas and Coppola continued to meet in San Francisco, and to discuss the fate of Zoetrope. To add to its problems, the company was embroiled in a complicated lawsuit brought against local unions by the left-wing film-makers to whom Coppola had incautiously given house room the previous year. They'd formed their own union, and Zoetrope's productions, such as they were, became the battlefield on which they struggled for jurisdiction. It cost Coppola another $40,000 to extricate himself from the firefight.

Patton brought Coppola numerous offers from Hollywood to script and direct films, but he turned all of them down. The most insistent came from Paramount, who wanted him to film Mario Puzo's bestselling novel *The Godfather*. Coppola thought it a potboiler, and refused repeatedly. Eventually Peter Bart, a Paramount staffer and, later, editor of the trade paper *Variety*, rang one last time.

Lucas was in the office that day, and Coppola, covering the mouthpiece, asked, 'George, what should I do? Should I make this gangster movie or shouldn't I?'

'Francis, we need the money,' Lucas said. 'And what have you got to lose?'

While Coppola was away filming *The Godfather*, Lucas moved into the Zoetrope offices. He was constantly on the phone, setting up *American Graffiti* and finding editing work for Marcia. None of the calls were on behalf of Zoetrope, so after a few weeks office manager Mona Skarger presented him with a phone bill for $1800. With only $2000 in the bank, Lucas had to borrow the money from his father. He was so angry and humiliated that he shunned the offices and sent Marcia in with the check. Coppola later claimed he hadn't authorized Skarger to demand payment: 'I would never have done that to a friend.' Lucas didn't believe him. Their friendship inched one step nearer a break, though really it was just another aspect of the general withdrawal from personal relationships which paralleled Lucas's abandonment of Los Angeles. 'George feels,' says Willard Huyck, 'that he made enough friends at USC, and doesn't need any more.'

One new friend Lucas did accept was a calm, indeed grave young man a few years older than himself named Gary Kurtz. Kurtz wore his beard even shorter than Lucas's, and cut it back severely from his chin in a style usually associated with the Amish. In fact, Kurtz was raised as a Mormon, and refused to fight in Vietnam from religious conviction. Having graduated from the USC film school in 1962, he was made a combat cameraman with the Marines and served three years 'in country.'

Kurtz was the same age as Coppola, whom he knew from their days with Corman, but in his gravity, stability, and morality the direct antithesis. 'I worked for Roger Corman as a student on lots of little films,' he says, 'most of which I can't even remember the titles of now; some of which we didn't even know the titles of then. Shooting little bits and pieces. That's how I met Francis. I was on *Dementia 13*, his first film. He shot most of it in Ireland but we did little bits of it in Los Angeles.

'When I got out of the Marines in 1969, I went back to doing a few low-budget films and doing odds and ends, and another friend of mine whom I'd worked with with Roger, Monte Hellman, wanted to do this film, *Two Lane Blacktop*. We got Universal to buy into it under their under-$1 million-budget program. I went up to talk to Francis about using his Techniscope equipment for *Two Lane Blacktop*. He said, "We've just finished shooting this film on Techniscope. I'll take you out to meet George, and he'll show you some of the material on the Steenbeck." We went out to Mill Valley. George was editing in his attic. He was very gracious. He showed me the footage, and we had a chat about Techniscope, and I went back to San Francisco. I called George a couple of other times about technical aspects of using Techniscope in the next week after that.'

Aside from *Radioland Murders* and *American Graffiti*, Lucas had one more idea: a science fiction story, a movie comic-book inspired by Edgar Rice Burroughs, the *Flash Gordon* serials and *Dune*, but shot in a style inspired by old Hollywood action films. At some point, wearying of turning images into words, he created an outline in collage, with images cut from comic books and science fiction magazines.

Lucas didn't aspire to compete with Hollywood science fiction like *Forbidden Planet* or *Planet of the Apes*. Another kind of science fiction film had always existed parallel to them. This strain was disreputable, catchpenny, its plots vulgar, its costumes cheap. It encompassed Ed Wood's *Plan Nine from Outer Space*, Roger Corman's *The Beast with a Million Eyes* and *Attack of the Crab Monsters*, and Japanese imports like *Godzilla*. Its market was revival houses or drive-ins, its audience teenagers with one hand up their girl's skirt and the other clutching a Coke.

Whenever Hollywood got more money for a science fiction film, it splurged on state-of-the-art special effects, good mainstream writers, well-known stars. *Forbidden Planet* was directed by the director of *Lassie Come Home*. Its scriptwriter wrote *Tarzan the Ape Man*. Its cameraman photographed Ernst Lubitsch's *The Smiling Lieutenant*. It starred Walter Pidgeon, one of MGM's oldest and most respected leading men. To do what Lucas proposed with his science fiction film, i.e. spend money not on making the product more intellectually respectable or scientifically authentic, but on amplifying the sleaziness and vulgarity, seemed absurd to Hollywood. One might as well take some cheap old car, give it a lustrous paint job, and tart it up with chrome and flashing lights . . .

In 1971, Lucas wasn't pushing the sf project too hard. He still hoped he might acquire the rights to the *Flash Gordon* comic strip and incorporate his ideas into a remake of the serial version. At the same time, he began looking at some of the work being done by new people at the edge of the sf movie world. Matthew Robbins and Hal Barwood, trying to find backing for a science fiction script called 'Star Dance,' had asked an artist named Ralph McQuarrie to create some concept paintings in the hope of interesting possible investors. The film never got made, but Lucas spent an afternoon in McQuarrie's tiny garage apartment going through slides of his work. As a technical artist at Boeing, McQuarrie had drawn the illustrations for the company's parts catalogue. After that, he did 'artist's impressions' of space and other planets for NASA and CBS News, and worked for the *Encyclopedia Britannica*. Lucas told McQuarrie about his still-untitled sf project. 'It sounds great,' McQuarrie said. 'I'd like to see it.'

In January 1971, Lucas was both flattered and offended when friends told him that an episode of Universal's TV series *The Name of the Game* broadcast on 15 January 1971 looked a lot like *THX1138*. In the feature-length TV film *LA 2017*, written by Philip Wylie, of which even the name recalled Lucas's film, magazine editor Gene Barry crashes his car en route to an environmental conference. He wakes up in the year 2017, when the people of Los Angeles have fled underground to escape air pollution and gang warfare. They live in sterile tunnels, ruled by an overlord. The film was shot with the long lenses characteristic of *THX*, and in a similar dreamlike style. The director was Steven Spielberg.

Lucas fought the current of his career that appeared to be carrying him inexorably towards science fiction, and shied away from being pigeonholed as an sf specialist. In discussions with potential backers, he tried not to favor the sf idea over his two other projects, *American Graffiti* and *Radioland Murders*, judging that *American Graffiti* in particular, obviously aimed at the young audience, would be easier to finance. His model was Federico Fellini's 1953 *I Vitelloni*. Like Lucas, Fellini had grown up in a provincial backwater – Rimini, on the Adriatic coast below Venice. As teenagers, he and his friends talked incessantly of leaving, but none could quite find the energy. In the end, only Fellini got away, making his fortune in Rome.

Fellini turned his youthful experience into *I Vitelloni* – literally 'The Young Calves', but more accurately 'the drones,' or 'the layabouts.' His four main characters, all old friends, loaf through the day, playing pool, drinking coffee, chasing girls. Only the quiet one who walks the streets at night, who goes down to the station to watch the trains come in, who reads while the others argue and dream, finds the courage to leave, and at the end boards the Rome train for an uncertain future.

Lucas imagined a similar story set in Modesto on a single day – the last day of the school year. The day of the senior prom. The last day some friends would ever see one another. Three of the four main characters, like Fellini's, were surrogates of people Lucas had known, though all had aspects of Lucas himself: the thoughtful Curtis, about to go to college on a scholarship, but unsure if he wants to leave; the dropout hot-rodder Milner, obsessed with cars and racing; Terry the Toad, class nerd, socially inept, especially with girls; and Steve, class president, king of the senior prom, and destined for a future in business. Lucas acknowledges that he had least sympathy for Steve, who was, he admits, 'written to add a love-story angle, and round it out to four people. It shows.'

Lucas gave his script outline to Jeff Berg, his agent at ICM, who circulated it, without much reaction, except to the title, which nobody liked – some thought a film called *American Graffiti* must be about feet. Lucas got used to catching the 9 a.m. PSA shuttle every Monday to Los Angeles, a change of underwear, socks and a clean shirt in his briefcase next to the script outline and budget, and spending a couple of days going round the studios.

The only executive to show any interest was David Chasman, vice president in charge of production at United Artists; but in the end he passed. Berg advised Lucas to get a full script written and try again. Busy with the last touches on *THX*, which Warners had now decided to open in March, he called Huyck and Katz. Would they write one on spec, or for very little money? They had to refuse: a British producer had offered Huyck a chance to direct their script for a horror film. The most they could offer was a four-page outline, which improved on Lucas's by giving a rough structure to his ideas. Casting around for someone to nursemaid the project while he finished editing *THX*, Lucas remembered the quiet man with the beard who'd produced *Two Lane Blacktop*.

Early in 1971, Charley Lippincott had a call from Gary Kurtz, whom he knew from USC. They had dinner, and Kurtz told Lippincott of Lucas's offer of work on a film about growing up in Northern California. Lucas, he said, had another idea too, a science fiction film, but Kurtz was vague about exactly what that entailed. Lippincott recommended Lucas enthusiastically, not only as a film-maker, but as a person. Kurtz had no better offers, so he signed on to develop *American Graffiti*, with the idea that if it got made, he would be its producer.

Warners opened *THX1138* on 11 March 1971, in the doldrums between the end of the Christmas/New Year break and the prime summer period. By stalling, brooding, lapsing into long silences, failing to return phone calls, and generally fighting a stubborn rearguard action, Lucas prevented Fred Weintraub from restructuring the film, but he couldn't stop Warners' veteran head of editing, Rudy Fehr, from amputating four minutes. The cuts infuriated him. His hatred of Ted Ashley simmered for years, and he refused even to consider working with him again until he apologized for his treatment of *THX*. Lucas wasn't alone in his loathing of Warners: 'Marty [Scorsese] was next door working as editor on *The Great Medicine Ball Caravan* where he was having a terrible time too, and Brian [De Palma] was making *Get to Know your Rabbit* and they were cutting his film to shreds too, so we started commiserating.'

Warners' publicity department eventually sold *THX1138* not on its 'freaks' but on its second-most futuristic image, the blank chrome faces of the cops. Lucas saw his film for the first time with a paying crowd on the day it opened, and was warmed by their enthusiasm. Warners screened it to critics only at the last minute. Arthur Knight's notice in the *Saturday Review* was loyally supportive, but reviews were generally sparse, appropriate to a film which wasn't going to be seen outside the student and art-house circuit. After a few weeks, Warners pulled *THX* from city screens, consigning it to the suburbs and drive-ins as the bottom half of a double bill with one of its many flops.

All the same, the film had drawn attention to Lucas. In April, the LA PBS Channel 28 ran *George Lucas, Maker of Films*, an hour-long documentary in which Lucas discussed his career with writer/critic Gene Youngblood. The film included *6.18.67*, the student version of *THX* and an extract from the feature. Rather than shoot in the studio, director Jerry Hughes took Lucas to Bronson Canyon, on the edge of Griffith Park, location for countless low-budget movies since the early days of cinema. A prescient opening showed Lucas and Youngblood chatting amid a jumble of rocks, only for the camera to pull back and reveal the 'HOLLYWOOD' sign looming unignorably above them.

Lucas was outspoken about the film business. 'Making films is an art, selling them is a business. I don't know how to sell films,' he announced. Nor, he said, did the producers: 'The people selling movies only want movies they don't *have* to sell, because they're lazy.' In a largely favorable review of the PBS film, the trade paper *Variety* remarked drily, 'Of interest would be the studio's viewpoint.'

In May, *Newsweek* devoted a two-page article to Lucas, who was now being seen by some as the acceptable face of New Hollywood. His soft-spoken manner and insistence in the Hughes documentary that 'most of the oddballs have been filtered out' made him an attractive alternative to off-the-wall adventurers like Dennis Hopper. By then *THX* was almost into profit, a goal achieved when Warners sold it to television, though all Lucas ever saw was his $15,000 fee. Warners' accountants ensured that only the most massive success ever paid off on 'net points.' 'It made money in the theaters but not in the accounting office,' Lucas said cynically, chalking up another black mark against Hollywood. *Newsweek* concurred in Lucas's cynicism. 'Apparently, Lucas is one of the victims of the youth backlash sweeping some studios,' wrote the magazine's Paul Zimmerman, 'which have decided to ride tight herd on the young directors they were searching for only recently to bail themselves out. But if obvious talent, demonstrated efficiency and a highly profitable product are not sufficient recommen-

The Stinky Kid. George Lucas at Downey High School, Modesto, 1960.

ABOVE Ramona Avenue, Modesto, where Lucas was born.

RIGHT Betty Salette's sculpture *American Graffiti,* erected on 'George Lucas Plaza' in 1997 to celebrate Modesto's best-known citizen.

LEFT USC days. Randal Kleiser menaces Debbie Burr, watched by Don Glut, in Randy Epstein's student film *The Pursuit* (1964).

BELOW Randy Epstein as Jimmy Olsen being saved by Superman (Don Glut) in Glut's student film *Superman and the Gorilla Gang* (1964).

George Lucas with James Garner (left) helping shoot the credit sequence of John Frankenheimer's *Grand Prix* while he was a USC student, 1965.

Lucas's vision of a dystopic future in his 1966 student film *THX1138 4EB* (LEFT) grew into the 1970 feature version *THX1138* (BELOW), with Robert Duvall and Maggie McOmie as doomed lovers in a sexless and regimented state.

dation for a young director, then the legendary irrationality of Hollywood is apparently still very much alive.'

In a bonus Lucas didn't expect, the Cannes Film Festival asked to
show *THX1138*. Following the riots of 1968 which had closed down
the festival, its president Favre Le Bret bowed to pressure from fire-
brands like François Truffaut and Jean-Luc Godard, and agreed to
include more work by young directors. The *Quinzaine de Realisateurs*,
or Directors' Fortnight, was outside the official competition, and thus
exempt from the requirement that a film should not have opened in
the country that produced it. The choice of *THX1138* had less to do
with its merit than with the pull which studios still exerted over this
most market-oriented of festivals, but Lucas was pleased just the same.
Marcia needed a holiday after editing Michael Ritchie's *The Candidate*,
so they withdrew their $2000 savings, bought backpacks and sleeping
bags, and caught a charter to Paris, with a stopover in New York.

In New York, Lucas took a chance and called the president of
United Artists, David Picker. As David Chasman in LA had shown
some interest in *American Graffiti*, it couldn't hurt to talk to his boss.

UA had no studios. Set up in the 1920s by Charlie Chaplin, D.W.
Griffith, Douglas Fairbanks, and Mary Pickford, it was designed to
fund and distribute independent productions. When Arthur Krim and
Robert Benjamin took over in 1955, they jettisoned UA's library of
cheap westerns and gangster pictures, and went after films being produced by such companies as Mirisch or Bryna, tied to stars like Kirk
Douglas.

David Picker was Old Hollywood – his uncle Arnold shared control
of UA with Krim and Benjamin. Picker had just become president in
1969, and was looking to put his stamp on the company, and Hollywood. He was ready to see a young director with a film at Cannes,
since he would be there too. They chatted about France. Lucas
explained that he and Marcia were travelling on a Eurorail pass, staying in campsites, and checking out all the Formula 1 car circuits, as
well as going to the festival. He gave Picker the *American Graffiti*
outline, and talked up his science fiction film.

In Cannes, they didn't have press passes, and George had to sneak
into the screening of his own film, which was a *succès d'estime*. So
enthusiastic was the audience's reaction that the festival scheduled a
press conference to introduce Lucas, but since he was at none of the

usual hotels, nobody could find him to give him the news, so he missed his own launching on the international film scene. Picker invited him and Marcia to the UA suite at the Carlton, and after hearing about George's problem, gave them his passes so they could see all the films they wanted. He also told Lucas he'd decided to recommend *American Graffiti* to his board. The Lucases went on to London, where Picker rang them with the news that UA would invest $10,000 in a first draft screenplay, with more to come if he liked the result. The call came on 14 May – Lucas's birthday.

Lucas called Gary Kurtz in Los Angeles with the good news. They mulled over who should write the script. Lucas suggested Richard Walter, who'd gone through USC with them and become a successful screenwriter. Walter recalls: 'At USC, I'd acted in a student film by a man named William Phelps – a freak-out crazed undisciplined black-and-white feature-length movie, sort of unwatchable, called *The Reversal of Richard's Sun*. It's about Revolution and all that stuff. There's a scene where I'm in a stairwell, sitting and looking through old 45rpm records: Little Richard, Jerry Lee Lewis, Chuck Berry – the early geniuses of rock and roll. There was an obsession at that time about labels; the trivia of it, and so on. Suddenly John Milius bursts in and breaks up the whole thing.

'I threw away the pages I'd been given and just ad-libbed. And after the screening, George, who's very close-mouthed and not effusive in praise, a very very deeply shy man, came over and said, "You were terrific in that thing."

'I was in New York, working on a screenplay called "Young Love," when Gary Kurtz rang, and said George wanted me to write this thing called *American Graffiti*. The first thing I said was, "What a dreadful title. It sounds like some Italian *neo-realismo* movie." Everybody hated this title but George; my first drafts say "American Graffiti: Working Title."

'Gary gave me the pages Willard and Gloria had done, and said, "Pay no attention to these pages. They're simply for the legal end of things." He gave me the parameters. It's Modesto, it's dusk to dawn, it's four characters. The two buddies are going to leave next morning, get out of this rathole of a town, but by morning they'll all chicken out but one. There wasn't much money involved, but I was to get all of it: $10,000.'

Walter says he was 'thrilled out of my mind, and flattered that George wanted me to do it.' He had dinner with Huyck and Katz, and told them of Kurtz's approach. They congratulated him, and told him to go ahead, ignoring their outline, which they'd written in haste to help Lucas out.

Walter didn't go to Modesto, but on the contrary, tried to talk Kurtz into setting the story in New York, and basing it on a novel he'd written. Called *Barry and the Persuasions*, it was about growing up in New York in a haze of fifties rock'n'roll, and inspired by Walter's own adolescence.

'Lukewarm middle America is the most boring thing I've ever heard in my life,' he told Kurtz. 'Let's do my story. Upper West Side, middle-class Jewish kid, rock'n'roll . . .'

Kurtz wasn't interested. Walter says: 'There are two polite ways of saying "Fuck you" in Hollywood. One is "Trust me." The other is, "Let's make that our *next* project." Gary winked at me, and said, "Let's make that our *next* project." I take some pride in the fact that I tried to talk him out of one of the most profitable films in movie history.'

Once Kurtz had refused *Barry and the Persuasions*, Walter acquiesced. 'I'll do some research,' he said. 'Read some fifties newspapers, listen to the music. Then when George comes back, we'll start working.'

'No,' said Kurtz. 'He's been *putzing* around with this thing too long. We must have a draft by the time he comes back in two weeks.'

'If you want it fast,' said Walter, 'get someone else. If you want it good, I'll do it.'

Kurtz compromised. He offered Walter $7500 for the first draft, and a guaranteed $2500 for the second, on which Lucas would work with him. Walter wrote twenty pages the first day, and had a first draft in nine days. 'I thought, "This is great. It's all over the place, it ain't half ready, but we can at least go on to stage two when he comes back." I sent it to my agent, Mike Medavoy, and I guess Mike gave it to George.

'George came over to see me at my house, and he really looked grim – George always looked as if he was ready to be executed – and I can tell he doesn't like this draft.' Asked what he disliked, Lucas said the script was 'nothing like his experience.' 'Which is not surprising,' Walter continues, 'since I'm a Jew from New York. What do I know from Modesto? We didn't have cars. We rode the subway, or bicycles.' Lucas later complained that the script 'had put in playing Chicken on the road instead of drag racing.' 'Well, it was great for character conflict,' says Walter. 'It was a homage to *Rebel Without a Cause*, and it seemed to me a perfect metaphor for the era of brinkmanship: East vs West; who blinks first?' For all his rejection of this idea, Lucas, when he shot *American Graffiti*, would stage the climactic drag race in a style visually similar to the Chicken run in *Rebel Without a Cause*.

The supposed raunchiness of Walter's screenplay also figured in many of Lucas's later criticisms. Walter agrees it had its share of sex. 'The main character was the Ron Howard character. He goes over to his girl's house to break it off. She seduces him, and there's a very sexual scene – which I know, from things I was told subsequently, really offended George. But hey, it's adolescence! Though not, I gather, George's adolescence. In my version, the Ron Howard and Cindy Williams characters go over the state line to Nevada, where you don't need your parents' permission, and get married.'

Walter offered to work with Lucas on the script, but Lucas refused. 'I've learned that I really have to write it myself,' he said. Walter recalls: 'George wanted it seamlessly to drift – which is adolescence too. He didn't want any long scenes. No scene should be more than two pages. I'd nominated all the songs to go with the various scenes. For the sock hop, I had Little Richard doing "We Gonna Rip it Up." He wanted me to drop all the songs. But he also wanted to end the deal there. He didn't want to pay the other $2500. I didn't need the money, but I felt betrayed. After I'd advised against it, after I'd advised of a more enlightened way to go, I'd done exactly what I'd been asked.

'I said, "I'm going to Mike [Medavoy]," but George said, "Don't call him! Don't call him!" Eventually he left. By the end of the week, Mike told me, "Lucas hates the script. He doesn't want to go forward to the second draft." I said, "He doesn't have to go forward to the second, but he has to *pay* for the second." Jeff Berg rang up and tried to get me to agree, and I threatened Jeff Berg's life!'

Lucas arranged a conciliatory lunch at Hamburger Hamlet on Doheny, his favorite hangout. When Walter wouldn't relent, he went back to Marin. A few months later, in July 1971, he rang Walter to say that since they were going to have to pay for it, they might as well have a second draft. He explained what he wanted in it, and told Walter, when he delivered the new version, that he felt it was 'vastly improved;' but Walter felt 'he was just going through the motions.'

When a producer or director claims credit for writing a film for which a screenplay already exists, the Screenwriters' Guild automatically holds an adjudication, to protect a writer from having a producer or director bully him into giving up his credit. The Guild was to adjudicate on *American Graffiti*, and would award sole credit to Lucas, and to Huyck and Katz, who wrote the final screenplay.

At ICM, Jeff Berg, touting Lucas as a director, received a screenplay co-written by Alan Trustman, who worked on the major success *Bullitt*. *Lady Ice*, the story of an insurance investigator who steals a diamond and gets involved with the daughter of a crime king, would be shot in Florida. The job paid $100,000, plus points. Given Lucas's lack of sympathy with crime films, and his inability to communicate with actors, it's hard to see why he was ever offered such a project. Lucas too was baffled and, after some discussion with Marcia, turned it down. Tom Gries made the film in 1973, none too successfully, with Donald Sutherland and Jennifer O'Neil.

There was never much chance that Lucas would take work as a contract director, as Coppola had done. *THX1138* had taught him he had no aptitude for it. 'I dislike directing,' he says. 'I hate the constant dealing with volatile personalities. Directing is emotional frustration, anger, and tremendously hard work – seven days a week, twelve to sixteen hours a day. For years my wife would ask why we couldn't go out to dinner like other people. But I couldn't turn it off. Eventually, I realized that directing simply wasn't healthy for me.' His diabetes had begun to manifest itself in weariness, confusion, and bad temper, all of which were exacerbated by the pressures of film-making.

Lucas rewrote *American Graffiti*. His version pushed it away from drama into a kind of imaginary documentary, softening the reality. When she saw the film, Lucas's mother remarked that life in Modesto, even in 1962, was never as lively as the film made out. 'Not everything in the movie really happened,' she said. 'But the main thing was, a lot of them were things that the boys *hoped* would happen. They would say, "Gee, wouldn't it be neat if we could do this?"'

The most obvious element to be absent from *American Graffiti* was parents. 'The thing that really made the film stand out,' says Charley Lippincott, who grew up in Oswego, near Chicago, a town not unlike Modesto, 'is the way adults were treated. For the most part, there's very little adult interaction. It's a kids' world.' If the adults are not authority figures, like the teacher supervising the dance or the traffic cop who stops Milner for a traffic offense, they're dummies, like the two lodge brothers responsible for sending Curt to college. In every case, the teenagers treat them with contempt.

Lucas sent the new screenplay to Picker, asking him to approve funding for a second draft, which Huyck and Katz were now ready to do (their horror film had fallen though, though Huyck did direct it in 1974 as *Messiah of Evil*, aka *Return of the Living Dead, Revenge of the Screaming Dead* and *The Second Coming*). Lucas was shattered when Picker almost immediately rejected it.

As the studios saw it, the youth boom had crashed as quickly as it had taken flight. *Easy Rider* made money, but the films pushed out in 1970 to capitalize on the new audience all flopped. In 1973, the year *American Graffiti* was released, it would be almost the sole film aimed at a young audience. Instead, the studios had green-lighted films about crime and violence, starring established personalities: *The Exorcist, The Day of the Jackal, Enter the Dragon* with Bruce Lee, Clint Eastwood in his most nihilistic western to date, *High Plains Drifter, Serpico,* and *The Sting.* The year's big money-maker was an old-fashioned disaster melodrama, *The Poseidon Adventure.* From the previous year, Coppola's *The Godfather* and Bob Fosse's *Cabaret* swept the Oscars.

Huyck and Katz agreed to write a new screenplay for Lucas on spec, and did a quick first draft in collaboration with him, shuttling pages between Mill Valley and Los Angeles. Once it was finished, Lucas pondered whether to send it to Coppola, but held off, taking it instead to American International, the cheap studio that funded Roger Corman, and had backed a number of biker films. They said they might come up with the money if Lucas rewrote the script to make it more violent and exploitational.

Jeff Berg circulated the screenplay to all the studios, which reacted in the same way as David Picker: youth films were finished. Only Ned Tanen at Universal conceded that it might have some remote possibility of success. When Lew Wasserman, the head of Universal, launched a youth division to make low-budget films by new young directors in 1969, he put Tanen in charge. His remit was clear. No film could cost more than $1 million, and ideally only $750,000. Everyone involved would receive the minimum union rate – 'scale.' They would be given no studio space, no facilities; they could shoot on location, and if they had problems, solve them there. On the other hand, they would receive a generous share of any profits, and, in theory, the final cut, though the small print gave Universal the right to make almost any changes it cared to in the interest of better sales.

Tanen, 'a classic climber' in the admiring words of *Life* magazine, had graduated from the mailroom at Lew Wasserman's MCA agency, via an advantageous marriage to the daughter of director Howard Hawks, to a spot inside Universal. He was one of Hollywood's most dour characters – 'clinically manic-depressive,' insisted producer Don Simpson. His mood swings were famous, and he regarded the movie business with a stoic's weary pessimism. Asked to sum up his experience of Hollywood, he growled: 'Negativity and illusion. The only words you need to know. Especially negativity.' All the same, he seemed the ideal person to head a youth program. The same age as Coppola, he didn't share conventional Hollywood prejudices. 'I guess I'm pretty stupid,' he said. 'I never believe anybody.' Verna Fields, one of his closest friends, said, 'Ned could see three sides to every situation.'

The first film of the youth project, foisted on Tanen by Wasserman, was *The Last Movie*, Dennis Hopper's next movie after *Easy Rider*. A kind of western, it needed, insisted Hopper, to be shot in Peru. It went grossly over budget, took forever to edit, and proved unreleasable. Subsequent films like John Cassavetes' *Minnie and Moskowitz*, *Two Lane Blacktop* (the Monte Hellman film produced by Gary Kurtz), Frank Perry's *Diary of a Mad Housewife*, Milos Forman's first US movie, *Taking Off*, Peter Fonda's *The Hired Hand*, and *Silent Running*, the environmental science fiction film that marked the directing debut of special-effects expert Douglas Trumbull, all drew good reviews, if not major interest at the box-office.

Lucas and Kurtz went to LA to see Tanen, who was relatively benign, even though his division was running down. *American Graffiti* appealed to him. He liked cars, and used to cruise himself, in Southern California. He took the project to Sidney Sheinberg, Wasserman's deputy, and voted to fund it. Sheinberg didn't hide the fact that he'd lost faith in the youth program. It hadn't produced another *Easy Rider*, and both he and Wasserman now believed that feature-length TV episodes and TV movies made 'in house' offered just as good a nursery for new talent.

Sheinberg's protégé Steven Spielberg had just made a splash with one of these films, a low-budget actioner about a driver pursued by an ancient tanker truck. *Duel* showed on 13 November 1971. Lucas was at a party at Coppola's place in San Francisco that night, and hadn't forgotten that the TV movie's director was the same Universal staffer who made the *LA 2017* episode of *The Name of the Game*, but decided it might be worth a look. 'Since I'd met Steven,' he said, 'I was curious about the movie and thought I'd sneak upstairs and catch ten or fifteen minutes. Once I started watching, I couldn't tear myself away. I thought, this guy is really sharp. I've got to get to know him better.'

At the Universal production meeting, Tanen championed *American Graffiti* against executives wary about pouring good money after bad. In particular, the music department wondered how Lucas hoped to secure rights to the rock songs he'd strewn so promiscuously through his script – the early treatment stressed that the film would be a MUSICAL (Lucas used the upper case intentionally), though one in which people didn't sing themselves. The musicians whose work Hopper and Fonda used in *Easy Rider* had wrung every cent they could from them. One executive estimated that music permissions alone could cost $500,000. But the board narrowly approved the project, providing Francis Coppola produced it, which would allow them to advertise it as 'From the Man who Gave you *The Godfather.*' *American Graffiti* was simply a sprat to catch that very lucrative mackerel.

As he left the meeting, Tanen knew this would be the youth program's last film. That didn't improve his temper, and the offer he made to Lucas was alarming in the bleakness of its terms. Universal would invest a total of $600,000 in the film, that sum to include all music rights, as well as fees for the actors. Lucas would get $50,000 for both co-scripting and directing, but would receive 20 per cent of any profits – 'net points,' in Hollywood terminology, which were only payable after the studio recouped its costs. The deal also gave Universal first refusal on Lucas's next two projects, *Radioland Murders* and the unnamed science fiction film.

Lucas bridled when Tanen told him he must have Coppola as producer rather than the relatively untried Kurtz. Having bypassed Coppola to take the script to Tanen, it would humiliate him to return, cap in hand, and ask for his support. Finally, Tanen himself agreed to fly to San Francisco, and prevailed on Coppola. He wouldn't have to do anything, Tanen wheedled. Kurtz would be line producer. He offered Coppola twenty net percentage points – exactly what Lucas would receive. Out of that, Coppola could pay Kurtz to manage the film, plus anyone else he felt might be needed to guarantee its quality, and pocket the rest. Huyck and Katz, the actors, and lawyer Tom Pollock, who would negotiate the music rights, would be paid out of Lucas's share. No stranger to such intrigue, Coppola accepted – providing Lucas asked him in person. 'When I had to come back to him and ask him to produce *Graffiti*, Francis was feeling good,' Lucas recalled sourly, chalking up another black mark against his old friend. One imagines a meeting like the first scene of *The Godfather*: the supplicant bowing before the don, kissing his hand, and the *capo di tutti capi* of New Hollywood growling, 'Why did you not come to me first?'

Coppola hired Haskell Wexler's TV production company to film *Graffiti* auditions. When people complained that he was feathering his nest from the work of others while doing little himself, he bridled: 'I had the job in Hollywood. I had the credits. I had the money. I had the houses. All of my young associates were broke, and I took them all with me and used everything I had to fund their, and my, projects.' Hollow laughter was heard around the Bay area – all the more so when Coppola's slice of *American Graffiti* paid him more than $3 million, even after he'd taken care of Kurtz.

With Coppola on board, Jeff Berg was able to squeeze another $150,000 out of Universal. In return, he had to concede some of Lucas's rights, among them that of final cut. Lucas and Kurtz were given a two-room office across the street from Universal, which was to remain the Los Angeles headquarters of Lucasfilm even after they'd finished *American Graffiti* and moved to Twentieth Century-Fox for *Star Wars*. Charley Lippincott had found a job as publicist on Alfred Hitchcock's last film, *Family Plot*, which Universal was also producing, so he saw something of Lucas, though not a lot. 'They were rarely there,' he says, 'because it's a George Lucas rule never to have an office at the studio for whom you're making the film.' The most presence they would ever have on the Fox lot throughout the production of the *Star Wars* films was two parking places.

Lucas set out to find locations and accumulate a cast. Coppola insisted on him hiring Fred Roos, an ex-agent who had cast *The*

Godfather. Roos, ambitious to become a producer – he would produce Coppola's *The Conversation*, and would go on to do a number of films for the relaunched Zoetrope, including *Hammett* and *Tucker* – became another Coppola collaborator put 'on the pad' of *American Graffiti*'s budget. But Roos more than earned his keep. Quietly-spoken, attentive, he saw thousands of films every year, and attended lots of plays. He'd cast numerous TV shows and films. His coups included spotting the young Jack Nicholson and placing him into the low-budget films that launched his career. He had also suggested Al Pacino and Diane Keaton for *The Godfather*.

'We decided to make a massive search for good kids,' says Roos; 'and that's what it was: massive. It went on for weeks and months.' He took Lucas to Bay area high schools, and supervised numerous 'cattle call' auditions for which hopeful youngsters were invited to turn up even if they had no theatrical experience. Among them was Mark Hamill, later Luke Skywalker in *Star Wars*.

Lucas found casting excruciating. He didn't know what to say to actors, and found their brashness alarming. He stayed in the background, letting Roos do the talking. If anyone asked what he thought of a performance, he answered reflexively, 'Great! Terrific!'

For Steve Bolander, the straight-arrow student who ends up turning his back on the outside world to remain in town and sell insurance, Roos suggested Ronny Howard. Already a veteran at eighteen, Howard had starred as little Opie in the long-running *Andy Griffith Show* on TV – a role found for him by Roos. 'I went for a meeting,' says Howard, 'and [Lucas] turned out to be unlike any director I'd ever met. He was wearing a school jacket and had a beard. We did cold readings, improvisations, video tests, everything. Five interviews and six months later, I was cast.'

Harrison Ford also had experience. The supervisor of Columbia's talent program had flunked him for lacking 'star quality.' After that, he earned a living as a carpenter around Hollywood, building recording studios and sundecks for people in the music and movie businesses. His clients included Roos, who picked him to play Bob Falfa, the out-of-town hot-rodder who challenges John Milner to a drag race.

'How much does it pay?' Ford asked. Lucas told him everyone was getting Screen Actors' Guild scale, $480 a week.

Ford was aghast. 'I'm already making $1000 a week as a carpenter, and I have a young family to support!'

He walked out. Later, Roos called back. They'd looked over the budget, and maybe they could improve the offer a little – to $500.

Another Roos discovery, ex-boxer Paul LeMat, had narrowly missed out on a part in *Fat City*, which John Huston had just shot in Stockton. A story of the low end of boxing, set in the tank towns of Northern California, it had the rough, cheap, natural look Lucas wanted. Roos proposed LeMat for John Milner, the drag racer. Lucas liked his casual arrogance, his automatic understanding that a cool guy carried his cigarette pack twisted into the sleeve of his T-shirt.

Richard 'Ricky' Dreyfuss had done stage work and a TV commercial, and had one line in *The Graduate*. His career had been interrupted by two years' military service. Pleading conscientious objections, he was put to work in the LA County Hospital, where he acquired an amphetamine habit that was to dog him for many years to come. Lucas offered him a choice of Curt or Terry the Toad. Dreyfuss chose the former. Terry, after another actor had proved to look dreadful in a TV test recorded in LA, went to Charlie Martin Smith, who everybody agrees embodied the gauche young Lucas to the life.

The women were easier to cast. An audition right in Lucas's home town, Mill Valley, produced Kathleen Quinlan, who played Peg, Laurie's wised-up girlfriend. At Roos's urging, John Huston had cast New York ex-model Candy Clark in *Fat City*. Now Roos suggested her to Lucas for Debbie, the gum-chewing, bubble-headed blonde with whom Terry strikes it lucky. Model Suzanne Somers had the mute role of the Blonde Angel who coasts around Modesto in a white Thunderbird and stirs Curt's imagination with romantic longings. Mackenzie Phillips was twelve when she was cast as Carol, the kid Milner is stuck with as he cruises town; under Californian law, Gary Kurtz had to become her legal guardian for the term of the shooting. For a number of other girls who became extras, the primary criterion was whether or not they would have their hair cut for the film.

Harrison Ford, as befitted the actor who would become the biggest star, proved the most demanding cast member. Lucas, whom he found so shy that at first he mistook him for a casting assistant, also wanted Ford to trim his hair. A military cut would make him look more an outsider among the Presley quiffs. Unwilling to abandon the emblem of his alternativeness, Ford counter-suggested that he stuff his hair under a white cowboy hat. Lucas agreed, so Ford felt free to improvise other parts of his role. Lucas suggested he might serenade Cindy

Williams when, on the rebound from a fight with Howard, she joins Falfa in his car, and Ford suggested using a song by one of his friends, Phil Everly of the Everly Brothers. When this didn't work, he burst into a fruity impromptu version of 'Some Enchanted Evening' in the phoney Italian tones of Ezio Pinza. Such casual and joky arrogance led Lucas to cast Ford as Han Solo in *Star Wars*.

In one of the film's major coups, Lucas persuaded Wolfman Jack to appear. His radio show provides an obligato to the film, and Curt seeks him out at his little cinderblock station outside town to plead for a dedication that will unite him with the mysterious Blonde Angel. Nobody had previously put a face to that bourbon-and-unfiltered-Camels voice, but after *American Graffiti*, the deejay's genial persona became a national commonplace. 'It made me legitimate,' he said later, somewhat mournfully. Omnipresent, moralizing, bearded, benign, Wolfman Jack is *American Graffiti*'s God figure, its equivalent of OMM in *THX1138* and Obi-Wan Kenobi in *Star Wars*. For all his later embrace of Eastern mysticism, there remained in Lucas more than a little of the Methodist.

Many people who saw *American Graffiti* assumed it was shot in or near Modesto, but Lucas never seriously thought of doing so. His home town had prospered since he left. The sleepy provincialism was gone from its downtown business area; even his father's company had moved to the sprawling outskirts that were devouring the walnut ranches. Cruising was discouraged, and the city council didn't welcome a film which might glorify it. Moreover, Lucas didn't fancy old friends peering over his shoulder and saying, 'That wasn't the way it was at all.' But above all, it was simply too far away. Like an army, a film unit depends on its supply lines, and to shoot in Modesto, eighty-five miles from San Francisco, would have hopelessly attenuated those of *American Graffiti*.

Gary Kurtz went looking for another location. 'I remember walking up and down the main street of every community in Marin and Sonoma Counties with my light meter,' he says, 'looking for places where the stores were pretty much old, and we had enough light level from the regular sodium vapor streetlights to get a basic exposure so you could see the cars.' He made a deal with San Rafael, an hour's drive north of San Francisco into Marin County, and twenty minutes from Lucas's home in Mill Valley. Lucas had shot in its Civic Center on

THX1138, and for $300 a night the city council agreed to close off part of Fourth Street downtown from dusk to dawn for the period he wanted to film.

The deal didn't survive the first week. When a bar-owner complained he was losing business, and threatened to sue, the council rescinded the film's permit. Kurtz negotiated a three-day reprieve, and frantically searched for a replacement town. Petaluma, on the Pacific side of the Marin Peninsula, was less nervous than San Rafael, and the production moved there.

Later, Lucas would claim he intentionally imitated the style of AIP and Z-movie producer Sam Katzman, who made *Rock Around the Clock*, but the truth was that circumstances forced him into the same cheap shooting and visual short-cuts that Katzman had used to save money. The low budget forced him to drop his most imaginative scenes, including an eerie opening in which the Blonde Angel, Curt's image of the perfect woman, drives through an empty drive-in cinema in her Thunderbird, her transparency revealing that she doesn't really exist. 'Since it would have been the first image in the film, people wouldn't have been aware she was a ghost,' says Lucas. 'It would have appeared real.' But he never shot it. 'Everybody thought I was crazy, and it would also have been expensive and technically difficult.'

With CinemaScope still too expensive, Lucas elected again for the Techniscope process. He asked Haskell Wexler to shoot the film, but Wexler declined. 'He didn't want to shoot Techniscope,' said Lucas, 'because he felt it looked grainy, and he didn't want to push it [photographically]. And besides, he was writing his own script and shooting commercials, and he didn't really want to go back to being a cameraman.' Lucas decided to shoot the film himself. 'He thought he could be the cameraman, and just hire some operators,' says Kurtz. 'Didn't work. After three days, the stuff was looking terrible. We were using very low light levels and it was extremely hard for the operators to see what they were doing. We had two cameras going, and we were using lights of two foot-candles in some scenes when the usual low light level is about two hundred foot-candles. It just looked mushy.'

Kurtz appealed to Wexler, who became, *de facto*, the film's lighting cameraman. 'It was a major feat for Haskell,' says Kurtz. 'He was doing commercials in Hollywood. He'd fly back and forth between

LA and San Francisco every day. He was really exhausted by the end of it. Every weekend, he was in despair at not getting enough sleep.' The two operators, Ron Eveslarge and Jan D'Alquen, stayed on, and received joint cameraman credit. Wexler only receives credit as 'visual consultant.'

Lucas told Wexler he wanted the film to look – Marcia's word was 'ugly,' but Lucas felt that wasn't quite it. 'Not ugly,' he said, 'but a sort of jukebox lighting, like a 1962 Hot Rods in Hell jukebox. As far as I'm concerned, Haskell is the best cameraman in the country. Most cameramen shoot pretty pictures, and everything looks very pretty, but it takes real genius to make something look ugly and have a very special feel.' Even by Wexler's standards, the result was unglamorous. Wexler himself dismissed it as 'looking like a television show.'

Some locations proved elusive. 'We looked everywhere for a round drive-in restaurant for Mel's,' says Kurtz. 'We just couldn't find one. Finally we located one in downtown San Francisco; if you'd turned the camera through 180 degrees, you'd have seen all these skyscrapers and tall buildings. It was in terrible shape. We had to repair the neon in the signs and repair the lightbulbs and paint it. When Haskell saw it for the first time, he decided, since we were going to do so much shooting there, to replace all the lightbulbs with photofloods.'

Ron Howard, who had ambitions to direct himself, subsequently realized with films like *Cocoon* and *Apollo 13*, watched Lucas closely. 'He shot everything with two cameras,' he says, 'so you never knew if you were on screen or off. So you gave 100 per cent every time you did a scene.' Lucas told Howard, 'I'm not really getting a chance to direct this film. I don't have time. I'm really gonna direct it in the editing room. That's when I'm going to make my choices.'

The twenty-eight-day shooting schedule imposed by Universal's starvation budget obviated subtleties. There was no camera car – for travelling shots, the cameramen unbolted the lid of a car's trunk, climbed in and shot through the windscreen of the car they were towing. For side shots, they hung precariously on a sling of webbing, hand-holding the camera, feet braced against the door. The studio was so nervous of costs that the electrician in charge of the film's generator had orders to turn it off at precisely six o'clock each morning, when rates went up and there should be enough natural light anyway.

One trailer served as both make-up and changing room. Candy Clark's blonde wig was too small. Rather than get another one, it was slit up the back and bobby-pinned together. Harrison Ford says, 'I well remember almost being fired for taking two donuts from the food tray when it was well understood that the limit was one per cast member.'

Location shooting on most Hollywood films tended to be staid, but New Hollywood introduced an element of *Animal House*. The day before shooting began, a member of the crew was arrested for possession of marijuana. LeMat, Ford, and Bo Hopkins, who played the lanky leader of the Pharaos, were drunk most days and every weekend. When they'd exhausted the fun of urinating into the ice machines of the Petaluma Holiday Inn, they raced one another to the top of its revolving illuminated sign, the winner planting an empty beer-bottle on the summit. Ford also roared round town in Bob Falfa's hot Chevy, and nearly got thrown in jail.

'Every day we would arrive and someone would say, "Have you heard what's happened now?"' recalled Cindy Williams. When Ford and LeMat, tossing empty beer-bottles into the parking lot from their hotel balcony, shattered the windscreen of a Cadillac, Richard Dreyfuss, who was getting dressed for a date with Clark, went to their room to complain. 'Finally thirty or forty minutes had passed since he was supposed to be there,' says Clark, 'when a knock came on the door, and he was standing there leaning on it, soaking wet with a great big knot on his forehead. Those pranksters had tossed him into the shallow end of the pool head-first. I had to give him my pancake make-up, as there wasn't make-up on *American Graffiti* because they couldn't afford it.' After this brawl, and a fire in one of the rooms which had every fire brigade in town converging on the hotel, Ford was ordered out of the Holiday Inn, and exiled to Howard Johnson's across town.

Disasters continued right to the end of the shoot. Kurtz, a vegetarian, dictated non-meat meals for the cast and crew, but some rebelled at the lack of hamburgers, so two parallel sets of catering had to be laid on. Paul LeMat ate vegetarian until an allergy attack brought on by walnuts in a salad put him in hospital. Grip Tony Coangelo fell out of the camera car and was run over, but was uninjured. In the final drag race, Falfa's car broke an axle on the first day. On the second, it went out of control and narrowly missed hitting one of the four cameramen shooting the scene. The plane in the final scene had a flat tire and couldn't get off the ground.

Lucas conceived his characters in terms very different from those of the typical Hollywood entertainment film. One sees why he rejected Richard Walter's well-made if contrived screenplay, with its standard boy/girl relationships. Though *American Graffiti* is the story of four men, it's their women who drive it. The men talk, the women act – roles symbolized by the joint distinction of Steve and Laurie. Steve, last year's class president, is a figurehead and administrator; Laurie, this year's head cheerleader, is a person of action.

Curt is the most abject of slaves to women. Salivating for his Blonde Angel, he pursues her all night, only to see her from the plane, borne away like all dreams. Terry is no less in thrall to sex. Debbie urges him into action from the very moment he picks her up, walking disconsolately down the street against the lighted shop windows. 'I love it when guys peel out,' she says, and he obediently burns rubber to please her. After that, getting her some alcohol at the price of becoming peripherally involved in a liquor-store robbery seems inevitable.

Carol is foisted on Milner, but she soon controls him with her gibbering sub-teen chatter and shrewd understanding of the importance to him of retaining his machismo. She'll acquiesce in the fiction that she's a cousin he's babysitting for the night, but only in return for his submission. Next thing, he's taking her on a tour of the local wrecking yard, and meditating on the inevitability of his death, probably in a pile-up so horrendous that, like the worst of the crashes suffered by these heaps of crushed Chevies and Fords, it will be filmed and shown in Driver Education class.

Cindy Williams and Candy Clark were incensed by Lucas's cavalier treatment of their characters, given their importance to the story. They don't figure in the epilogue, where, next to their carefully posed class photographs, Lucas describes the fates of his four main male characters: Curt, a writer living in Canada; Steve, selling insurance in his home town; Milner, dead in a car crash; Terry, missing in action in Vietnam.

Once shooting ended, Lucas scraped together enough money for a 'wrap' party, at which he showed twenty minutes of edited material. The crew of Hollywood pros weren't impressed by what looked to them an amateurish effort, and most of the cast were too exhausted to care. Dreyfuss was only glad it was over. Lucas's failure to communicate on the set made him wonder if he hadn't already mentally edited out his character. 'Am I still in this film?' he once asked Lucas. At the end, dismissing *American Graffiti* as 'a little movie that wouldn't make sixty dollars,' Dreyfuss left for Canada to make what he regarded as a serious, adult story, *The Apprenticeship of Duddy Kravitz.* Only Harrison Ford retained his enthusiasm. At the end of the screening, his voice could be heard over the applause, shouting, 'This is a fucking *hit!*'

$$\boxed{II}$$

The Road to the Stars

Where we're going, you don't need roads.

Christopher Lloyd in *Back to the Future*, screenplay by
Robert Zemeckis and Bob Gale

Lucas wanted *American Graffiti* edited by Marcia – 'I made it for you,'
he told her – but Tanen insisted on Verna Fields. She had just cut
Spielberg's road movie *Sugarland Express*, and so, he argued, had a
handle on this new style of cinema. But Tanen was also preoccupied
with supervising a lavish version of *Jesus Christ Superstar* being shot
in Israel. As one of his oldest confidantes, Fields would be a reliable
informant within the Lucas/Coppola camp who could report back to
him if, as had happened with *THX1138*, Francis's attention wandered
and he gave his young director his head.

Marcia was assistant editor, but, except when he dropped by on
his way to another session of recording sound with Murch, she and
the driven Lucas seldom spoke during the post-production. Richard
Walter and his wife visited on their way back from a trip to Oregon,
and stayed one night with the Lucases in Mill Valley. 'But we never
saw George,' says Walter. 'He arrived home after we'd gone to bed,
and left before we got up.'

Coppola wanted Lucas to cut the film at Zoetrope, but Kurtz drew
the line at this. 'We didn't want to work in the city,' he says. 'There
was no parking. And George thought Francis wanted too much to
rent space. The warehouse was not friendly enough. Francis was very
gregarious. He had Christmas parties and Easter parties at his house,
and invited everybody. But driving into San Francisco was always a
bit of a problem. We didn't want to be downtown. The suburban

atmosphere of the small villages in Marin County was much more conducive to working.'

Instead, Lucas persuaded Coppola to buy a house in Mill Valley and convert the coach-house behind it into cutting rooms. 'It was a granny flat that had once been the chauffeur's quarters,' says Kurtz. 'We had two editors and an assistant editor, plus a kind of mini-office and a coding machine.' During the most intense part of the editing, Kurtz slept on the coach-house floor, but later he rented the house itself and moved his family in. The place became an informal center for friends and relatives. Coppola organized *bocce* games and barbecues. People sunbathed. For lunch, they walked along the river into Mill Valley. It was as close as Lucas ever came to recreating the feeling of Laterna. To encourage Marcia and Verna Fields, Coppola Xeroxed some of the stratospheric checks he was receiving for *The Godfather* and taped them to their Moviola.

Lucas's plan for the structure of *American Graffiti,* to cut between the four male characters in strict rotation, telling their stories in parallel, didn't work. He hadn't anticipated that placing one of Terry's social disasters next to Curt's explanation of romantic longings could make the latter seem affected and ridiculous. After a long argument with Marcia, he reluctantly accepted a less strict approach. It yielded, in Fields' words, 'one hell of a picture,' but it ran 165 minutes. 'After that,' said Lucas, 'all of our editorial efforts were in cutting almost an hour out of it but keeping the same pace that was in it originally and keeping the stories in balance.' Each new cut rendered it incoherent once more, so Lucas and Marcia restructured it again.

As soon as it was clear that *Graffiti* was on track, Fields left to work on other films, including Spielberg's *Jaws,* a success so huge that Universal nominated her to head a new in-house youth department, replacing Tanen's program. The acclaim made Fields even more grandiose about her contribution to the new wave of American films. Her lectures on their shortcomings, illustrated by snaps of her fingers to show where the cuts should have come, became tedious. Claims that she 'saved' *Jaws* with her cutting incensed Spielberg. 'The shameless credit grabbing would rock you back,' he sputtered of the race to climb aboard the *Jaws* bandwagon. 'There are several individuals whose careers have taken off as a result of their avowed contributions . . . when the sad fact is that these people did the least work of all.'

When Eastman Kodak wanted to feature Fields in an advertisement hailing women in the industry, Spielberg persuaded Julia Phillips to substitute Marcia Lucas.

While Marcia chipped away at *American Graffiti* through the last months of 1972, Lucas and Murch concentrated on the sound. Where later films with rock soundtracks were content to let the music accompany the action as if it had been composed for it, *Graffiti*'s music lingered on the edge of audibility. In this it paralleled its characters, who, because of the night-time setting, often hover in half-darkness in the background or at the edge of the frame, only pressing forward if they have something to say. When the music bursts out, as in the opening 'Rock Around the Clock' at Mel's Drive-In, or when – shades of *60 Cycles* – 'Green Onions' by Booker-T and the MGs pumps out as a caravan of cars rolls into the dawn for the climactic drag race, the effect is like an adrenaline rush.

Murch suggested making Wolfman Jack's radio show the backbone of the film. When he broadcast from Tijuana, the Wolfman's signal would fade in and out, at the mercy of the weather or topography. 'He was an ethereal presence in the lives of young people,' said Gary Kurtz, 'and it was that quality we wanted and obtained in the picture.' Murch recorded a two-hour studio session with the deejay, complete with commercials, phone calls and his repertoire of howls and exhortations. To achieve a muffled, attenuated, distant effect, as if it was being heard from a passing car, he played the program back through a speaker attached to a Nagra tape recorder and re-recorded it in the open air with a hand-held microphone; he called this 'Worldizing,' a term that, thankfully, never caught on. For days, Lucas and Murch paced and prowled in the space between the Mill Valley house bought by Coppola and the coach-house where Marcia was editing. 'George held that speaker and would slowly move it from side to side,' says Murch. 'I stood about fifty, seventy-five feet away with another tape recorder and a microphone, and did the same thing. The goal was for us to be only occasionally – if at all – in synch.' It was during the later sound-mixing sessions that, according to legend, Lucas asked for 'Reel Two, Dialogue Two,' abbreviated on the can to 'R2-D2.' 'Good name for a character,' he is supposed to have said, scribbling in his notebook.

Every song heard in the film required permission from its record company. Elvis Presley's management refused to negotiate, but fortunately Dennis Wilson of the Beach Boys had acted with another rock singer, James Taylor, in Monte Hellman's *Two Lane Blacktop*, which Gary Kurtz produced. Kurtz persuaded Wilson to let Lucas use Beach Boys tunes like 'All Summer Long' for $2000 each, a bargain rate, and this broke the logjam. Lawyer Tom Pollock negotiated a deal in which every group received the same low fee; but even minimal payments mounted up, and Lucas was forced to halve his wish-list of ninety songs. This was still too much for Universal, and Tanen only agreed to the $90,000 tab for music rights if Coppola personally underwrote it – another example of Old Hollywood's myopia about the changing audience, since *American Graffiti*'s soundtrack album would be the film's most lucrative spin-off.

That Coppola's word, valueless six months before, was now worth $90,000 showed how far and how quickly his stock had risen in Hollywood following the success of *The Godfather*. In August 1972 he launched the Directors' Company, a triumvirate of himself, Peter Bogdanovich and William Friedkin, to produce and control their own films. There were no more charismatic names in the crop of new young directors. Bogdanovich's *The Last Picture Show* and Friedkin's *The French Connection* had not made as much money as *The Godfather*, but they returned generous profits on small investments. Moreover, Bogdanovich was at work on a promising comedy, *Paper Moon*, and Friedkin on *The Exorcist*. Suddenly, a package deal of the sort dismissed so summarily by Warner-Seven Arts a few months before looked like the bargain of the century. Paramount put up $31 million, and the three directors promised to deliver twelve pictures over the next six years.

Coppola immediately started work on *The Conversation*, the convoluted drama about professional eavesdropping which he'd tried and failed to make with Ray Stark. Arrangements for the release of *American Graffiti* were left to Kurtz. At Christmas 1972, Lucas decided the film was ready, so Kurtz set up a preview. He chose the eight-hundred-seat Northpoint Theater in San Francisco, and assembled a demographically balanced audience.

The 10 a.m. screening on Sunday, 28 January 1973 would not only be the film's first public airing, but also the first time anyone from Universal had seen it. Ned Tanen and his chief aide flew up that morning on the same flight as a Lucas contingent that included

Robbins, Barwood, and Jeff Berg. They found Tanen grouchy and distracted. He refused to sit with them on the plane, and when his limousine failed to arrive, declined to share a cab to the cinema. 'He was furious before he even saw the movie,' says Robbins.

Tanen had reason to be impatient. After its flirtation with *Easy Rider*, Hollywood was in full flight from youth. Lew Wasserman had installed Richard Zanuck and his partner David Brown as a sort of rump feature unit within Universal which for years had produced almost exclusively for television. *Jaws* was their triumph, and now they were making *The Sting*, a comedy crime movie set in the thirties with Robert Redford and Paul Newman, and a music score of Scott Joplin piano rags. It was a far cry from Modesto, hot cars and Wolfman Jack. To Tanen, this seemed an absurd time to be releasing a teenage hot-rod and rock movie, especially since no other studio was making them, not even Universal. There wasn't a top box-office star under forty, and Tanen could be forgiven for feeling aggrieved at being stuck with the dying gasp of a fad that looked as irrelevant as the hula hoop.

At the theater, the audience was in the mood to be entertained. Tanen, Coppola, Kurtz, Lucas, and the LA contingent didn't sit together, so had no way of gauging the others' reactions, but none doubted that the audience loved it. Despite two breaks in the first reel and a soundtrack often out of synch, they were delirious from the first notes of 'Rock Around the Clock' over the credits.

As the film ended, everyone connected with the production hurried to the lobby to assess the mood of the departing crowd. One of the first people to bump into Tanen was Kurtz. 'Ned came out with his aide Alf Yartkus,' says Kurtz, 'and he said, "This film is not ready to be shown to an audience."'

Coppola and Lucas joined them, and Coppola innocently asked how Tanen had liked the film. Tanen rounded on him. 'You boys let me down,' he raged. 'I went to bat for you and you let me down.'

Lucas was as astonished as Kurtz. 'I was in shock,' he said.

But, characteristically, Coppola attacked. 'You should go down on your knees and thank George for saving your job,' he blustered. 'This kid has killed himself to make this movie for you. And he brought it in on time and on schedule. The least you can do is to thank him for doing that.' Working up to a climax, he said, 'I'll buy the film. This movie's going to be a hit!'

He reached for his checkbook, or at least groped for it in his jacket.

Like much that Coppola did, the gesture was flamboyant but futile, since the pocket was empty. 'Francis doesn't carry checkbooks,' says his assistant Mona Skarger – a habit shared by Lucas, who kept a single check in his wallet for emergencies. But the confrontation ended the argument. Tanen and his assistant climbed into their limousine and drove away, leaving the film's team and its supporters staring at one another among the chattering audience, still high on the experience they'd just shared.

Coppola's defense of the film impressed Lucas. It almost made up for his earlier failures. 'Francis really stood up to Ned,' he said. 'I had given him a bad time when the Warners thing came down over *THX*. I really held that against him – "You're gonna let them cut it, you're not gonna go down there and stop 'em" – and when *Graffiti* came along I said, "Here we go again." But Francis did what he was supposed to do. I was pretty proud of him.'

The gesture wasn't without cost to Coppola. He and Tanen didn't speak for another twenty years. Coppola also kicked himself for not having followed through on his offer to buy the film. He'd have been a millionaire many times over.

Of everyone associated with the movie, Kurtz was probably the most shaken by Tanen's outburst. 'I couldn't believe it,' he says. 'I'd known Ned from *Two Lane Blacktop* and before. I was probably more closely associated with the studio than anybody on that picture.'

Three or four days later, he called Tanen. 'This is ridiculous,' he said. 'The preview went very well.'

'You packed the audience,' Tanen said accusingly.

Kurtz was incensed. 'What are you talking about? We went out of our way to get a cross-section of demographics. I'll show you the list. We had almost a thousand people there, and yes, some of them were teenagers: the kind of people who would enjoy this film. But a lot of them weren't.'

A week later, Kurtz visited Tanen at Universal. He urged him, 'Come back up and we'll run the film reel by reel, and you tell us what you think.'

The second screening in San Francisco found Tanen more tractable. His suggested changes were relatively trivial. He wanted to cut the moment when a pushy used-car dealer, noticing that Terry has pulled up near his lot to check some minor damage to the back of his borrowed car, hectors him to trade it for a Corvette. Tanen argued that this dissipated the humor of the crash, and slowed the tempo. So, in his view, did Steve's mocking defiance of a teacher supervising the sock hop. When the teacher orders Steve and Laurie not to dance so close, Steve insults him, then, when the teacher threatens suspension, reminds him he graduated the previous year. Tanen also loathed Harrison Ford's improvised solo on 'Some Enchanted Evening' – a dislike echoed by the song's writers Rodgers and Hammerstein, a representative of whose publisher had been at the preview and threatened to withdraw its permission. Most ominously, Tanen wanted to remove the entire scene where Milner takes Carol on a tour of the car junkyard.

Returning home to Mill Valley, Lucas raged to Marcia about the randomness of Tanen's choices. Who knew if cutting those few scenes would make any difference? Using a metaphor he'd return to repeatedly, Lucas said, 'You write [a film], you slave over it, you stay up twenty-eight nights getting cold and sick. It's exactly like raising a kid. You raise a kid for two or three years, you struggle with it, then somebody comes along and says, "Well, it's a very nice kid, but I think we ought to cut off one of its fingers." So they take their little axe and chop off one of the fingers. They say, "Don't worry. Nobody will notice. She'll live, everything will be all right." But I mean, it hurts a great deal.'

Marcia, more pragmatic, and more inured to the Hollywood system, favored accepting the cuts and moving on to another film, but Lucas was adamant. 'He refused to participate,' says Kurtz. 'I ended up having to do it, and having to deal with the studio all the time. It was a nightmare. It was Kafkaesque. There wasn't any reason for anything. I'd heard all the stories [about studio interference], but I thought that, in a hard and fast situation, reason would prevail. Not a chance.'

Tanen threatened to call in Universal's ace cutter, William Hornbeck, for radical surgery. In fact Hornbeck had already seen the film, and told Tanen it was 'totally unreleasable.' Kurtz hurriedly prevailed on Verna Fields to supervise the cuts, and mollify the irascible Tanen. After prolonged negotiations, complicated by a Writers' Guild strike which shut down work at Universal – they had to meet with Tanen in a suite at the nearby Universal Sheraton hotel – they excised the three short scenes, and moved the junkyard sequence to another part of the film.

'What we got out of it,' says Kurtz bitterly, 'was a film two and a half minutes different, and I would defy anyone to see both versions together and notice any difference. The studio wasted all of our time when it could have released the original version. Everyone would have been happy and we'd have made another picture for Universal, and it would have been hunky dory.' Once the film was a success, Lucas restored all the cuts, but his resentment remained. He told Kurtz he would never speak to Tanen again, and was virulent in his public criticism of the executive.

The reaction of Lucas and Coppola astonished and offended Tanen. Old Hollywood never washed its dirty linen so publicly, and even the most aggrieved kept their resentment private, on the understanding that the studio press office would disguise the rift as 'creative differences.' The game of musical chairs in which executives discarded by one company automatically found work at another depended on loyalty to 'the industry,' not to any one studio or producer.

But the staff of American Zoetrope and, later, Lucasfilm, honored only their chief, who became endowed with an almost mystical significance. Sid Ganis, vice president of marketing for Lucasfilm in the eighties, said, 'At Lucasfilm, every one of us is working for George, and he knows it. When I worked at Warner Bros, Ted Ashley was my boss: George is my *leader*. I watched one of the secretaries who met him for the first time look at him as though he was a deity.'

The beginnings of a team had begun to coalesce around Lucas, as they had once gathered around Coppola. People who shared his commitment to Marin County as a place to make movies, or who couldn't find work in heavily unionized Hollywood, were drifting north. Walter Murch was a founding member. He settled in Bolinas, in a house looking out on its lagoon, and, like John Korty, converted an old barn into a studio. Green pasture surrounded the house, with horses grazing on it. At low tide, you could dig for clams in the beach in front of the house. Willard Huyck and Gloria Katz also gravitated toward Lucas. They were looking to make their name in screenwriting, and finding it as difficult as all newcomers. They would become, in effect, Lucasfilm's house writers, always available to do a treatment or a quick polish.

What united all these people, besides a chance to enter big-time film-making via the back door of a San Francisco film industry, was an allegiance to a less rigidly adult cinema. Hollywood was middle-aged, and so was its product. Even Coppola, for all his professed radicalism, shared the studios' preference for the well-made three-act film, the literary adaptation, the epic. In returning to Hollywood to make *The Godfather*, he threw in his lot with that sort of consensus cinema, which Steven Spielberg, Bogdanovich, Friedkin and many of the new young directors shared. By staying in Marin and making *American Graffiti*, Lucas committed himself, for the moment anyway, to films on the European model, small-scale, individual, and independent.

The period between finishing a film and releasing it is traditionally fruitful for pitching new projects. Nobody knows whether the film will do well or not, but a little discreet networking can ensure a climate of optimism. There was no shortage of people ready to talk up George Lucas as the next big talent. It helped that his career hadn't crashed and burned with Zoetrope as had that of Carroll Ballard, reduced to doing episodes for the educational TV series *Sesame Street*, or John Korty, reflectively picking up the threads of his old career in the barn at Stinson Beach.

Tom Pollock, the lawyer who worked on the thorny problem of music permissions for *American Graffiti*, incorporated Lucas as a company. Never meant to be anything more than a shell to minimize taxes, Lucasfilm Inc. retained its clumsy name – widely criticized as 'English-sounding' – even when it became one of the world's most valuable corporations.

Lucas told his agent Jeff Berg that only two projects really interested him – his science fiction movie and the Vietnam film, *Apocalypse Now*. Lucas was high on it. 'It's the kind of film the government will probably run me out of the country for making,' he said. 'It's not about massacres or anything like that. It's about Americans. Like a super-John Wayne movie. It's the same argument as *The Wild Bunch*: an anti-violence film. Francis says the way to make an anti-violence film is to have no violence in it, but I feel there should be so much violence in it you're disgusted.' Berg was sceptical. The war was reaching a climax. There were rumors of a ceasefire, and a complete withdrawal by America and its allies. But to Lucas the very idea of an American surrender made the story even more attractive.

John Milius says, 'It was always the plan that I would write it, George would direct and Francis would produce. The idea was, we would have got the cooperation of the army, and filmed around the army. We'd shoot in 16mm and get very gritty and real, and look more like documentary. We'd star someone like Warren Oates; Kurtz would have been somebody like Sterling Hayden. [George] denies it now, but we wanted to go to Vietnam and shoot the film while the war was on. This was *cinéma vérité*: getting close to real events, having films shot in and around the events. He and Gary Kurtz spent a tremendous amount of time.'

For Milius, shooting *Apocalypse Now* in Vietnam would be his last chance to get in the war. But while Coppola havered, giving his time to the Directors' Company and preparing to shoot *The Godfather II*, the political climate changed. Formerly so cooperative, the army no longer welcomed cameras observing the rout of the South Vietnamese army and the steady retreat that would lead to the public-relations disaster of April 1975, with desperate refugees scrambling on the roof of the American Embassy for the last helicopters out of Saigon.

Lucas abandoned all hope of making *Apocalypse Now*, though Walter Murch believes he actually transformed the material, visualizing a sort of Vietnam in outer space that would become *Star Wars*. 'I was interested in the human side of the war,' agrees Lucas, 'and the fact that here was a great nation with all this technology which was losing a war to basically tribesmen.' Murch believes, 'He took that situation, and transposed it not only out of Vietnam, but to a galaxy far away and a long long time ago.'

In reviving his science fiction project, Lucas ditched one important element. Italian producer Dino di Laurentiis had bought the rights to Alex Raymond's *Flash Gordon* comic strip for Federico Fellini, and though Fellini never filmed it, de Laurentiis wasn't prepared to sell them. Lucas revised his ideas and wrote a new outline, which he now handed to a puzzled Jeff Berg.

Headed 'The Story of Mace Windu,' it began: 'Mace Windu, a revered Jedi-bendu of Ophuchi who was related to Usby C.J. Thape, Padawaan learner to the famed Jedi . . .' The rest was equally tortuous, a ramble through worlds of fantasy which, though familiar enough to readers of comic books and space opera, baffled men whose primary reading matter was deal memos and *Variety*.

Lucas set the story in the thirty-third century, a period of upheaval.

An eleven-year-old princess, her family and retainers are fleeing from the evil Empire across a desert planet. With them are two Imperial bureaucrats captured by the man who guards the princess, a battle-scarred old warrior named Skywalker. They're heading for the space port of Gordon, carrying the 'clan treasure,' including two hundred pounds of treasured 'aura spice.' In the desert, they link up with a group of rebel teenagers. Skywalker trains them to fly one-man 'devil ships,' which protect the party from attack as it flees toward the friendly planet of Ophiuchi. Ambushed and wrecked on a world called Yavin, the fugitives battle a race of aliens who fly on huge birds. The princess is captured and taken to the imperial capital, Alderaan. Skywalker enlists the help of a cantankerous old human farmer who has married an alien. With his help, he bluffs his way onto Alderaan with a group of the boys, and rescues the princess, who honors them in a huge ceremony at which she reveals her 'true goddess-like self.' Afterwards, the drunken bureaucrats stagger down an empty street arm in arm, 'realizing that they have been adventuring with demigods.'

Like most people in Hollywood, Jeff Berg knew nothing about science fiction; but he could tell that this film wasn't anything like *2001: A Space Odyssey*, *Planet of the Apes*, or the other films that Old Hollywood made under that label. There were no lofty sentiments, no social satire. He might have seen its roots in comic books, and perhaps understood that the idea of a priceless 'spice' recalled Frank Herbert's novel *Dune*, but beyond that, it was *terra incognita*. He certainly didn't recognize the debts to Akira Kurosawa and *The Hidden Fortress*. Oddly, however, it made sense when Lucas talked about it. Berg admits, 'I knew more about the story based on what George had told me than what was in that brief treatment.'

Berg suggested Lucas rewrite the outline, removing the elaborate back-story and stressing the elements that might attract studio investment, notably exotic characters and interesting special effects. In May 1973, Lucas handed Berg thirteen double-spaced pages. For the action, he'd borrowed even more liberally from *The Hidden Fortress*, but also from the best-known Hollywood adaptation of Kurosawa's work, *The Magnificent Seven*, John Sturges's 1960 western version of *Seven Samurai*. For the first time, the project carried the name 'The Star Wars.'

The outline rounded up most of what Lucas wanted for the film.

'Mace Windu' was gone, though he would turn up in Episode I, *The Phantom Menace*, which Lucas directed in 1999. Instead, the hero is Anakin Starkiller, brash son of Kane Starkiller, one of the few surviving Jedi-Bendu knights, a group of samurai with reputed mystical powers. Kane Starkiller is a Six Million Dollar Man, only one step from the junkheap. Progressively mechanized over centuries of battle, he's down to only the head and one arm of his human body.

On the run from the New Galactic Kingdom and its warriors, led by renegade Jedi Darth Vader, the Starkillers take refuge on the planet of Townowi with King Kayos and his military commander, silver-bearded General Luke Skywalker, another Jedi survivor. Kane begs his old friend to teach his son the Jedi ways.

In a piece of plot lifted from *THX1138*, children of the future are educated by transfusing them with a serum that drips knowledge direct into the bloodstream. To placate the 'chrome interests' who hold the balance of galactic economic power – to a longtime admirer of classic American cars such as Lucas, no other metal possessed such intrinsic value – King Kayos agrees to have the memories of Townowi's greatest scientists condensed into capsules of liquid by 'Bloodory's Distillation,' and handed to the chrome barons for dissemination among their own children. Hoping he's averted war by this gesture of appeasement, Kayos sends his fourteen-year-old daughter Zara to school on the other side of the planet. When the Empire double-crosses him and invades, Anakin is sent to carry Zara to safety. Joined by her two young brothers, two bickering robots, ArtwoDetwo and SeeThreePio, and Skywalker – a less-than-magnificent seven – they flee across a planet at war. On the way, Skywalker contacts a representative of the underground, 'a huge green-skinned monster with no nose and large gills,' named Han Solo.

Berg found the new version more comprehensible, but, if anything, even more potentially expensive. Photographic special effects were still relatively basic, and most science fiction films relied on models integrated into the action by the travelling matte technique, which, if done poorly, left a wavering blue halo around every object. Stanley Kubrick had set new benchmarks in *2001: A Space Odyssey*, but at the cost of thousands of hours manipulating models inch by inch against backgrounds created by regiments of art students stippling white paint onto black cardboard with toothbrushes.

Lucas and Berg pondered who might back such an ambitious project. Universal had no taste for epics, least of all from a director whose recently-finished film, they were convinced, was a disaster, and might prove unreleasable. Nor did United Artists, which had shown no interest in any market younger than middle age.

If any major studio might be responsive to this kind of material, it was Twentieth Century-Fox, where Alan Ladd Jr, son of the Hollywood star, had just taken over as head of production. While Ned Tanen was still fretting over the cuts to *American Graffiti*, Berg and Lucas smuggled a print to Ladd. From what they told him, he gathered – erroneously, as it turned out – that Universal wanted to sell it. He watched it that week, and rang back with an offer to talk about Lucas's future projects.

'Laddy' combined Old Hollywood with New. Like most executives, he'd learned the business at the dinner table, watching his stepmother, agent Sue Carol, shrewdly manage his father's career, maximizing his meager talent, disguising his toneless voice, his shortness, his chronic alcoholism, his almost total inability to act. Isolated by his father's drinking and his stepmother's resentment of him, Ladd Jr became self-sufficient, inclined to make his own way. In common with New Hollywood's smartest film-makers, he found refuge in old movies, viewing and re-viewing the classics until he could reel off their credits from memory.

He became an agent like his mother, joining CMA in the early sixties, learning about producing in England, then following other agents like his friend Guy McElwaine into studio management. Softly spoken, reserved, impeccably and stylishly dressed, a fanatic for football on TV, Ladd became one of the new breed of producers, like Francis Coppola and Julia and Michael Phillips, around whom coteries formed – with one difference: he was an outsider on the inside, head of production for Twentieth Century-Fox.

In the seventies, Fox was in decline. After the departure of its founder, Darryl Zanuck, the studio's backlot had been sold off for real estate, to become the massive development of Century City. What remained came under the cautious management of Dennis Stanfill, an accomplished bean-counter but with no creative talent for making movies. Trailing a succession of expensive flops, Fox seemed headed for disaster until Ladd joined in 1971.

Though United Artists had backed out of funding *American Graffiti*, it still had an option on *Star Wars*. Lucas and Berg deliberated over

ways to extricate themselves. Eventually Berg realized that if the outline baffled him, it would leave UA's David Picker totally in the dark.
He simply sent it to Picker, with a request that UA consider advancing
$25,000 to fund a full screenplay. Picker's refusal was courteous but
quick. Lucas was now free to submit the project elsewhere – which
meant, unfortunately, to Ned Tanen at Universal, which had an option
too.

Again, Berg simply sent the outline to Tanen, with a request that
he fund Lucas to write a full screenplay. Tanen gave it to a studio
reader, whose response is a classic piece of Hollywood fence-sitting.

> To my mind, we're really rolling dice with this kind of a
> project. But I think the concept here (at least in terms of what
> has been done so far with the genre) is rather exciting, and
> combined with the potential action inherent in the piece, it
> seems to me an attractive possibility in many ways.
>
> On the other hand, a great deal of this screenplay (above
> the special effects and make-up problems) is going to be very
> difficult to translate visually. I'm thinking particularly in terms
> of our robot 'heroes' Threepio and Artoo.
>
> And even if all visuals and special effects work perfectly,
> the story could be ultimately no more than an interesting
> exercise if the audience doesn't completely understand the
> rights and wrongs involved, and just as important, have abso-
> lute empathy with young Luke Starkiller. And it is in these
> areas I believe the script still needs work. Action and adventure
> abounds. We still need more from the characters.
>
> Bottom line: if the movie works, we might have a wonderful,
> humorous and exciting adventure fantasy, an artistic and very
> commercial venture. Most of what we need is here. The ques-
> tion, in the end, is how much faith we have in Mr Lucas's
> ability to pull it off.

Tanen didn't have that kind of faith. He declined to produce 'The
Star Wars,' a decision which cost Universal the most popular film
series in the history of cinema.

Lucas, having extricated himself from his contractual obligations
to submit the project to UA and Universal, pitched it to Alan Ladd
Jr, and found a matching enthusiasm based on a shared love of old
movies. Ladd recalled, 'When he said, "This sequence is going to be

like *The Sea Hawk* or this like *Captain Blood* or this like *Flash Gordon*,"
I knew exactly what he was saying. That gave me confidence that he
was going to pull it off.' At the end, Ladd told Lucas, 'I don't understand this movie but I trust you and I think you're a talented guy. I'm
investing in you. I'm not investing in this script.' Lucas says, 'I don't
think he ever actually understood [*Star Wars*] until he saw it.'

Ten days later, Lucas signed a preliminary seventeen-page 'deal
memo' with Twentieth Century-Fox. He would be paid $50,000 to
write 'The Star Wars,' and a further $100,000 to direct it. Gary Kurtz
would produce, for $50,000. A new company hurriedly formed by
Tom Pollock, the Star Wars Corporation (in effect, Lucas) would
own 40 per cent of the profits on a film it was estimated would cost
$3.5 million – the lowest budget by far of any film Fox was producing
that year, and a drop in the bucket compared with what it was spending
on *The Turning Point* with Shirley MacLaine and Anne Bancroft, or
Julia with Jane Fonda and Vanessa Redgrave.

Lucas felt free to breathe at last. He had money to live on, and to
work, even if *American Graffiti* failed. His thoughts turned to other
films he might direct while he was writing the *Star Wars* screenplay,
and he asked Coppola if they could go ahead with *Apocalypse Now*,
but shooting it in the United States rather than Vietnam. Coppola
shocked him by saying he'd only do it if he and Lucas each got
25 percent of the profits, but that Lucas pay Milius out of his share.
Lucas was furious: 'I couldn't possibly have made the movie under
those conditions.' He felt that Coppola only proposed such a deal in
order to freeze him out of a film he had now decided to make himself.
Another shovel of earth rattled on the coffin of a friendship.

In the spring of 1973, *THX1138* was broadcast on network TV. To
many people, it looked better on television than it had on screen.
'Instead of looking mutilated and fragmented, like most movies
chewed upon every few minutes by commercials,' said the critic Joseph
Gelmis, '*THX1138* was the first film I'd ever seen swallow the commercials. Whole. They were incorporated into George Lucas's vision
of hell on Earth: a Big Brother society using video conditioning as an
instrument of mind control ("Be Happy, Buy More!").'

Gelmis rang around Hollywood to find out what Lucas had done
since *THX*. He learned about *American Graffiti*, and arranged to preview it the following week in Los Angeles. An old-time publicist

screened it for him. Afterwards, he confided to Gelmis, 'We don't know what the hell to do with it.'

Gelmis suggested, 'Why not put it in theaters immediately, run ads with the word "FUN" displayed in large letters, and stand aside so as not to be trampled?'

Unconvinced, the publicist disappeared, mumbling. Gelmis sought out Gary Kurtz, who was in town haggling over the cuts. 'Universal doesn't understand the movie,' Kurtz told him, and arranged for the critic to meet Lucas.

Gelmis took the Lucases to lunch in Sausalito, and got the impression that they were glad of a free meal. He didn't know what to make of the couple: Marcia with her large and playful malemute, Indiana, and Lucas, who had just turned twenty-nine, looking like a high-school boy in sneakers, white sweatsocks, a pink, long-sleeved sweater, and a button-down striped shirt hanging out over non-flare denims. His only concession to his age was a neatly trimmed beard, but spectacles with heavy tortoise-shell rims and his thick black hair combed in a big pompadour undercut its effect.

Lucas's halting conversation echoed his downbeat appearance. 'I'm a film-maker, anyway, not a director,' he told Gelmis. 'I like the physical part of making the movie. I might be a toymaker if I weren't a film-maker. *THX* relied on what I knew best – visuals, not story or character. *Graffiti* was done to test myself with personalities. My next film – hopefully, "The Star Wars," a $4 million space opera in the tradition of Edgar Rice Burroughs – will be an attempt to deal with plot.'

Lucas didn't mention *Apocalypse Now*, which had joined Coppola in the icy limbo to which he consigned all those elements of his life over which he could not exercise total control. Gelmis left confused. Maybe *THX* was a flash in the pan. Whether Lucas would stay in the industry or disappear like so many other promising USC graduates would depend on the reaction to *American Graffiti*.

Universal scheduled another public preview of *American Graffiti* on 15 May, at the Writers' Guild theater in Beverly Hills. This time, Kurtz did what Tanen had unjustly accused him of at Northpoint – packed the audience. 'Normally, fourteen stodgy old men sit in a room and that's it,' said Lucas. 'So, we said, OK, we'll show them the movie. But we want to show it with an audience of at least a couple of hundred people – crazy kids, everybody's secretary.' With the help of Wolfman Jack, Kurtz assembled such a crowd, who loved the movie. He immediately held five or six more such screenings, always with the same reaction. But still Tanen dragged his feet.

Alan Ladd Jr had no such reservations. He'd seen from the first moment that *Graffiti* was a potential hit, and the previews simply confirmed that. He rang Tanen and offered to buy the film if he didn't want to release it. Tanen was taken aback, even more so when Paramount made a similar approach. Reluctantly, he decided that maybe *American Graffiti* had something, and sent it to distribution. To the end, however, he never liked the film. 'I'm basically manic-depressive by nature,' he confessed, 'so I guess I just don't get it.'

With the summer season at its height, Universal favored a mass national release that would exploit the large drive-in market while the weather held. It ordered hundreds of prints, and launched an ad campaign featuring the roller-skating waitresses of Mel's Diner and the slogan 'Where Were You in '62?,' which disguised the film's bitter-sweet mood.

Kurtz protested that *American Graffiti* deserved a big-city release in advance of the wider one, if only to gather some – hopefully – enthusiastic criticisms. Universal agreed to invest $500,000 in prints and publicity, and to open it at two small cinemas in New York and Los Angeles two weeks before the general release. In Los Angeles, they chose the Cinerama Dome, a geodesic cinema fitted with a panoramic screen for the three-strip Cinerama process. Tanen took one look at Lucas's low-lit images sprawled across the vast screen, flinched, and ordered a new venue found. The film moved to the Avco in Westwood, an upper-middle-class suburb next door to the UCLA campus, and popular as a launching pad for new films.

American Graffiti opened on 1 August 1973. Fearful of a negative reaction, Lucas left for a holiday in Hawaii, but Kurtz, who was in New York, stayed up till midnight to read the reviews. They were ecstatic. Charles Champlin in the *LA Times* called it 'one of the most important films of the year, as well as the one most likely to move you to tears. What is so striking and so admirable about [Lucas] and [Huyck and Katz's] re-examination of the last hours of settled youth is the affectionate but unfalsified tone of the reminiscence, which recalls the passing moment with amazing exactitude but also with detachment. The past has been put in perspective; it has also been revarnished to fit the fancies of a later time.' *Time* magazine felt that 'few films have shown quite so well the eagerness, the sadness, the ambitions and small defeats of a generation of young Americans.'

The film set a first-week record of $35,000, and continued to rack up the steady grosses which would soon reach $55 million. By the 1990s, it would have grossed more than $200 million, the most profitable return on an investment in the history of motion pictures. The success wasn't achieved overnight, as would be the case with *Star Wars* and *Raiders of the Lost Ark*. The film simply kept attracting audiences wherever it was shown. Once it opened across the continental United States, the effect intensified. Some cinemas ran it exclusively for two years. Outside America, however, *American Graffiti* had only modest success. In Europe, people tended to agree with critic David Thomson that it was 'a movie full of the prospect of Muzak cinema, a light show without delight or distress. Boredom and malice have been subtly erased, along with misery and ecstasy – all the real, untidy ingredients of adolescent experience.' Lucas had hit a nerve, but it was a uniquely American one.

Lucas agreed to a charity preview in his home town for the local Heart Association. The high society of Modesto paid $10 a head to see the film, then share champagne and, according to the *Bee*'s reporter, soggy canapés with Lucas, his family and Marcia in a nearby shoe store. Mayor Lee Davies presented Lucas with the key to the city. 'Little did I think,' he said patronizingly, 'when I saw George playing with his home movies out on Sylvan Road that he would one day sell one of them.'

Lucas responded, 'I owe everything to Modesto. If I hadn't grown up here and cruised Tenth Street . . .' The sentence trailed off, as did Modesto's reaction to the film. Most concluded it was no big thing. The *Bee*'s film critic Fred Herman dismissed it as a trivial piece, set in 'a made-up Modesto in fall, 1962, as a made-up Downey High School is holding a "welcome back" dance and the city's teens are gathering at a made-up drive-in before cruising a made-up Tenth Street.' He went on, 'The stars are nice clean-cut kids whose names probably will not be remembered.' He found the music 'monotonous. Of forty-two period numbers by thirty-five groups, I recognized only "Rock Around the Clock," popularized seven years earlier, and "At the Hop," a hit from Woodstock, seven years later.' He rated *Graffiti* 'worthy of inclusion in the recent deluge of nostalgia flicks, although

I hope it will be the last for a while. Try to ignore those ads that put 1962 in the dim, distant past and ask, "Where were you . . . ?"' This review and another in the *San Francisco Chronicle*, calling *American Graffiti* 'the worst film of the year,' upset Lucas out of all proportion to their influence, since these were the papers his parents read. 'It was my first real success,' he said, 'and they made it so that it wasn't a success to all the people I care about.'

National admissions kept building through the late summer. Checks started arriving from Universal, each one larger than the last. In 1973, the Lucases earned less than $20,000 between them. Lucas still owed his father $2000 for the Zoetrope phone bill, and he'd also borrowed from friends, and from his lawyer Tom Pollock.

Almost immediately, the principals began to bicker about the profits of *American Graffiti*. Coppola tried to renegotiate his deal to pay Kurtz half of his 10 per cent. With more justice, he also felt that Haskell Wexler – who had come on the production after the initial deal, and directly as a result of Lucas's inability to shoot the film himself – should be paid out of Lucas's share. Since he had wanted Wexler to shoot *The Conversation*, Coppola suggested Lucas pay the cameraman 3 per cent, and Coppola pay the other 2. Lucas had agreed, and paid up, but Coppola delayed payment, as he had with Kurtz. Both Kurtz and Wexler only got their money after protracted and acrimonious argument.

In another gesture not typical of Hollywood, Lucas also gave away some of his points in the film. He split one of them ten ways, among the main performers. The Huycks also received a share. Verna Fields, Walter Murch and Fred Roos got new cars, others $10,000 checks or gifts.

Now that *American Graffiti* was a hit, Universal tried to mend its fences. Tanen made conciliatory noises. Lucas didn't respond. In January 1974, Sid Sheinberg, Universal's head of production, cabled Lucas: 'I personally consider *American Graffiti* to be an American Classic.' This gesture too was ignored. 'George had a very Old Testament view of not forgiving,' Kurtz recalls. 'Once he was wronged, he would always remember it.'

By the end of 1973, Lucasfilm – and Lucas – was worth $4 million, only a fraction of what Universal had made from the film, but a fortune to Lucas. $300,000 went into the Star Wars Corporation as working capital. The company hired its first employees: Bunny Alsup, Kurtz's sister-in-law, became Lucas's secretary, and Lucy Wilson kept the books. The Lucases also bought their first house. San Anselmo, a few miles from Mill Valley, had retained its turn-of-the-century charm, and many of its big family mansions. Lucas and Marcia's eye had been caught by one at 52 Park Way. Built in 1869, it was too big for only the two of them and Indiana, but Lucas fell for its Victorian gingerbread trim, multiple black-shingled roofs and overall *Addams Family* character. He and Marcia would live on the upper floors, he decided. The lower floors would become his writing room, and cutting and screening facilities – not just for Lucasfilm, but for other film-makers he expected to join him there. Marcia christened it Parkhouse.

Though almost all his money went into safe corporate investments, Lucas began, tentatively, to speculate. A friend from film school offered him a share in SuperSnipe, a comic-book shop on the Upper East Side of New York. Lucas invested in it. To most people, this seemed frivolous, the sort of thing someone new to big money might do out of *folie de grandeur*, only to tire of it after a few months and let it languish; but intimates knew how seriously he took everything, including comic books. It would have needed a crystal ball to foresee that SuperSnipe would be the seed of Lucasfilm's merchandising empire, the profits of which would outstrip even those of the *Star Wars* films.

In January 1974, Lucas went to New York to collect the New York Critics' Award for the screenplay of *American Graffiti*, presented by Marshall Efron, who had had a small role in *THX1138*. Never comfortable speaking in public, Lucas said dryly that he had come to get a close-up look at the critics. 'He peered at us as though we were a zoological exhibit,' said Joseph Gelmis, 'thanked us in a bemused tone, as if he'd faced some personal challenge and survived.'

In February, Hollywood confirmed *American Graffiti*'s status as a hit by giving it a scattering of Academy Award nominations. Lucas received one for Best Director, Huyck and Katz for Best Original Screenplay, Candy Clark for Best Supporting Actress, Verna Fields and Marcia for Best Editing, and the film was nominated as Best Picture. However, at the Oscar ceremony on 2 April 1974, the film was upstaged in more ways than one. It soon became clear that the year's big winner wouldn't be *American Graffiti* but *The Sting*, which picked up Best Original Screenplay, Best Art Direction, Best Song and Best Costume Design. Marcia wept when the Best Editing award went to the same film, but Lucas seemed unperturbed when George Roy Hill was named Best Director.

As it came time to open the envelope containing the Best Picture winner, David Niven introduced Elizabeth Taylor. She had just stepped out when a naked man 'streaked' across the stage behind him – Robert Opal, thirty-three, had bluffed his way backstage on a fake press pass. Niven ad-libbed imperturbably: 'The only laugh that man will probably ever get is for stripping and showing off his short-comings,' but Taylor was flustered. 'That's a pretty tough act to follow,' she said. Reading the nominations from the Autocue, she stumbled over the first name. '*American Graffiti*. Universal-Lucasfilm Limited . . . Limited? What does that mean? I'm really nervous; [the streaker] upset me. I think I'm jealous.' Recalling her duties, she opened the envelope and said, 'Oh, I'm so glad. It's *The Sting*.'

Old Hollywood continued to snub the newcomers for years, fobbing them off with technical awards. For decades, Spielberg would be denied an Oscar as Best Director. Lucas would be nominated for *Star Wars*, but would lose to Woody Allen, just as Spielberg lost to Federico Fellini in the year he was nominated for *Jaws*. In both cases, Hollywood's establishment chose outsiders as a lesson to the upstarts. Mortified by his continued isolation, Spielberg campaigned, intrigued and lobbied for decades until the Academy gave him its Best Director Oscar in 1993 for *Schindler's List*. By contrast, Lucas ignored the whole process. Being denied the award was, to him, just another reason to treat Hollywood with contempt, and to beat it at its own game.

$$\boxed{12}$$

I am a White Room

Pulp can always be recycled.

John Sladek on 'Clichés' in *The Encyclopedia of Science Fiction*

Lucas went home to San Anselmo and started writing the science fiction film.

His new writing room at Parkhouse was on the ground floor, at the rear. It looked out over a large sloping yard, with another vacant lot at the foot. He could see for miles, to Mount Tamalpais, a small peak which blocked the fogs that otherwise would have rolled up the valley from San Francisco, only eleven miles away.

On one wall of the room hung a portrait of Sergei Eisenstein staring meaningfully at a strip of film held up to the light; on another were two framed posters for *THX1138*. The rug was white, and a houseplant drooped in the corner. A gumball machine on a bookshelf dispensed sugarless gum, the only kind permitted diabetics. A table, a chair, and a 1941 Wurlitzer jukebox made up the rest of the furniture. Coppola also had a Wurlitzer in his office. Lucas loaded his with fifties rock'n'roll on 78rpm, Coppola with records of legendary Italian tenor Enrico Caruso.

The rest of the house, decorated by Marcia, was Early Norman Rockwell: natural wood, dark green carpet, white and buff walls. The main cutting room, adapted from what had been a parlor, still resembled one, with a giant clock, houseplants, an open fire – as little like a typical Hollywood editor's lair as one could imagine.

'It was a house by itself, on an isolated piece of property,' says Gary Kurtz. 'We could rent out rooms to other pictures, but it was only local; it wasn't a matter of advertising in the Hollywood trades for clients. First of all, it was always dubious whether we could legally have that as an office, since it was zoned as a single family residence, so we just didn't tell anybody. And nobody cared, really. San Anselmo is kind of lackadaisical about that kind of thing.'

Michael Ritchie, whose feature *The Candidate* Marcia had edited, Hal Barwood, and Matthew Robbins hired space at Parkhouse, but as much to show support for a friend as for convenience. Though he'd imagined Parkhouse evolving into a feel-good alternative to American Zoetrope, Lucas's enthusiasm for such a project was waning. People who'd known him since college were finding, behind the mask, a man they didn't recognize. As he often admitted, Lucas held grudges, and he had a grudge against Hollywood.

Not long after Lucas moved in, someone acquired the vacant lot lower down the hill and built two houses close to Lucas's property line. 'He didn't like the fact that they were built,' says Kurtz, 'and he bought them, just to keep them out of other people's hands. We used them for offices and editing rooms for a while. We used the garages for storing posters and film clips, and the houses for meeting rooms.' Parkhouse became the halfway stage on the road to Skywalker Ranch, Lucas's ultimate Xanadu, an empire not only run to his rules, but built to them as well.

Already, Lucas was becoming an inspiration to a new generation of filmgoers. David Fincher, later the director of *Alien*[3] and *Se7en*, lived near Parkhouse as a boy, and saw him most mornings. 'Here was this guy who'd made my favorite movie, *American Graffiti*, going out every morning in his bathrobe and horn-rimmed glasses, picking up his *San Francisco Chronicle* on his driveway. Suddenly being a movie director wasn't some magical, far-away thing.'

Every day, Lucas religiously put in eight hours at his desk, even if he only stared at a blank page or shuffled his notes. When he wrote, it was still with a hard, sharp pencil in a high school 'blue book,' lined in blue and green – the sort handed out at exam time, and sold by his father to thousands of Modesto kids over the years. Lucy Wilson, office manager as well as book-keeper, brought him dozens of samples before he located the exact blue of the book cover, the precise texture of the page, the necessary sharpness of the pencils. Only when he'd recreated that Monday-morning mood of the test that must be passed could Lucas start work.

When there was something to type, he passed the book with its tiny printed capitals to Bunny Alsup. Lucas had *Bartlett's Familiar Quotations, Harper's Bible Dictionary, Roget's Thesaurus, Webster's Dictionary* and *Screenplay: The Foundations of Screenwriting* by Syd Field on his desk, but from his erratic spelling and disjointed ideas, Alsup judged that he seldom consulted them. When ideas wouldn't come, he snipped distractedly at his hair with the office scissors. Alsup soon learned to read the signs: 'George was either very happy or very frustrated.' He could have called in any number of people to help him, but the dispute with Richard Walter over *American Graffiti* had made him wary. Nobody was getting a share of the new film unless he personally presented them with it.

Promptly at six each evening, he climbed the stairs and collapsed in front of the TV for the *CBS Evening News* with Walter Cronkite. Vietnam was seldom off the screen, and Lucas watched with morbid interest, aware that any chance of making *Apocalypse Now* as semi-documentary was evaporating before his eyes. The Vietnamese would be in Saigon before Francis raised the money.

Unless there were guests, he and Marcia seldom ate dinner together. She made him a tuna-salad sandwich the way his mother used to, on white bread with the crusts removed, and he went to bed. By ten, he was asleep in front of the bedroom TV. Some Fridays, at Marcia's urging, they entertained friends at a barbecue. Gary Kurtz and his wife Meredith usually came. 'The core group was Matt Robbins, Hal Barwood and Walter Murch,' says Kurtz. 'Michael Ritchie was in Mill Valley. He came sometimes. John Korty too. That was the main group.' Occasionally they were joined by the Huycks, up from Los Angeles.

While the women cooked, the men talked shop: serious guys with beards, nursing beers and Cokes, turning their faces away as smoke drifted from the spitting steaks. Mostly they discussed Francis, the Directors' Company, and his shift toward the Hollywood he'd professed to despise. Murch and Carroll Ballard were ambivalent about Coppola. Working with him had won Murch a reputation among film editors. Coppola was also about to produce Ballard's first feature, *The Black Stallion* – though so far he'd rejected every screenplay. Those of the group who were not being helped by Coppola pointed out that, if you asked him for a light these days, he handed you a book of matches with the lordly inscription 'Francis Ford Coppola. The Godfather.' He drove everywhere in a blue Mercedes limousine with the numberplate 'FFC' – a gift from Paramount. The studio had doubted his claim that *The Godfather* would make more than $50 million. 'When it does,' Coppola said with his usual bluster, 'you owe me a limousine.' Once the gross passed that figure, he selected the car and had the dealer bill Paramount.

Everyone agreed that becoming rich hadn't ameliorated Coppola's old tight-fistedness with collaborators. He offered Ballard a paltry $10,000 to direct *The Black Stallion*. Only after prolonged negotiation could Ballard work it up to $35,000, plus seven net points – worth, in effect, nothing.

When it came to American Zoetrope, Coppola was more generous. He'd bought Columbus Tower, a historic 'flatiron' on the edge of San Francisco's Chinatown, and installed the studio there. Decorated in an ornate style somewhere between *art nouveau* and baroque, surmounted by an improbable cupola and a flagpole, the building was a landmark for newcomers navigating their way up San Francisco's hilly streets.

He'd also plunged on a new house in the city, with a screening room where he entertained friends like Lucas and Scorsese, impressing them with his ability to call up the Pacific Film Archive and order any rare film which interested them – every film fan's dream. Later, he acquired a mansion in the Napa Valley, with a vineyard. Next door, Robert Mondavi was remaking the tradition of American wine. Coppola became a wine-maker himself, naming his prize red 'Rubicon', after the river symbolically crossed by Julius Caesar as the irrevocable step on his way to seize power in Rome.

Visitors to Parkhouse confirmed that Francis intended to direct *Apocalypse Now* himself, probably in the Philippines. John Milius was rewriting his 1969 screenplay. It followed Willard, a Special Forces officer, as he sails upriver with orders to assassinate Kurtz, a charismatic colonel who's surrounded himself with a private army on the Cambodian border, and who refuses to accept orders. The first version had Willard falling under Kurtz's spell, and the two men blazing away at the American planes sent to bomb his base, an ending which Lucas would have favored had he directed the film; but Milius's rewrites made the conclusion more operatic, with a Kurtz who owed more to *Citizen Kane* than to Joseph Conrad.

Each week brought a new *Apocalypse Now* story. Steve McQueen was slated to play Willard, then Al Pacino, then James Caan, with Marlon Brando as Kurtz. When they all cried off, Coppola offered Kurtz to Pacino, who also turned that part down. Brando wouldn't return Coppola's calls. Coppola, furious, picked up his five Academy Award statuettes and threw them out the window.

Since he would have produced the film if Lucas had directed it, Gary Kurtz was losing almost as much as Lucas by Coppola's decision to make it himself, but he shrugged off such opportunism with Buddhist fatalism. 'The project belonged to Francis,' he says. 'He was free to do what he wanted with it.' Lucas wasn't that detached. He felt betrayed.

After the barbecue, Lucas would gather the men in his office and read them parts of the *Star Wars* script. The women weren't invited. 'What it boils down to is, he's a male chauvinist pig,' says Bunny Alsup. This at least was one element of the Zoetrope model which Lucas had retained. Except for Marcia, women had no place in Lucas's professional life above that of secretary or aide. His personal discomfort with women rendered them near-invisible.

Afterwards, Lucas taped his friends' reactions to the screenplay. Michael Ritchie said frankly that he didn't understand a lot of it. 'It was very difficult to tell what the man was talking about,' he recalled. Barwood and Robbins were troubled by Lucas's changing the two kidnapped bureaucrats into robots. After the cops in *THX1138* and all those cars in *American Graffiti*, wouldn't people think of him as someone more comfortable with machines than emotions? Lucas pushed the robots further back in the story, and drew young Starkiller to the fore, but only a little.

If the story lacked passion and sentiment, it was because he did too. And the robots were there because he loved machines. All the characters were, in some sense, people in his life. Darth Vader 'was really a combination of Death Water and Dark Father,' he acknowledged – no surprise to anyone who knew his relationship to the stern Lucas Sr. And the name Luke? 'I used that because I was identifying with the character.' As for the Empire, one had only to look to Los Angeles, and the studio apparatchiks who would cut off your children's fingers, to find his model. Later, when the film was a hit, Lucas would scale up its metaphors from the purely local to the international. 'It was based essentially on the Richard Nixon, Adolf Hitler idea,' he would say of the Empire's subversion of the galactic order established by the Jedi knights.

With each change, the script came closer to *The Hidden Fortress*, to the point where Lucas and Kurtz briefly considered buying the remake rights. They decided instead to play down the parallels, though Japanese-isms still abound, from the style of the swordplay to words like 'Jedi,' suggested by 'Jidai Geki,' the term for period TV samurai stories. Grizzled old General Skywalker, scratching himself as he overawes the boy rebels with his swordsmanship, was essentially Toshiro Mifune from *Yojimbo*.

When Lucas reduced the parallels, the script's resemblances to Edgar Rice Burroughs became more evident, so these too were minimized, rather than risk the wrath of ERB Inc., the corporation which guarded the rights to Burroughs' work. Similarities to Frank Herbert's *Dune*, like the 'aura spice' and the concept of Tatooine as a spice planet, disappeared when Dino di Laurentiis acquired the rights to the book, though references to 'spice freighters' and 'the spice mines of Kessel' lingered in dialogue. Other people pointed to *Wizard of Oz* parallels, with Leia as Dorothy, Chewbacca as Toto, and C-3PO the Tin Man.

Every few weeks, Lucas packed a spare pair of underpants, some deodorant and his notebook into a briefcase, flew to Los Angeles, and showed the script to the Huycks. 'We'd say, "George, this character doesn't work," says Willard Huyck, 'and George would say, "Uh-huh" and make a note, and then he'd fly home.' Most people thought Lucas was wasting his time. 'They said, "George, you should be making more of an artistic statement,"' recalled Lucas. 'People said I should have made *Apocalypse Now* after *American Graffiti*, and not *Star Wars*. They said I should be doing movies like *Taxi Driver*.' Everyone had read Paul Schrader's bleak script about a Vietnam vet driving a hack in New York city and taking up the gun to oppose, as he sees it, the evil lapping round his chin. Martin Scorsese's enthusiasm for it was equally well known, though he hadn't yet found someone to back it.

Lucas felt toward Scorsese and the other wilder members of New Hollywood much as Schrader's hero Travis Bickle did toward the pimps and lowlifes of Manhattan. On one of Lucas's visits to Los Angeles, Milius invited him to a preview at MGM. Lucas took Charley Lippincott, who'd found a niche at Universal promoting films to the fan and alternative press. Among the films he'd helped sell were *The Death of Grass* and *Westworld*, with its evocative bumper-sticker assuring the public, 'Westworld. Where nothing can go worn gg . . .'

As USC graduates found toeholds in the industry, they discovered the value of short haircuts and the standard executive suit, collar and tie. Lippincott was no exception, but success had not tamed Milius. Nor was personal hygiene high on his agenda. When he met Lucas and Lippincott at the screening, it was quickly evident he'd neither shaved nor bathed in days.

'I'm not sure I want to see John again for a while,' Lucas murmured as they left the screening. 'What do you think's wrong with him?'

'He's just . . . John,' shrugged Lippincott. But Lucas clearly found his old friend disgusting.

For someone who aspired to make a science fiction epic, Lucas's reading in the field was patchy. He knew Orwell's *1984* and Huxley's *Brave New World* from his English course in junior college, though he probably never did more than dip into Tolkien's three-part *Lord of the Rings*. He was happier with conventional science fiction, particularly the more fanciful variety, low on science, high on adventure, generally dismissed as 'space opera.' (In discussing *Star Wars* with Fox, Lippincott, by then in charge of marketing, forbade even the use of this term, and coined another – 'space fantasy.')

The debt to Burroughs is evident in the early drafts of *Star Wars*. Both are set in an *Arabian Nights* society of emperors and princesses, and desert worlds dotted with palaces. Both mix high technology with low; swords against spaceships. The names of Burroughs' characters and places – Matai Shang, Holy Hekkador of the Holy Therns, Ras Thavas of Toonol, the Temple of Issus, erected by the Therns on the shores of the Lost Sea of Korus – resonate with Han Solo, Chewbacca the *wookiee* and Jedi knight Obi-Wan Kenobi.

Initially, Lucas didn't visualize *Star Wars* as an epic, or imagine it going beyond one film. Downey High School hadn't taught *The Iliad*, *The Odyssey*, or the *Anabasis* of Alexander. If Lucas knew anything of world-spanning journeys by bands of heroes who attained their goal only after fighting whole armies, evading monsters and outwitting the magicians or, occasionally, gods who gave them orders, it was from their popular-culture versions: the Classics Illustrated comic-book editions of Homer, or 'peplums' churned out by Italian studios in which American bodybuilders, incarnating Hercules, heaved polystyrene rocks in outfits cast off from some Hollywood-funded extravaganza.

Then there had been the films of Ray Harryhausen, a disciple of *King Kong*'s creator Willis O'Brien. Harryhausen had settled in Britain, from where, every few years, he released a new fantasy of Sinbad or Jason routing creatures animated from brightly-painted rubber or by men in monster-suits (inside the Minotaur in *Sinbad and the Eye of the Tiger* was Peter Mayhew, later Chewbacca in *Star Wars*).

Many of Lucas's generation fell under Harryhausen's spell. One of the proudest boasts of Mark Hamill, Luke Skywalker in the *Star Wars* trilogy, was of having published an interview with Kerwin Matthews, star of *Sinbad and the Eye of the Tiger*, in a magazine for fantasy-movie enthusiasts. A generation of young fans felt likewise inspired. They followed Harryhausen into special effects and stop-motion animation, creating a reservoir of hobbyists eager to work for little more than bench space and the occasional hamburger.

Harryhausen's films wore their status with a cocky pride; they might not be Homer, but, in a world that hardly knew of those giants of the ancient world, they were all you could get. Lucas sensed the same sweep and grandeur in the *Flash Gordon* serials of the thirties, and in Alex Raymond's comic strips that inspired them; some of Raymond's original artwork was among Lucas's most valued possessions. Flash may only have been a college football player whisked into a universe of Wing Men, Clay Men, Orangopoids, the seductive Princess Aura and her evil father, Ming the Merciless, but he fought and won with all the style of Ulysses or Alexander. And, as the serial trailer at the head of *THX1138* pointed out, he was American.

Even more evident were parallels with the 'Fourth World' comic books of Jack Kirby launched in 1971 as *The New Gods*. Kirby, a veteran of numerous other comic series, imagined a future world where a superhero, Orion, battled with a villain, Darkseid, who turned out to be his father. Darkseid, opposed by the gods of the New Genesis, searched for the Anti-Life Equation. Kirby invented characters with names like Mark Moonrider, and a Doctor Doom, who resembled Darth Vader. John Morrow, a Kirby scholar and editor of *The Kirby Collector*, believes: 'There are just too many similarities for me to believe Kirby wasn't some kind of an influence on Lucas.'

In May 1974, Lucas finished the first screenplay of 'The Star Wars,' cautiously identified as 'Rough Draft 5/74.' At 132 pages, representing roughly the same number of screen minutes, its size alarmed Gary

Kurtz, as did its scope. It began with an extended fight with 'laser swords' and 'laser pistols' on the surface of a desolate planet as the Starkiller family is ambushed by forces of the Evil Empire, and progressed to space battles and planetary invasions. It had all the defects of a first-time screenplay – too many characters, too much plot, and dialogue that made the pulp magazines of the thirties like *Thrilling Wonder Stories* and *Amazing Science Fiction* seem reticent. The names too were a ragbag of pulp and comic-book coinings – Starkiller, Skywalker, Kessilian, Aquilea, Vader, Valorum.

All the same, it was a full screenplay, and Lucas and Kurtz, while sending a copy to Alan Ladd Jr at Fox, also began to canvas opinions – even, with some misgivings, from Coppola. Coppola made cordial noises. The idea of a pre-teen heroine piqued his interest. It was ironic, then, that sex became the first element of the screenplay to be toned down. Since he loathed writing intimate scenes, Lucas reasoned, maybe he should drop the princess altogether. In the next rewrite, she disappeared, but nobody liked the all-male cast, so he restored her, this time as fourteen-year-old Zara. In subsequent drafts, she inched up to 'a beautiful young girl of sixteen' named Leia, with untapped psychic powers of goddess-like force. Coppola would be disappointed when Lucas made Leia nubile. 'George became frightened of some of his own good ideas,' he says. 'I think he shied away from his innovations somewhat.'

Lucas emasculated his heroes, too. In early versions of the script, young Starkiller is aggressively horny. General Skywalker discovers him having a quickie with an aide in a computer closet, and reminds him of the Jedi code.

GENERAL: You are trained well, but remember, a Jedi must be single-minded, a discipline your father obviously never learned, hence your existence. Clean yourself up. Discipline is essential. Your mind must follow the way of the Bendu.

Within two more drafts, young Starkiller was Bendu to the bootheels. Embracing celibacy, he's devoting all his energies to a quest of Arthurian single-mindedness, driven by the sexless veneration of a virgin princess who, in the final versions of the story, turns out to be his sister, and thus supremely unavailable.

By July 1974, Lucas had finished a 'First Draft' of the screenplay. On 18 January 1975, a 'Second Draft' appeared. In addition, the thirteen-page outline of May 1973 was periodically given a new cover sheet, though the contents remained the same, down to spelling errors, like a cantina filled with 'weird and erotic Aliens.'

'When Charles Manson was in the news,' Lucas recalls, 'people who knew about the name Starkiller started asking, "Are you making a movie about mass murderers or something?" I said, "OK, I won't use that name."' The Starkillers briefly became 'Akira Valor,' the son 'Justin,' and the Jedi the 'Dai-Noga.'

In these versions, Darth Vader isn't a renegade Jedi but part of a rival warrior clan, the Knights of Sith. R2-D2 and C-3PO become briefly A2 and C3; and, right up to the second draft, the former could talk, rather than communicating in beeps and squeals. The two princes, who spent most of the first two versions being lugged about in drugged immobility, were discarded as, literally, excess baggage, along with Akira/Kane Starkiller, whose only function in the story had been to sacrifice himself to save one of them. King Kayos and his queen, the chrome interests and 'Bloodory's Distillation' also disappeared.

In their place came attempts at light relief, like the dialogue between Huu Tho, the aged anthropologist on Yavin, and his wife Beru.

THO: Beru, where's the thanta sauce?
BERU: I swan! I put it right here in front so you'd see it. Here's some bum bum extract. It's very mild.

Han Solo metamorphosed from green-faced alien to 'a burly-bearded but ruggedly handsome boy dressed in a gaudy array of flamboyant apparel,' and then 'a tough James Dean-like star pilot, a cowboy in a starship; simple, sentimental and cocksure.' His companion was the seven-foot-tall *wookiee* Chewbacca. 'Chewie' was partly suggested by Marcia's dog Indiana, which sat beside her in the passenger seat of her car, and which she once referred to as 'our large furry co-pilot;' but also by Aslan, the stern but kindly lion of C.S. Lewis's Narnia fantasies which began with *The Lion, the Witch and the Wardrobe*.

For a draft or two, the *wookiees* – sometimes 'wookees' or 'wookies' in his notional spelling – preoccupied Lucas. A friend, radio deejay Terry McGovern, who played the schoolteacher in *Graffiti*, coined the name while recording background voices for *THX1138*. He joked about having run over a wookiee in the street, and Lucas jotted it down. The back-stories Lucas invented for his characters made Chewbacca a prince, son of Auzituck, chief of the Kaapawkum, and over two hundred years old. Rescued from slavery by Han Solo, he becomes his lifelong friend.

Mark Hamill recalled that 'one of my favorite earlier versions of the *Star Wars* screenplay had a clever device to offset the technology of the whole thing so that audiences wouldn't think that this was going to be another *2001*. It started with a helicopter shot of an enchanted forest and they push the camera through the window of a tree and you see a mother *wookiee* trying to breastfeed this squealing baby *wookiee*. He keeps gesturing toward the bookshelf and there's all this *wookiee* dialogue going on. She goes and points to one particular book and the baby gets all excited. She takes the book off the shelf and we see it's titled *Star Wars*. She opens the book and that's when the ship comes overhead and the film we know starts.'

Gary Kurtz remembers this idea, and why it was discarded. 'As soon as we got to discussing it over dinner one night, we realized what a fatal mistake that would be. When we found how difficult it was to get just one *wookiee* costume looking right, we never considered creating a whole planet of them.'

Only hardware survived every change. Much as he struggled to humanize his characters, Lucas would always be happiest with machines. He might not know what his characters were thinking – or, even less, feeling – but he knew precisely what they drove and what they fought with. The hovering 'Land Speeders' appeared in the completed film just as he described them in the first outline. The warriors of Yavin flew on 'jet sticks,' destined to be the Speeder bikes of *Return of the Jedi*, and a twelve-minute race between land vehicles on Tatooine would be the high point of *Star Wars I: The Phantom Menace*. The preferred weapon would always be the 'laser sword.' Some incidents which showed off these gadgets existed from the first outline, in particular a face-off in the spaceport cantina, whose alien drinkers are all too ready to draw a raygun at the smallest slight.

However seductive its technology, *Star Wars* needed much more if it was to succeed. Artless adventure wouldn't prevail against the mysticism of Spielberg's *Close Encounters of the Third Kind*. Universal's reader had been right: understanding 'the rights and wrongs' of the story was crucial. Lucas needed a rhetoric, a philosophy, a creed.

Apologists for and interpreters of *Star Wars* insist that 'the Force,' the all-pervasive power on which the heroes rely to defeat the Empire, was there from the start, and provided the primary motive for making the films. Lucas fosters this idea. 'There was no modern mythology to give kids a sense of values, to give them a strong mythological fantasy life,' he said later. 'Westerns were the last of that genre for Americans. Nothing was being done for young people that has real psychological underpinnings and was aimed at intelligent beings.'

But in fact Lucas had no such intentions at the outset. If anything, the whole idea of religion was alien to him. He had gone to church as a boy, and even attended Catholic mass a few times at USC, but the last time he'd been in church was to be married. He was no mystic – he knew what a Chevy or an Arriflex would do, but a soul . . . ?

The Force wasn't mentioned in the script's first drafts. It first appeared in the Second Draft of January 1975, a year after Lucas started writing. People in early scripts occasionally say 'May the force of others be with you' instead of 'Good luck,' but *what* force is never mentioned. Lucas himself didn't begin expounding the Force until well after the film's release. In 1977, he was still saying vaguely, 'The Force is really a way of seeing, it's a way of being with life.' All evidence suggests that the secret of *Star Wars*' extraordinary longevity and the fidelity of its following, indeed the basis of George Lucas's later near-guru status, was an afterthought.

It was the season of psychedelia, of dope, of gurus so wise they could change your life. Visitors to San Anselmo carried creeds with them like dust on their shoes. They pressed copies of Carlos Castaneda and Khalil Gibran into Lucas's hands, along with texts from the Hare Krishnas, the Scientologists, the Moonies, and fashionable sf novels, like Robert Heinlein's *Stranger in a Strange Land*, about a charismatic sect whose adherents indulge in ritual cannibalism. Someone told him about *The Hero with a Thousand Faces*, by anthropologist Joseph Campbell, though apparently Lucas never read it, but heard some extracts on an audiotape in his car.

Campbell argues that every epic, no matter what culture created it, rests on two or three characters and a personal conflict, usually between father and son, which embodies the eternal battle between good and evil. Could Obi-wan Kenobi, Lucas wondered, be a figure often mentioned by Campbell, the older mentor and guru? Initially, Gary Kurtz didn't favor the idea: 'The fear was that any religiously based, any theologically based character would require lots of explanation and exposition that was detrimental to an action adventure.'

Lucas put it into the Second Draft anyway, but in a form so cumbersome that it bore out Kurtz's fears. Luke Skywalker, now recognizably the character of the film, explains the source and significance of the Force to his younger brothers, Biggs and Windy.

> LUKE: In another time, long before the Empire, and before the Republic had been formed, a holy man called the Skywalker became aware of a powerful energy field which he believed influenced the destiny of all living things . . .
> BIGGS: The 'Force of Others!'
> LUKE: Yes . . .

In this version, the Force has two aspects: Bogan, the evil, and the good, Ashla (from C.S. Lewis's Aslan). Skywalker, apparently unburdened by the celibacy imposed in earlier versions, had twelve sons, to whom he passed this knowledge. They became the Jedi-Bendu, and 'brought peace and justice to the galaxy' – by what means isn't specified. All this ended in the Clone Wars when the Great Senate, in league with the Power and Transport Guilds, allowed knowledge of Bogon to fall into the hands of the Sith Knights, personal bodyguards to the emperor. The Sith hunted down the Jedi – though not the father of Luke, Biggs and Windy, 'The Starkiller,' the search for whom becomes a theme of the film. Once he finds him, Luke will give him the Kiber Crystal, which has the power to amplify the Ashla force a hundred times.

'Anybody who read those drafts,' recalls Kurtz, 'said, "What are you doing here? This is absolute gobbledegook."' He urged Lucas, who later defined his religion as 'Buddhist Methodist', to go for something simpler and more universal. 'Comparative Religion is one of the things I studied in university,' says Kurtz. 'I also studied the Buddhist and Hindu sects, and studied Zen and Tibetan Buddhism, and also Native American spirituality; shamanistic methods and so on. I got out a lot of my old books, and we talked about it. If you trace back most religious thought to the teachings of the great prophets, whether Judeo-Christian tradition, or Muslim, or even Hindu or Buddhist, you start to see lots of similarities. The core philosophies are very very similar. The most obvious one is the Buddhist tradition about karma – the karmic action that comes out of cause and effect. So the Force is an amalgamation of lots of different things.

'I saw Ben Kenobi as a shaman, really, rather than a character tied to any conventional religious background. The American Indians look upon God as the Great Mystery – that's what they call him. [Their religion] is about the universal energy you can draw on through individual effort. You draw on the energy of the Great Mystery in the dances and tribal prayers. [I thought] this would be a good way to connect with this, since it's simple enough that you don't have to go through weeks and weeks of explanation trying to get some sense of what the religious philosophy is. And it's true enough, in the sense that it's based logically in a real belief system. We wanted to avoid that problem of imposing some sort of religious messiah on our characters so that we could have some sort of religious history. So there is a Joseph Campbell connection, but it's just one of many.'

There remained large chunks of back-story for which there was no place in the film: the nature and structure of the Empire, Luke's background, the Jedi – none were explained. Lucas tried to spell them out in dialogue, but once actors got hold of the script, the idea was abandoned. Piling exposition into their lines simply made them unsayable.

Lucas and Kurtz chose a radical solution. They wouldn't explain anything. 'We decided,' says Kurtz, 'that we were making a *Flash Gordon*-type action adventure, and that we were coming in on Episode Four; at that time there was no thought of a series or prequels. We're just racing through the story, not explaining anything. This is just the life that these people lead. We're not explaining technology. We're not explaining philosophy. We're not explaining religion. Like George's idea to shoot *THX1138* in Japan, it was a way of not having to tell the audience everything. Whether they get it or not is immaterial to the story. What you get out of it is what you bring to the cinema, and you read into the thing the things you want to read into it.' Had they but known it, Lucas and Kurtz were obeying one of the oldest conventions of the epic: to commence *in media res*; while the story was actually taking place. It had worked for Homer and the *Kalevala*. Why not for *Star Wars*?

Since nothing needed to be explained, *Star Wars* became in effect a documentary about another universe. While Luke, Han, Leia, and Kenobi adventured in the foreground, a whole world passed by behind them, unremarked. John Dykstra, who would manage the film's special effects, saw it from the start. 'The outlandish places [the story] goes are taken for granted. The film depicts a common way of living, and everybody does it. It makes it more believable, quite frankly. You know, "I'm gonna go out and get in an old P38 X-Wing:" that's all pilot talk and that's all standard stuff, and people can relate to it. It wasn't, "I'm-going-to-go-out-and-get-in-my-supersonic-ultralight-Speedsaber-Fighter-Number-3." There were laser swords, but it was more like, "Here, kid, take your father's old laser sword." And it's got a leather case . . . The aliens walked around. They were just *there*. George threw so much stuff away in those shots. Something was always going on in the background . . . so there was always something of interest in there that wasn't presented for production value. It wasn't, "Please note. We just spent $10,000 on this robot. You must look at it." It just rolled by in the dust in the background.'

With little to do until they had another project, Marcia was bored. Much of her time was spent propping up Lucas's frail ego. After each new criticism of his script, he fell into another fit of depression and sat in his writing room for hours. Marcia asked Brian De Palma, one of the more outspoken of Lucas's friends, to cheer him up: 'George thinks he has no talent. He respects you. Tell him he does.'

Lucas hated interviews, but Marcia encouraged him to do them as a way of raising his spirits, though the prevailing feeling, fostered by *auteurist* criticism, that Lucas created every aspect of his films, irritated her. Passing through his office just as one journalist used the term 'master director,' she snorted.

'Doesn't he like that description?' the writer asked.

'Oh, he loves it,' she said.

Asked in 1980 by a journalist whether or not Marcia worked for him, Lucas gave an uncomfortable and schematic summary of their relationship:

> It's difficult to work in a creative sense with someone you're married to. The closest thing I can relate it to is redecorating your house. There are two issues that most people come clos-est to divorce on. One is how to raise the kids, and the other is what color the living room should be. It's very emotional because you're not talking about rational things, you're talking about the essence of what you are. 'I am a green room.' 'I am a white room.' Or 'I don't like Chinese' or 'I love Swedish

modern.' Making a film is like that. It's easier with Marcia because I'm still essentially the boss. I am the director and the director is the boss, and she has to respect that. Obviously, when you're married, she has an advantage nobody else has.

Lucas thought Marcia should start a family; she wanted to work. Martin Scorsese had just shot *Alice Doesn't Live Here Any More*, about a middle-aged widow who goes on the road with her son in an attempt to revive her early ambition to become a singer. In the interests of making the film more 'honest,' the producer signed as many women as possible to the unit. Sandy Weintraub was associate producer, Toby Rafelson the art director, and Scorsese asked Marcia if she would cut the film. Obsessive about his effects, he already knew exactly how it would look, shot for shot. He wanted a foil and sparring partner more than an editor. But Robert Getchell's script stirred thoughts of independence in Marcia. And Scorsese, with his generally wild style, offered an interesting change from making tuna sandwiches for George. Against Lucas's strenuous objections, Marcia took the job.

13

For Sale: Universe, Once Used

The key to a successful entertainment phenomenon usually isn't the what or the how. It's the when.

Louis Menand, 'Pop Technology: How *Star Wars* Changed the
World,' in *Slate*, 18 February 1998

In 1975, science fiction in Hollywood lay dead in the water. Dystopias
dominated the few fantastic films being made, with the emphasis on
an earth blasted by pollution and ecological disaster. In *Silent Running*,
directed, as part of Ned Tanen's 'youth' program, by special-effects
man Douglas Trumbull, Bruce Dern, the custodian of the last forests,
now roaming the solar system, refuses to destroy his greenhouses and
instead takes off on a voyage of discovery with three small comic
robots. Called Huey, Dewey and Louie, after Donald Duck's nephews,
they were operated by three Vietnam amputees.

In England, actor Cornel Wilde directed *The Death of Grass*, a
version of John Christopher's *No Blade of Grass*, about a plague which
destroys all vegetation. *Damnation Alley*, adapted – remotely – from
a novel by Roger Zelazny, showed the world's last Hell's Angel piloting
a huge recreational vehicle across a desert infested with giant killer-
cockroaches.

The Stepford Wives, *The Terminal Man* and *Westworld* betrayed
a deep distrust of artificial intelligence, prefigured by the runaway
computer HAL9000 of *2001: A Space Odyssey*. In the first film, robots
replace the wives in a small American town; in the second, from
Michael Crichton's novel, a computer chip in George Segal's brain,
fitted to eradicate a malfunction, drives him to multiple homicide;
while in *Westworld*, also by Crichton, the robot whores, knights, and

gunmen of a computerized theme park run wild and wipe out their clients. Other sf movies – *A Boy and his Dog, Death Race 2000, Rollerball, Logan's Run* – were no less jaded. Hollywood had seen the future, and it sucked.

Critics of Lucas's *Star Wars* concept almost never grasped the two fundamental differences that separated it from other science fiction films of the seventies: it was optimistic, not dystopic; and it took place not on a planet, but mostly in space. 'There was a sense of adventure,' said Charley Lippincott. 'And what I didn't realize until later on, there was a sense of surprise, of wonder. You were seeing something new; just like *2001*. You were seeing something new, but something you may have thought about – or dreamed about. But you're gonna actually see it.'

Science fiction films, especially those with monsters and alien creatures in them, supported a lively fandom, many members of which were eager to become part of it. Future *Star Wars* sfx men Dennis Muren, Richard Edlund, and Ken Ralston were all tinkering, experimenting, dreaming. Once *Star Wars* succeeded, art director Michael Minor wrote angrily to the *Hollywood Reporter*, pointing out how Lucas's film drew on 'a host of fresh *underground* talent [his italics], new artists and technicians, new model-builders and make-up wizards, many of whom, like myself, have for years worked a commercial here, a *Star Trek* or porno there, under the table and no credit – not in the old Hollywood – for credit would have meant expulsion.'

'Lucas really lucked out with that,' says Jon Davison, producer of the *Robocop* films and *Starship Troopers*, 'because there were across the country a whole series of kids who were then in their early twenties who had all seen the Harryhausen pictures when they were new, all wanted to do special effects, all loved effects and fantasy movies, and had made things in their garages or, if they were lucky, had worked on a commercial or done tabletop stop-motion stuff in their bedrooms, and were all there waiting for somebody to come along and say, "Follow me. Come, let's do this." They were this great eager workforce. They would have done it for nothing, and they probably did do it for nothing. To do effects of a space movie with creatures . . . you wouldn't have to pay these kids.'

Having inaugurated the seventies with widely advertised public auctions at which they sold the props and costumes accumulated over generations, studios spent most of the decade closing their special effects and animation departments. In 1973 and 1974, the Academy didn't even bother to award Oscars for special effects. Having failed to beat television during the seventies with epic stories and giant screens, the movies decided to capitulate, and make films mainly for the new medium. Features would be modest, intimate, and set in the real world. A 1970 article in *Life* magazine, 'The Dream Factory Woke Up,' scorned standing sets, prop and costumes stores, and trick photography studios. 'Bogus reality in fantastic abundance – but who needs it?' sneered the writer as he toured studio warehouses. 'Today's movie makers and audiences want their reality absolute. This can be achieved most easily and cheaply by shooting on location instead of in a studio.' Marvin Davis, vice president of Gulf and Western, stated truculently, 'These kids aren't going to the movies to take home dreams.'

When studios did make fantastic films, the special effects were perfunctory. Most directors tried to avoid them altogether, with multiple dissolves, superimpositions, color separations. As for creating a fantastic world from scratch like Fritz Lang in *Metropolis* or the Hollywood serial-makers of the thirties, nobody knew where to start. Warners once employed a hundred special-effects technicians and eleven full-time matte artists. Now there were none. Background painters and matte artists Albert Whitlock, Glenn Robinson, Bill Abbott, and Frank van der Veer now worked freelance on films like *The Towering Inferno*, *Logan's Run* and the remake of *King Kong*, but everyone assumed the art would die with them.

Coasting on their credit with Universal, Kurtz and Lucas used the old *American Graffiti* office as their LA headquarters while they tried to sell 'The Star Wars.' On weekends, they went back to San Anselmo, where Lucas continued to rent out space for local film-makers. One of them was Philip Kaufman, who was in the same young director program from which Steven Spielberg emerged. Chicago-born, and eight years older than Lucas, the intense, intellectual Kaufman had more in common with Coppola and De Palma than Lucas, but he knew Marin, and had even, at a low point in his career, delivered mail in Mill Valley. He had just spent a dispiriting eight months at Paramount developing the TV series *Star Trek* into a feature, only to be informed by the producer, 'Forget it. There's no future in science fiction.' (After *Star Wars* was a hit, Paramount would rush to make *Star Trek: The Motion Picture*, directed by Robert Wise.)

Kaufman and Lucas began kicking around original ideas for screenplays. Lucas admired MGM's 1950 film of H. Rider Haggard's *King Solomon's Mines*, starring a suave Stewart Granger as white hunter Allan Quatermain. He also had a soft spot for the same studio's thirties adventure stories, often featuring Clark Gable or Spencer Tracy (sometimes Gable *and* Tracy) as happy-go-lucky adventurers in the far corners of the globe. Usually in leather jackets and battered felt hats, they beat up villains in bar-room brawls, patronized and exploited the locals, romanced American girls far from home, and still managed to shoot the newsreel film, drill the oil well or rescue the heroine. In turn, these heroes could be traced to the serials of the thirties, of which Lucas had a dim memory from *Adventure Theater* and Don Glut's screenings at USC.

An image from one of these serials caught his eye, and he had an enlargement made. It showed a man in the obligatory felt hat and leather jacket leaping from the back of a galloping horse onto a truck. In Britain, independent producer Harry Saltzman and Albert 'Cubby' Broccoli were pumping out adaptations of Ian Fleming's novels about super-spy James Bond, but otherwise nobody was much interested in action adventures. Maybe there was room for a film that returned to those innocent days.

Lucas and Kaufman began filling yellow legal pads with notes for such a story. They imagined a hero as smooth as Gable, but able to hold his own in a fight. An adventurer, but with a sentimental side. More intellectual than Gable, too. They made him an archaeologist. But what was he looking for? Kaufman suggested the Ark of the Covenant. Lucas looked blank. Methodism had little truck with the Old Testament, and he'd never heard about the coffer in which the Israelites carried the tablets of the Law that Moses brought down from Mount Sinai, together with Aaron's rod and a pot of the manna which fell from heaven and sustained them in the wilderness. But Kaufman was Jewish, and, more important, so was his childhood orthodontist, who'd told him the story to keep him from fidgeting in the chair.

They were well into preliminary work on the story when Clint Eastwood offered Kaufman the direction of a western, *The Outlaw Josey Wales*. Kaufman chose the cast, picked the locations, determined the look of the film, and the wardrobe; but once shooting began in October in Arizona and Utah, he fell out with Eastwood, first over the female lead, Sondra Locke, then over Kaufman's thoughtful, deliberate direction. Within a month, Eastwood had fired Kaufman and taken over the direction. By then, however, Lucas had shelved the adventure story and was deep into *Star Wars*.

Charley Lippincott, about to start work as publicist for Hitchcock on *Family Plot*, was another old friend to drop by Lucas's office across the street from Universal. Lucas confided some details of *Star Wars*. 'You've got to read it,' he said, and gave him a draft screenplay.

Lippincott read it over the weekend, and on Monday told Lucas, 'It's terrific. I'd love to work on it.'

'But you're too big to work on a film like this,' Lucas said.

'No, I'd love it,' said Lippincott.

Lucas, with every sign of astonishment, said, 'You *would?* Oh, wow!'

A few days later, Lippincott ran into Lucas again in the lobby of the Black Tower, the monolith of black glass that housed Universal's executive offices. Lucas began picking his brains about merchandising toys, games, and clothing derived from *Star Wars* and its characters. 'We must have stood there for two hours, talking, while people are passing by,' says Lippincott. 'George was saying, "We could make stuff up for the movie and sell it. We could have these three stores. We could have a store in San Francisco and a store in Westwood and we could have one in New York" – because he owned a share of the SuperSnipe comic-book shop.'

Lucas's enthusiasm surprised Lippincott. 'No studio had a regular functioning merchandising unit except Universal, because of TV. Fox had had one, but the last big merchandising push was the *Dr Dolittle* movie [in 1967], which failed.' The toy company Mattel created three hundred *Dolittle* items – dolls, watches, kits, and items of clothing – but most were still gathering dust in the warehouses. The biggest seller on the market when *Star Wars* came out was a figure based on the TV show *The Six Million Dollar Man*. A few *Star Trek* fans sold T-shirts and 'Star Fleet Manuals' by mail, or at science fiction conventions, and there was a lively market in posters, stills and memorabilia; but the studios thought it pointless to create and merchandise spin-offs. If they ever decided to do so, they could license some manufacturer, and collect a royalty – though, more often, the studio paid soft-drink retailers or a hamburger chain to feature a film on their packaging.

But Lippincott could see that Lucas's story might succeed in the world of merchandising where others had failed. '*Star Wars* had what the toy people call "play value." It had depth of character. It had characters interesting to kids. It had a variety of characters, human and non-human. It had a great villain. It had all these things that a lot of the cartoon shows had.' Lucas never saw *Star Wars* toys as simply a lucrative spin-off: to him, they were his best chance of making a profit from a film that would probably not do all that well at the box office. In June 1977, when *Star Wars* had barely been released, he said, 'In a way, this film was designed around toys. I actually make toys. If I make money, it will be from the toys.' When the business magazine *Fortune* profiled him in 1980, it would note with some confusion that Lucasfilm was 'hardly more than a toy company which licensed *Star Wars* products.'

'It's safe to say,' wrote industry journalist James Surowiecki twenty years later, 'that *Star Wars* single-handedly created the film-merchandising business . . . It's a classic example of a company creating a market rather than responding to an existing one. No one knew how much kids wanted action figures until they were offered them.'

Meanwhile, Gary Kurtz was looking for technicians. He asked Ken Miura, the teacher of sound at USC, for his best mixer. Miura recommended his teaching assistant Ben Burtt, and Kurtz hired him immediately. Lucas told Burtt to forget the electronic fizzes and sizzles of conventional science fiction soundtracks. As much as possible, all the sounds were to be natural. He wanted the spaceships' motors 'to sound real, to sound squeaky and rusty.' This would be a used universe. Burtt spent a year gathering noises, ranging from the snuffling and howling of bears and wolves to exploding missiles and planes taking off from an aircraft-carrier's deck. Manipulated electronically, they would create the soundscape of Lucas's future.

Special effects promised to be the film's most difficult element. Technology had progressed in the decade since *2001: A Space Odyssey*, but it remained expensive and time-consuming. The best people, like Douglas Trumbull, who had achieved the psychedelic effects at the end of *2001* with his 'slit-scan' camera, were booked up years in advance.

In spring 1975, Kurtz and Lucas talked to Trumbull, and to the reigning chiefs of model animation and mask-making, Jim Danforth and Bill Taylor. Always happier if he could show rather than explain, Lucas assembled a reel of clips from World War II and Korean War movies of aerial dogfights to show what he hoped to duplicate in space. Everyone who saw it agreed it would take years to do, and would cost a fortune. According to Rose Duignan, director of marketing of Industrial Light and Magic in the nineties, the reaction was, 'No way. The technology's not here. You're dreaming.'

Lucas didn't agree. He believed the cinema could achieve these effects. Moreover, he proposed to be around to make sure they were done right. 'I don't know how we're going to do all this stuff,' he told Danforth. 'Maybe we'll darken a studio and throw models at a camera, but whatever we do, I'll be right there with you.' Both Danforth and Trumbull were alarmed by Lucas's insistence on being involved in the process at every step. Danforth backed out immediately. 'Not on my film you won't,' he said at Lucas's suggestion of involvement, and walked out. Trumbull remained interested, but his attitude was adamant: if you hired him to do your special effects, *he* did your special effects, without you looking over his shoulder.

Lucas and Kurtz turned to the second rank – people who'd worked with Trumbull and Danforth. One of them was John Dykstra, six feet four inches tall, bearded, radical, an ex-rocker with long flowing hair who'd gone through a phase of doing experimental photographic projects with Jim Morrison and the Doors before serving an apprenticeship with Trumbull at his company Future General on *Silent Running* and doing effects on Robert Wise's *The Andromeda Strain*. A maverick, he'd studied industrial design at California State College at Long Beach – Spielberg's school – but, like so many in New Hollywood, never graduated.

Dykstra was working on a system which he hoped would solve the oldest problem of superimposing model shots onto backgrounds – precision. On *2001*, special-effects technician Wally Veevers shot the space scenes with methods pioneered before the Second World War. You hung models on wires, and moved toward them with the camera. Almost no film had shots in which both model and camera moved at the same time; there was simply no way in which the movements could be duplicated exactly on the next take, a necessity if the model had to be optically superimposed on a starry background. For that sort of precision, Veevers mounted the camera on a twenty-two-foot-long worm gear, like a giant micrometer. The calibrations ensured it could be returned to exactly the same point for each shot, but it was a wearisome technique. Some shots took hours to film.

Dykstra saw that it would be far simpler to keep the model stationary and move the camera around it, and that worm gears could be replaced by electronics. His Dykstraflex system operated by 'motion control.' He demonstrated its capabilities to Lucas and Kurtz. The basis was the 'stepper' motor, developed for use on production lines, where a large number of objects might need to be turned under a paint spray, or rotated for the application of a label. The stepper turned in precise increments, and could repeat the same movement *ad infinitum*. It could also be taken off the line, rewired, and put to work doing something else.

Dykstra mounted his camera on a gimbal at the end of a small crane and added a stepper motor. Then he put a model on a stand, and attached another motor, allowing it to swivel. Motors could also be put inside the model, to rotate individual components, like a turret. The camera ran on a forty-foot motorized track. To record the movements of the motors and repeat them on subsequent takes, he linked the camera to a twelve-channel computer tape which registered the position of every motor at each frame of the film. 'Now that we have a positional map for each frame,' he explained, 'we can run the camera as often as we'd like, knowing that the camera and subject positions would track the map exactly, based on the frame count.'

By today's standards, the Dykstraflex was primitive. 'You've got to remember that motion control was not PC-based,' says Dykstra. 'There was no keyboard entry, no "Good morning, thanks a lot for coming to work." It was all hard-wired electronics, with microprocessors that were hooked to switches and buttons, [and] somebody sitting at a box and pressing the buttons in the right sequence to make all this stuff record.'

Lucas recognized some of the electronics from the Oxberry animation camera he'd used at USC. In a leap of imagination, he understood what this equipment could do. He could shoot a moving model with a moving camera, then shoot another moving object with precisely the same camera movement, and, by superimposing them on the same piece of film, create a dogfight in space. Even though a lot of bugs remained to be ironed out, he hired Dykstra to head the special-effects team for *Star Wars*.

Buying up old VistaVision cameras, whose negative area was larger than that of the conventional 35mm camera, Dykstra incorporated them into the system. 'We took archaic cameras,' said Dykstra, 'built before we were even born, and we created hybrids of them by bolting different parts together. Nobody else was inventing cameras to make films in 1975. We were there when a genre was being born and reborn.'

Kurtz leased a 15,000-square-foot, two-story building on Valjean Avenue near Van Nuys airport, a desolate spot in the Valley's sprawling dormitory suburbs, and installed Dykstra and eight helpers, a number that would expand over the next year to seventy-five. Looking for a name that would disguise the warehouse's function and suggest it was simply in the business of wholesaling electronic components rather than making movies, Lucas came up with Industrial Light and Magic.

One end of the ugly, flat-roofed building was offices, the other a giant, airless warehouse space. There was no air-conditioning, and yellow overhangs above the office windows did nothing to keep out the sun. Temperatures often rose to a baking 120 degrees, but the site's remoteness and low rental recommended it. Except for Dave de Patie and Friz Freleng turning out their popular *Pink Panther* cartoons in a building on the same industrial park, there wasn't a film company in sight.

This was just as well, since ILM was non-union – a dangerous policy in a town where unions resented seeing their traditional status and perquisites eroded by the newcomers. One of the projects on which Charley Lippincott worked for Fox was *Fighting Mad*, a Roger Corman production directed by Jonathan Demme on location in Fanfield, Arkansas. Demme gave an incautious interview which mentioned his non-union crew, and the one IATSE member in town, a movie projectionist, blew the whistle, forcing costly new hirings. Though everyone at ILM was sworn to keep their mouth shut about the company's non-union status, anonymous callers threatened to firebomb the Van Nuys facility. Kurtz and Lucas opened tentative negotiations with IATSE, but it had no interest in recruiting what it saw as a gang of hobbyists and crazies.

Looking for a production manager, Kurtz approached Jim Nelson, who'd worked with him on *Two Lane Blacktop*. Sensing that Fox's $3.5 million was being eaten up day by day by Dykstra's expensive equipment and rental on the Van Nuys facility, he asked Nelson if he could start the following Monday. Nelson, in the middle of a picture, refused, particularly when Kurtz told him the salary – $25,000 a year, compared to the $100,000 he could expect from a year's work on any normal production – on top of which he would have to pay his own health insurance and social security, leaving a meagre $224 a week to live on. Kurtz and Lucas convinced him by, Nelson claims, promising him 'associate producer' credit on the film, a valuable step up in the Hollywood hierarchy.

Meanwhile, Jeff Berg and Tom Pollock hammered out the contract with Fox. Each new twist in the negotiations brought anguished phone calls from Lucas. 'He rang me once,' says Willard Huyck, 'and said, "I don't think I'm going to do this movie. They don't want to give me the rights to the sequels." I said, "George, you're lucky just to be making the movie. Make the first one and worry about the sequels later." But he said, "No, it will be better if I control the sequels."'

Other sticking points, though less urgent ones, were merchandising and the rights to the soundtrack album. Lucas and Kurtz resolved these with a concession that astonished Fox. The deal memo allotted them $50,000 each to write and produce the movie, with an additional $100,000 to Lucas to direct. They would also receive 40 per cent of the profits. Studios expected these figures to be bargained upward in the bickering over profit thresholds and distribution fees, and accordingly set them low. When Lucas and Kurtz offered to accept the original low figures if Fox conceded them the merchandising and soundtrack rights, the studio, hardly believing its luck, agreed to cede Lucas 60 per cent of merchandising rights, rising over two years until by 1979 he owned them all.

Lippincott is dismissive of Fox's merchandising expertise. 'Fox, like most of the studios at that time, had no real merchandising department as we know it today. They had a guy who just went over deals that were brought to them.' Marc Pevers, vice president in charge of licensing at the time, has always strenuously denied that he let the money machine of *Star Wars* slip through his fingers. When Dale Pollock made such a claim in his biography of Lucas, *Skywalking*, Pevers sued. In 1999, he wrote an acerbic letter to the *Los Angeles Times* contradicting its statement that 'Fox famously traded away the merchandising and sequel rights for *Star Wars* to Lucas for lower writing and directing fees.' According to Pevers:

The facts are that, as detailed in the original production-distribution agreement between Twentieth Century-Fox and Lucas, Fox administered the merchandising rights to *Star Wars*. Lucas did have the right to approve all licensing deals. When the sequel rights were renegotiated, Fox relinquished the licensing rights to Lucas in 1979, not in 1977. As vice president of Fox Licensing, I was responsible for the licensing campaign for the initial theatrical release of *Star Wars* in coordination with Charles Lippincott of Lucasfilm. Both Dennis C. Stanfill, Fox CEO, and Alan Ladd Jr, Fox's president of theatrical production, strongly supported my efforts well before the release of *Star Wars*. Lippincott and I made joint presentations to the toy industry in New York during February 1977. Foolishly, few toy companies expressed any interest and many did not even bother to attend our presentations. However, as a result of these presentations, we concluded what ultimately became a precedent-shattering master toy license with Kenner Products Co. I negotiated this license, which remained in effect throughout the first two *Star Wars* sequels.

The fact remains that Fox did sign away to Lucasfilm an unprecedented share of and control over merchandising. The concession helped soften the blow inflicted by the bean-counters, who, now that they'd analyzed the screenplay, estimated that *Star Wars* would cost not $3.5 million but $7.8 million. Almost before anyone could digest this, the figure rose again, to $10 million. Ladd's staff urged him to back out. Fox already had one mega-project in production, *The Towering Inferno*, a joint production with Warners, which involved burning down a skyscraper. At $10 million, *Star Wars* was too great a risk, especially since science fiction was notoriously slow at returning its investment: as of November 1975, *2001: A Space Odyssey* had just gone into profit, seven years after its release. They pressed to keep the budget at $8.7 million. At a budget meeting, Jim Nelson blurted out, 'I don't know why we're arguing about $2.5 million. This film will make $100 million.' Everyone laughed. Even Lucas was embarrassed. He shrank down in his chair, and mumbled that he'd be happy if it grossed $35 million.

Kurtz and Lucas threatened to take the film elsewhere if Fox didn't approve $10.5 million, but privately they were delighted with the figures. Fox had costed each sfx shot as if shooting a spaceship against a starry sky would involve building the model, hanging it on wires in front of a blue screen, filming it with a full camera crew, handing it to an optical printer operator to superimpose it on the background, then sending it to the lab. Dykstraflex, if it fulfilled all Dykstra's hopes, could halve such costs. Lucas took to joking that *Star Wars* was 'the most expensive low-budget film ever made.'

Lucas and Kurtz decided to tough it out with Fox. Had they known it would be twelve months before the first sfx shots were made, and that even those would be useless, they might have been less sanguine.

While *Star Wars* was building momentum, John Milius and Steven Spielberg, both of whom had contracts with Universal, were embarking on major projects. Unlike Lucas and Kurtz, who had to rub along in an office, Milius and Spielberg occupied a bungalow like those of Alfred Hitchcock and Don Siegel – though, indicative of their tentative place in the Universal scheme of things, they had to share it. Old Hollywood tolerated these upstarts, but it didn't have to like them. Billy Wilder, another bungalow resident, grouched about the new breed of boy directors playing with toys, and taking the money that might have been used to finance adult films.

Milius had his surfing epic, *Big Wednesday*, and Spielberg was looking for a film to follow *Jaws*. For a while, he contemplated a period swashbuckler in the style of Errol Flynn, but discarded this and announced that he too would make a science fiction film. Called variously 'Kingdom Come' and 'Watch the Skies,' it was being written by Paul Schrader, and would involve, it was promised, the most lavish spaceship effects ever seen. Douglas Trumbull would achieve them.

If Lucas felt resentment at Spielberg's coat-tailing, it was softened by the differences between *Star Wars* and the film that would become *Close Encounters of the Third Kind*. Spielberg wanted to show how an ordinary man reacted to the arrival of galactic beings. Lucas dreamed of extraordinary people on planets and galaxies distant in both space and time. His earliest outlines already carried the introduction, 'Long long ago in a galaxy far far away, an incredible adventure took place.' Spielberg and Schrader would fall out when Schrader refused to send into space 'the sort of man who might run a McDonald's franchise,' and Spielberg said, 'That's exactly the kind of man I want.'

The difference between Spielberg and Lucas was obvious to Charley Lippincott: 'Spielberg sees his audience as twelve years old. Lucas sees his audience as fourteen. That's an enormous change, going from pre-teen to teenage. Those two years are crucial.' *Star Wars* made far more money from its toys, games and associated spin-off items than from seats sold. Spielberg's films never inspired the same loyalty, and produced no successful series of games or toys.

One might have guessed the films would be different from the two men's first attempts at creating imaginary worlds. As a teenager, Spielberg, the extrovert, persuaded his family and friends to appear in his 8mm feature *Firelight*, shot with as much realistic detail as he could achieve in Scottsdale, Arizona, and screened it at the local cinema. Lucas, the introvert, created an environment in a garage, using lighting and decor to create a mood, but no live performers. But one thing united them. Both charged for the experience, and made money. In their hearts, each knew he had more in common with the other than with mercurial visionaries like Coppola, Milius and De Palma. Rather than doing his best to undermine Spielberg, Lucas began to think of him as another Wexler, Kassower, Murch – someone he could learn from, even collaborate with.

ILM attracted young sfx enthusiasts like a pole magnet. Peter Kuran was typical. Brought up on *Famous Monsters of Filmland*, he'd begun making 8mm monster movies with clay models in the basement of his parents' home in New Jersey. After high school, he got into Cal-Arts, the Los Angeles college launched with money from the Disney studios. Following a few months interned at Disney, he was told by a friend at DePatie-Freleng that an sfx facility near them was hiring. Kuran showed Dykstra his 'reel,' assembled so quickly that the splices kept breaking. 'I don't think Dykstra was very impressed,' said Kuran, 'but I told him I was willing to work a week for free, and I remember seeing a sparkle in his eye when he heard that.' Kuran ended up working on two of the *Star Wars* trilogy, and forming his own company.

The amateurism of the people Dykstra was hiring lulled Lucas into believing ILM could do the film's estimated four hundred effects shots for even less than the $3 million allocated. 'Having been a clever film-maker who did things on his own,' says Matthew Robbins, 'George's idea was that ILM was going to be this little squad of techies. They'd figure out how to make these shots in a garage for $1.98. I remember Dykstra saying, "If it were up to George, we would have hung a black backing, and put the ships on broomsticks and waved them around. Like twelve-year-olds." I think George actually did propose that. Dykstra, of course, knew they were going to have to hire a lot of people and buy a lot of equipment.'

In effect, ILM would create modern special effects almost from scratch. Optical technology had leaped ahead since *2001*, whose techniques now seemed almost medieval: even Kubrick's office Xerox machine had been an early model which routinely burst into flames. For the lights inside his spaceship models, Kubrick used tiny lamps and 16mm projectors, which caused overheating, buckling, and occasional fires. ILM pioneered the use of fiber-optics, which fed cold light to the most inaccessible corners of a model. *Star Wars* would use the same hand-painted glass matte paintings as the Kubrick film, but would exploit the larger negative size of VistaVision to superimpose additional images – as many as eighteen during the space battles. Above all, Dykstraflex promised to reduce to routine the shooting of space sequences, which had kept *2001* in production for five years.

Even though most of the film would be special effects, *Star Wars* needed real sets and locations: the interior of Han Solo's spaceship, the *Millennium Falcon*; and numerous meeting chambers, control rooms, engine rooms and holding cells on the Empire's flagship; as well as a cantina in the spaceport of Mos Eisley; and the desert home of Luke Skywalker's adoptive parents and of the old Jedi Obi-Wan Kenobi.

Kurtz estimated he'd need at least thirty sets on about ten sound stages – more than any Hollywood studio could provide. He went to Italy, but one look at the dilapidated Cinecittà complex outside Rome, with its dusty prop stores of antique statues and its overgrown backlot littered with peeling plaster façades and the rusting remains of Federico Fellini's wilder creations, convinced him this was no place for a futuristic film. In May 1975, he flew to London, where Lucas joined him.

In the boom days of the sixties, the studios littering London's rural outskirts had flourished, helped by Hollywood money and some investment from the British government, which levied a few pence on each cinema admission and allocated it to films using British technicians and talent. Pinewood built the biggest sound stage in Europe for the more lavish scenes of the James Bond films, while Elstree, at Borehamwood, housed *2001*. But British film-making had suffered even more than Hollywood in the massive reallocation of resources to television. In June 1972, sixteen films were in production in British studios. In July 1973, with the retreat of American money, the number had dropped to six.

In 1972, MGM promised to invest £170,000 a year in Elstree, but when its board brought in cost-cutter James Aubrey, dubbed 'The Smiling Cobra,' one of his first acts, in October 1973, was to cancel MGM's $30,000 a week underwriting. Elstree's owners, the electronics company EMI, immediately slashed its 479 staff by half. EMI was rich enough as a result of its recording and medical equipment operations to keep Elstree running, but the board couldn't believe that making films in Britain had a future. They preferred to set up a Hollywood operation under producers Michael Deeley and Barry Spikings, who were authorized to invest in promising major projects. The first of them was Spielberg's *Close Encounters*, which Spielberg, faced with the same problems as Kurtz and Lucas, had decided to shoot in a massive dirigible hangar in Mobile, Alabama.

Kurtz visited Pinewood. Its setting, in the well-kept grounds of an elegant country house with a panelled dining room and a bar worthy of a gentlemen's club in Mayfair, was attractive, and the giant Bond sound stage an added plus, but the owners insisted Lucas employ their lighting, sound mixing, and support technicians as part of any deal, so he passed. Shepperton and Twickenham were too small, though Lucas thought the former's giant 'H' Stage might be large enough for the finale, where Princess Leia honors her heroes before an assembly as big as one of Leni Riefenstahl's Nuremberg rallies.

This left Elstree, where Kubrick had made *2001*. It was losing almost £1 million a year, and in 1975 EMI closed it altogether, hoping to sell the land for an industrial park or shopping mall. They might have done so but for an outcry from Britain's trade unions, who at that time had enormous power, particularly as Harold Wilson's Labour government was dependent on their support. In 1975, Wilson launched a 'working party' to investigate ways of helping British film-making. EMI reluctantly kept Elstree open, but fired everyone. If producers wanted the place, they could rent it 'wall to wall,' supplying their own technicians – which suited Lucas perfectly.

'England was not only somewhat cheaper to shoot,' says Robert

Watts, who'd worked on *2001* before becoming line producer on *Star Wars*, 'but they had something very difficult to find at that time in the US: eight or nine stages in one studio available at the same time. That was a very key aspect from a financial standpoint. The film required a large amount of stage space. Though the Hollywood stages were larger, they were almost constantly occupied.'

Physically, little about Elstree was attractive. Bunny Alsup rated it 'drab, ugly, cold, depressing.' The nearest town, Borehamwood – dubbed 'Boring Wood' by Harrison Ford – lacked even a decent restaurant. 'But they couldn't have found a better location for privacy,' Alsup said. 'No one walked in off the street.' Kurtz struck a deal to use Elstree for seventeen weeks from March 1976, and also booked Shepperton's 'H' Stage for the same period.

Early in 1973, Richard Zanuck and David Brown had bought a script by Willard Huyck and Gloria Katz called *Lucky Lady*. A comedy about rum-running during Prohibition, it was planned as a vehicle for Paul Newman, perhaps directed by Spielberg. Two years later, while Lucas was preparing *Star Wars*, Zanuck and Brown revived the project, this time with Burt Reynolds in the lead, and directed by Stanley Donen. On their return to Hollywood, Lucas and Kurtz dropped by its set at Fox, and admired the production design, by a forty-year-old Englishman named John Barry. Barry – credited as 'Jonathan Barry' in the US, to avoid confusion with the film composer – had just designed Donen's English production of *The Little Prince*, a box-office flop, but interesting for Lucas, since Antoine de Saint-Exupéry's fantasy was set on a barren planet, locations for which Barry had found in Tunisia. Lucas was equally impressed with Barry's work on Kubrick's *A Clockwork Orange*, assembling that film's extraordinary anthology of pop-art visuals. A forager and eclecticist, Barry had a flair for juxtaposing incongruous items to create disturbing effects, which suited *Star Wars'* 'used universe,' retro-fitted and jerrybuilt. Lucas hired him as production designer, along with his assistant, Norman Reynolds. Their first job was to travel through Spain and North Africa, finding locations for Luke's desert home planet, Tatooine.

Star Wars was racing toward the point where Lucas needed to start casting. The script still wasn't right, so he begged Huyck and Katz to clean it up, promising them a point each as a reward. They junked his worst solecisms, threw out extraneous characters and tightened up the remaining dialogue.

With the help of casting director Diana Crittenden, and Fred Roos, who was also working on *Apocalypse Now* with Coppola, Lucas started seeing actors. For Roos's convenience, they used the Goldwyn studios where Coppola also had his production office.

Apocalypse had bogged down in logistical problems. Saigon was in Communist hands, and a humiliated US Army now scorned his script, based on what an internal memo called 'a series of some of the worst things, real and imagined, that happened during the Vietnam War.' Cornered, Coppola did a deal with the corrupt Marcos regime in the Philippines, which promised unstinting help, including the use of its Huey and Cobra helicopter gunships, supplied by the US to fight Communist insurgents.

Ever the empire-builder, Coppola was expanding his offices even as he worked on the film. He'd decreed a new and more imposing door, and when Lucas called by one day with Richard Dreyfuss, whom he'd briefly considered for Han Solo, he was surprised and embarrassed to find Harrison Ford on his knees, surrounded by lumber and sawdust. Ford had had a small part in *The Conversation*, and Coppola had promised him another one in *Apocalypse Now*. In the meantime, he'd offered him some casual carpentry. Ford was furious when Roos asked him to do the job. 'I'm not working on a fucking door when Lucas is there,' he said. Roos insisted, and Ford, since he'd had only minor roles since *American Graffiti*, acquiesced; he needed the work.

It took Ford some time to realize that all this was a Roos subterfuge to prod Lucas into casting him as Han Solo. 'I kept saying, "George, he's right under your nose,"' said Roos. Eventually Lucas saw the light. 'Harrison was there outside working all the time, banging on things,' he said. 'I just said at lunchtime or sometime, "Would you like to read some of these things? Because I need somebody to read against all these characters."' When Ford began to read Han opposite a series of actresses, the space cowboy character made sense. Ford was never a particularly accomplished actor, one critic dismissing his technique as 'a small but familiar repertoire of apologetic shrugs, hesitations and lopsided smiles,' but the mocking braggadocio of the young blockade runner came naturally to him.

Lucas still wasn't convinced. 'He really wanted Christopher Walken for Han,' says Willard Huyck. The thirty-two-year-old Walken, with his crooked, sleepy smile and air of manic malevolence, struck everyone as an odd choice. 'Very evil, but with a sort of eccentric look,' says Huyck, 'a delicious quality that was sort of extraterrestrial.' Then little-known except for a small role in Sidney Lumet's *The Anderson Tapes*, Walken had just finished Paul Mazursky's *Next Stop Greenwich Village*. He went on the shortlist for Han Solo, and remained there until late in the casting. As soon as Lucas decided against him, Woody Allen cast Walken as Annie's suicidal brother in *Annie Hall* who confesses his urge to drive right into the headlights of an approaching car.

Lucas recalled, 'I saw an actor every five or ten minutes – for six months.' Diane Crittenden said frankly, 'We were looking for people who would work for no money. We contacted colleges and drama schools. We had boxes and boxes of pictures that came in unsolicited.' Crittenden pressed for John Travolta as Han, but Lucas thought him too much of an individual. He briefly considered a Eurasian Leia opposite black actor Glynn Turman, who'd attracted attention in one of the many *American Graffiti* clones, *Cooley High*. The idea died when he became worried that audiences might read Han's early scorn of Leia as being due to racial prejudice.

Cindy Williams lobbied Roos for the role of Leia. She'd done well out of *American Graffiti*, winning a role in the TV sitcom *Laverne and Shirley*, but that, and her age, made her less attractive to Lucas. As well as hoping to avoid using anyone from the earlier film, he still remembered the prepubescent Leia of his earlier drafts. Williams found herself rejected with a humiliating, 'We want a young Cindy Williams.' Ex-*Penthouse* centerfold Terri Nunn was briefly in the running, but Lucas felt she lacked the arrogance and abrasiveness needed for Leia. Marcia recommended thirteen-year-old Jodie Foster, who played a shoplifting teenager in *Alice Doesn't Live Here Any More*, and who Scorsese had chosen as the teenage hooker in *Taxi Driver*. Lucas screen-tested her, but felt her coltishness wasn't right for the part. After the first weeks, he had seen nobody with the tomboy quality Leia needed. As a test, he handed some of them a heavy .45 pistol. Most couldn't even hold the weapon convincingly, let alone shoot it.

Once it became known that Lucas and Roos were auditioning unknowns, other directors in search of new talent asked to sit in on the interviews. Brian De Palma was looking for girls for *Carrie*, his adaptation of Stephen King's novel about a high-school girl with psychic powers, and Spielberg wanted someone for the wife of Richard Dreyfuss in *Close Encounters* – eventually Teri Garr.

Sometimes it seemed every good-looking girl in Hollywood was waiting to see these young directors. Scores of hopefuls were marched through the office at Goldwyn. De Palma and Lucas agreed between themselves that one of them would open the ritualized conversations of such meetings and the other close it, but some candidates were so unpromising that they were still groping for their résumés when one of the pair interrupted with the standard, 'Well, we're not deciding anything today. Thanks for coming in.'

Sex was all over New Hollywood, as readily available as the omnipresent cocaine, itself a sexual stimulant and aid to male endurance. Marcia and Lucas discussed the fact that, during casting, he would be exposed to some of Hollywood's most attractive women, many of whom had got where they were on their backs, not their talent. They agreed that, should either of them have an extra-marital affair, they would confess it to the other; but nothing was further from Lucas's mind, a fact dramatized when he tested Amy Irving. A foxy-eyed young Lauren Bacall lookalike with masses of dark hair, Irving well knew herself to be both attractive and intelligent. DePalma wasn't blind to her appeal, and eventually cast her in *Carrie* and, later, *Fury*. Spielberg, who was sitting in on the auditions that day, also sensed her sexual challenge. Only Lucas was indifferent, dismissing her as too glamorous and knowing for *Star Wars*. Spielberg, however, was smitten. Later, he confessed to Julia Phillips, 'I met a heartbreaker last night.' Shortly after, Irving became his lover, then, after a stormy relationship, his wife.

It was Roos who proposed Carrie Fisher as Leia. The daughter of Eddie Fisher and Debbie Reynolds, and just twenty, she'd kept a puppyish plumpness that made her look younger, an attribute she'd used in her one movie role, a single scene in Hal Ashby's *Shampoo*. Warren Beatty played a priapic Hollywood hairdresser, Fisher the daughter of Lee Grant, one of Beatty's 'heads.' Finding him in the kitchen as she walks in after a game of tennis, she divines his character instantly and, over milk and cookies, asks curtly, 'Wanna fuck?' Even at just five feet two inches, she had a body sufficiently impressive for Matthew Robbins to provisionally cast her in a film he wanted to make about models, and despite reservations about her weight, Lucas put her on the *Star Wars* shortlist.

For Luke, his alter ego in the film, Lucas wanted someone who replicated his relationship with Allen Grant back in Modesto; who would exist happily in Solo's shadow but still contribute in the fight against the Evil Empire. Mark Hamill had been in television for five years, including a regular stint in the daily soap *General Hospital* and a starring role in a series called *The Texas Wheelers,* as one son of an indolent and scheming Jack Elam; another son was Gary Busey, whom Milius used in *Big Wednesday.* ABC pulled the show in October 1974 after airing only four episodes, so by the summer of 1975 Hamill needed work badly enough to submit to a cattle-call audition.

'There were guys literally everywhere,' he says, 'in age from sixteen to thirty-five.' At twenty-four, Hamill was still fresh-faced and blond, a classic California beachboy. He thought he was up for the part of the high-school Lothario in *Carrie,* eventually played by John Travolta. 'They weren't going to let us read; you had to look right first. So I walked in, and [De Palma and Lucas] were both sitting there. Brian said, "So tell us a little about yourself." And I went through the litany. George didn't say anything. I thought he was Brian's gofer or something. In fifteen minutes, it was all over.'

But Hamill's naïveté impressed Lucas. He told Diane Crittenden he had an 'all-American boy' quality that fitted the character of Luke. A few days later, Hamill received six pages of script – from *Star Wars,* not *Carrie* – and instructions to return for a video test. His hopes rose, though he was, it turned out, only one of fifty called back. They included Nick Nolte, considered for Han, and William Katt, though Lucas's early favorite for Luke was Will Seltzer, another fugitive from television whose first series, *Karen,* had just collapsed.

Paul LeMat implies he also had an offer to play Han. 'The worst decision I ever made was in 1976,' he said. 'I was working for the man who was running for District Attorney so I didn't wanna leave town during the primary season in 1976. And guess what movie they were making in London in 1976? Of course I thought at the time George Lucas would continue directing so it was only a matter of time before he would want me for another movie. Lo and behold, he quit directing.' But no other evidence suggests LeMat was a serious candidate for any part in *Star Wars.*

Hamill couldn't believe the script. 'Han Solo says, "Look, I've held up my side of the bargain. I'm turning this ship round," and I say, "But we can't turn back! Fear is their greatest defence. I doubt that the actual security there is any greater than it was on Aquileia or Salis, and what there is is probably directed against a large-scale assault." Who talks like that?'

Carrie Fisher called her test dialogue 'space triple-talk, killer lines.' Hauled onto the bridge of the Empire's flagship after her capture, Leia has to tell Grand Moff Tarkin, 'Oh, Governor Tarkin. I should have expected to find you holding Vader's leash. I recognized your foul stench when I was brought on board.' For the first take, the line came out, 'Omigod, I came on board and there was this smell, and of course it turns out to be you.' Lucas took her aside and said, 'This is all very real and very serious.' Lucas visualized Leia, despite her size and youth, acting and thinking like the queen she would become. 'He wanted me to be proud and frightening,' says Fisher, who never managed the transformation. 'I was not a damsel in distress; I was a distressing damsel.'

Fisher agreed to deliver the dialogue she was given, but Harrison Ford, whom Lucas called back to test with Hamill, refused. 'You can *type* this shit,' he told Lucas, 'but you can't *say* it.' For the test, he and Hamill condensed their lines to something like conversation. Occasionally, Lucas refused to let them alter a line he felt particularly meaningful. After a few such cases, Hamill said, 'George, how about I do the dialogue, but I won't *listen* to it?' Lucas agreed.

Hamill never overcame his contempt for the *Star Wars* trilogy. 'These movies didn't give me much pride in my craft,' he said. 'I had to act on stage to get that. Special-effects movies are hard on actors. You find yourself giving an impassioned speech to a big lobster in a flight suit. Only later do you see how silly it looks.'

Nervous about a cast of near-unknowns, Alan Ladd Jr urged Lucas to include somebody better known in the cast, if only in a supporting role. The most obvious was Obi-Wan Kenobi. A late addition, he replaced old General Skywalker. Since he had to explain the film's mystical subtext, the script made him an improbable amalgamation of guru, shaman, magician, warrior, father figure and god, with a little Dr Dolittle thrown in. When the part had had more action and less rhetoric, Lucas imagined Toshiro Mifune in the role, but now he needed someone with gravitas.

Conveniently, Alec Guinness was doing one of his rare Hollywood stints, playing the butler Bensonmum in *Murder by Death,* Neil Simon's spoof of country-house murder mysteries. Roos had a *Star Wars* script delivered direct to his trailer at Columbia. Famously described as 'an empty bottle' who didn't come to life until he assumed a role, Guinness was sixty-two, but still a comparatively minor name as far as Hollywood was concerned, despite his Best Actor Academy Award for *Bridge on the River Kwai* in 1957. Playing Prince Feisal in David Lean's 1962 *Lawrence of Arabia* made him briefly fashionable, and in between that film and Lean's *Doctor Zhivago* in 1965, he played the philosopher-emperor Marcus Aurelius in Anthony Mann's *The Fall of the Roman Empire.* Otherwise, he worked mostly in Britain, and on stage. His film reputation rested largely on Ealing comedies like *The Lavender Hill Mob,* which he'd made in the forties, and which still played on TV – a sore point with Guinness, who got no residuals from them.

By no means as reticent and formal as he seemed, he'd spent a dangerous World War II in the navy, and was delighted to be offered a film role that offered a physical challenge. According to his friend Peter Ustinov, Guinness had been so piqued that another actor dared compete with him for the role of Hitler in the 1973 *Hitler: The Last Ten Days* that 'he rented a Hitler outfit from a celebrated costumier, made up with his usual brilliance, and went into the London streets in the vicinity of Little Venice, to have photos made of himself as Hitler. He strode, his hands clasped before him, he ranted, he gazed over the canal as though it marked the jagged peaks of Berchtesgaden, he saluted the raging crowd at the Nuremberg rally, he enjoyed moments of relaxation with Eva, and picked up imaginary babies to bestow prickly kisses on their innocent cheeks. And, being Alec Guinness, he attracted not the slightest attention among the passers-by.'

After checking out Lucas with friends who told him of *American Graffiti*'s enormous success, Guinness agreed to a lunch on his last day in Hollywood. Awed, Lucas said barely a word, which recommended him to the star, who promised to think about the role if Kurtz and Lucas rethought the money – the $1000 a week everyone else was receiving would certainly not tempt him, unless they threw in a share in the profits. Guinness wouldn't finally agree to take the part until almost the first day of shooting, and his 2¼ per cent of the producers' 40 per cent would make him one of Britain's richest actors.

With the casting of Guinness, Lucas effectively recreated his child-hood on film: a world of stern fathers, loving but distant mothers, and wayward but essentially good-natured boys, too decent – and too busy – for sex. A *Flash Gordon* with no Dale Arden; with Ming the Merci-less, but no Princess Aura.

Its certainties contrasted with those of his own personal life. While he was casting, Scorsese asked Marcia to cut *Taxi Driver* with him in New York. She agreed, which sent Lucas into a jealous panic. In Manhattan, she would be exposed to all the excesses for which Scorsese and Schrader, not to mention the city, were famed: dope, sex, a generally excessive lifestyle. Why, he suggested, couldn't she stay in San Anselmo and get pregnant? Marcia countered that she had her own career to think of, and that while she wanted children, Lucas had hardly been around enough during the last year to conceive one.

Lucas wanted her to cut *Star Wars*, but Marcia pointed out that, with the film still obviously not ready, there would be plenty of time for that. She told Scorsese she'd do *Taxi Driver*, and flew to New York. Spielberg was in town, pursuing John Belushi to star in *1941*. He dropped in at the cutting room, obviously in awe of Scorsese, and respectful of what he and Marcia were doing. The gap between people like Scorsese and Schrader, the true believers, rigidly devoted to seri-ous, adult films, and the triviality of *Star Wars* struck her forcibly.

Later, Schrader would bemoan the split between Lucas and Spiel-berg on one side, and Scorsese, Milius, and Coppola on the other, which started to open around 1975. 'We came up full of piss and vinegar and politicization,' he said, 'and we really felt that we were going to create a new brand of movies. Now, if you look at the film-makers of my generation – Walter Hill, Phil Kaufman, John Milius, George Lucas, Spielberg – by and large you see a kind of middle-age creeping in, a kind of establishment attitude and a lack of eagerness to take risks and challenge and upset.'

'Put Some More Light on the Dog'

Another fine mess you've got me into, Stanley.
Oliver Hardy to Stan Laurel, *passim*

When Charley Lippincott finished with *Family Plot*, Lucas tried to hire him as a special publicist and marketing expert, paid by Fox, but responsible only to the production. Fox protested that it had plenty of publicists already, any one of whom could handle *Star Wars*; but Lucas's previous experiences had made him adamant about having his own people in positions of power. Under protest, Fox accepted Lippincott, but only if he worked on a couple of their films as a test. He spent two weeks with Fox productions, one of which, a biopic about rocker Buddy Holly, he was instrumental in closing down because of irregularities in the location shooting. After that, Fox admitted Lippincott knew his business, and late in 1975 he became one of the first employees of Star Wars Corporation, as vice president in charge of marketing.

'They weren't sure when they were going to start the movie,' says Lippincott. 'ILM was functioning, but George and Gary were paying for it out of their own pocket, because Fox wouldn't, since there wasn't yet an official start for the production.' Fox was still fretting over whether or not to back the film. Ladd trusted Lucas to deliver on time and budget, but his financial comptroller Ray Gosnell counselled caution. From a high point of $13 million, the budget had retreated to $10.5 million, $3 million of it for special effects, but Gosnell still thought this too high, and though Kurtz's provident deal with Elstree helped pare it back to $7,887,000, doubts remained.

Remembering how Lippincott had compiled a reel of experimental films to nail down Warners-Seven Arts' backing of *THX1138*, Lucas suggested they prepare a visual aid on *Star Wars*. Technical artist Ralph McQuarrie came back to mind, and Lucas commissioned a series of paintings to convey how the film might look on screen. In three weeks, McQuarrie came up with a set of sketches which he refined into five paintings in acrylic and gouache, twenty-two inches long by ten inches high, to suggest the effect of wide-screen.

McQuarrie worked only from descriptions and the current version of the script, so his paintings crystallize Lucas's vision of *Star Wars* at the end of 1975. Debts to *Metropolis*, *Dune*, and Kurosawa are still evident. C-3PO resembles the robot figure from Lang's film, the desert backgrounds suggest *Dune*'s Arrakis, and the fight scenes between robed figures wielding light sabers are straight from *Yojimbo*.

Lippincott made fifteen copies of each set of pictures, and placed them in black vinyl portfolios sealed with a label printed 'The Star Wars.' In December 1975, Ladd submitted them, and the project, to Fox's CEO Dennis Stanfill and the board. Ladd's presentation, delivered in his trademark near-inaudible voice, convinced almost everyone, but McQuarrie's paintings, the originals of which Ladd propped up around the boardroom, played a key role. Just as an 'architect's impression' of a new building, meticulous down to the last tree and artfully posed group of residents, doesn't reveal a shortage of elevators or insufficient parking, the cool pastels and shadowless golden light of the visualizations gave no hint that the figure of C-3PO or the blades of the light sabers might be difficult to film.

The board's objections were minor. One was the title. Couldn't they find a better one than 'The Star Wars?' 'Give us a list,' said Lucas curtly when this was passed on, 'and we'll think about it.' Nobody did, and the question never arose again, though Lucas did decide, after the film was in production, to drop 'The.'

Star Wars' only opponent on the Fox board was the sole African-American, John H. Johnson, publisher of *Ebony*, *Jet*, and other magazines for the black community. His objection was understandable. Not a black, Hispanic or Asian face would be seen in the first of the trilogy, just as, in *THX1138*, the only blacks had been creations of TV: 'holograms,' lumbering and non-human.

Anybody who knew Lucas would not have been surprised. The *Star Wars* universe would be Modesto writ large, without nations, without societies, and without blacks – indeed, mostly without common people of any color: warrior elites fight the battles, and all we see of the rest are bandits and scavengers. The Rebel Alliance's members are manly, forthright, decent, healthy, clean-limbed, sensibly dressed, pious, and, except for Alec Guinness and Anthony Daniels, the voice of C-3PO, American. Those of the Empire are rigid, uniformed, devious, masked, occasionally deformed, and, from Ian McDiarmid's Senator Palpatine, later the Emperor, voiced by Clive Revill, through Peter Cushing's Grand Moff Tarkin, to Kenneth Colley's Admiral Piett, Julian Glover's General Veers, and assorted officers, British to the heels of their jackboots.

Even after the board's endorsement, Fox continued to haggle over minor points. Final approval only came through on New Year's Day 1976, to the enormous relief of Lucas and Kurtz; at least if the film never got made, this committed Fox to covering the $1 million already spent from their own pockets.

The end of casting left Lucas with two possible teams: Christopher Walken, Terri Nunn, and Will Seltzer; or Harrison Ford, Mark Hamill, and Carrie Fisher. Since some of the others by then were already committed elsewhere, Lucas chose Ford, Hamill, and Fisher, all of whom could start shooting in London in March. Harrison Ford got his revenge for the humiliating circumstances of his casting. He accepted $1000 a week ('This was promoted as a low-budget movie,' he said curtly. 'It certainly was – for actors'), but refused to sign for two sequels. Out of fear at being trapped grinding out joyless carbons of this trivial story, he vastly increased his income from the remaining two films of the trilogy.

Lucas immediately sent Fisher to a health farm to shed ten pounds – 'Like losing a leg to someone of my build,' she complained. Fat remained a problem until she discovered cocaine, which had the useful side-effect of reducing her appetite, and the more long-term one of putting her in the Betty Ford Clinic. Harrison Ford kept working at his carpentry right up to leaving for England. He was renovating the actress Sally Kellerman's kitchen, and, confident he'd be back in a couple of weeks, left the job half-finished. Once it was clear he'd gone for good, Kellerman moved his tools, ladder, and paint pots to the garage, and painted 'Harrison Ford Left These' on the wall above.

In London, John Barry started constructing the sets. Shepperton's

'H' Stage would house the hall where Leia honors her champions. It was an enormous expense for a few minutes of screen time, but Lucas sensed the film needed such a finale, a reminder that Han and Luke weren't lone adventurers but representatives of a movement encompassing planets. In the end, he couldn't afford enough extras to fill the space. Most are cardboard cut-outs.

He also cut corners on weaponry. The laser pistols were facsimile World War I 'broomhandle' Mauser automatic pistols, and the Imperial stormtroopers' automatic weapons rebuilt war-surplus Sterling 9mm submachine guns filled with blanks to give a realistic kick. These ejected streams of shell casings which, Lucas assumed, could be erased optically – a vain hope, since they can clearly be seen bouncing on the ground in some of the Death Star scenes.

Barry used Elstree's two largest stages for the spaceport at Mos Eisley and the Death Star interior. The rest of the sets were corridors, down which people in *Star Wars* spend an inordinate amount of time running. This faithfully reflected the cheese-paring style of early movie serials, but the claustrophobic effect would return to haunt Lucas, and for the 1997 Special Edition reissue, newly-sophisticated special effects added windows, and glimpses of the universe outside.

Naval engineers in Portsmouth built Han Solo's ship, the *Millennium Falcon*, and shipped it to Elstree in sixteen sections. Modelmaker Colin Cantwell had produced a series of designs, including one for the *Falcon*, but Lucas rejected them as too streamlined, though they would find more favor with him when he made *Part I: The Phantom Menace*. In particular, the *Falcon* looked like a spaceship used for the British TV series *Space 1999*; it was adapted into the blockade runner which is the first vessel seen in the complete film. In its place, Lucas suggested a sort of flying saucer, something like a hamburger – a flattened sphere with a division around the edge, maybe with a pickle-like ovoid off to one side for the bridge. Cantwell's modelmakers elaborated on this, adding two 'horns,' which suggest the burger had a slice of pizza sandwiched inside. Another vehicle was supposedly inspired by two chilli dogs lying in a fast-food joint's standard cardboard tray.

To emphasize the contrast between the gleaming black and gray of the Imperial fleet's interiors and the vessels of the Rebel Alliance, Lucas told the design crew to dirty everything up. They added rust and grease to the *Falcon* and other ships, which in any event were already painted an overall matte-gray on the outside, since any light reflected from a model would show up as a hole, and would expose the blue screen against which the model was photographed. Technicians also nicked, scraped, scuffed, and scarred R2-D2, as well as the white armor of the stormtroopers. Before each take, actors rolled in the dust until their clothes looked as if they'd slept in them. To make sure everyone shared the same sense of style, Kurtz made the design staff watch *Fellini Satyricon*, which depicted imperial Rome as squalid, grimy, and crumbling. He also showed them *THX1138*, to general bafflement: 'That isn't the George Lucas I know,' said John Stears, who designed the light saber and the film's robots, including C-3PO.

Since 90 per cent of *Star Wars*' costumes were uniforms, Kurtz hired John Mollo, who advised Stanley Kubrick on the uniforms for *Barry Lyndon* and was an expert military historian, though inexperienced in other areas of film. He modelled the Imperial uniforms on those of the Japanese army of the 1920s. For the rest, he was content to be guided by Lucas, who urged him to see some Kurosawa and Eisenstein movies, and provided him with comic-book pages from *Flash Gordon*.

Mollo had little to do with the film's most memorable costume, Darth Vader's helmet and robes. These were conceived by Ralph McQuarrie, who'd gone onto the payroll and would remain a fixture of Lucasfilm. Lucas, McQuarrie recalls, described Darth Vader as 'coming in like the wind, kind of sneaky, yet big and impressive . . . With the desert setting so prominent, I think George at first envisioned him as a Bedouin-like character. He suggested that maybe Vader could be in a silk robe that always fluttered as he came in, and he might have his face covered with black silk and have some kind of big helmet like a Japanese warrior. I reminded George that the first time we see Vader, he's boarding one spaceship from another, and I asked, "How's he going to breathe out there in space?!" So my illustrations show a breathing mask with a downward-curving snout and big goggles. John Barry and his designers developed it still further with a mask that gave Vader a tremendously monumental stature, and I think George felt that keeping Vader always in his mask would be fascinating – like an actor in an old Greek tragedy. But it all came to pass because I thought he needed a mask to breathe.'

McQuarrie visualized Leia in a skin-tight suit with a gunbelt hung low over her hips, but Lucas wanted her demure. Mollo's softly draped white robe with a kirtle was straight out of *Prince Valiant*. He topped it with a wig copied from Princess Fria's in Alex Raymond's strip *Flash Gordon in the Ice Kingdom of Mongo*, complete with coiled plaits over the ears. A bra would have looked anachronistic under such a costume, so Fisher's ample breasts were restrained with adhesive gaffer tape, every film's all-purpose fix-it material.

Harrison Ford refused to wear his outfit. By McQuarrie, and also inspired by Alex Raymond, it made Solo a dandy in elegantly tailored clothes with a favorite *Flash Gordon* fashion feature, a high pink collar. Ford preferred black trousers shoved into high boots, a white shirt, and a vest or lightweight coat in black, with his laser pistol slung low on his hip – an intergalactic gunfighter. As Luke Skywalker, Mark Hamill wore tight white trousers and boots under a Japanese-style tunic with a tie belt, made from a plain rough fabric normally used for lining curtains. To many people, Mollo's Oscar for the *Star Wars* costumes seemed as little earned as the one he would win in 1983 for *Gandhi* – 'For what?' queried journalist Rex Reed sarcastically on that occasion. 'Wrinkled sheets, burlap sacks and loincloths?'

Other costumes and masks were devised by Stuart Freeborn, who also handled special make-ups, particularly those for the scene closest to Lucas's heart, in Mos Eisley's cantina. A veteran who'd created Alec Guinness's controversial make-up for Fagin in David Lean's 1948 *Oliver Twist*, a parody of the hook-nosed Jew so exaggerated that American distributors at first refused to release the film, Freeborn had also worked on *Dr Strangelove* and the pioneering apeman make-ups for *2001: A Space Odyssey*.

Since nobody was left in Elstree's special-effects department, Freeborn used the studio's old schoolroom, a relic from the days of child actors, to set up his own workshop with his wife Kay, his son Graham, Nick Maley, Charles Parker, Chris Tucker, and Sylvia Croft. Lucas, too busy to conceive make-up designs, left it to them. Stuart Freeborn visualized the creatures, Graham modelled the masks in clay, and the whole team worked on turning the originals into foam latex shapes. Parker, with Tucker, who'd begun his career at Madame Tussaud's waxworks and went on to model John Hurt's face and body for *The Elephant Man* and the werewolves of *The Company of Wolves*, mounted them on polystyrene skulls, painted them and fitted them to the performers. Croft added the teeth.

Lucas visualized a crime boss named Jabba the Hutt. Slug-like, but the size of a cow, Jabba would be a major villain, and the nemesis of Han Solo. As models, he gave Freeborn some photographs of giant insect larvae, bloated with eggs, and a queen bee surrounded by solicitous drones. Freeborn put off constructing this elaborate creature. For the scene where Jabba and his men waylay Han as he's about to leave Tatooine with Luke and Kenobi, Lucas shot a burly actor in furs playing Jabba, intending to superimpose the monster later, but Freeborn never designed Jabba, let alone tried to build him, and Lucas dropped the scene.

To light the film, Lucas retained Geoffrey Unsworth, the amiable cameraman who'd shot *2001: A Space Odyssey*, *Cabaret*, and *Murder on the Orient Express*, but at the last minute Unsworth elected to shoot *A Matter of Time* in Rome for Vincente Minnelli. Gil Taylor replaced him. Kubrick's cameraman on *Dr Strangelove*, Taylor also shot Roman Polanski's *Macbeth*, and *Frenzy* for Hitchcock, but his speciality was black-and-white, and he had no experience of or interest in genre pieces like *Star Wars*. Moreover, working with the doctrinaire and humorless Kubrick had soured him on American directors. Before *Strangelove*, Kubrick even submitted Taylor to a test, quizzing him on technique, and checking his answers in a copy of the trade magazine *American Cinematographer*, an insult Taylor never forgave. In Lucas and Kurtz, both unsmiling and earnest, he felt he saw Kubrick all over again.

The greatest drain on Lucas's pocket, and the least productive, was Industrial Light and Magic. In twelve months, John Dykstra had created more problems than he solved. Every new development in computer or camera technology instigated a wave of tinkering and retro-fitting which slowed down progress still further. Fox kept an eye on ILM's expenses, but, not understanding the first thing about special effects, concentrated on trying to monitor the cost of converting the Van Nuys space and paying Dykstra's seventy-five eager but often maladroit young helpers. Arguments about stationery and film stock raged between Dykstra and Fox's accountants.

Relations weren't helped when a contingent of studio suits arrived one day to find Dykstra, a startling figure in shorts, with hair long enough to sit on, raising a refrigerator towards the roof of the warehouse on a forklift, then, cheered on by his staff, letting it crash to the floor. The ageing unit had failed, they explained, and everyone kinda wondered how it would sound dropped onto concrete.

In the parking lot, production manager Jim Nelson installed a giant container from a World War II surplus store as an improvised swimming pool. ILMers rigged a 747 escape chute to the roof and greased it with cooking oil. One lunchtime, as staff in their underwear were lining up to take a plunge, Alan Ladd Jr and Fox executives Jay Kanter and Gareth Wigan arrived. A technician wearing an alien fish-head mask directed them to Nelson. 'We were way behind schedule, way over budget,' says Nelson. 'They were not happy. I told them the place was like an oven. We went into the building and fortunately it was about 120 degrees in there. The tour didn't take long, and they all got back into their air-conditioned limo. I think they thought it was good for employee relations to let us keep the pool.'

Ladd sent over two of Hollywood's senior special-effects men, Linwood Dunn and John Love, to report on the facility. 'I have no doubt that you guys can do the work,' Dunn told Dykstra's deputy Richard Edlund, 'but what you really need here is somebody to help you schedule.' Scheduling was the last thing on their mind, however, and the advice went unheeded.

Even Lucas was roused to shouting as 1975 became 1976, and it was increasingly clear that the Dykstraflex equipment wouldn't be ready in time. He decided to shoot the film with old-fashioned travelling matte, and told Dykstra to produce back-projection 'plates' – short film clips – of starry space and dogfights against which he could film his actors at Elstree. Scenic artists were set to work painting scenes on glass at $5000 a plate. Just before Lucas and Kurtz left for London, Dykstra delivered some film, but, to Lucas's fury, it was unusable. 'The ships looked like little cardboard cut-outs,' he said, 'and the lasers were big and fat, and looked awful.' After hurried discussion with line producer Robert Watts, he decided to start shooting with the Tunisian sequences, hoping that would give Barry time to finish his sets.

In the midst of this sea of problems, Lucas continued adjusting the script to his cast and his budget. The Revised Fourth Draft, dated 15 January 1976, is almost the film as shot. After all his sorting through other sources, Lucas had returned for his story to the oldest of cinema's traditional models and structures, the western. At every turn, the story recalled *Rio Bravo, Shane,* and particularly *The Magnificent Seven.* Luke is the callow young gunman; Kenobi the tough old sheriff; Han Solo a gambler, experienced beyond his years and apparently interested only in money until the chips are down. Add the evil, sneering villain, inevitably in black; the spunky young heroine; Solo's monosyllabic redskin pal; and a couple of bumbling Mexicans for comic relief, and the recipe's complete. In the *Los Angeles Times,* Charles Champlin would write, 'The sidekicks are salty, squatty robots instead of leathery old cowpokes who scratch their whiskers and say "Aw shucks" a lot, and the gunfighters square off with laser swords instead of Colt revolvers. But it is all and gloriously one, the mythic and simple world of the good guys vs the bad guys, the rustlers and the land grabbers, the old generation saving the young with a last heroic gesture, which drives home the message of courage and conviction.'

While Lucas geared up for the first days' shooting of *Star Wars,* Coppola was in the last stages of preparing *Apocalypse Now.* He, his family, and his crew left to start principal photography in the Philippines on 1 April 1976, almost the day Lucas began work at Elstree; but Coppola wouldn't finish until May 1977, practically the day *Star Wars* opened in American cinemas. Both films had disastrous production periods which left their directors physically and emotionally depleted, but after that, the results would be very different. *Star Wars* made Lucas rich and famous, a force in New Hollywood, while *Apocalypse Now* just as effectively terminated Coppola's power.

In London, despite the meager fee offered – a flat $1000 a week for featured players, and Equity minimum for the rest – numerous actors turned up to audition for *Star Wars.* Most couldn't afford to pick and choose. British cinema admissions were down thirteen million from the year before, and the only movies being made were modest filmed stage plays and an apparently inexhaustible succession of scaled-up TV series.

The gossip about *Star Wars* wasn't promising. In December 1975, *Newsweek* published a round-up of new Hollywood science fiction which described it as 'a $9 million movie about a juvenile gang rumble against Fascist oppressors of the galaxy.' Lucas was quoted as calling it 'a shoot-'em-up with rayguns.' Peter Cushing, veteran of numerous horror films, agreed to play Grand Moff Tarkin, but apart from Alec

Guinness he was the only well-known name in the cast. Eddie Byrne and Bill Hootkins belonged to London's American expatriate community. Jeremy Sinden, Dennis Lawson and Ken Colley had survived working for Ken Russell. None of them imagined *Star Wars* as more than the futuristic gang-war film described in *Newsweek*.

Since the costumes of Darth Vader, Chewbacca, and the two robots did most of the acting, few performers would become so famous and yet remain so anonymous as the men who played them. Dave Prowse, a six-foot six-inch-tall weightlifter, held the title of Britain's Strongest Man from 1965 to 1970, after which he became a competitor in professional Highland games, tossing tree-trunks and stone cannon-balls. He'd made his film debut in 1967 as Frankenstein's monster in the brawl that concluded Charles Feldman's chaotic *Casino Royale*, and repeated the role in *Horror of Frankenstein* and *Frankenstein and the Monster from Hell*. In between, he played hangmen, torturers, and strongmen, almost never speaking a line, since his Devon drawl contrasted comically with his massive frame. Spotted by Stanley Kubrick's casting director demonstrating exercise equipment in Harrods department store, Prowse appeared, again mostly mute, in *A Clockwork Orange* as the athletic male nurse to a paralyzed Patrick Magee – his finest hour until *Star Wars*.

Lucas, who'd never seen Prowse in anything but *Clockwork Orange*, offered him a choice of Vader or Chewbacca. Hoping to escape from faceless roles, Prowse didn't need to hear more than that Chewbacca would spend the whole film in a suit of angora wool and yak hair before deciding on Vader. He only learned at his first costume fitting that he'd be just as invisible as Vader, a fact that rankles to this day.

To achieve the effect of McQuarrie's drawings of Vader, John Mollo rummaged through a British costume warehouse and came up with a German World War II steel helmet, a set of motorcycle leathers, a monk's cloak and a gasmask. The headgear metamorphosed into a glossy plastic helmet recalling one worn by the invading German knights in *Alexander Nevsky*, crossed with a Japanese *mempo* war mask. 'It was very hot,' says Prowse. 'The trousers were quilted leather with a seam all the way down, on top of which I wore four layers of canvas and leather, then a breastplate and two cloaks, one of which was left off at the end. At first my head turned around in the mask without it moving, so they padded it with foam rubber.'

Graham Freeborn told Nick Maley he was having trouble with the character of Chewbacca. The tallest man they could find was six feet ten, and Freeborn was contemplating putting him into high boots and adding a false skull to reach the height demanded by Lucas. Maley remembered an amiable giant who'd played the Minotaur in Ray Harryhausen's *Sinbad and the Eye of the Tiger*, and the part went to Peter Mayhew, a seven-foot two-inch hospital porter, the second-tallest man in Britain; the tallest, Chris Greenaway, was an accountant, and not interested in a film career. Like Prowse, Mayhew would never be seen, since the role of Chewbacca, like that of Snug in the play within a play in *A Midsummer Night's Dream*, is 'nothing but roaring.' One of Maley's first jobs was transforming Mayhew. Chewbacca's similarity to Marcia's malemute, who'd inspired the character, was more than casual. Lucas supplied Freeborn with a photograph of the dog and asked him to copy it.

Ralph McQuarrie had already sketched Chewbacca, Vader, the stormtroopers, the two robots, and Greedo, the killer who confronts Han Solo in the cantina and is killed by him. The other creatures had no names, so the maskmakers created some. These stuck until Lucasfilm, to satisfy the hunger of fans for information on every aspect of the film, christened the characters and gave them personal histories. Mutant humans with split noses had been simply 'Uglies' to the mask unit, but the barman retrospectively became 'Wuher,' the one who picks a fight with Luke 'Ponda Baba,' and the one at the end of the bar with a hookah 'Dannik Jerriko.' Two of the creatures first called 'snaggletooths' were renamed 'Takeel' and 'Zutton,' and two 'croakers' became 'Hrchek Kal Fas' and 'Sai'torr Kal Fas.' Freeborn's 'rat alien' became 'Snitch Garindan.' A 'bat alien' was christened 'Kabe,' and a 'fly alien' 'Tzizvvt.'

Much of the make-up was cheap, and looked it. Combing the film later, eagle-eyed fans found numerous examples of characters with one alien claw and one human hand, or of real eyes glimpsed through fake ones. The Greedo who draws on Solo isn't the same Greedo who explodes when he's shot; for that, Freeborn made up a dummy that, like the film's many casual make-ups created 'on the day,' doesn't stand much scrutiny. The 'sand people' who attack Luke in the desert, later dignified as 'Tusken Raiders,' and the Jawas who scavenge the two robots, employed monks' robes from the costume store, in plentiful supply in an industry where three or four horror films or fantasies with medieval settings were usually in production somewhere. To make them look alien, Freeborn added rough masks, or, in the case of the Jawas, improbable glowing eyes.

A succession of short people tried out for R2. Lucas chose Kenny Baker, more for his size – at three foot seven inches, he was the shortest man in Britain – than for any talent, since he would be neither seen nor heard inside the dustbin-shaped shell designed by British toymaker Tony Dyson.

Lucas visualized his two comic 'droids as the cybernetic equivalent of the comedy team of Bud Abbott and Lou Costello. R2-D2, like Costello, would be short and fat, emitting cartoon-like peeps and whines when distressed, while C-3PO would be Abbott, fast-talking, wisecracking, with a pronounced New York accent. Their relationship replicated that between Lucas the tinkerer and various 'big brother' figures like Allen Grant and Francis Coppola; Lucas himself even made R2-type noises from time to time. After the film was released, Lucas recorded 'biographies' for its characters as background for the artists drawing the comic-book versions. R2-D2 was 'primarily a repair robot,' he explained. 'Essentially he is just a plumber' – very much Lucas's vision of himself as a teenager in Modesto.

C-3PO was more difficult to cast. Knowing Lucas wanted someone who could 'do' a robot, casting agents sent mimes rather than actors. Lucas was sitting through yet another interminable impression of a clockwork man winding down when Anthony Daniels arrived. Daniels could actually act. After drama school, he spent six months with BBC radio's repertory company, doing voices in everything from sitcoms to Shakespeare, before joining London's leading youth theatre, the Young Vic. He was playing one of Tom Stoppard's (and *Hamlet*'s) strolling players in its revival of *Rosencrantz and Guildenstern are Dead*, but, more important, doubling as the English ambassador to the court of Denmark, when he tried out for *Star Wars*.

Daniels sat patiently while Lucas, ignoring him, made notes about the departing performer. When they finally talked, both were non-committal. Daniels wasn't sure he wanted to play a machine. As for Lucas, he remained wedded to an American C-3PO, though once he met Daniels, the idea of a fastidious, prissy diplomatic robot with a cut-glass English voice took hold. He called him back for a second audition, during which they discussed McQuarrie's paintings. Looking at McQuarrie's vision of C-3PO, like a gilded boy from an eighteenth-century opera, Daniels asked wistfully, 'Could I play him?' Lucas smiled and said, 'Sure.' 'It was months and months later,' says Daniels, 'that I found out that he hated what I was doing. He kept thinking that he could change it later.'

The robot's thirty-pound outer shell rode on a full-length skin-tight vinyl suit. Daniels submitted to a full-body plastercast to fit the costume, then had to do a second when the first went wrong. His body was shaved, leaving him to scratch his way through the remaining performances of *Rosencrantz*. Meanwhile, C-3PO's outer skin was manufactured from plates of fiberglass; Tunisia's heat would melt plastic.

In Tunisia, June to August is hot and dry. Temperatures can rise to 90 degrees. From December to February it's cooler, but also wet. Late spring and early summer were the ideal times to shoot. Because of his problems with ILM's sfx plates and John Barry's sets, Lucas was early, and, inevitably, it rained. Desert wadis suddenly became rivers. Trucks were bogged down in salt lakes that turned overnight into swamps. Hotels were disgusting, the food unreliable. Everyone came down with stomach problems, and Stuart Freeborn had to be flown back early to London with pneumonia. He spent two weeks in hospital, during which no work was done on the vital cantina masks. Bunny Alsup too collapsed with dysentery.

Kurtz had allowed eleven days for the Tunisian shoot. On the twelfth, a C130 Hercules would arrive to freight the crew and equipment back to London. Extra time on the ground would be charged at $10,000 a day. With the well-developed sixth sense of the seasoned technician, the crew sensed Lucas's fear. 'I made this movie on the seat of my pants,' he said. 'I didn't really know what I was doing.' All were nonplussed by his habit of wearing a baseball cap, even indoors. Part of the New Hollywood uniform, the caps hadn't yet caught on in England. It made Lucas just a little harder to take seriously. As usual on any British set, the crew referred respectfully to 'the Guv'nor,' but, far from trying to help, they, and particularly Taylor's men, did everything they could to impede Lucas. 'A lot of the English crew, especially Gil Taylor's, were very rough,' says Gloria Katz, who came to Elstree for rewrites after Lucas returned from Tunisia. 'We were there on the set when they were shooting Chewbacca, and they were saying things like, "Put some more light on the dog."' Trying to be diplomatic, Kurtz didn't push Taylor to a showdown, a fact which, Lucas came to feel, disadvantaged the production. It was a process already familiar from Lucas's dealings with other partners, whom he gradually marginalized as their importance to him as 'big brothers' began to diminish.

The sky in Tunisia was often overcast, for which Lucas was grateful, since he sunburned easily. Taylor resorted to traditional camera tricks to render the soggy sands more mysterious. One was shooting through a nylon stocking – a device so antique that the technicians who, twenty years later, were restoring *Star Wars*, spent weeks trying to identify the exotic filter Taylor had used, until Lucas explained. Since they were unable to precisely match the mesh of that particular stocking, they had to write image-processing programs that spread the light as the nylon net did, adding rings of color to give the spectral range.

Mostly, Tunisia provided desert backgrounds – gullies, defiles and dunes for the scenes in which Luke buys and chases the robots, meets Kenobi, and flees with him from the spaceport at Mos Eisley. Near the village of Matmata, on the Mediterranean coast 250 miles south of Tunis, the Berber people had built pit-like dwellings twenty feet deep, with rooms hollowed out of the sides, to escape the heat. One of these became Owen and Beru's house. John Barry designed a low, domed entrance and some 'vaporator' towers, supposedly for extracting moisture from the air, which, scattered across the table-flat landscape, gave it a Tanguy-like effect. The pit dwelling itself offered little more than some attractive mosaics, so he had to fill it with the impedimenta of a twenty-third-century dirt-farmer. Back at Elstree, these scenes were matched with some domestic interiors. Also at Matmata, Lucas shot the exteriors of the bar at the Hôtel Sidi Driss, which would become the Mos Eisley cantina. Kenobi's home was at Chott el-Djerid, a desolate area of stony canyons. It never looked good on film, and one of the 'improvements' of the Special Edition was a painted exterior showing a domed house of castle-like dimensions squatting in the barren wastes. Lucas also envisaged a scene in the Jawa village, set in a complex of four-story-high fortified granaries called *ksars*. 'Little tiny windows, little tiny doors; it was a Hobbit village,' he said. But it simply became too expensive, though he would return to the *ksars* for *The Phantom Menace*.

Both Luke's landspeeder and the tank-like sandcrawler in which the Jawas cruise the desert looking for scrap proved almost useless on location. For the landspeeder, McQuarrie imagined a sleek, finned vehicle, but Lucas revised it into a flat tub with three rear-mounted jet engines. To make it seem to float on a cushion of anti-gravity, a cantilever arm supported it, but no matter how carefully Lucas framed the shot, it never looked convincing. He had to use a version with wheels, hoping they could be erased in the sfx lab. The sandcrawler was superbly designed, a rusting, top-heavy hulk rolling on giant treads, but a windstorm blew the flimsy structure to pieces before Lucas had all his shots. By then, observers in neighboring Libya had complained to Tunisia about a giant military vehicle lurking on its borders. 'There are some wars that have started with less provocation than that,' says Kurtz.

Lucas also hoped to show the fauna of Tatooine, in particular a lizard-like beast of burden called a *dewback*, and the *bantha*, something between a yak and an elephant. They never managed a *bantha*, and the one *dewback* was a life-sized dummy with a stick jutting from one side of its head to lever it back and forth. The polystyrene skeleton of a huge reptile arranged in the sand did suggest monsters just beyond the nearest dune, but the lack of convincing alien animals or any sense of Tatooine as part of the 'used' universe always galled Lucas. Back in America he would shoot scenes with a *bantha*, and, for the 1997 Special Edition, add the rusting hulk of a crashed spaceship, visualized by McQuarrie but never included in the original. ILM's animators would also generate half a dozen *dewbacks*.

The light saber gave John Stears enormous trouble. He first designed a weapon lit from inside, with a multi-sided revolving blade, some faces silvered, others clear. The drawback was its fragility. If two blades clashed together, they broke. Fight arranger Bob Anderson had to develop a new technique to create realistic battles. On *The Empire Strikes Back*, Lucas would abandon these cumbersome creations in favor of oval blades faced with the highly reflective 3M material used in front-projection, which threw back light from a lamp above the camera lens. When this didn't satisfy him either, he resorted to adding the glow with animation, the system used in both *The Empire Strikes Back* and *Return of the Jedi*.

The actors loathed Tunisia even more than Lucas did. 'The first day I put the costume on in Tunisia, I walked ten paces and couldn't walk any more,' says Anthony Daniels. 'The whole weight of 3PO's fiberglass legs was across my feet. The weight of the arms rested on my thumbs. For months, I lost almost all feeling in my thumbs.' He endured eight-hour days on location, sweating furiously, unable either to drink or to relieve himself without help. The sixteen plates of the suit grabbed and caught, and the knees never did bend correctly. Lucas and Kurtz spent half the production kneeling in front of Daniels, trying to free the joints. Finally they gave up, and he developed a stiff-legged waddle that got him around, though inelegantly. Almost worse was the isolation imposed by the suit. 'I couldn't turn my head more than twenty degrees to the right or left, so I had tunnel vision. I felt totally alone. People would come up and stand near me and say the most outrageous things, as though I wasn't human. They forgot there was a human inside, that I needed a drink or some food.'

Kenny Baker was no happier inside R2-D2. All its noises would be added later, so he had no way of communicating, a fact which added to his claustrophobia. The sole motive for him being inside was to operate the motors which made R2 run, but when these failed on the sandy and uneven Tunisian landscape, Lucas took him out, and the machine was simply towed around on hidden cables. Daniels found it disconcerting to deliver all his lines to a silent, metal companion. Eventually they worked out a compromise. For close-ups, Baker climbed into the machine and bounced it around by throwing himself against its walls. This rocking motion created a sort of walk as his weight shifted from one track to another. Suddenly the little robot had body language, which helped to humanize it.

Back in London, Lucas became more morose, uncommunicative, and emaciated. 'George doesn't really communicate that directly with people on the set,' complained Daniels. 'He prefers to have everything on film, or in some kind of digital format so he can weave you around in whatever sort of formation he wants.' Gloria Katz, used to his moods, says, 'I've never seen him so depressed – to the point where you would wonder, "Is he going to make it through this movie? Is he going to get up in the morning to go to the set?" So much of what George visualized he was not able to achieve. He was in a state of constant frustration.' He developed a chronic cough, and chest pains.

Even Marcia, who had come to London and rented them a cottage in sedate Hampstead, couldn't allay his growing sense of doom. 'You know you're not going to get 100 per cent,' he told her, 'but you think maybe you'll get 70 per cent or 80 per cent. I'm getting 40 per cent every day.' His mood wasn't helped when, while they were away in

Tunisia, burglars broke in and stole his video equipment. Even on the heights of Hampstead, they felt stifled in the hottest summer ever recorded in England.

On the set, the mood ranged from weary resignation to outright rebellion to a manic hilarity. In one scene, Luke, Chewie, Han, and Leia are trapped in a half-flooded trash compactor. Luke is dragged underwater by an unseen monster called a *dai-noga* – Lucas recycling a name he'd used for the Jedi in earlier drafts of the script. The *dai-noga* was supposed to be, in Lucas's words, 'a giant sort of filmy, clear, transparent jellyfish kind of thing that came shooting out of the water, with all these jelly-like tentacles with little veins running through them. So the special effects people came up with this giant eight-foot high, twelve-foot wide brown turd that was bigger than the set, and that didn't work. We finally got it down to just one tentacle. That was all they could really accomplish.'

When Ford blew his first take of the scene, he glanced apologetically at Lucas and, taking a piece of the polystyrene 'scrap metal' that half filled the space, jammed it into his mouth. Hamill started gnawing on a bar of plastic steel. Lucas didn't laugh. He just remained standing nearby, 'looking depressed,' according to Hamill, 'and shaking his head.' Hamill picked up a piece of green styrofoam, and to the tune of 'Chattanooga Choo Choo,' started to sing, 'Pardon me, George, could this be *dai-noga* poo-poo?' Lucas didn't smile. He simply put his foot on Hamill's chest and shoved him under the water.

Carrie Fisher was already deep into drugs. Percodan got her up in the mornings, and she openly smoked marijuana between shots. Cocaine, with occasional jolts of LSD, kept her going through weekends of partying. Between shots, she'd sing songs from Hollywood musicals in imitation of her mother, or play giddy word games – Is Marvin Gaye? Is Lorne Greene? Is Anna Mae Wong? The script for her final scene described her as 'staggeringly beautiful.' Fisher sarcastically amended this in her copy to read simply 'staggering': 'I felt this new wording more approached what I could bring to the character.' She and Harrison Ford became intimate. 'They had a nice little relationship going there,' says Dave Prowse. 'Whenever anyone couldn't find Harrison, you'd say, "Have you tried Carrie Fisher's changing room?"' Fred Roos wasn't surprised. 'Those two were always going to get on. They have the same cynical, jaded view of the world.' Hamill, hot for Fisher himself, was resentful.

Nobody rated the film, or Lucas, very highly. 'We all thought it was rubbish,' said Anthony Daniels. Peter Mayhew agreed: 'We had no idea what was going on. When they said, "The spaceship is going through an asteroid field," nobody knew what that visualized like. We were told to do this, stand there. It was difficult to realize what it all meant.' Fisher complained of Lucas's monotonously repeated direction, 'Faster and more intense.' When he lost his voice, she suggested he have two small blackboards lettered 'Faster' and 'More intense,' and simply hold up one, or both together.

Fisher mocked her role as the one woman in a universe of men – 'The only girl in this sort of adolescent boy's fantasy.' Tauntingly, she said, 'How about a big cooking scene? Baking some space food. Or how about me sewing my costume back together? A shopping scene, maybe, on a mall planet. Give me a girlfriend and we'll talk about how cute Han is.' Lucas wasn't amused; this was *serious*. As a joke, Hamill began playing Luke in the hushed tones and affectless style of Lucas himself, and was rewarded with a rare beam of approval. He'd finally realized what everyone else knew all along: Luke was Lucas, just as Darth Vader was his father and the universe a scaled-up Modesto.

Half the time, the actors spoke their lines to blank walls, or at clipboards held by grips on the other side of the set – remote-control acting, increasingly common as special effects invaded the film business. Fisher recalls, 'I watched my planet blow up as a blackboard with a circle drawn on, and a bored Englishman holding it up.' A BBC journalist came to interview Ford: 'I walked off the set at lunchtime,' Ford remembers, 'and he said, "What's this picture about?" And I sat there with this microphone in my face and realized I don't *know* what the fucking picture was about.'

Taking their lead from Gil Taylor, with his E-type Jaguar, country-squire manner and casual assumption of command – he'd flown combat missions in World War II – the crew became rebellious. Taylor didn't discourage them. 'I've had good relationships with most of the directors I've worked for,' he said. 'I attempted it with George, but he doesn't make friends easily. Every day we would go to rushes, and never did George say he liked anything. I don't think he ever paid anyone a compliment.' Lucas appealed repeatedly to the crew to work overtime in order to make up lost time, but they stuck religiously to their schedule of eight-hour days, with two obligatory breaks for tea. Again, Lucas felt that Kurtz didn't sufficiently impose his authority.

With Huyck and Katz, Lucas was still paring down the script. In the Fifth Draft, with which he'd begun shooting, Luke had friends on Tatooine, including Biggs Darklighter – the last vestige of his brother in earlier versions – who has already gone to the Space Academy, but is back on a visit. Lucas shot a scene in which Luke, staring moodily into the Tatooine sky with its twin suns, catches a glimpse of the Imperial cruiser pursuing Leia's blockade runner. He hurries to the nearby town of Anchorhead to tell Biggs, who's in the local pool hall with a glamorous girl, played by Koo Stark, star of soft-core porn movies, but later to become more famous as a girlfriend Prince Andrew smuggled into Buckingham Palace.

Lucas refused to send daily rushes to Hollywood, the practice that had led to many of his problems on *THX1138*. Instead, the editor periodically supplied completed sequences. When Alan Ladd Jr saw the Anchorhead scene, he was on the phone immediately. What was Lucas making – *American Graffiti* in space? Koo ended up on the cutting-room floor with Garrick Hagon, who played Biggs, and his friends (Jay Benedict and Anthony Forrest), but Lucas couldn't remove the references to him. Arguing with his aunt and uncle at dinner about leaving Tatooine to join the Academy, Luke says, 'You said the same when Biggs and Tank left.' Later, he says to C-3PO, 'Oh, Biggs is right. I'm never gonna get out of here!' Biggs reappeared as one of the rebel pilots who attack the Death Star. Describing how they intend to race along a narrow channel in the outer surface of the Death Star, Luke tells him, 'It'll be just like Beggar's Canyon back home' – referring to a game they played on Tatooine, bombing sand creatures from their speeders. He's horrified when Biggs becomes one of Darth Vader's victims. The removal of Biggs always irritated Lucas, and for the Special Edition he would restore the friends' reunion in the hangar before the raid.

Huyck and Katz pointed out a fundamental flaw in the screenplay. For the second half, only Luke, Han, and Leia have anything to do. Marcia suggested disposing of C-3PO, but Lucas demurred – to him, the 'droids were the film's true heroes. Then she and the Huycks proposed killing off Kenobi. After he'd introduced Luke to the Force and explained the recent history of the galaxy, the old man was redundant. Why not have him die in a confrontation with Darth Vader, and return as a disembodied presence? Kurtz broke the news to Guinness, who, seeing his entire role going the way of Koo Stark's, threatened

Where were you in '62? A montage of the elements that made *American Graffiti* (1973) the most profitable movie ever shot: the rollerskating waitresses of Mel's Diner, deejay Robert Weston 'Wolfman Jack' Smith, the climactic drag race, and the film's young stars, Ron Howard, Cindy Williams, Richard Dreyfuss, Charles Martin Smith, and Paul LeMat.

The Force of Others. Lucas and some of the people who helped make *Star Wars*.

RIGHT Alec Guinness as sage Obi Wan-Kenobi, on Tunisian location with Lucas.

ABOVE Harrison Ford as Han Solo, Carrie Fisher as Princess Leia, Peter Mayhew as Chewbacca, and Mark Hamill as Luke Skywalker.

RIGHT Lucas with Gary Kurtz, producer, collaborator, and another of his many 'big brothers.'

BELOW Lucas adjusts a raygun for Diane Sadley Way, playing bounty-hunter Greedo. Stuart Freeborn's make-up obliged her to breathe through a straw.

BOTTOM Lucas poses with an obviously exhausted Carrie Fisher and Mark Hamill outside Mann's Chinese Theater on Hollywood Boulevard after *Star Wars* proved an undoubted hit. Anonymous actors wore the costumes of Darth Vader, C-3PO, R2-D2, and Chewbacca, a fact resented by Dave Prowse, Anthony Daniels, Kenny Baker, and Peter Mayhew, who created those roles.

ABOVE LEFT Lucas with Francis Ford Coppola (center), his earliest mentor, and Akira Kurosawa, one of his inspirations for the *Star Wars* films.

LEFT Walter Murch, among Lucas's earliest friends, and a long-time collaborator, holding the two Oscars he won for Sound and Film Editing of *The English Patient*, 1997.

ABOVE Marcia Lucas, *née* Griffin, stood by her husband throughout his early career, and edited his films, until they divorced in 1982.

RIGHT AND BELOW
Michael Eisner as head of
Paramount gave the green
light for *Raiders of the Lost
Ark* (1981) and the subse-
quent series that launched
Harrison Ford's Indiana
Jones.

Just friends? Lucas with Steven Spielberg, director of the *Indiana Jones* films; collaborators but also, as their body language suggests, long-time rivals.

The three directors of the *Star Wars* cycle: Irvin Kershner, who made *The Empire Strikes Back*, Lucas, and Richard Marquand, tractable young English director who let Lucas have his way in the making of *Return of the Jedi* (1983).

Kershner, Gary Kurtz, Lucas, and Lawrence Kasdan on the set of *The Empire Strikes Back* (1980). Kasdan was the dramaturg Lucas had been searching for. His script for *Raiders of the Lost Ark* notched a new benchmark for action comedy.

to quit. Kurtz and Lucas squared it with his agent, arguing that Guinness dead would make a more powerful impression than as the invalid, wounded in a battle with Vader, envisaged in the original.

In Hollywood, *Star Wars* was increasingly an object of scandal and concern. Some executives at Fox were even trying to persuade Ladd to cut his losses and sell off the film to a group of West German investors. In December 1976, the US government outlawed film production as a tax shelter for foreign companies, but made a politically diplomatic exception of West Germany. Columbia's canny head of production David Begelman partly financed *Close Encounters of the Third Kind* with German money, and at Fox, one of its lawyers, Donald Loze, was set to sell a $24.2 million package of films to German investors, including *Star Wars*.

To offset the negative publicity about the film, Kurtz flew a group of American journalists to London, including Donald Goddard of the *New York Times* and Charles Champlin from the *Los Angeles Times*. Champlin, who had reviewed *American Graffiti* so warmly, called Barry's sets for the Death Star and the *Millennium Falcon* 'awesome,' and extolled Lucas's concept of a 'used' future; his headline was 'Used Future Present and Accounted for.' Though Kurtz stressed they were 'trying for a high energy level rather than the technical perfection of *2001*,' and complained, '$7 million, but it's like doing a $600,000 epic for Roger Corman,' Champlin assured readers that 'the special effects will take full advantage of some new advances in computer-controlled stop-motion animation.'

The article appeared on 20 June, too late to reassure Ladd Jr, who, disturbed by the rumors, had flown to London himself and visited the set. Lucas screened him forty minutes of the completed film. Without music or special effects, it looked dreadful. 'I just wish you had never seen this stuff,' Lucas said disconsolately afterwards. But Ladd wasn't so pessimistic. He even suggested Lucas shoot some extra footage while he had the sets up – for the sequel. Lucas smiled wanly. He'd be astonished if he even got the first film finished.

Once he was back in Hollywood, Ladd revised the release date. The film was already five weeks over schedule. He'd hoped for a release at Christmas 1976. Now they would be lucky to have it by summer 1977.

★　　★　　★

The opening of *Star Wars*, where Darth Vader boards Leia's ship, was shot last. Considering its importance, work on the sequence began disastrously. Barry cannibalized other sets to create some sort of interior, but the result looked as cheap as Roger Corman at his most penny-pinching. Since the Vader mask only provided pinholes to see through, and the brace round his neck prevented him from looking down, Dave Prowse could barely see what he was doing. Striding confidently into the corridor, he tripped over a stuntman and fell headlong. Stormtroopers piled on top of him.

After that, Lucas demanded two new and larger corridors for the rebel ship. They would cost $50,000, and would take two weeks to build, which exasperated Fox. Lucas also estimated that even after the new sets were done, he'd need a further two weeks to film in them. Fox approved the new sets, but ordered shooting to be wound up in one week. Even with two extra camera crews working, Kurtz acting as second-unit director, and Lucas pedalling between sets on a bicycle, he still didn't finish on schedule. Allowed three extra days, he had time to film the invasion of the rebel ship, but nothing else. 'I ended up with an 80 per cent-shot movie,' said Lucas.

The English crew, more than ever convinced they had participated in the creation of a monumental flop, remained relentless to the last. Traditionally, the 'wrap' party at the end of shooting is a *gemütlich* occasion during which gifts are exchanged, casual affairs terminated, eternal friendship sworn. It is also, when the production has been unpleasant, a chance to settle scores. One unpopular director was presented with a parcel which turned out to contain his ostentatiously labelled director's chair chopped into little pieces. On this occasion Gary Kurtz received a huge box which, as he unwrapped layer after layer of paper, turned out to contain only a false mustache reminiscent of Adolf Hitler's. He was unamused.

The *Star Wars* team arrived back in Los Angeles like the remnants of a defeated army. None of the actors imagined the film would be a success. Fisher, strung out on dope and on Harrison Ford, and stuck in an acrimonious relationship with her domineering mother, didn't work for the three years it took to launch the next film in the series, *The Empire Strikes Back*. Harrison Ford returned to supporting roles, first in *Heroes*, backing up Henry Winkler as a crazed Vietnam vet, then in *Force Ten from Navarone*, a follow-up to the successful World

War II adventure *The Guns of Navarone*. He also replaced Kris Kristofferson as a US Air Force officer in *Hanover Street*, a wartime weepie that put his career back almost as far as *The Conversation*.

Before he left for England, Hamill had signed to appear in ABC-TV's sitcom *Eight is Enough*, due to begin transmission in March 1977. The hour-long show starred Dick van Patten as a Sacramento newspaperman bringing up eight children with his wife, played by Diana Hyland. Hyland, the lover of John Travolta, was an old friend of Hamill's, and had got him the job, but he now recognized that the contract, which ran for seven years, would be the death knell of his feature aspirations. He tried to get out of it, and when ABC wouldn't negotiate, refused to appear in the first episode. ABC sued. 'They decided to nail me to the wall as a test case,' says Hamill. 'They threatened to cancel the series and sue me for damages. I felt desperate.' He began drinking heavily, and medicating himself against depression. When he saw people from *Star Wars* at screenings around Hollywood, he shrank from even discussing the film, which promised to be his last big-screen appearance.

Lucas knew little or nothing of his cast's personal problems. He was entirely occupied with ILM. Dykstra's people had only managed to get the cameras working during the last few weeks. Of a projected four hundred effects shots in the film, they'd produced three. Of these, only one, the scene of the escape pod leaving Leia's ship with the robots on board, was usable. Lucas was livid.

On the plane back to San Francisco from Los Angeles after receiving this bad news, he began to get chest pains. As soon as they landed, Marcia rushed him to the Marin General Hospital. They kept him overnight but discharged him next morning, declaring him to be suffering from hypertension and exhaustion, both exacerbated by his diabetes. Lucas resolved that *Star Wars* would be the last film he directed. The physical cost was simply too high. But first, he had to finish it.

Saving *Star Wars*

C-3PO: Sir, the possibility of successfully navigating an
asteroid field is approximately three thousand, seven
hundred and twenty to one.
HAN SOLO: Never tell me the odds!

From the script of *Star Wars* by George Lucas

The key to completing *Star Wars* was clearly ILM. After more acrimonious discussions with Dykstra, and an appalled tour of the ramshackle Van Nuys installation, Lucas removed him from day-to-day
supervision. 'George, who was very much his father's son in terms of
business, felt he was being ripped off,' says Matthew Robbins, 'that
all the expenses and technical mumbo jumbo were about creating an
empire for John Dykstra, founding John Dykstra Inc.' Lucas was also
guiltily aware that much of the chaos stemmed from his own casual
conviction that any technical problems would melt away in the heat
of his enthusiasm and belief, and that 'simply throwing models at the
camera' would be enough.

Dykstra insists that Lucas's return coincided with the motion-
control equipment finally starting to work. Lucas didn't agree. Without
his intervention, he believed, shooting would have dragged on for
months more. 'John, it seemed to me, became obsessed with the
research work,' he said, 'to the exclusion of the practical matter of
shooting the movie effects.' Lucas accelerated the pace by introducing
simple business methods. As Linwood Dunn had warned a year
before, ILM lacked any real understanding of scheduling. With as
many as eighteen separate exposures on a single frame, technicians
were accustomed to wait hours, even days, for the previous exposure
to return from the lab before adding another. Lucas ordered them to

keep working. Under Dykstra, work had stopped every morning as the whole staff assembled to see the previous day's 'dailies.' This became a thing of the past. Film was snatched from the lab and viewed the moment it arrived. 'We needed quick turnaround on the dailies,' said Lucas. 'We needed hourlies.'

For two weeks, a penitent Lucas stayed in Los Angeles, living in a Van Nuys motel and personally overseeing ILM's work. Dykstra remained in formal command, but Jim Nelson brought in George Mather, a no-nonsense pro, as production supervisor. Among the treasures of the Lucas Archive is Mather's 'bible,' a ring-backed binder with a page of script pasted to each leaf and, facing it, the matching storyboard or illustration. It's emblematic of the new discipline Lucas imposed.

A rough production line and a command structure quickly developed. Richard Edlund and Dennis Muren headed two teams that worked almost round the clock, one from 8 a.m. to 6 p.m., the other from 3 p.m. to midnight. Model work came under Joe Johnston and Steve Gawley, who had the job of realizing in balsa, clay, and plastic the weapons, props, and vehicles visualized by Ralph McQuarrie or Colin Cantwell. Stumped on how to achieve the necessary near-microscopic surface detail in plastic foam, the new generation of movie modelmakers bought thousands of plastic Airfix model kits for aircraft, armored vehicles and ships. Jumbled together in new and arresting configurations, these, and other scraps of formed plastic, made convincing spacecraft. The Jawas' landcrawler rolled on treads from Panzer tanks. They moulded the star destroyers' thrusters from the plastic eggs which held a popular brand of women's stockings, and R2-D2 and C-3PO fled the blockade runner in an escape pod made from two plastic paint-buckets.

Model work remained the most craft-oriented of all special effects skills, and correspondingly vulnerable to accident. A fragile model could be crushed by a careless movement, and the need to fill the spaceships in particular with lights, motors, and wiring made fire a constant threat. It was a problem that not even the introduction of cooler fiber-optic lighting entirely solved. On *Return of the Jedi* in 1983, the larger models, in particular the giant Imperial cruisers, had to be air-conditioned. A cameraman disliked the hissing of the airhose and uncoupled one Imperial starship from its cooling system. It melted, and cost $150,000 to replace.

★   ★   ★

Once ILM was up and running, Lucas began returning to San Anselmo for weekends, and commuting to Los Angeles every Monday. He called it 'one of the worst periods of my life. I was spending three or four days a week down in Los Angeles, editing, working, and finishing the film in San Francisco, flying back down, flying back up. It was a real mess.' Staff at ILM came to dread his arrival to look over the weekend's work. Progress was accepted without comment, failure with contempt. Passing people in the corridor, Lucas ignored them. To reduce conversations still further, he had three rubber stamps made up which he slammed on the drawings that crossed his desk: 'WONDERFUL' signified acceptance; 'OK' meant 'needs more work;' 'NOT SO GREAT' equalled 'do it again.'

By coincidence, Marcia was also in Los Angeles, helping Martin Scorsese cut *New York New York* at the Goldwyn studios. She worked in relays with Richard Chew, Walter Murch's assistant on *The Conversation*, and Paul Hirsch, with whom she'd cut *Carrie* for Brian De Palma. Strung out on cocaine, Scorsese was a nightmare to work with, the drug impairing his normally razor-sharp instincts. 'I was just too drugged out to solve the structure,' he later confessed.

Lucas hired cutting rooms next to Scorsese's, and Marcia began alternating. She worked from 8 a.m. to 8 p.m. on one or both films, after which Lucas took over for the graveyard shift. They based themselves in a small Beverly Hills apartment bought with money from *American Graffiti*. Marcia occasionally left a note: 'Can we meet for breakfast?' but more often George's 1967 Camaro was pulling up out front as Marcia left for work. Their marriage had contracted to a fringe aspect of *Star Wars*.

When Marcia had finished a rough cut of Scorsese's film, Lucas came in to watch it. Scorsese recalls, 'He said we could add $10 million to the box-office receipts if we'd give the film a happy ending and have the man and the woman walk away together. He was right, but I said it just wouldn't work for the story. I knew that he was going for something that was extremely commercial, but I had to go another way.' Marcia would later tell Charley Lippincott that she'd never edit another of Lucas's movies. 'If she ever had to work with him again,' says Lippincott, 'she felt it would be the end of their marriage.'

While Spielberg had been completing *Close Encounters of the Third Kind*, he invited Herb Lightman, editor of the magazine *American*

Cinematographer, to visit the set. Lightman brought with him thirteen-year-old Patrick Read Johnson from Wadsworth, Illinois. His mother had written to Lightman, explaining that her son spent all his time watching and making fantasy films. Could he show him around Hollywood? Spielberg, once a gawky provincial 8mm moviemaker himself, invited Johnson to visit Trumbull's workshops. The boy even helped modelmaker Greg Jein feed bundles of fiber optics into the giant mother-ship model. Later, Lightman took him across to ILM. 'Some college kids are shooting models on sticks,' he told him. 'We're not sure what the hell it is, but they call it *Star Wars*.'

Dykstra had obligingly screened the latest cut for them. With no special-effects sequences, ILM made do with World War II combat film. Instead of Ken Ralston's X-Wing and Tie fighters – named because they resembled bow-ties – and the *Millennium Falcon*, control of the galaxy was contested by Spitfires, Messerschmitts, and Zeros. (This was far from the first such screening. Before Lucas clamped down on security, almost everyone in the sfx community saw at least part of the film. Just how many is indicated by the fact that among the objects which decorate the complex exterior of the mother ship in *Close Encounters*, visible as the ship passes over Melinda Dillon hiding in the rocks, is R2-D2.) The experience inspired the thirteen-year-old Johnson to become a feature-film-maker. With some encouragement from Spielberg, Disney released his first feature, *Spaced Invaders*, in 1989.

Once Lucas took over the reins again, he forbade such generous access. Camera operator David Robman, hired to shoot the painted backdrops of the Death Star and its surrounding Imperial spacecraft, had trouble finding out what the story was about. 'On my first day, I asked Ken [Ralston] if there was a shooting script I could read. He replied there was only one script in the entire building and it was kept under wraps due to its unique nature.' Fortunately, enough people had read it to give newcomers the basic plot points.

Dykstra had covered five hundred square yards of the parking lot with a model of the Death Star's heavily armored exterior. Cast in foam in two-and-a-half-inch squares, it was comfortably large, with enough room for his cameras to pan and crane into every crevice, particularly the canyon down which the rebel fighters speed to drop their crucial bombs. Since Marcia had to integrate these sequences into the film, Lucas asked her to look it over. One glance was enough for her to see that the model, while fine for speeding tracking shots, was far too large for everything else – on film, it would have the unconvincing gray monotony of model battleships in old John Wayne movies. She suggested a much-reduced shooting area, the size of six ping-pong tables. ILM took her at her word, and joined six tables together with gaffer tape, on which they constructed a scaled-down Death Star exterior. Now too small to crane into, the model was mostly filmed in tracking shots from a camera in the back of a moving pick-up.

Hollywood was becoming aware of the science fiction fan community, and was trying to tap into it. In 1972, Spielberg attended a World SF Convention to introduce his futuristic *Name of the Game* episode *LA 2017*, and was struck by the enthusiasm, knowledge, and, above all, wealth of the teenage fans. Unlike himself at their age, they had money to spend. The market already supported numerous professional magazines like *Cinefantastique* and *Starlog*, specializing in advance information and behind-the-scenes reports on upcoming sf films. Publicist Jeff Walker, who later worked for Lucasfilm, says, 'There's an entire market segment that thrives on knowing the stuff beforehand, that was created by Steven, and George, and [*Star Trek* producer] Gene Roddenberry.'

Roddenberry was the first producer to recruit sf fandom. When the network axed his series *Star Trek* in 1968, he organized a campaign of letter-writing and highly publicized protests by fans which forced it to think again. The starship *Enterprise* flew once more, and *Star Trek* became the most successful science fiction series ever broadcast on television.

Charley Lippincott, Gary Kurtz, and Mark Hamill attended the 1976 World SF Convention in Kansas City, hoping to stir up similar interest in *Star Wars*, but found it an uphill struggle. Bill Warren, one of the journalists writing for the sf market, recalls the occasion vividly. 'I wandered up to the small, badly located room the convention had allocated for Gary and Charley in the Kansas City hotel. They had some props and costumes – and Mark, who, when I entered the room, was chattering away to a couple of pretty girls. I was about to introduce myself when he saw my name badge and shouted, "You're Bill Warren. You write for *Cinefantastique*, the greatest magazine in the world!"

'I mentioned that *CFQ* editor Fred Clarke was downstairs in the dealers' room. Mark dashed out the door and was running down the hall when Charley caught up with him and said, "You can't leave now, Mark; you're the exhibit." Later, they let him out on parole, and I took him to meet Clarke – who was cold, distant, and unresponsive, although Mark was so excited he didn't notice (I think).

'There was a dealer selling plastic rayguns with barrels that lit up, about which Mark became (typically) very enthusiastic. He told me that the guns in *Star Wars* were real .45 pistols, re-dressed to look like rayguns. Lucas wanted the guns to clearly have heft when they were picked up – but Mark wanted a raygun that felt like a raygun. The dealer was sold out, and Mark got all excited, almost jumping up and down and exclaiming, "But I gotta have one! I'm Luke Sky-walker!" The dealer shrugged and asked, "Who's Luke Skywalker?"'

Fox distribution staff began offering *Star Wars* to cinema owners, whose promises to show the film – 'guarantees' – would be the barometer of its potential success. At Fox's sales conference, Lippincott showed slides of McQuarrie's artwork and talked about the film, to uniform indifference. Fox's 1976 releases, including duds like *The Blue Bird*, *The Duchess and the Dirtwater Fox*, and *Mother, Jugs and Speed*, had turned distributors against the studio. Ladd launched some more prestigious projects, but of its 1977 releases, the most promising were *Julia*, adapted from Lillian Hellman's *Pentimento* and starring Jane Fonda and Vanessa Redgrave, directed by Fred Zinnemann, *The Turning Point*, with Anne Bancroft and Shirley MacLaine, but above all *The Other Side of Midnight*, a showy international romance based on Sidney Sheldon's *roman à clef* about the life and loves of Greek shipping magnate Aristotle Onassis. *Star Wars*, without any stars and, besides, part of a devalued genre, looked like a throwback to the sixties.

After his presentation, Lippincott lunched with people from Films Incorporated, which distributed Fox films on 16mm to the film-club and college market. 'A whole bunch of young people who worked for the exhibitors, maybe about eight people, came and sat with us. They loved the concept of the movie. They understood it. They were all for it. It wasn't the older big-cigar group. This was a core of real enthusiasts. And it was like a breakthrough. I thought, "*We* are the Rebel Alliance!"'

Fox hoped for $10 million in guarantees. It got $1.5 million.

Desperate, the sales staff took off the gloves. A few cinema owners were told curtly, 'Take *Star Wars* or you won't get *The Other Side of Midnight.*' Exhibitors protested at this return to the bad old days of block booking, and Fox was later fined $25,000 – for the offence, ironically, of trying to force exhibitors to show the most profitable film they'd ever screen.

Lucas continued to fret over the shooting he hadn't had time to finish at Elstree. In particular, he disliked the cantina sequence, left incomplete after Freeborn's collapse in Tunisia and premature departure from the film. 'None of us felt that the full potential of the scene was fulfilled when the main-unit shoot was completed,' Nick Maley admits. Kurtz twisted Fox's arm, and persuaded them to invest another $100,000 in new shooting.

Rick Baker, a master of the monster suit, had just won a reputation on John Guillermin's remake of *King Kong*. Producer Dino de Laurentiis commissioned a sixty-foot-high mechanical ape, but it never worked and, moreover, looked appallingly fake. Its appearance was confined to a single, very distant long shot. The Kong suit Baker created and wore, electronically operating its facial features, saved the film. Lucas asked Baker to add some new creatures to the cantina. Baker assembled a team that included Jon Berg, Laine Liska, Doug Beswick, Tom St Armand, Rob Bottin, and Phil Tippett, then a young model animator trying to break into movies. 'Rick just threw together a shop, taken from a bunch of things that he already had sitting on his shelf,' says Tippett. Lucas particularly wanted a band, so Baker created masks for three apparently mouthless aliens playing something like oboes. He added five more creatures designed by Ron Cobb, including one resembling a strip of leathery carpet, upright, artfully folded, and sentient.

Cobb was typical of the people who became caught up in *Star Wars*. He'd done covers for *Famous Monsters of Filmland* in 1965 and 1966, but was best known as a political cartoonist for the alternative *Los Angeles Free Press*. While *Star Wars* was shooting in London, Cobb and his partner Dan O'Bannon, who'd been at USC during Lucas's last postgraduate year, where he mastered the new field of computer graphics, were in Paris, working on a planned film of Frank Herbert's *Dune* with flamboyant Mexican director Alexandro Jodorowsky. When it collapsed in 1975, they began designing the movie that became

Alien. While Cobb did creatures for *Star Wars'* cantina sequence, Lucas hired O'Bannon to design the computer read-outs which show the Death Star inching toward the rebel stronghold on Yavin.

The strict budget only allowed two days' shooting on a tiny studio on La Brea. 'George got an insert stage together,' says Phil Tippett, 'and Carroll Ballard came down and shot the material. We actually performed the parts ourselves. We got into our monster outfits and acted it out, which was a fun day.' In this case, 'fun' was a relative term. 'We were sweating like mad,' Tippett recalled. 'The masks filled up with moisture, causing us to choke on our own juices. We couldn't get any air and we couldn't see anything because the eyepieces were fogged.' Gary Kurtz saved them by cutting airholes in the masks with a razor blade.

Visiting Baker's studio, Lucas noticed some of Tippett's stop-motion figures. 'Hey! You guys do this type of stuff?' he asked. Eager to break into movie special effects, Tippett offered him free use of the models. Lucas decided to use them for a game of holographic chess played by Luke and Chewbacca on the *Millennium Falcon.* It launched the career of Tippett, subsequently the Oscar-winning creator of creatures and machines for the last two *Star Wars* films and *Jurassic Park.*

Once he'd put the cantina sequence on track, Lucas concentrated on the other major weakness, the Tatooine desert sequences. In particular, the scenes with Luke's landspeeder irritated him. The vehicle never looked convincing, and ILM showed no signs of being able to erase the wheels convincingly. The best they could do was to create a fuzzy orange zone under the vehicle, like a heat haze. With a camera crew under Tak Fujimoto, Lucas set up a shoot in Death Valley. It was Fujimoto who suggested adapting an old stage illusion by fitting a mirror underneath the speeder. It reflected the ground, which the audience would take for the desert beyond.

Lucas hoped to film the *bantha,* and some new scenes with R2-D2, who, because of malfunctioning remote-control equipment, was never seen in the original film to move more than a yard at a time. Lucas was all set to leave for Death Valley when, at 3 a.m. on that January morning, the phone rang. Kurtz was calling with the news that Mark Hamill had driven his BMW over a seventy-foot incline on the Antelope Freeway near Los Angeles. Nobody was sure if he'd live. Inured to disaster and too tired to contemplate the significance of his star's injuries, Lucas left for Death Valley anyway, with a stand-in to replace Hamill.

For the *bantha*, they'd hired an elephant from the zoo at the Marine World theme park, draped it in the same material as Chewbacca's outfit and fitted it with giant plastic horns, but the animal hated the costume, and kept shrugging it off. All they would get was one usable image, a long shot of the beast standing dumbly on a dune. It was no more than Lucas expected. As Han Solo might have said, 'I have a bad feeling about this.'

After that, only one sequence remained unfilmed. Lucas visualized the rebels hiding out on Yavin, a jungle planet with the remains of an ancient civilization. His model was Tikal, in Guatemala, and though Kurtz pleaded with him to save at least a little money by doing it closer to home, Lucas clung to his original idea. Richard Edlund was sent with a second unit to get shots of a sentinel perched above the jungle with the remains of Mayan temples in the background.

Hamill survived his crash, but his face was mutilated. 'My nose was wiped right off,' he says, 'and my face had to be rebuilt.' In three operations, surgeons gave him a new nose cartilage from part of his ear. ABC, convinced he was finished, released him from his *Eight is Enough* contract, though in fact his face, except for a slight lop-sidededness and a marginally flattened nose, was good enough to appear before the cameras. His mental state was less easily treated. Diana Hyland visited him in hospital, but, unlike other friends who commiserated, ordered him to stop feeling sorry for himself and to get to work remaking his life. It was advice she was uniquely qualified to give, since she'd been fighting breast cancer for more than a year, and had already had one mastectomy. After the Christmas break, she'd returned to Los Angeles and found the cancer had spread to her spine. Her doctor gave her six months to live, but she died on 26 March, after filming five *Eight is Enough* shows. Hamill, chastened, began psychotherapy with his older brother, a psychiatrist.

Charley Lippincott was battling heavy weather in selling *Star Wars* to the merchandisers. As far as the comic-book, toy, and publishing worlds were concerned, science fiction had died in the cinema and been resurrected on television. They could sell books, toys, and merchandise based on *The Six Million Dollar Man* because TV series normally ran for at least a year, giving them time to supply the shops and keep items on the shelves until (hopefully) the fad took hold. A film, however, might close in a fortnight, leaving them, as had *Dr Dolittle*, with warehouses of unsaleable merchandise.

Of course, if Lippincott was representing Fox, that was a different thing. Would the studio guarantee to take back any unsold merchandise? Lippincott had to explain that he didn't actually work for Fox, but for Star Wars Corporation. When one major exhibitor at a toy fair heard this, he ordered Lippincott off his stand.

Major manufacturers, like the biggest, Kenner, gave him a polite welcome, but were no more enthusiastic. A film due to open in the spring or summer of 1977 gave them no time for design or packaging. Christmas was the big sale time for toys. Could Lucasfilm guarantee that *Star Wars* would still be popular then? Even so optimistic a booster as Lippincott couldn't go that far. Lucas didn't help when, visiting Kenner with Lippincott, he explained earnestly how the *Millennium Falcon* was inspired by a hamburger, and lectured executives on the mystical significance of the burger to the new generation of filmgoers.

Nor could manufacturers see what there was to sell. Lucas's first ideas, a mug shaped like the head of Chewbacca and an R2-D2 cookie jar, looked naïve. As for the characters and vehicles of the film, did they light up, have detachable limbs, make interesting noises, glow in the dark? Well, no, Lippincott admitted. Only the light sabers looked promising, but manufacturers were dubious about them. Would they survive the sort of wear inflicted by battling ten-year-olds? Kenner eventually signed to market a limited range of figures and other *Star Wars* toys – the most important decision the company ever made.

Lippincott was only marginally more successful with publishers. For the comic books based on the film, he targeted the biggest in the business, Marvel, and its flamboyant boss, Stan Lee. A forty-year veteran of writing and publishing comics, Lee combined Roger Corman's nose for profit with the flamboyance of a TV evangelist. He dumbfounded British journalists by announcing, 'Aren't I the most wonderful person you've ever interviewed?' In the future, he assured them, schoolteachers would tell their class, 'Today we are going to study the classics, and that wonderful human being, Stan Lee.'

The 'classics' for Lee were his comic books with their superhero characters: Spiderman, the Incredible Hulk, the Silver Surfer, the Fantastic Four, and Captain America. Driven by Lee's relentless energy, Marvel tapped precisely the mood Lucas and Lippincott hoped to exploit with *Star Wars* – what writer Clancy Sigal called 'that lonely, pathetic sense of involuntary power which hit America's adolescents at just about the time when they began to constitute a definable "teenage market" – catered for, concentrated upon and all too often made the objects of adult fears and ambitions.'

Most of Lee's characters were TV stars as well, in animation (*Spiderman*, *The Fantastic Four*) or, from the next year, live action (*The Incredible Hulk*). The year *Star Wars* was released, the market sustained almost three hundred Lee spin-off items, from models of the superheroes to posters, candy, calendars, and T-shirts, including one devoted to Lee himself.

Fox wanted all the publishing spin-offs from *Star Wars* put up for auction, but Lippincott gambled on his intimate knowledge of science fiction and comics. Marvel was the best, and he called Lee for an appointment – only to be fobbed off. Lee didn't want to see McQuarrie's artwork, the film's script, or Lippincott's slides. Above all, he was unresponsive to the idea that the first comics should come out before the film, to alert the teenage audience and build up preliminary interest. Nobody had ever done this, and Lee wasn't about to be the first. 'Gee, I'm not terribly interested,' he said. 'Why don't you come back when you've shot the movie?'

Through the SuperSnipe shops, Lippincott knew Roy Thomas, who had been editor at Marvel before taking over the highly successful *Conan the Barbarian* series. Thomas agreed to set up a meeting with Lee, providing Lippincott let him edit the *Star Wars* comics. Lippincott agreed and, once in front of Lee's desk, was able to hammer out a deal of sorts. Marvel would publish six *Star Wars* comic books, three before the film and three after, but Lucasfilm would get no money until sales of each title topped 100,000. Few comics did half as well, but Lippincott acquiesced, demanding only that the contract be renegotiable once the film was released. He also persuaded Lee to use Lucas's preferred artist, Howard Chaykin. He left with the feeling that he'd got his foot in the merchandising door only at the risk of having it sliced off if *Star Wars* didn't become the hit they all hoped for.

'I went back to Fox,' says Lippincott, 'and they told me I was a fool. I was wasting my time making comic-book deals.' However, with Marvel behind him, he felt confident in approaching publishers to bring out a novelization of the script. Conventional wisdom about novelizations was divided. Stanley Kubrick had been so concerned that Arthur C. Clarke's book version of the *2001* script would reveal too much before release that he dragged his feet until Clarke's publishers had to pulp its printing; the best-selling novel didn't appear until months after the film hit the theaters.

A *THX1138* novelization by respected sf writer Ben Bova had flopped, but Lippincott believed a *Star Wars* novel would sell and, more important, trigger advance interest in the movie. Ballantine Books under veteran sf writer Lester del Rey and his wife Judy-Lynn had one of the strongest sf lists in the world, and Lippincott knew both of them well. He had no trouble getting an appointment in the late summer of 1976, and found Judy-Lynn more than accommodating. She was leaving Ballantine at the end of the year to start her own imprint, and was looking for low-priced, high-profile material. If Stan Lee was prepared to gamble on *Star Wars*, why not her? As for the script Lippincott showed her, who could say what kind of film it would make? 'It was an interesting story,' she said later, 'but nothing to make you jump out of your skin.' Nor did Lucas inspire her as a creator, any more than he had impressed Kenner's executives. 'In the hands of a yo-yo,' del Rey said curtly. 'Who needs it?'

Lucas had already offered the book to his old USC classmate Don Glut. 'I had heard he was making *Star Wars*,' says Glut. 'I rang him at the studio and asked him, "Is there anything I can do on this?" I didn't know what. He called me back and said, "The best I can offer you is, you could write the novelization."

'I said, "What's the deal?" He said, "The deal's not really great, but it's been imposed on me by the studio and the publisher. Ghost-written, a flat fee of around $5000, and no royalties."' Glut turned it down. 'And for the next few years I kept kicking myself, like Lugosi after he turned down *Frankenstein*. What would have happened if I'd taken that?'

With Glut out of the picture, Del Rey suggested Alan Dean Foster. The thirty-year-old Californian had already novelized *Dark Star*, John Carpenter's sf black comedy, and turned out a series of paperbacks in the *Star Trek Log* series.

'My agent, Virginia Kidd, got a call from Tom Pollock,' says Foster. 'Tom was George Lucas's representative at the time. I had a contract where I couldn't say I was the author, and had to lie to a lot of people about it.' Foster didn't mind the $5000 fee – the advance on his 1974 novel *Icerigger* was only $3000.

'I went down to Industrial Light and Magic which, at the time, was in a little warehouse, and met George Lucas – who, to this day, is the nicest guy I've ever met in the film business – who took me through and showed me this whole wall of material, like World War II tanks and model kits and things, which they were picking parts off of to build the ships and models for the movie. George showed me the Death Star, which was this beachball thing.'

Unfazed by the amateur feel of the production, Foster started work, using the second-to-last screenplay, updated by Gary Kurtz as the story changed. Even so, the novel, which he delivered at the end of summer 1976, varied in numerous details from the finished film. By November it was on the stands, under Lucas's name, in a printing, generous for such a paperback, of 100,000 copies.

In the fall of 1976, Lucas decided *Star Wars* was in good enough shape to show to members of the Fox brass, and to friends. At the head of the film, he'd added a crawling introduction which, in imitation of the old *Flash Gordon* serials, spelled out the back-story. ILM was still producing effects sequences, so he left in some of the World War II combat footage.

A large contingent of marketing, advertising, and publicity staff, led by Alan Ladd Jr and his wife Patty, came to Parkhouse to see the film. The screening took place at night, and they chartered a bus, the driver of which got lost in the maze of small towns and delivered them two hours late. Already tired and dispirited, the executives watched aghast as *Star Wars* unrolled on screen. None could remember a production so obviously marked for disaster.

But Ladd was elated. Marketing head Johnny Friedkin recalls, 'On the bus back to the airport, Laddie was going up and down saying, "Great, huh?"' Loyal yes-men, the group hastily agreed, though gossip in the commissary next day was poisonous. News leaked of this almost guaranteed turkey, and a few people in the investment world began taking a position in Fox shares. If *Star Wars* flopped, Ladd, who had pinned his reputation to the film, might be forced to resign, perhaps putting the studio into play as a possible takeover target.

Such rumors merely made Ladd's staff more eager to put up a cheerful façade. At a later Parkhouse screening, many of the guests, who included financial comptroller Ray Gosnell, Johnny Friedkin, and executives Ashley Boone and Tim Deegan, took advantage of Ladd's absence to sleep through it. But still, as soon as they arrived at San Francisco airport, most were on the phone to Ladd telling him he undoubtedly had a hit on his hands. Ladd began talking about opening the film early in 1977, to get in ahead of *Close Encounters*, scheduled for the end of the year. With effects sequences still only half completed, nobody was confident that it would be ready much before the summer – and, moreover, a summer which would see the release of *The Deep*, from Peter Benchley's follow-up novel to *Jaws*, and a new James Bond film, *The Spy Who Loved Me*.

With the dialogue scenes now mostly in the can, Lucas turned to fine-tuning the performances. Some of the voices recorded in Britain no longer satisfied him. That of Shelagh Fraser, who played Aunt Beru, he found too low, and had her dubbed over. He also rethought the voice of Darth Vader. Though Carrie Fisher and others joked about Dave Prowse's slow, deep rural tones, dubbing him 'Darth Farmer,' Prowse insists to this day that Lucas promised him Vader's dialogue as well as his costume. 'Lucas told me that my voice would be processed and metalicized,' he says. It's evident, however, that Lucas always imagined Vader with a deep, resonant voice.

For a while, Lucas thought of Orson Welles, but opted instead for James Earl Jones, another graduate of the Stanley Kubrick school – he'd had a small role in *Dr Strangelove*. Prowse believes the decision was racially inspired: 'I think [they realized] they had dropped an enormous clanger and cast the entire film without a black person,' he says – which may well be true. Jones took the job for $10,000, but refused screen credit. Later, when his voice became inextricably associated with the Vader character, he claimed he'd felt his small involvement didn't merit credit; but at the time he was more concerned that any association with this near-certain flop might compromise his career as a serious Broadway actor.

Anthony Daniels' voice still rankled too, and Lucas, stubbornly faithful to the idea of C-3PO as a Bud Abbott soundalike, called in satirist Stan Freberg to record a dozen variations, none of them satisfactory. Eventually, he decided that Daniels' voice couldn't be separated from the character without doing more damage than if it remained.

Ben Burtt had been diligently assembling a battery of sound effects and voices. He hired Larry Ward, a linguist from Berkeley, to read passages in Quechua, the tongue of the Incas which was making a comeback as Venezualan and Guatemalan immigrants arrived in Los Angeles. Played backward, it became the language of the bounty-hunter Greedo. The Jawas jabbered in Zulu, speeded up. Chewbacca's roar was mostly bear, with a little badger, walrus, and seal. R2-D2 spoke with the squeak of dry ice rubbed against metal, and air blown into water from a pipe. The thrum of the light sabers was the sloweddown hum of a TV tube.

The laser gun gave most trouble. Burtt still hadn't found the precise sound when he went hiking with his family in the Poconos Mountains. 'On top of this one mountain was a large radio antenna, with those big metal cables that are used to stabilize the tower. As my father and I walked along, one of our backpacks caught on the wire, and it plucked the wire and made it vibrate. And I thought, "Oh my God, a laser gun."

While the film was in preparation, Lucas accompanied screenings with a 'temp. track' compiled by editor Paul Hirsch. It included some of Gustav Holst's spacious, awed music from his suite *The Planets*, and, for the more grandiose moments, extracts from Alex North's martial music for *Cleopatra*. Hirsch accompanied Han's reappearance from his secret smugglers' hold after hiding from the stormtroopers with some of Bernard Herrmann's music from *Psycho*. Once he was ready to commission the music, Lucas looked for someone who could recreate the sumptuous studio scores of the forties, composed by Max Steiner and Erich Wolfgang Korngold, the Viennese *wunderkind* who left a classical career in Vienna to write the scores for such Errol Flynn romances as *The Adventures of Robin Hood*, and who, like many of his generation, drew his main inspiration from Richard Strauss. Such writers were thin on the ground. Most new movie composers like Johnny Mandell, Henry Mancini, and Dave Amram came out of jazz. Not ashamed to follow in the footsteps of his greatest rival, Lucas in March 1976 asked Spielberg to introduce him to John Williams, who'd scored all Spielberg's films.

Williams came over to Lucas's tiny office across the street from Universal. Nothing he'd composed in a long career resembled what Lucas envisaged for *Star Wars*, but then, his *Jaws* music differed radically from his folksy score for Spielberg's first cinema feature, *The Sugarland Express*. Williams was, in fact, a brilliant *pasticheur*, capable of working in almost any musical style. He sat through the whole film without sound, alone in a preview cinema, then spent three days at San Anselmo going over it scene by scene with Lucas. In the end, he'd write ninety minutes of music for the 123-minute film.

Early in 1977, Lucas invited a group of friends to San Anselmo to see the film. Alan Ladd Jr flew up independently, but Lucas suggested that Spielberg, Scorsese, Willard Huyck and Gloria Katz, Brian De Palma and *Time* film reviewer Jay Cocks meet him at the Burbank airport and go up together. All except Scorsese arrived at Burbank, to find the airport fogged in. When the fog lifted, Scorsese still hadn't shown up. Some put down his absence, charitably, to his fear of flying. Others suspected he shrank from having to criticize Lucas's film when *New York New York* was in even more trouble.

At Parkhouse, the group watched *Star Wars* in appalled silence. 'When the film ended, people were aghast,' says Katz. Marcia was in tears. Quoting Peter Bogdanovich's catastrophic attempt at a sophisticated thirties-style New York musical, which had done much to destroy the Directors' Company, she sobbed, 'It's the *At Long Last Love* of science fiction. It's awful.' Katz shushed her. 'Laddie's watching,' she hissed. 'Just look cheery.'

Ladd returned to Los Angeles. The others went to a Chinese restaurant. 'We all got into these cars to go someplace for lunch,' says Huyck, 'and in our car everyone is saying, "My God, what a disaster!"' Over lunch, the autopsy continued. 'The crawl was about three times longer,' Huyck recalls. 'It looked like it had been shot on somebody's driveway, and the camera was on a wheelbarrow.' Everybody scorned the Force as the worst kind of gimcrack mysticism.

De Palma was particularly scathing. 'What are those?' he demanded of the coiled plaits the size of stereo earphones clamped over Carrie Fisher's ears. 'Danish pastries?' Of Darth Vader's first shot he snorted, 'That's your villain? That's the best you can do?' Katz says, 'Brian wouldn't let up. He was out of control. He was like a crazed dog.' Nobody was really surprised. De Palma had behaved much the same at a preview of *Taxi Driver*, laughing uncontrollably during dialogue scenes between Cybill Shepherd and Robert de Niro, setting off the rest of the audience.

Lucas, apparently unconcerned, stolidly ate his meal, but what he heard confirmed his worst, unacknowledged fears. Now that he looked at it objectively, the resemblances to a Walt Disney movie seemed magnified. It combined the worst qualities of *Island at the Top of the World* and *The Computer Wore Tennis Shoes*, and no adult audience would ever take it seriously. Disney considered $15 million an acceptable gross for such a film, and he'd be happy if *Star Wars* did that well. Secretly, however, he thought it might, like *THX1138*, just break even, while Spielberg's more sophisticated *Close Encounters of the Third Kind* would make the money.

De Palma and Cocks offered to rewrite the crawl. Lucas agreed. Later, Fox would suggest that a narrator intone the words as they inched across the screen, for the benefit of those who couldn't read. Lucas refused. 'They're going to have to learn to read sooner or later,' he said mockingly. 'Maybe *Star Wars* will give them an incentive. Maybe we have a valuable tool here. Maybe a whole generation will learn to read just so they can figure out what's going on in *Star Wars*.'

Throughout the post-mortem, Spielberg was the only one with anything good to say about *Star Wars*. 'That movie is going to make $100 million,' he said in the car on the way to the restaurant, 'and I'll tell you why – it has a marvellous innocence and naïveté in it, which is George, and people will love it.' Over lunch, he repeated the claim. When even Lucas looked sceptical, Spielberg, according to John Williams, said, 'I'm going to put in an envelope the figure for gross earnings for the first six months of the film, just to prove you're all wrong.' (Others who were present recall Spielberg and Lucas estimating the probable grosses of each other's films, writing their guesses inside matchbooks from the restaurant, and trading them.) 'When Lucas opened it,' says Williams, 'he found Spielberg had written "$33 million."' (Spielberg remembers $16 million.) By then, *Star Wars* had grossed more than ten times that.

Hearing of the previews, Dennis Stanfill demanded Lucas screen *Star Wars* for the Fox board. He and Kurtz did so, but dubiously. 'The only way to do it,' says Kurtz, 'was to run the work print with the mixed soundtrack we had up to that point with a temporary sound mix on the last reel. And in the end, the lights came up and they walked out. There was no reaction at all. We looked at each other and said, "Uh-oh."'

But Ladd's optimism prevailed. 25 May 1977, the Wednesday before Memorial Day, was fixed as the release date, and Ladd even authorized the production of ten 70mm prints for those cinemas able to show the epic format. Fox put together a trailer, which was released before Christmas 1976. 'They didn't understand the movie at all,' Lippincott told *Variety*. Lucas and Kurtz felt that Fox missed the whole point of the film. Lucas made another trailer, using Holst's *The Planets* as background music. 'A whole lot of people showed up at a theater in Westwood and hated the trailer,' said Lippincott. 'Buck Henry was there. Gene Wilder went. Everybody else. They all hated the trailer.' Spielberg told him the audience at a screening of Fellini's *Amarcord* had booed the trailer. But Mark Hamill saw it with another audience that cheered. Lippincott intuited the truth: 'Adults hated the trailer and the kids loved it. And I knew then that we were right on target. We had the kids.'

Fox started to remove the trailer from the theaters. 'By the time Easter rolled around,' says Lippincott, 'there were less than a hundred trailers playing around the country. Fox wanted a new trailer, but we wouldn't make a new one. It was a constant battle. We got the trailer back out for Easter. Fox didn't understand who the audience for the film would be. They thought *Damnation Alley* was going to be the science fiction hit of the summer. You laugh, but it's true.'

Fox claimed their marketing surveys showed women didn't like science fiction films. Lucas offered to make a trailer just for them, including clips from *Gone with the Wind*, Errol Flynn swashbucklers, and the epic western *Cimarron*. The studio was still dithering when the film opened, and their doubts became irrelevant.

Just after Christmas 1976, Lucas and Kurtz flew to London to hear John Williams record his score with the eighty-seven-piece London Symphony Orchestra. In response to Lucas's call for Korngoldian sentiment and Holstian bombast, the composer had pulled out all the stops. Traditionally, science fiction film music relied on futuristic squeals and burbles, or the *misterioso* keening of electronic instruments like the Theremin or Ondes Martinot; but Williams had taken Lucas at his word and gone back almost a hundred years to create a rich pastiche of Richard Strauss, chromed in brass, with a swashbuckling march theme right out of Strauss's *Don Juan*.

'Everything visual was going to be unfamiliar,' Williams had reasoned. 'What should be familiar was the emotional connection that the film has through the ear to the viscera. This I have to credit George with: the idea of making the music, as a composer would say, solidly tonal and clearly melodic, acoustic rather than electronic.' Not that

Williams took the score's bombast entirely seriously. 'For a musician, something like *Star Wars* is fun,' he admitted later. 'It's an opportunity to do fanfares and flourishes. So it's welcome. We had the London Symphony Orchestra, and they all left their serious music-making and came out to Denham Studios. We got the brass out and had great fun, with ruffles and flourishes and drums.'

Lucas didn't find the music playful. Hearing it for the first time with the full orchestration awed him. 'It was the one part of the film that turned out even better than I thought,' he said. Ringing Spielberg in Los Angeles, he played him half an hour of it over the phone. The experience crushed Spielberg. He'd chosen Williams to score *Close Encounters*, but this preview convinced him Lucas had got all his best stuff. Once he and Williams got around to discussing *Close Encounters*, Spielberg pressed for more conventionally modern music. Williams responded with urgent string passages reminiscent of Bernard Herrmann, and ominously questioning horn motifs that rise in a crescendo, only to stop short, with a bump, as if of astonishment. Garnished with references to *Pinocchio*, including a pastiche of that film's 'When You Wish Upon a Star,' the *Close Encounters* score became as different from *Star Wars* as Williams and Spielberg could make it.

With the music laid and the special effects finished – if none too expertly in some cases – Lucas and Kurtz felt ready to screen the film in public. Lucas wasn't optimistic. 'Previews always mean recutting,' he said.

They chose 1 May 1977, and the Northpoint cinema in San Francisco, where they'd previewed *American Graffiti*. A group from Fox, including Alan and Patty Ladd, came up for the preview. Like everything about Old Hollywood, there was a ritual to such events. Audiences were expected to watch in attentive silence, then file out to the lobby to fill in cards detailing their response. During the screening, members of the distribution staff prowled the cinema, ears alert for spontaneous reactions. Critics often saw the films at the same screenings. Based on their reaction and the audience cards, the studio would open the film in three or four big cities, then, if it proved popular, nationally.

But New Hollywood had already started to shake up this system. The teenage audience didn't want to wait for reviews, if indeed they read them at all. They chose films based on word of mouth, and clips on TV. To have seen the latest big film became a point of honor, and young audiences would flock to it the moment it hit a local cinema, lining up around the block for days if necessary. Soon, a studio would be able to gauge from the first weekend's figures how a film would do nationally. Those which didn't 'open' could be replaced before the next weekend. The previews of *Jaws* had been a straw in the wind. When its crowd went wild, Universal's brass held a hurried meeting in the men's room to authorize reshooting, order more prints, commission more advertising, and increase the price of the film to exhibitors.

Kurtz's demographically chosen audience bemused Ladd Jr: 'Rotarians, Kiwanians, YMCA, teachers,' he recalled. (It also included two spies from Columbia's San Francisco office, whose reports would do much to launch the film in Hollywood.) Some murmured as the words 'A long time ago in a galaxy far, far away . . .' appeared in simple white lettering on the black screen, but perked up as the soon-to-be-familiar *Star Wars* logo appeared in block outline capitals against a black background, accompanied by Williams' stirring march. The crawl puzzled many, but when, as if swooping from overhead, Princess Leia's blockade-running ship appeared from the top of the screen, followed by the prow, then the vast bulk, of Darth Vader's destroyer, engulfing the sky, the crowd gasped collectively. 'As the first spaceship went across the screen, they started applauding,' says Ladd. 'I didn't expect that. It brought tears to my eyes. They cheered and screamed.'

Marcia had warned George, 'If the audience doesn't cheer when Han Solo comes in at the last second in the *Millennium Falcon* to help Luke when he's being chased by Darth Vader, the picture doesn't work.' Long before then, when the *Falcon* jumped to light speed, they were cheering, and when Han rescued Luke, they stood on their seats and waved their arms in the air like a baseball crowd after a home run. Ladd had given up smoking, but as soon as the film was over, he floated into the lobby and, elated, lit up. The Lucases joined him, dazed. Editor Paul Hirsch walked over to the group. Deadpan, he said, 'I guess we won't recut it after all.'

16

Twerp Cinema

> Meanwhile, at the Effingham truck plaza, and in the Western Avenue four o'clock joint where Arab numbers runners throw stools through the back bar, dangerous men would stuff the jukebox for John Williams' *Star Wars* march, and sit with their hands white-knuckled around their beers, hunching their shoulders and thinking the ineffable.
>
> Sf writer Algis Budrys on the popular reaction to *Star Wars*

The week before release of *Star Wars* wasn't auspicious. In what, at the time, looked like yet another setback, the *Time* cover promised by Jay Cocks fell through at the last minute when the editors elected to feature a snap election in Israel instead. The story still appeared, but the only reference on the cover was a 'snipe' on the upper corner saying simply 'Best Film of the Year.' But hundreds of thousands bought the magazine to learn what the film was, and swelled the mass of sf fans who went to see it the first weekend.

That *Time* should even think of featuring *Star Wars* warned some at Fox that they had underestimated Lucas. On 3 May, Donald Loze, the lawyer negotiating the possible sale of upcoming Fox films to German investors, rang Bel Aire Associates, who were handling the American end of the deal, and explained that *Star Wars* was no longer on the table. Loze insisted it was purely a matter of the paperwork being too complex to complete before the film's release, but Bel Aire smelled a rat, and its principals later sued Fox, unsuccessfully, for $25 million.

'People ask why *Star Wars* only opened in forty theaters,' says Fox executive Gareth Wigan (it was actually only thirty-two). '*Star Wars* only opened in forty cinemas because we could only get forty theaters to book it.' There were no billboards. Fox issued two basic posters before release, both with nothing but text. One read, 'May the Force be with You,' the other, 'A long time ago in a galaxy far far away . . .' An early design showing a sword-wielding warrior against a red planet, with a girl at his feet and the Death Star in the background, and still using the title 'The Star Wars,' was never produced. Only when the film proved a hit did Fox create the familiar poster of Luke leveling a laser pistol at the viewer, and Leia and Han blazing away in either direction behind him.

Every cinema in the actual suburb of Hollywood refused *Star Wars* – a disaster in the eyes of Fox, since a film that didn't open in Hollywood proper wasn't deemed to have opened at all. Fortunately, Universal's *Sorcerer*, the long-awaited adaptation of Henri-Georges Clouzot's 1953 *The Wages of Fear* by William Friedkin, and his first film since *The Exorcist*, wasn't finished on time. Ted Mann took *Star Wars* for Mann's Chinese on the understanding that he'd only keep it on for the month it took to deliver *Sorcerer*, and even less if it flopped.

The film's censorship classification further cooled the enthusiasm of some exhibitors. At Northpoint, Charley Lippincott had sat behind a young girl who cried when Darth Vader picked up a rebel officer with one hand and throttled him, and later used the Force to choke one of Tarkin's aides. He remembered how the violence of the original *Flash Gordon* serial had distressed him when he was seven or eight. Fox assured Lucas he could expect a 'G' rating, making the film available to all ages, but Lippincott persuaded Kurtz and Lucas to take the unprecedented step of requesting a 'PG.' A friend on the rating board told Lippincott that most of its members slept through the screening of what they automatically regarded as a kids' movie, and, waking, voted to rate it 'G.' The request to raise the classification baffled them. Every other director, as Steven Spielberg would do, successfully, with *Indiana Jones and the Temple of Doom*, lobbied to reduce their films' ratings, thus broadening the audience. But the one mother on the board agreed with Lippincott, and understood how children might react.

Privately, Lippincott was already convinced the film would be a hit, though he couldn't rationalize his conviction. In February, someone stole three models of the X-Wing and Tie fighters, worth $70,000, from ILM. Early copies of the trailer, prototype T-shirts, then an entire stormtrooper outfit also disappeared. In April, another thief grabbed three hundred original transparencies and six thousand duplicates from Lippincott's office. The thief offered to sell back two thousand of them for $4000, but before Lippincott could respond, the deal was taken off the table; someone else had offered more. To Lippincott, all these were favorable signs; nobody stole anything from *The Other Side of Midnight*.

In the weeks leading up to 25 May, Lucas rushed to get *Star Wars* mixed and ready for the theaters. At Walter Murch's urging, he'd recorded in Dolby stereo, which complicated the mix. A week before the release date, he still had no final print. As he and his crew looped dialogue and sound effects into the 70mm copies at the last minute, Fox became increasingly panicky.

The editors entered that zone, familiar to anyone who ever cut a film, where language ceased to function. Only the lines of dialogue, endlessly repeated, had any reality. Zombie-like, they muttered automatically, 'Here they come,' to almost any question asked. Carrie Fisher visited the cutting rooms: 'George was lying on the couch, and he'd been up for something like thirty-six hours. They were threatening to take the film out of his hands, cut the negative and go right to the theaters. And he looked up at me and said, "I don't ever want to do this again."'

A few weeks before, Lucas had held the traditional preview for cast and crew. He wasn't there himself, a fact which offended many who'd worked on the film for little or nothing. Mark Hamill attended, his face still heavily bandaged. Alan Dean Foster came too, still unable to tell anyone he'd written the novelization, though the first printing of 100,000 in February, with its cover of Ralph McQuarrie's Darth Vader mask, had already sold out. To Lippincott's irritation, Ballantine/Del Rey refused to print more until the movie opened. Once they did, it went into four more printings in June alone, and by August had sold two million copies.

In the lobby, Foster met Gary Kurtz, and jokingly suggested he precede the film with one of Chuck Jones's best cartoons, the 1953 *Duck Dodgers in the 24½ Century*, in which Daffy Duck encounters Marvin Martian, a minuscule helmeted alien armed with some awesome weaponry. 'He kind of laughed, and left,' says Foster. But Kurtz took the suggestion, and screened *Duck Dodgers* before the film all over the world.

Another screening was held on the Fox lot for members of the science fiction community. Journalist Bill Warren was there, and loved the film. On his way home with fellow sf fan Allan Rothstein, he said, 'Do you think we should buy stock in Fox?' Rothstein reflected. 'Naw. It's only going to appeal to people like us who are into science fiction,' he said at last.

Asked in later years if he could remember the day *Star Wars* opened, Lucas said, 'Like it was yesterday. I was tired, stressed, and thinking about nothing but all of the things I hadn't done and should have done.' He and Marcia took a break to eat dinner at Hamburger Hamlet, opposite Mann's Chinese. 'I noticed this huge line that went around the block. I didn't know what it was. I had forgotten it was opening that day; that was how out of it I was.'

After dinner, Lucas went back to the Goldwyn studios and kept mixing. When the East Coast cinemas closed, Alan Ladd Jr phoned him excitedly with their grosses. 'Wow . . . wow . . . wow . . . wow . . . gee, that's pretty amazing,' said Lucas, periodically putting his hand over the phone to whisper orders to the sound engineers. When he hung up, he said, 'I'm still going to hold my breath for a few weeks. The movie's only been released for five hours. I don't want to count my chickens before they're hatched. I expect it will all fall apart next week.'

At 10 p.m. he called Mark Hamill. 'Hi kid,' he said. 'Are you famous yet?' Then he asked him to come over to the cutting room to loop one more piece of dialogue. As the limo drove Hamill past the Avco cinema in Westwood, where people had been queueing since 8 a.m., and where they still stood in line for the seventh and last screening of the day, he could barely contain the urge to roll down the window, lean out and yell, 'It's meeeeee!'

Marcia went out, and returned with two bottles of champagne. Jay Cocks stopped by with congratulations. So did Brian De Palma. 'Shall we call Francis and spread the gloom?' he joked. They discussed the problem faced by Mann's Chinese, having to yank *Star Wars* after a month in favor of *Sorcerer*.

'It took Billy three years and five continents to bring us *Sorcerer*,' De Palma said, mocking the film's advance hype.

'And all it took me was two years and one garage,' mused Lucas.

★   ★   ★

On the Memorial Day weekend after *Star Wars* opened, Doris Payne, Chicago branch manager of Fox cinemas, toured her theaters. At the Eden in Northbrook, she found chaos. Crowds had begun gathering at dawn, and the staff were swamped. Helped by her daughter and stepdaughter, Payne started to take tickets and police the exits, where kids without the price of admission were trying to wrench open the doors. Her husband took a snow shovel from his car and began cleaning up the popcorn boxes, candy wrappers and drink cups that filled the lobby and corridors ankle-deep.

In Los Angeles, manager Albert Szabo at the Westwood Avco hired sixty extra people to handle the crowds. Some days, they turned away as many as five thousand. At Mann's Chinese on Hollywood Boulevard, people waiting in line brought picnics and held impromptu parties to relieve the boredom. The management hired maintenance crews to clean up the debris. In Honolulu, a tropical downpour drenched the queueing fans for two hours. Nobody abandoned their place.

In San Francisco, Al Levine, manager of the Coronet on Geary Boulevard, said, 'I've never seen anything like it. We're getting all kinds. Old people, young people, children, Hare Krishna groups. They bring cards to play in line. We have checkers-players, we have chess-players. People with paint and sequins on their faces. Fruit-eaters like I've never seen before. People loaded on grass and LSD. At least one guy's been here every day. It's an audience participation film. They hiss the villain, they scream and holler and everything else. When school's out, the kids'll go crazy.'

Producer Jon Davison, then working at Roger Corman's studio, was in line on opening day. 'Everybody from Roger's who I knew had taken the day off work to go to the Chinese. I was the boss, and I was leading the charge to cut work. It was the movie we had all been waiting to see. It was the movie we had hoped somebody was gonna make. It's the movie we'd have loved to make ourselves.'

Fox wasn't awed by regiments of teenagers queueing round the block. That was the fools' gold of sf films, inflating the first weekend's figures, which then plunged once every fan had seen it. What did impress them were the groups of serious professional guys from the industry like Davison who deserted the office *en bloc* to see the film, and the party from the *Playboy* mansion, led by editor/publisher Hugh Hefner, arriving at Mann's Chinese in limos, watching the film from the back rows, then sitting through it a second time closer to the screen. Even more astonishingly, Senator Edward Kennedy, country and western singer Johnny Cash and boxer Muhammad Ali all waited in line at their local cinemas to see a film the company regarded as worthless.

As with *American Graffiti*, Lucas had decided to leave town after the opening, to avoid the grisly ritual of waiting for the weekend reviews, and fielding the commiserations of enemies or friends. 'The ball is back in the studio's court,' he told a reporter from the *Los Angeles Times*. 'I've given this my best shot. We are off to the sun.'

With the Huycks, he and Marcia booked into the Mauna Kea hotel in Hawaii, an arrangement he wasn't about to cancel, despite the evidence piling up that he had a hit. In Hawaii, he kept track of the grosses with growing incredulity. Even when Ladd Jr rang to confirm the same reaction everywhere, Lucas counselled caution – the second weekend would tell them whether it had 'legs.' Fox's Tim Deegan, also taking a Hawaii break, was getting the same news from a friend at *Variety*. Its editor, Art Murphy, told him, 'It was the biggest opening in history; the projections are that it will be the biggest movie ever.' Fox authorized the production of more prints and started organizing a wider distribution. By August, *Star Wars* would be screening in eight hundred theaters.

Shortly after trading opened on 23 May, the New York Stock Exchange suspended sales of Fox shares at $11.50 on rumors that Nashville trader Claude Cockress Jr was taking a position prior to launching a takeover bid. Once this rumor was discounted, dealers began a frenzy of trading. Six million Fox shares, about half the issued stock, would be bought and sold over the next three months, and by June the price had soared to $24⅝. Among the most vigorous buyers were executives of Universal; following an early preview of the film they'd turned down, the men who had rejected *Star Wars* secretly began investing in Fox.

Lucas still religiously watched the *CBS Evening News*, so nothing confirmed his success as conclusively as Walter Cronkite's report on the phenomenon of *Star Wars*. The press coverage jolted exhibitors into advertising, holding extra screenings, and generally fanning the national interest long enough for the news to spread by the vital word of mouth.

The next day, realizing at last that they were rich, the Lucases went into town, determined to splurge, only to find nothing on sale but souvenirs, shells, and suntan lotion. Yogurt shops were doing big business, however, and Lucas wondered if he might invest in one. Or perhaps a chain. Once he got back to California, he satisfied a lifelong ambition by starting a collection of racing cars.

Spielberg called to congratulate him. Supervising the special effects and soundtrack of *Close Encounters* had exhausted him. Also, by shooting clay pigeons with John Milius he'd developed the hearing deficiency tinnitus, making his ears ring constantly. It exacerbated his weariness, causing him, he confessed, to lose his 'sense of judgment and objectivity.' But he'd carried on, 'continu[ing] to make decisions, not all of them the right ones' until his staff, diplomatically, suggested he take a break.

Lucas suggested he and Amy Irving join them in Hawaii. Spielberg agreed. The day they arrived, 29 May, the three couples had dinner together. The subject of children came up. Amy said that she, like Marcia, wanted a family, and Spielberg was no less evasive on the subject than Lucas. Marcia hoped the holiday would revive their relationship. 'Getting our private life together and having a baby,' she had told a friend firmly. 'That is the project for the rest of this year.' But George dissembled. From having actively tried to persuade her to get pregnant as a way of keeping her from working with Scorsese, he now blew cool on the whole idea. Until then, his pretext for avoiding fatherhood had been financial. 'This film-making stuff may be a fluke thing,' he'd said righteously. 'I'm not going to have a family until I feel more financially secure.' Free now to do anything he wanted, he found that fathering children wasn't top of his list.

Inevitably, the table talk soon switched to projects. After *Jaws* began to rack up worldwide grosses which, at the time of their meeting in Hawaii, totalled $458 million, Spielberg had been in the same position as Lucas, and knew the cycle of emotions he would experience over *Star Wars*: relief that the film had succeeded; elation at that success; then an anti-climactic let-down; and finally the shrewd calculation of where to go next. Spielberg urged Lucas to start thinking about his next project while the honeymoon period persisted – or, as he could have put it, 'Cut to the chase.'

Lucas hesitated. He'd reached a crossroads in his career. A rich man now, he could realize what he'd always claimed was his ambition

– to make cheap, personal films with a few like-minded people in conditions of rural calm. But rationalizations for going on immediately to a big film weren't hard to find. To turn one's back on a hit was *hubris*. The gods might punish you for refusing their offer of immortality. And one had a duty to stretch one's talent, to explore places one never could have done as an unknown.

Physically exhausted, Lucas never wanted to sit in the director's chair again, even to make little pictures about simple people. But, nagged his interior voice, did that mean he need stop making films? He and Spielberg could be the architects of New Hollywood, putting their stamp on the world cinema of the twenty-first century. Overnight, in his own mind, Lucas transformed himself from director to producer. 'If I do a sequel,' he'd tell the press in a few weeks, 'I'll be a sort of executive producer. I'll approve the rough cut, and I'll say, "You're doing great," and that kind of stuff.'

In Hawaii, Lucas and Spielberg spent most days on the beach, ritually building a sandcastle, though Lucas, still sensitive to the sun, did so in a wide-brimmed hat and gloves. It was a significant choice of diversion, since what they were really doing was building New Hollywood.

For Spielberg, Lucas had metamorphosed overnight from an ambitious friend to someone with the capacity to be either a valuable ally or a dangerous rival. A consummate career tactician, Spielberg moved to consolidate his position. Old Hollywood, he argued as he moulded the castle battlements, had controlled things for too long. It was time the newcomers took charge. The establishment had effectively destroyed Coppola, but with *Jaws* and *Star Wars* he and Lucas had snatched the ultimate power in the film universe, and they had to exercise it while they could.

Above all, they needed financial control of their films. As things stood, the investors took everything, then gave back as much – or as little – as they cared to. That Lucas should own only 40 per cent of *Star Wars* was insulting. He should own 100 per cent, and pay the studio what he thought they deserved for having provided the money to make it.

Until now, studios enjoyed that power because the film-makers weren't rich enough to finance their own films, and needed advance payments to live. But Spielberg and Lucas were now rich enough to stump up their own budgets if necessary, and to waive advances. As the sandcastle walls mounted higher and the fortifications became more complex, they planned a new kind of deal, a new way of making movies.

But what movies? The Lucas mythology would foster the idea that he always intended a saga in as many as twelve episodes, but while he was making *Star Wars*, the idea of further films in the series was more academic than real. When he thought of sequels, it was in terms of *Star Trek* – not an epic but a continuing series, perhaps animated, and intended for TV. The 1977 version carried no subtitle at the head of the opening crawl. It wasn't until the film was re-released for the first time in July 1978 that he added '*Part IV: A New Hope.*'

His first thought was to tell the story described in the crawl: the rise and fall of the Jedi, the evolution of the Empire and the Rebel Alliance: 'I said, "Gee, I could do these back-stories too. That would be interesting." That's where the [idea of] starting in episode four came [from], because I said, "Well, maybe I could make three [films] out of this back-story." That evolved right around the time the film was released, after I knew it was a success.

'Then everyone started saying, "Are you going to do sequels?" I said, "Gosh, sequels. I guess I could do sequels. I could do three of what happens later on." But that was really an afterthought. [I thought] "I don't have scripts, I don't have any story." The only notion on that one is: wouldn't it be fun to get all the actors to come back when they're like sixty or seventy years old, and make three more that are about them as old people?' Then Lucas grinned as he realized that when Ford and Hamill were in their seventies, he'd be even older.

Spielberg recognized the vacuum in Lucas's ideas, and hurried to fill it. When the two collaborated on their film – already a foregone conclusion, in his mind at least – perhaps it should be something that combined the action and humor of *Star Wars* with a more earthbound story. At their first dinner in Hawaii, Spielberg had mentioned that he wanted to direct a James Bond film. He'd offered to make one for Saltzman and Broccoli, but they turned him down. Maybe he and Lucas could do something in that line.

Pausing as he molded new battlements on the castle, Lucas said, 'I've got a better film than that. Have you ever heard of the Ark of the Covenant?'

Because they saw *Star Wars* as the doom of their kind of cinema, many old friends of Lucas viewed its success sourly. Coppola, tongue in cheek, wired Lucas in Hawaii, 'Send Money. Francis,' but privately he mocked the film in the same terms as had De Palma. He and his friend Dennis Jakob called it 'twerp cinema.'

The mass enthusiasm for this cinematic comic book appalled William Friedkin. Catching the trailer of *Sorcerer* at Mann's Chinese, where it was due to open the following week, he and his wife Jeanne Moreau sensed the audience's relief as the curtains closed on his dour images, and the excitement as they reopened on Darth Vader's destroyer rumbling from over their heads like the harbinger of doom. Outside, Friedkin chatted with Ted Mann, who warned him that if *Sorcerer* didn't draw the kind of crowds now massed on the sidewalk four deep, *Star Wars* would be back within a week. When *Sorcerer* opened, Fox moved *Star Wars* to its Egyptian cinema, further down Hollywood Boulevard, but once *Sorcerer* flopped, Mann brought it back.

Old Hollywood found *Star Wars* alarming, but for different reasons. Irwin Allen, dean of Hollywood special-effects movies, the producer of *The Poseidon Adventure* and *The Towering Inferno*, was incredulous. 'I don't understand it,' he said to Fox executive Gareth Wigan as the audience exploded in applause. 'There's no stars, there's no love story, what are they clapping at?' A contingent from Disney also saw the film – 'Virtually the whole studio,' said Adam Beckett, one of the engineers on *Star Wars*. 'They were planning to do a science fiction film about a mile-long spaceship that might get sucked into a black hole. They were saying to each other, "Where did all these people come from? There's a gang of people out there who did this impossible stuff! We've never heard of these guys." The story is they decided to drop their space epic when they saw *Star Wars*.' If so, Disney later changed their mind, since their film, provisionally called 'Space Station One' but retitled *The Black Hole*, was released in 1979, and proved to be a giant flop.

Once the *Star Wars* bandwagon began rolling, critics hurried to climb on board. In *Time*, Jay Cocks had called it 'a combination of *Flash Gordon*, *The Wizard of Oz*, the Errol Flynn swashbucklers of the '30s and '40s and almost every western ever screened – not to mention *The Hardy Boys*, *Sir Gawain and the Green Knight* and *The Faerie Queene*. The result is a remarkable confection: a subliminal history of the movies, wrapped in a riveting tale of suspense and adventure, ornamented with some of the most ingenious special effects ever contrived for film.' In the way of critics determined to like a film despite its faults, Pauline Kael found even the cast admirable, as if Lucas had gone out of his way to find incompetents, and calculatedly directed them to give lumpen performances: 'Lucas has got the tone of bad movies down pat; you never catch the actors deliberately acting badly, they just seem to be bad actors, on contract to Monogram or Republic.'

Less-convinced critics saw that *Star Wars* wasn't simplistic by design. This was Lucas working at the peak of his powers, and the disproportion between the naïveté of his creation and the frenzy of its reception alarmed them. *Time* magazine's Richard Corliss, just back from the Cannes Festival, was asked to assess the film. After the intellectual onslaught of Europe's greatest film event, he found Lucas's fantasy laughable: 'All these dense factoids about Galactic Empires and Death Stars – it was like some nightmare of a pop quiz in a course I hadn't taken. The sets were Formica, the characters cardboard; the tale had drive but no depth, a tour at warp speed through an antiseptic landscape.' Stanley Kauffmann wrote, 'This picture was made for those (particularly males) who carry a portable shrine with them of their adolescence, a chalice of a self that was better then, before the world's affairs or – in any complex way – sex intruded.' The disbelievers searched for irony, perspective, even the timid cynicism of *American Graffiti*, and, not finding them, wondered how to take the film. Was it no more than an animated comic strip, as diverting and technically inventive as *Duck Dodgers in the 24½ Century*, but not intended to elicit anything more than a Chuck Jones cackle?

Supporters of *Star Wars* claimed that the vacuum in meaning was filled by the Force, which was already attracting adherents, though Lucas himself never professed it. The very insubstantiality of this most diaphanous of belief systems appealed to adolescents. Here was a religion that, like Scientology, claimed to supersede every creed, every philosophy, every human aspiration – not, like L. Ron Hubbard's synthetic creed, by illuminating their fallacies with the white light of science, but by subsuming all existing faiths. The Force was a belief roomy enough for Christianity, Buddhism and Islam to nestle in its ample folds. Tongue in cheek, Coppola would suggest to Lucas that he launch a religion based on *Star Wars*, and settle down like Hubbard to bask in his godhood. Once Skywalker Ranch was built,

Lucas invited Joseph Campbell to lecture there, impressing John Williams, for one: 'Until [Campbell] told us what *Star Wars* meant – started talking about collective memory and cross-cultural shared history – the things that rattle around in our brains and predate language, the real resonance of how the whole thing can be explained – we regarded it as a Saturday-morning space movie.'

Although Lucas claimed he had created *Star Wars* to endow mankind with the mythology it lacked, his behavior became less and less philanthropic with the film's success. Over the next decade, he became obsessively proprietorial of his characters and ideas, ruthlessly pursuing anyone using them without permission and payment. By the end of the century, Lucasfilm would claim that even the memories of actors and technicians who worked on the first films belonged to the corporation. The very words 'star wars' became a trademark, and Lucas sued when Ronald Reagan adopted them as the tag for his orbiting anti-ICBM laser weapons. Real mythology, by its very nature, is communal, and open to interpretation by all. But Lucas permitted no other writers or film-makers to employ his characters, except under the most stringent and expensive restrictions. He hadn't given us a mythology; we could only rent it.

Lucas vehemently denied that *Star Wars* and *Close Encounters* infantilized the film industry. On the contrary, he insists, by enriching cinema owners it encouraged a new diversity. 'Of the billion and a half dollars that *Star Wars* made,' he told film historian Peter Biskind in 1997, 'half of it, $700 million of it, went to the theater owners. And what did the theater owners do with that? They built multiplexes. Once they had all these screens, they had to book them with something, which meant that the art films that were being shown in tiny places in the middle of nowhere, suddenly were playing in mainstream cinemas, and started making money . . . So in a way I did destroy the Hollywood film industry, only I destroyed it by making films more intelligent, not by making films infantile.'

The reality was very different. Multiplexes didn't show art films, but used their multiple screens to maximize their income from blockbusters. When Spielberg released *The Lost World* in 1997, one New York cinema showed it round the clock on every one of its eight screens, with a new session starting every thirty minutes. With the once-thriving art-house network wiped out, foreign films all but disappeared from American cinemas, particularly if they had subtitles.

Filmgoers, it seemed, could no longer read, nor concentrate on any scene that took longer than three minutes, unless it involved a chase.

New York New York opened a few weeks after *Star Wars*, on 21 June. The Lucases came to Manhattan for the premiere. There was no skimping on hotels any more. Lucas – 'fresh from Hawaii,' noted *Rolling Stone* – sat in the Sherry Netherland giving interviews while crowds queued round the block for *Star Wars*. By contrast, Scorsese's film won small crowds and grudging reviews. These depressed Marcia, as did Scorsese's deteriorating health. He was on Lithium to level out his cocaine-induced plunges into despair. From this anguish would come *Raging Bull*, his best film and a contemporary masterpiece, but for the moment Marty seemed to Marcia and his friends a sacrifice to New Hollywood. '*Star Wars* was in,' Scorsese said somberly. 'Spielberg was in. We were finished.' William Friedkin agreed: '*Star Wars* swept all the chips off the table. What happened with *Star Wars* was like when McDonald's got a foothold – the taste for good food just disappeared.' Marcia sided with them. In 1997, she would confess, 'Right now, I'm just disgusted by the American film industry. There are so few good films, and part of me thinks *Star Wars* is partly responsible for the direction the industry has gone in, and I feel badly about that.'

Leaving Los Angeles

What a director does with [his] freedom tells a lot about
the man.

Stephen Zito, 'George Lucas Goes Far Out,'
American Film, April 1977

During the summer of 1977, Lucas began growing into his role as a
prince of the cinema. Friends and supporters were rewarded with a
share of his new millions. With forty points to give out, he could
afford to be generous. In any event, he felt he had nothing to lose;
when Tom Pollock cautioned him, Lucas said, 'Look, the studios are
going to cheat us out of everything anyway; what's the difference?'

Altogether, Lucas gave away 25 per cent of his share in *Star Wars*.
By contract, Kurtz received five points. Everyone who worked on the
set got a minimum of a twentieth of a point, and Lucas gave some
people in the office not directly involved with the film a two hundredth
of a point. Huyck and Katz got two points. Tom Pollock got one. Alec
Guinness already had 2¼ points. Hamill, Ford, and Fisher divided two
points between the three of them. Ben Burtt got a quarter-point for
his work on the sound, and John Williams a full point. Other members
of the staff, down to the janitors, received smaller sums. Alan Dean
Foster got a $50,000 handout, and James Earl Jones a $10,000 bonus.
In a spirit of comradeship that harked back to the earliest ideals of
New Hollywood, Lucas also exchanged points with friends. Spielberg
and Milius each got one, and in return offered Lucas points in *Close
Encounters* and *Big Wednesday*.

Lucas estimated the value of a *Star Wars* point at around $300,000,
but Mark Hamill, not long after the film's release, put his annual

income from his points at around $680,000. In 1980, Alec Guinness's share was estimated to be worth $2,880,000, but though the actor would complain that much of his income went in taxes, he's estimated to have grossed about $6 million from his participation in Lucas's films.

Oddly, the film didn't rocket all its stars into the top echelon. Fame made Carrie Fisher feel 'helpless,' she said; famous, but 'in a weird way, because I'm this children's cartoon character. It hasn't translated into jobs.' Lucas suggested her to Randal Kleiser for his film of the rock musical *Grease*, inspired by *American Graffiti*, but Kleiser preferred the white-bread charm of Olivia Newton-John. Already visiting a shrink three times a week, Fisher slipped more deeply into drugs.

Hamill fared even less well. 'I had a part that made such an impression on people,' he said, reviewing his career in 1997, 'that I felt I had to break that impression.' Lucas even suggested, deadpan, that he retire; he could always announce that he'd been lured back by a good role if one came along. Hamill tried, only to find that, if a good role did appear, producers wouldn't let him take it. Peter Yates wanted him for the starring part in *Breaking Away* (1979), as a working-class boy in rural America besotted with Europe and its promise of romance, but Alan Ladd Jr blocked the casting. Hamill complained, 'He didn't want me to do it because he felt it was more important to get someone that you could immediately say, "That's a kid from high school," and not, "That's the kid from *Star Wars*."' Alan Parker also turned Hamill down for a part he coveted as Billy Hayes, the young American jailed on drugs charges who escapes from a Turkish prison, in *Midnight Express* (1978). 'I don't even get a chance to fail,' said Hamill. He fired his manager of seven years, who, he claimed, 'was always looking for a good deal, while I was looking for a good role.'

Instead, after a period during which, he confessed, 'I went to Las Vegas to date thirty-eight-year-old showgirls. I wanted to scale all these women,' Hamill tried New York. He took an apartment in the Dakota, the fashionable block on Central Park West where John Lennon and other celebrities lived. After playing in the musical *Harrigan 'n' Hart*, he missed out on replacing Tim Curry as Mozart in *Amadeus*, but became the eighth and last actor to feature in a long-running production of *The Elephant Man*. The title role had become prey to stars from other fields looking for a change of pace, among them David Bowie. Producer Richmond Crinkley advertised Hamill's casting with posters of him in his Skywalker costume and the ad line, 'And the Force continues . . . on Broadway!' But it only continued for three weeks with Hamill, after which the show closed for good. He made a few more sf film appearances before finding his niche in the *Wing Commander* series of interactive CD-ROM space adventures. The first two grossed $100 million, his share of which made him financially independent for life.

Only Harrison Ford became a major star, a destiny foreshadowed in the days following *Star Wars'* release. A few days after, he dropped into Tower Records on Sunset Boulevard to buy an album, and was mobbed. He turned up at the home of Jeremy Kagan, his director on *Heroes*, with his clothes in tatters, still stunned by his unaccustomed fame.

Sent on a promotion tour to New York, Ford arranged to meet an old friend, Earl McGrath, a rock and roll manager and one-time carpentry client, at the Sherry Netherland hotel. As they headed out for dinner, Ford told him, 'I've got a car outside.'

'We don't need a car,' said McGrath – until he saw the mob. Ford hustled him into the limo, which accelerated down Fifth Avenue, pursued by hundreds of fans.

A year later, Ford still wasn't used to his fame. When a reporter pointed out to him that his likeness was on a million lunchboxes, schoolbook covers, drinks cups and paperbacks, he said wearily, 'I'm on bedsheets now, too. It's everywhere. I just walk past it. I really don't relate to it.'

The demand for *Star Wars* merchandise had become a frenzy. Diffident at first about Williams' music and soundtrack albums in general, Fox produced a mere two thousand copies of the two-disc set with its insert poster, only to be swamped by the demand. By late June, they'd shipped 200,000 units. For the film's first run, Mann's Chinese declined to stock the $1.50 souvenir program produced by George Fenmore Associates, but after *Star Wars* returned to follow *Sorcerer*, they ordered five thousand, which brought the number in circulation to half a million. Marvel scrambled to negotiate for more titles in the comic-book series, painfully aware that, with sales over the 100,000 threshold on each of the first six titles, they had to begin paying Lucasfilm royalties.

Manufacturers were ready to put the *Star Wars* logo on anything that might sell. Factors Etc. marketed T-shirts with 'May the Force be with You' and 'Wookiees Need Love Too,' but every cinema line had a furtive vendor selling rip-offs. Though Fox approved a line of *Star Wars* jewelry, the charm bracelets and barettes never sold. Fox also refused an offer to package whiskey in bottles shaped like R2-D2, at a loss of $750,000 in potential royalties, but Lucas did license Darth Vader and Obi-Wan Kenobi tankards. He insisted that all candy and gum bearing the *Star Wars* emblem also be available in sugarless form, and initially banned sugared breakfast cereals, though by the time of *Return of the Jedi* he would bow to pressure from manufacturers and authorize Kellogg's 'C-3POs,' with reduced sugar.

Vietnam had sensitized Americans to the idea of kids playing with weapons, and parents' groups campaigned against war toys. The first toy light-sabers were lightweight inflatable tubes, to protect children from injury. Kenner later replaced them with stiff plastic. When they displayed their ideas for the first *Star Wars* toys, Lucas asked, 'Where are the guns?' Bernie Loomis of Kenner explained the company's misgivings at length. When he finished, Lucas simply repeated, 'Where are the guns?' Loomis said resignedly, 'You've got the guns, George.' Kenner's versions of the Mauser-based laser pistol and a laser rifle both became big sellers.

Crowds continued to flock to the film in the cities, but once it fanned out into smaller communities, the momentum slowed. Lippincott re-accelerated it with a press junket that brought provincial journalists to Los Angeles to meet the stars. At Mann's Chinese, in a nationally publicized ceremony, R2-D2, C-3PO, Chewbacca, and Darth Vader, watched by Hamill and an obviously exhausted Fisher, had their footprints immortalized in cement – the first non-humans to be so honored since Roy Rogers' horse Trigger planted a hoof thirty years before. Lucasfilm announced that Dave Prowse, Anthony Daniels, and Kenny Baker would give no interviews, in order to preserve a sense of mystery. In fact, all three were still in England. For the Mann's ceremony, other actors wore their costumes, a fact that incensed the originals.

As summer cooled into fall, it became obvious that *Star Wars* had 'legs' to spare. Jon Bon Jovi, not then a major name in rock, issued 'R2-D2, I Wish You a Merry Christmas.' Kenner, with nothing to sell, but foreseeing a holiday season in which *Star Wars* would be the film of the year, hurriedly prepared an 'Early Bird Certificate Package.'

Buyers got a box with illustrations of a dozen *Star Wars* figures on the lid, and, inside, a cardboard stage, some decals, a *Star Wars* Club card and a mail-in form entitling them to figures of Luke, Leia, Darth Vader, and R2-D2 once Kenner manufactured them, which turned out to be two months later. Despite the illusory nature of the gift, 600,000 boxes were shipped, and enough sold at $16 each (compared to $8.98 for the double album of Williams' music) to show Kenner a profit. Meanwhile, they put more than thirty *Star Wars* products into development, including a board game, jigsaw puzzles and paint-by-number sets.

Kenner skilfully targeted the *Star Wars* figures at the lower end of the market. Their *Six Million Dollar Man* figures were eight inches tall; those from *Star Wars* were less than half that, and correspondingly cheaper. There were also ninety-two of them, encouraging repeat sales. In 1978 alone, Kenner would sell 42,322,500 figures and, over the next eight years, 250 million of them. By 1981, *Newsweek* reported that the *Star Wars* films had 'generated $1 billion in retail sales of spin-off products, of which 6 to 15 per cent goes to Lucasfilm.' The figure was perhaps an overestimate, as Lucasfilm's average take from merchandising remained around 7 per cent. However, the statistics revealed the fact, puzzling to the film industry, that *Star Wars* merchandise was enormously more profitable than admissions – as if the film was simply a giant commercial for its toys, comic books and clothing.

As with *American Graffiti*, the distribution of the spoils of *Star Wars* aroused enmities and rivalries. Lucas handed out almost no bonuses at Industrial Light and Magic. John Dykstra got nothing – inducing, said one report, a condition 'something like apoplexy.' In postproduction, Lucas had also fallen out with Jim Nelson, who believed, following his early discussions with Kurtz and Lucas, that he would receive associate producer credit. When Lucas said he'd contributed nothing 'artistic' to the film, and would be listed among other minor functionaries, a furious Nelson took his name off the film. 'I liked George,' Nelson said. 'But George is very difficult to work with; you must agree with George, and if you don't agree with George, then George doesn't like you. Dykstra would argue with George all the time, and so would I. It didn't work.'

Once *Star Wars* was launched. Lucas announced that he proposed to close the Van Nuys facility and move ILM to San Rafael, with

Dennis Muren and Richard Edlund in charge, Dykstra launched his own company, Apogee Inc. Most of the old ILM people signed on, but a number followed Lucas north, intrigued by the idea of getting in on the ground floor of a new enterprise. Aside from Muren and Edlund, animator Peter Kuran, Bruce Nicholson, who headed up the new optical department, electronics expert Jerry Jeffress, modelmaker Lorne Peterson, Phil Tippett, and stop-motion specialist Jon Berg, together with some junior people, made the move to Marin. Ralph McQuarrie drew a change-of-address card. It showed a landspeeder with C-3PO and R2-D2 at the wheel leading the Jawas' sandcrawler and a *bantha* ridden by a Tusken Raider on the road out of Los Angeles. The only human figures in the picture are *Star Wars* characters. Already Lucas seemed anxious to emphasize that the only reality of his new world would be the one created out of his imagination.

While Spielberg was working on the post-production of *Close Encounters*, Lucas sent him a summary of the Ark of the Covenant story he had worked out with Philip Kaufman, together with notes on five possible sequels. He visualized films built around a hero who combined the casual glamor of Clark Gable with the suavity of Cary Grant. He'd named him 'Indiana,' after Marcia's dog, but dithered about the surname, eventually deciding on 'Smith.' An archeologist, Smith would quarter the globe, searching out ancient civilizations and looting their treasures, before returning to his job as a college professor, trading his dusty leather jacket and battered fedora for evening clothes and a top hat.

Lucas called in Charley Lippincott. 'He told me, "You're the one person who really knows movie serials,"' says Lippincott, 'and he would pick my brain about serials. He'd hint about it but never tell me exactly what he was doing. I never showed serials to George at USC like Don Glut did, but he knew I knew serials very well, and that I'd even seen the [Louis] Feuillade serials [from the early part of the century] at the French Cinématheque, and so I had maybe a different perspective on them than Don.'

Lucas and Spielberg sat through all twelve episodes of Universal's 1941 *Don Winslow of the Navy*, a dispiriting experience. The enchantment lent by distance evaporated as the cheesy settings, bumbling acting, and tortuous plot twists unrolled. 'These things sure don't hold up after twenty-five years,' sighed Lucas.

Lucas's image of the hero troubled Spielberg, who felt it was pitched too high for the twelve-to-fourteen-year-olds who'd make up the film's market. The personality which most readily sprang to mind when Spielberg thought about Indiana was Fred C. Dobbs, the unshaven, unwashed, panhandling drifter played by Humphrey Bogart in John Huston's *The Treasure of the Sierra Madre*. Kaufman had visualized an Indiana who could rummage in a girl's underwear as casually as he looted a tomb. Lucas wanted somebody at the other extreme, an archetype like the legendary beings of *Star Wars*, so driven by abstract concepts like Fate and the Force that they barely existed below the navel. It was evident that this film would require a lot more work than had been envisaged on a Hawaiian beach.

The Ark of the Covenant film wasn't Lucas's only project at the end of 1977. He told journalist Stephen Farber that he wanted to try a slapstick comedy: 'Woody Allen, Laurel and Hardy, Abbott and Costello, Harold Lloyd, Buster Keaton, all rolled into one. It's been a long time since anybody made a really goofy comedy that had people rolling in the aisles. It's very hard to do, which is why nobody does it, but it's a challenge; it's like climbing that mountain.'

He already had a couple of vehicles in mind. One was *Radioland Murders*, a comedy murder mystery suggested by the 1942 *Who Done It?*, in which a couple of soda jerks, played by Abbott and Costello, solve a murder in a radio station. He'd already discussed it with the Huycks, who were going to write the script. A better idea occurred to him in 1976, when the first full issue of a comic book called *Howard the Duck* appeared from Marvel.

Written and created by Steve Gerber and drawn by Frank Brunner, it was a product of the ecumenical spirit in which new comic artists revived and relaunched heroes of the past. Jack Kirby had brought Superman into the pantheon of Marvel superheroes, and would co-opt his sidekick Jimmy Olsen as a character in his 'New Gods' stories. *Howard the Duck*, though Marvel tried to avoid admitting it, was a widening and broadening of Disney's Donald Duck. Plucked from another planet where ducks, not apes, have evolved into the dominant race, Howard, three feet tall, cigar-chewing, tough, and horny, is dumped in Cleveland, Ohio, where he's befriended by Bev, a singer in a rock band who becomes his mentor and mistress. Howard became a cult comic hero, blossoming into a daily strip and a number of foreign translations. Lucas thought there was a film in Howard, and checked with Marvel on the rights. It turned out that Stan Lee had sold them to Universal-TV as part of a package that included *The Incredible Hulk*, so he shelved the idea, and turned to the Ark of the Covenant story.

Also in 1977, Universal had reissued *American Graffiti*, which found a whole new audience. Lucas took the opportunity to restore the cuts made before the first release, and to mix the sound, as originally intended, in stereo. Nobody commented on the restored material, least of all Ned Tanen, now head of Universal.

Tanen also pointed out that Lucas still owed Universal two more films under his contract, and suggested a sequel to *American Graffiti* as the first. 'More *American Graffiti* really got made because of pressure from the studio,' says Gary Kurtz. 'After the reissue of *American Graffiti* did well, they said, "What about doing a sequel?" George said, "No, I don't think that's a good idea." But the studio said, "We have the right to make a sequel without you." And he said, "Well, I don't want to see that either." So he reluctantly agreed to do that.'

Meanwhile, Alan Ladd Jr also badgered Lucas to commit to a second *Star Wars* film, and the sooner the better. This project tempted Lucas far more than the *American Graffiti* sequel, since, if it wasn't made within two years, all the sequel rights reverted to Fox. Lucas already had a treatment for the second episode. Suffused with defeat and despair, it began with a vengeful Vader tracking the rebels to their ice planet hideout. They escape, and scatter. While Luke undergoes training with the Jedi master Yoda, Obi-Wan Kenobi's old teacher, Vader pursues Han, Leia, and the 'droids across the universe. Betrayed to Vader by his old friend Lando Calrissian, Han is sold to Jabba the Hutt as a trophy to decorate his palace. Having discovered that Vader is really Anakin Skywalker, and his father, Luke faces him in a lightsaber duel, and barely survives, losing a hand. The film would end with Vader triumphant, the rebels disorganized, and Han, Leia and Luke at opposite corners of the universe.

To write the screenplay, Lucas needed someone more comfortable with pulp science fiction than any of the people who'd worked on *Star Wars*. He had no ideas until a friend handed him a science fiction novel and said, 'Here's someone who wrote the cantina scene in *Star Wars* better than you did.' The novelist was Leigh Brackett. Lucas found she was still living and working in Los Angeles with her husband, Edmond Hamilton, also a science fiction writer, and asked her to come in.

Brackett was in her early sixties, a plain, no-nonsense lady who looked as if she might run a rural hardware store. But she had written novels like *Queen of the Martian Catacombs* and *Black Amazon of Mars* for such pulp magazines as *Planet Stories,* and her book *The Sword of Rhiannon* was a classic of sword-wielding heroic fantasy which outdid even Edgar Rice Burroughs.

'Have you ever written for the movies?' Lucas asked.

Straight-faced, Brackett said, 'Yes, I have.' She began enumerating her credits, most of them films for Howard Hawks: *Rio Bravo, El Dorado, Hatari!,* and the classic *The Big Sleep,* which she co-wrote with William Faulkner.

In the awkward silence that followed, Lucas said, 'Are you *that* Leigh Brackett?'

'Yes,' Brackett said. 'Isn't that why you called me in?'

'No,' said Lucas, embarrassed. 'I called you in because you were a pulp science fiction writer.'

After that, there was no doubt that Brackett would script the second *Star Wars* film, provisionally titled *The Empire Strikes Back.* Lucas gave her his carefully detailed treatment, imbued with a morose tone very different to the first film. Brackett took the job, though she had been diagnosed with cancer – another factor that contributed to the darkness of her screenplay.

A few days after the release of *Star Wars*, Coppola wrapped *Apocalypse Now*, after 238 days of shooting and $27 million spent. To finish the film, he'd borrowed $10 million from the Chase Manhattan bank at 20 per cent interest, secured on his home and everything else he'd accumulated from the success of the *Godfather* films.

In the Philippines, Carroll Ballard had visited Coppola with the final screenplay of *The Black Stallion.* Coppola approved it, then had second thoughts and asked Melissa Mathison to rewrite it. Ballard gritted his teeth, accepted the revisions, and was rewarded with a minuscule $2.7 million budget. He was shooting the film in Toronto when Coppola, taking time off from editing *Apocalypse*, decided he wasn't happy with Ballard's footage, and flew in by private jet with Mathison and a retinue that included a couple of French film critics.

'It was like Hitler flying into Nuremberg,' said Ballard, who was grateful when Coppola, widely publicized as working twenty-hour days 'helping' the director, in fact spent his time partying, and left without changing one word of the script.

Back in San Francisco, the editors told Coppola that his friend and assistant Dennis Jakob, as emotionally unsteady as Francis himself, had been sneaking into the cutting room and re-editing the film. When Coppola warned him off, Jakob stole part of the workprint, burned it, and mailed some of the ashes to Coppola each day for a week.

'You should make a film about *that*,' Coppola told Lucas when they met after Coppola's return from Toronto. The two men remained friendly, and even talked about collaborating on something – not necessarily a film. According to Coppola, Lucas came to him and said, 'Oh, I'm gonna have all this money. We can do all the dreams we always wanted to do, and I want to do it with you.' Coppola told him, 'Well, George, you wait until you get the dough, and then we'll see if you still feel that way.'

They talked about buying the Mann cinema chain, or even the Fox studios, where Dennis Stanfill, the chairman, and Alan Ladd Jr were locked in a power struggle. But they could never decide on a project. 'Now I was clearly in the subordinate position,' says Coppola, giving his analysis of why their relationship had changed. 'About six months later, there was less of that talk, and then there was a period of falling out. I never understood what it was about.'

Very clearly, it was *about* what Lucas saw as Coppola's hijacking of his Vietnam project. As if Coppola sensed his culpability, the spirit of Lucas hovered over *Apocalypse Now*. Harrison Ford played a cameo as the sinister, soft-spoken Special Services officer present when General J.D. Spradlin orders Martin Sheen to terminate Kurtz, and the actor, sensing Coppola's mood, gave himself a name-tag that read 'Colonel G. Lucas.'

Lucas's attention turned to *More American Graffiti*. He worked out a rough plot in which each of the four main characters from the first film responded in a different way to the sixties, and began looking around for someone to write and to direct it. Toward the end of 1977, he thought of a strategy that would both satisfy Universal's desire for a sequel and inflict a subtle revenge on Coppola. He would make *More American Graffiti* as much as possible a Vietnam picture, and beat Coppola at his own game. The pretext already existed in the epilogue to the first film, where Terry was described as missing in action in Vietnam.

While Coppola continued to agonize over *Apocalypse*, Spielberg released *Close Encounters* on 15 November 1977, to phenomenal success. On 31 October, financial journalist William Flanagan had written in *New York* magazine that, 'in my humble opinion, the film will be a colossal flop. It lacks the dazzle, charm, wit, imagination, and broad audience appeal of *Star Wars* – the film Wall Street insists it measure up to.' Reflecting the experience of Fox investors in the run-up to the release of *Star Wars*, Columbia stock, which had climbed from $7 a share to $18 after good early response to *Close Encounters'* previews, slumped to $15 following Flanagan's report. On the Tuesday before the film's release, the New York Stock Exchange, as they had with Fox, suspended trading in Columbia shares; not because of frantic buying, but because the computers were swamped with 'sell' orders – which would be bitterly regretted by the vendors when Spielberg's film had audiences queueing in the snow until midnight to see it.

The physical act of writing literally pained many in New Hollywood. Some were undiagnosed dyslexics, or victims of related reading difficulties, the rest simply ill-educated by a system that put no premium on literature. They communicated best in conversation, just as they derived their greatest mental stimulation from visual arts like comic books and movies. Spielberg 'wrote' his screenplays by chatting with writers in front of a tape recorder. His collaborators, who included the writing teams of Robert Zemeckis and Bob Gale, and Matthew Robbins and Hal Barwood, then went away and put the script together.

Once Spielberg became a success, the writers on whom he'd relied had begun to ask for help in return. Such was his clout in Hollywood now that Ned Tanen would back almost any low-budget film by any first-time director if Spielberg put his name on it as executive producer, and promised to finish it if the director couldn't. On this basis, Universal funded *I Wanna Hold Your Hand*, the first film directed by Robert Zemeckis. Spielberg also agreed to help Matthew Robbins, who'd directed only one film, the unsuccessful *Corvette Summer*, though he did so with less enthusiasm. Older than Zemeckis and Gale, and correspondingly more desperate, Robbins and his writing partner Hal Barwood were less easy to sell. Also, many people bridled at Robbins' peremptory manner.

Late in 1977, Spielberg received a screenplay by someone he'd never heard of. Called *Continental Divide*, it was a Howard Hawks-like comedy about a tough Chicago sportswriter on the run from some criminals who, for his safety, is sent by his editor to the high Rocky Mountains to write a story about a reclusive ornithologist studying the nesting habits of eagles. Since the ornithologist is a pretty girl, the two fall into a romance.

Six months before, the author of *Continental Divide*, Lawrence Kasdan, had been working in a Los Angeles advertising agency, and loathing it. *Continental Divide* reflected his admiration of classic Hollywood movie-making. Spielberg was reminded of forties and fifties comedies like *Woman of the Year* and *Pat and Mike*, that had starred Spencer Tracy and Katharine Hepburn. They'd been among his favorite films when he was growing up. He sent a copy to Lucas, who agreed it was brilliant, and also cheap; who could fail with a story about two people in a hut on top of a mountain? Maybe, he suggested, this guy Kasdan, young, hungry, and cheap, would be good to script *More American Graffiti*.

Spielberg had a better idea. He called in Kasdan for a talk. 'I went out to see him where Zemeckis and Gale were making *I Wanna Hold Your Hand*,' says Kasdan. 'He was sitting on the kerb, and we met for the first time. He said, "I'm doing this movie with George Lucas and I want you to write it. An adventure thing, like the old serials," and I said, "Wow. Great." And he said, "But you've got to be careful, because George is going to try to get you to write the sequel to *American Graffiti*. I showed him *Continental Divide* and he really loved it, but I don't want you to do that. We've got to concentrate on this other thing." I said, "OK." My head was just spinning.

'So, we went to this meeting at Universal. There was this guy Frank Marshall, whom I'd never met. He'd been working for Walter Hill, and they wanted him to produce this movie. Steven was interested in him, and George had gone out and got him. So we're sitting around, Howard Kazanjian, Steven, George, Marshall, and me. George said, "I'm going to do this thing. It's like the serials, and it's named for my dog Indiana, and the guy has a whip, and we didn't know what he should be chasing after, but Phil Kaufman told me that his orthodontist told him about the lost Ark of the Covenant, and Steven's gonna direct it, and we think you should write it." I was a month out of advertising, and here were these two guys who, at the time, were the center of the earth. Frank Marshall and I walked out of there. We'd just met, but I said, "Did we get that job?" and he said, "I don't know." We had to see if the agents got a call.'

The agents were called, and Kasdan and Marshall got the jobs. 'I liked the sound of it from the get-go,' says Kasdan of the Ark story. 'It wasn't about comics and serials. To me, it was all about adventure movies, which I loved. It was about *Seven Samurai* to me. In fact there's a lot of Kurosawa in *Raiders*. It was decided that we were going to go off to the house in Sherman Oaks which Jane Bay owned, and George and Steven and I were going to sit for a week and work out this story. I felt I'd fallen into heaven.'

Howard Kazanjian had been at USC with Lucas. He and his girl-friend used to double date with George and Marcia. Kazanjian become one of the top first assistant directors in Hollywood, but after working with Alfred Hitchcock on his last film, *Family Plot*, Hitchcock suggested he think about going into production. Lucas hired him to produce *More American Graffiti*, and the two men started looking for a writer. With memories of Richard Walter on the first film, Lucas wanted him to be a Californian, about thirty-five – in other words, his age – and best known for writing comedy.

Among the scripts that crossed Kazanjian's desk over the next few months was one by Bill Norton. Both Kazanjian and Lucas knew him. He'd been in Gloria Katz's class in the UCLA film school, and graduated just one year after Lucas left USC. He lived in Venice, California, at the heart of West Coast hippie culture, wore his hair long, and sported a droopy mustache. In 1971, he'd directed and written *Cisco Pike*, with Kris Kristofferson as a fading pop star black-mailed by crooked cop Gene Hackman into dealing drugs. After its failure, he never got another feature going, but continued to write, in particular on Sam Peckinpah's 1978 trucking film *Convoy*, and Richard T. Heffron's *Outlaw Blues* (1977).

Norton looked to have all the right counter-cultural credentials, so Kazanjian offered him the chance to write *More American Graffiti*. Summoned to San Anselmo for one of the week-long script confer-ences that had worked so well with Kasdan and *Raiders*, he found that Lucas had already roughed out most of the story, which wove together the lives of John Milner, Terry the Toad, and Steve Bolander as they lived through three New Year's Eves – 1964 for Milner, 1965 for Terry, and 1966 for Steve. The dates were crucial, since the end of *American Graffiti* announced that Milner died in a collision with a drunk driver in December 1964, and that Terry was listed as missing in action at An Loc in December 1965. Logically, a fourth section should have dealt with Curt, whom the first film described as having become a writer living in Canada. However, while everyone else from *American Graffiti* had agreed to reprise their roles, Richard Dreyfuss refused. Having won the 1978 Best Actor Oscar for *The Goodbye Girl*, he felt that this remake could only set back his career.

In the new film, Milner has graduated to professional drag racing. Matched against a slick professional team in a New Year's Eve race-off, he wins against all the odds, only to be killed driving home. In Vietnam, Terry is a wised-up, embittered grunt who, as the film starts, is trying to shoot himself in the arm to get a medical discharge. After falling out with his commanding officer, who sentences him to latrine duty for the rest of his tour, he fakes a Viet Cong bomb attack and, declared missing, heads off into the jungle, vowing to hide out in Europe until the war's over.

Steve and Laurie are married, with two children, and living in San Francisco. When Steve refuses to let Laurie get a job, she runs away to her younger brother's house in Berkeley, and finds herself caught up in an anti-Vietnam demonstration. Steve pursues her, is himself arrested at the demonstration, then breaks all of them out by stealing the police bus in which they're held.

Lucas covered Curt's absence from the film by inventing a younger brother, Andy, for Laurie, and by following Terry's girlfriend Debbie as she rattles round the crash pads and rock shows of Haight-Ashbury. It was this section with which Norton felt most comfortable, and it's correspondingly more detailed than the rest, with Debbie working as a topless dancer and doggedly trailing after her languid lover Lance, finding bail money to get him out of jail after a marijuana arrest, crashing a New Year's Eve concert at the Fillmore, and ending up playing tamborine in a rock band. At the end of the film, she's the only one whose position has improved: the post-credit round-up says she's now a country and western singer.

Lucas told Norton he wanted each of the film's four sections shot in a different style – an idea he'd contemplated but abandoned on the first film. The drag racing should look bright and open, like Elvis Presley's *Viva Las Vegas*, complete with blondes in tight T-shirts: he suggested Panavision, 50mm lens, almost no camera movement. For the Haight-Ashbury sequences, he wanted psychedelia: wobbling multi-colored light shows, gaudy tie-dyed clothing, hippieness rampant. Kazanjian suggested they might shoot these sequences in split-screen, showing three separate images, so that an event could be seen from different perspectives. It had worked in Michael Wadleigh's film of Woodstock. Lucas enthusiastically agreed. For Laurie and Steve in the demonstration, Lucas proposed something more like Haskell Wexler's style on *Medium Cool*: long lenses peering into the action, leaping back from grainy close-up to panoramic scenes of police baton charges and crowds fleeing clouds of teargas. For the Vietnam sections, he wanted even more realism: they should look like combat footage, and be shot in 16mm – exactly as he and Coppola had planned to do *Apocalypse Now*.

As he left San Anselmo, Norton was, like everyone else, uneasily aware of the multiple hidden agendas of *More American Graffiti*. 'Stick it to Universal' was clearly one of them; 'Outdo Coppola' another. Critics had hailed Coppola's *Godfather II* as superior to the first film, in part because of its intricate pattern of flashbacks, switching between Vito Corleone as an ageing don, a rising career criminal in turn-of-the-century New York, and a boy in Sicily. *More American Graffiti* would, Lucas hoped, trump him on that score. John Milius for one doesn't doubt Lucas's intention to surpass *Apocalypse* by coming out with a more 'authentic' picture of the war, but made in the US, and on a modest budget: 'I always thought that was a bad thing that he goes and makes *More American Graffiti* and tries to bring it out before Francis. He wants to steal Francis's thunder, you know?'

In his dealings with Fox, Lucas also began exercising his new power. Knowing they would agree to almost anything in return for *The Empire Strikes Back*, he had Tom Pollock work out a package. His old agents, ICM, pointed out that having negotiated the first deal, they had a right to also represent him in the second, but Lucas angrily rejected their overture. What need did he have of agents when the studios were besieging him with offers?

Pollock actually wrote the deal with Fox, but Lucas dictated the terms. He had deposited all his profits from *Star Wars* in his own name, rather than that of Lucasfilm, but would lend $20 million to Lucasfilm, which would then use it as collateral for a line of credit to finance the film, estimated to cost $18.5 million. In return, he got 50 per cent of the gross profits, rising to 77 per cent as the film made money. Fox would pay all the cost of prints and publicity out of its 25 per cent, but Lucasfilm owned merchandising and spin-off rights, as well as those for television and home video sales. In addition, after seven years the film would revert to Lucas. Pollock handed Ladd the contract on Yom Kippur. 'This is your day of atonement,' he told him. Ladd signed, knowing that if he didn't, Lucas would make good on his threat to take the film to one of the many other studios salivating to produce it. On the other hand, exhibitors had already pledged $15 million in guarantees, so Fox could hardly lose.

The flop of *New York New York* and *Big Wednesday*, and the continuing problems of *Apocalypse Now*, widened still further the gap between New Hollywood's haves and have-nots.

When *Big Wednesday* failed, Lucas felt betrayed. Asked if he regretted having swapped a point in Milius's film for one in *Star Wars*, he said, 'I guess it just proves I'm a good friend but a bad investor.' Privately, however, he asked Milius to return the point. 'I told him I'd spent it on my divorce,' his old friend said tersely. 'After the exchange of points, he just disappeared out of my life. I just never would hear from him or see him. I guess he felt it was a bad business deal.'

Switching Lawrence Kasdan onto what would become *Raiders of the Lost Ark* had left *Continental Divide* hanging, so Spielberg suggested that Matthew Robbins and Hal Barwood make it for Universal, perhaps with John Belushi playing the sportswriter. A series of meetings began, presided over by the sardonic, capricious Ned Tanen. Kasdan watched in dismay as the Hollywood sharks devoured these two weakly flopping victims. 'Steven didn't really support Matthew and Hal all that much,' he says, 'and Ned Tanen just tortured them. No combination of casting satisfied him. It was going to be Peter Falk and Jill Clayburgh . . . They could never put the thing together, and Tanen just sat there. I went to those meetings. That was my first exposure to executives in Hollywood. I was amazed at how Ned was torturing these guys. Steven was never at these meetings, and Matthew wound up losing the movie. It was Matthew and Hal's fault. They would never drive anything to a conclusion. It was a real education for me, because I felt they were not being effective, and that Ned was playing with them.'

★   ★   ★

When the Oscar nominations were announced early in 1978, Spielberg and Lucas found themselves matched in an unsought three-way contest with each other and, jointly, with Old Hollywood. Not unexpectedly, the Academy voters, overwhelmingly middle-aged and devoted to the studio system, gave most of their endorsement to good old-fashioned pictures like *Julia* and *The Turning Point* (eleven nominations each), and Neil Simon's comedy *The Goodbye Girl* (five nominations). An influx of New Yorkers and stage people into Hollywood gave Woody Allen's *Annie Hall* an unexpected five nominations. But *Star Wars* received nominations for Best Picture, Best Director, Best Supporting Actor (Guinness), Best Screenplay Written Directly for the Screen, Best Art Direction (John Barry, Norman Reynolds, Leslie Dilley, and Roger Christian), Best Sound (Don McDougall, Ray West, Bob Minkler, and Derek Ball), Best Original Score, Best Editing (Paul Hirsch, Marcia Lucas, and Richard Chew), Best Costume Design (John Mollo), and Best Visual Effects (John Stears, John Dykstra, Richard Edlund, Grant McCune, and Robert Blalack). *Close Encounters'* Melinda Dillon was nominated as Best Supporting Actress, Spielberg as Best Director, Vilmos Zsigmond for Cinematography. It also received nominations for Art Direction, Sound, Original Score, Editing, and Visual Effects.

As 29 March, Oscar night, approached, Lucas affected indifference to the awards, but privately he was nervous. 'When *Star Wars* was up for an Oscar,' says Don Glut, 'I had a call from Randal Kleiser, inviting me to a party. Kleiser was just going to do *Grease*. George was nervous, and he wanted to surround himself with people he knew; people from the old days. So he basically had a cinema department reunion party the night before the Academy Awards.'

On Oscar night itself, the popularity of *Star Wars'* characters proved too much for the Academy to resist, and R2-D2 (wearing a bow tie) and C-3PO presented the Special Achievement awards. Voted on by specialists only, they included one to Ben Burtt for his sound effects on *Star Wars*. Dykstra was honored too for the Dykstraflex camera, and Frank Warner for his sound effects on *Close Encounters*. But both films were snubbed for the major awards. *Star Wars* won for Art Direction, Sound, Original Score, Editing, and Visual Effects; *Close Encounters* for Cinematography alone. *Annie Hall* was named Best Picture, Allen Best Director, and Diane Keaton Best Actress. *Julia* took almost all the rest. It was a pattern that would continue for the next decade. Science fiction films would have to be content with technical and craft awards until enough newcomers infiltrated the Academy to oust the old guard.

Francis and Eleanor Coppola watched the awards ceremony on TV. Coppola told her, 'Since George didn't win any of the major awards himself, he'll be back. He won't just retire into moguldom as he's been saying. He'll come back, he'll make another film. He likes to win.'

He was right. When the British Oscar-winners got back to London, they held a celebration party at which all nineteen of their statuettes – members of teams received a statuette each – were lined up on a table. 'And the next morning,' said John Mollo, 'we had a production meeting on the second movie.'

In early summer 1978, a TV production company, Smith-Hemion, approached Lucas with the suggestion of a *Star Wars* special, to air on the November Thanksgiving weekend. Traditionally, early evening on Thanksgiving is a prime spot for children's programming, and advertisers clamor for spots. Smith-Hemion had experience in juvenile TV: one of its principals, Dwight Hemion, directed a successful 1975 TV adaptation of *Peter Pan* with Mia Farrow. They also had a connection with the Canadian animation company Nelvana, which would later produce two animated *Star Wars* series, one based on R2-D2 and C-3PO, the other on the *ewoks*, furry creatures developed for *The Return of the Jedi*, the last of the trilogy.

Preoccupied with writing and planning *Raiders of the Lost Ark*, Lucas agreed to cooperate with *The Star Wars Holiday Special*, at least to the extent of supplying all the original stars still in the US – only Guinness and Cushing didn't appear – and allowing Smith-Hemion to use their characters and costumes, as well as out-takes from the film as background footage. He also suggested the story, hoping, according to Lenny Ripps, who wrote the first script, for 'a sweet and sentimental vision of a holiday season.' Once Smith-Hemion chose a director, David Acumba, Lucas attended a few production and script meetings, though Ripps claims he never contributed more than a list of things he didn't want included, and a few possible additions, many of them from early drafts of *Star Wars*.

Lucas's story resurrected the idea, abandoned early in the planning of *Star Wars*, of a planet inhabited by *wookiees*. As scripted by Ripps, it followed Han Solo and Chewbacca as they raced across the universe to this world, Kashyyyk, for the *wookiees'* most important annual festival, 'Life Day,' their equivalent of Thanksgiving. As Han and Chewbacca dodge Imperial patrols in the *Millennium Falcon,* Chewy's wife Mala, his father Itchy, and son Lumpy periodically check by videophone with Leia and Luke for news of his progress. Imperial stormtroopers arrive to search their rooftop house, supposedly looking for 'rebels,' and leave one of their number behind on guard. Once Chewy appears, he tips the interloper over the balcony. Han embraces everyone, and the family and friends settle down to celebrate the festival, during which Carrie Fisher sings, abysmally, 'The Life Day Song,' a vocal version of John Williams's *Star Wars* theme.

There was immediate enthusiasm about the special from CBS. Kenner, now struggling to keep up with orders for *Star Wars* merchandise, became the sustaining sponsor, and started designing four new action figures based on Chewbacca and his family. Originally planned to last an hour, the program doubled in length as more advertisers climbed on board. To spin out the story, Lucas and Ripps added comic episodes during which Chewy and Han revisit locations from the film, including the cantina on Mos Eisley, where Bea Arthur, star of the TV series *Maude,* plays a bartender who joins an alien client in a duet and dance. Other cameos featured comedian Harvey Korman and Art Carney (as a grocer), singer Diahann Carroll, and the group Jefferson Starship. R2-D2 also appeared to plug Kenner's *Star Wars* toys. These additions still didn't bring the program up to length, so Smith-Hemion commissioned Nelvana to make a twenty-minute animated film which Lumpy watches while he waits for his father. It showed the adventures of Han and the rest of the *Star Wars* characters, including Darth Vader and Boba Fett, the masked bounty-hunter who would become one of the *Star Wars* universe's least likely leading characters.

When Lucas saw the completed special, he was horrified, but by then it was too late to stop the broadcast, though he did remove his name as screenwriter. The program went out on the evening of 17 November 1978. Reaction ranged from incredulous to appalled. Kenner axed its projected line of *wookiee* figures, and CBS never repeated the show. No history authorized by Lucasfilm mentions it, and Lucas has never permitted its issue on videocassette, though bootleg copies circulate widely of the only commercial and artistic disaster to bear the name 'Star Wars.' Lucas has reportedly said that if he had a hammer and enough time, he would cheerfully smash every one.

18

Writing *Raiders*

Don't ask me. I'm making this up as I go along.

Indiana Jones, in *Raiders of the Lost Ark*. Script by Lawrence
Kasdan, from story by George Lucas and Philip Kaufman

In the house at Sherman Oaks, Kasdan worked with Spielberg and Lucas on the Indiana Smith film. The three sat talking for two weeks in front of a tape recorder, then Kasdan took the resulting hundred-page transcript home and wrote the script.

They never resolved the conflict between Cary Grant-Indy and Humphrey Bogart-Indy. Kasdan compromised on a character neither as suave as the first nor as leathery as the second. His model was Clark Gable – not the stocky, graying, post-war Gable, nor even the easy, laconic Gable of *Gone with the Wind*, but the little-remembered star of 1930s adventure films like Jack Conway's *Too Hot to Handle*. Gable played a newsreel cameraman sufficiently unprincipled to fake scenes of carnage during the Japanese invasion of China, and to do everything he can to frustrate his competitor Walter Pidgeon. He has his comeuppance when one of his stunts discredits aviatrix Myrna Loy, but redeems himself by helping Loy rescue her brother from savages on the Amazon.

'Gable was an odd mixture, because he wasn't an athlete or a muscular guy,' says Kasdan, 'but he always had an enormous masculinity that never left him. That could be most evident of Gable in *Too Hot to Handle*, which I've seen four times. Gable had this attitude of "Here's the adventure. Let's go!", which I think is also true of Ford in *Raiders*. In fact, the scene where the natives are chasing Indy during *Raiders*' beginning is very similar to a sequence in *Too Hot to Handle*.'

Up until the fourth draft of the script, effectively the version Spiel-berg used to shoot from, Indy remained half grave-robber, half lounge-lizard, a dichotomy dramatized by his accommodations: a poky office at the college cluttered with papers and artefacts; and a home furnished in high *art deco*, complete with blonde in evening gown, both financed by selling loot from his excavations. Kasdan disliked Lucas's idea of a venal Jones. 'I had to write, under duress, a different version of the scene where Brody [Jones's college supervisor] goes to his house,' he says. 'George wanted Indy to be a playboy, so Jones was going to answer the door wearing a tuxedo. Then, when Brody went into the house, he would see a beautiful, Harlow-type blonde sipping cham-pagne in Indy's living room. My feeling was that Indiana Jones's two sides, professor and adventurer, made him complicated enough without adding the playboy element. One of the factors that's so great about Harrison's performance is that he makes that combination believable. He didn't overdo it. There's real charm to Ford's perform-ance as the professor, yet you can also believe what Indy does later on is part of the same person. Luckily, that "playboy" scene was never shot.'

The story of *Raiders* opens in 1936. Indiana Jones, professor of arch-eology at an ivy-covered American college, spends his spare time rooting through tombs, the plunder from which his friend and superior, Marcus Brody, buys for the college museum. In the opening sequence, Jones is delving into the temple of the Chachapoyan war-riors in Peru, supposedly two thousand years old, in search of a small, solid-gold fertility idol encrusted with jewels. He escapes the ancient builders' intricate booby-traps, still puzzlingly efficient after centuries, only to have the idol stolen by his arch enemy, Belloq, a suave French-man always a day ahead of him – and in a clean, well-ironed shirt at that.

Back home, Indy is introduced by Brody to two US Army Intelli-gence officers. They tell him that Adolf Hitler, a believer in psychic phenomena, is on the track of the Ark of the Covenant, rumored to be buried in the Egyptian city of Tanis, which hordes of Nazis are even now excavating, with the help of Belloq. The clue to the Ark's location lies in the Staff of Ra, part of which belongs to a General Tengtu Hok, in Shanghai, and the other to American archeologist Abner Ravenwood.

Indy dons his working clothes of leather jacket, fedora and whip, and heads for China via flying boat. 'In 1936,' says Kasdan, 'Shanghai was a battleground between the Japanese and the Chinese. General Hok was such an outlaw, though, that he was aligned with the Japanese. I had Indy being taken to Hok's museum by two CIA agents. Indy then broke into the museum, where he saw a complicated alarm system, part of which was a ten-foot-diameter gong. Suddenly, two samurai burst in on Indy. Indy shot the first warrior and then had an interesting confrontation with the second samurai involving Jones's whip and the Japanese's sword. Indy wound up choking him with his whip. Indy took the fallen samurai's sword and used it to break open the glass container holding the medallion-half. That, naturally, set off the gong alarm. Hok came running into the room, holding a sub-machine gun, which he then started firing at Indy. Indy managed to push the gong off its hook and then rolled it across the floor, running behind it, using it as a shield. The gong was so heavy that it cracked the marble floor as it was rolling. There was also a tremendous amount of interesting noise as the blasting of Hok's gun merged with the almost musical sound of the bullets bouncing off the gong.'

Indy heads for Nepal by DC3 – a scene much shorter in the film than in Kasdan's script. 'Originally, we had Indy falling asleep. Suddenly, all of the other passengers – a little old lady, a European, some Chinese – got up and tiptoed and parachuted off the plane! All of the passengers were in on it. Indy was left by himself on the plane, heading towards a crash in the Himalayas. He finally woke up and then couldn't get into the cockpit. Indy pulled out an inflatable raft and wrapped it around his body. He didn't inflate it inside the plane, because it would have been too big for him to jump out the doors. Indy jumped out of the plane, pulled the inflator, and landed in the snowy Himalayan Mountains. He then rode the life-raft down the slopes.'

Ravenwood, the American archeologist, is dead, but Marion, his daughter – and, it emerges, once Indy's lover – runs a saloon, The Raven, just above the snowline in Nepal. Their painful reacquaintance and reconciliation, during which Marion reveals that after her father died in an avalanche, she'd been forced to work in The Raven – 'I wasn't the bartender,' she says ambiguously – is interrupted by the Gestapo in the person of a character named Belzig, transformed in the film into the sniggering Peter Lorre clone Toht. In the resulting firefight, Indy gets the medallion, but Belzig retains an impression branded onto his hand after he incautiously grabs it from a pool of burning booze.

Indy and Marion go to Egypt, where Indy recruits his old friend Sallah, 'the best digger in Egypt.' Between them, they find the Ark in the ruins of Tanis's Well of Souls, only to have it snatched back by Belloq, who leaves Indy and Marion surrounded by the Ark's guardian snakes. They escape, and Indy pursues the Ark first to Cairo, then to some Nazi submarine pens on a remote island. In the process, he's dragged halfway across the Mediterranean lashed to the periscope of a Nazi submarine with his whip. 'Indy got to the pen by swimming to the sub and then climbing on top of it until he reached its periscope,' says Kasdan. 'I know that part was filmed, because I saw it at one of the first previews. It's since been cut. What I'm not sure was ever shot was how Indy lashed himself to the periscope with his whip. I liked that a lot, because it made good use of the whip.

Indy enters the heart of the island through a flooded tunnel, and sees Belloq wiped out, with all his helpers, when he opens the Ark, unleashing its awesome force. Indy and Marion survive, fleeing with the Ark in a mining cart along the Nazis' supply tunnels. Back in Washington, the Ark, deemed by the US Army too dangerous to tamper with, is relegated to a warehouse choked, implies the final image, with millions of such secrets.

As Kasdan wrote, the link to serials became more tenuous, and was finally discarded, as it had been in *Star Wars*. *Raiders of the Lost Ark* would be *sui generis* – a new creation that fertilized an entire school of action cinema. Only the 1979 *Mad Max*, by Australian director George Miller, would have as many imitators, and Miller's retro-fitted world, carrying Lucas's vision of the used universe to its logical conclusion, owed its existence to Lucas anyway. Miller's partner and producer, Byron Kennedy, visited Hollywood on a scholarship during the production of *Star Wars*, met Lucas, and returned to Australia inflamed with the gospel of a junk future and Joseph Campbell's concept of the shaman hero. Miller responded with a post-apocalyptic desert world of tribal bike-riders warring over petrol, and a maimed hero who, instead of Luke Skywalker's electronic hand, has a braced leg.

While Kasdan wrote *Raiders*, Leigh Brackett was making heavy weather of *The Empire Strikes Back*. The easy ways of Howard Hawks didn't prepare her for Lucas's tight control. Her health was also failing as cancer took hold. She delivered a first draft of the script in March 1978. When Lucas rang to talk about it, her husband told him she was in hospital. She died shortly after.

The script wasn't what Lucas had hoped for. Hawks liked dialogue scenes, but narrative bored him. His work embodied Scott Fitzgerald's dictum, 'Character is action.' *Rio Bravo*, *El Dorado*, and *Rio Lobo* all shared the same plot, to the extent that Hawks took a print of the first on location for the two others, in case he forgot anything. *Hatari!*, the African animal-trapping adventure Brackett wrote for him, was made over two years, and never had a script – Hawks simply bought scenes from her, then went to Africa and shot them. The main problem in editing was separating sequences in which John Wayne wore a blue shirt from those where he wore red.

Marcia had planned a holiday for herself and George in Mexico with Michael Ritchie and his wife for Easter 1978, but Lucas, shunning the sun as usual, spent his time in the hotel, rewriting Brackett's script. When they returned home, he and Marcia signed the papers to buy the decrepit Bulltail Ranch near Nicasio, in northern Marin County, to create what would become Skywalker Ranch. Early in January 1979, the trade paper *Boxoffice* announced that Marin County had approved amendments to zoning laws that would allow Lucas to build a 'think tank' for film-makers on the ranch. The Board of Supervisors imposed thirty-seven conditions on Lucas, one of them that he 'make available the forces of Darth Vader for zoning enforcement.' Supervisors assured Lucas he could shrug off this particular demand, but others would prove less easy to avoid. The stage was set for a long-running conflict with the entrenched conservatives of Marin.

'I went up to San Anselmo to deliver *Raiders*,' recalls Kasdan, 'and George took me out to lunch. He said, "Leigh Brackett, who wrote the first draft, has just died, and I don't have a screenplay for *Empire*. I didn't even like what she was doing. And I gotta get going here. We're scheduled for production. Will you write it?"

'I said, "You haven't even read *Raiders*. What if you don't like it?" And he said, "If I don't like it, I'll call you up tonight and cancel this offer."'

Even as he said this, Lucas knew he wouldn't hate the *Raiders* script. As Spielberg had intuited, Kasdan was the screenwriter they'd been waiting for. He admired genre movies and Kurosawa films as much as they did, but understood them better. He could extract the nerve of Mifune's character from the shell in which Kurosawa enclosed it, and transplant it, still living, into an American hero. He had a sense of humor that didn't flinch from broad action comedy but was equally at home with Hawksian banter: so much so that a playful sex scene – the one where Marion soothes Indiana's injuries, asking, 'Where does it hurt?' – could be lifted from the *Continental Divide* script and used in *Raiders* without appearing out of place.

Lucas explained to Kasdan that he couldn't pay much up front for the screenplay, but would guarantee him profit participation. Increasingly, Lucas used his points not as bonuses but to tempt above-the-line personnel to waive salaries, thus reducing the start-up costs of a film. The principle soon became integral to New Hollywood.

Kasdan found rewriting Brackett a chore. 'It was sort of old-fashioned,' he says of her script, 'and didn't relate to *Star Wars*. The characters all had the right names, but the story's spirit was different.' Lucas's rewrites didn't help: 'There were sections in the script which, when I read them, made me say to myself, "I can't believe that George wrote this scene. It's terrible."'

In November, Kasdan delivered the script. *Star Wars* had its share of gloom, but the script of *The Empire Strikes Back* approaches the Gothic, with numerous sequences set in tunnels, caves, and hidden chambers. It begins in cold, on the rebels' hideout on the ice planet Hoth, and ends with Han Solo flash-frozen. The action in between takes place in a series of unpleasant locations, including the bone-littered lair of a *wampa* ice-beast, the swamp planet of Dagobah, and the belly of a monstrous space slug. Even the planet Bespin's Cloud City, setting for the final showdown, is, despite the fact that it hangs insubstantially above its planet, mostly corridors (Lucas added windows and outdoor scenes when he did his Special Edition).

At the start, the rebels have taken refuge on Hoth, where they operate from a base hollowed in the ice, venturing out only on the back of a local animal, the *tauntaun*, and battling the *wampas*, a dangerous Hoth equivalent of the polar bear, which periodically infiltrate the ice tunnels of the base. On patrol, Luke notices what looks like a meteorite (actually one of Vader's robot spies) and goes to investigate. He's surprised by a *wampa*, which slashes his face – a device to explain Hamill's scars from his auto accident.

He wakes to find himself hanging upside down in the creature's lair, ready to be butchered. His limited ability to call on the Force gets him out, and he staggers into a blizzard, to be rescued by Han, who slashes open his dead *tauntaun* and puts Luke into its stomach cavity until he can erect a shelter. They return to base just in time to join the mass evacuation as the Imperial fleet lands, and its lumbering Walkers – assault vehicles like robotized dinosaurs – crush their hideout.

The phantom voice of Obi-Wan Kenobi orders Luke to Dagobah, where he will start his Jedi training under Kenobi's old teacher, Yoda. A wizened alien midget, Yoda is soon as exasperated with the impatient Luke as Luke is with Yoda, who can lift Luke's entire X-Wing fighter out of a swamp with the power of his mind, while his student has trouble suspending a few rocks. A dreamlike walk through the swamp confronts Luke with his Dark Side, a phantom Vader who, when Luke decapitates him, is revealed as . . . himself! Later, Darth Vader reveals that he is Luke's father.

Meanwhile, Han, Leia, R2-D2, and C-3PO are fleeing from the Imperial fleet. Plunging into an asteroid field, Han dives the *Millennium Falcon* into a welcoming cave, which turns out to be the open mouth of a space slug. After some uneasy moments in its intestinal tract, they escape one step ahead of a bite big enough to excavate the Grand Canyon. They take refuge on Bespin's Cloud City, run by Han's old friend and rival Lando Calrissian, original owner of the *Falcon*. But Vader is there before them. C-3PO is caught and dismembered, and Han tortured in the expectation that Luke will sense his pain through the Force, and rush to save him.

Luke arrives, and finds himself fighting a duel with his father. They hack at one another through the bowels of the city. Luke survives, but loses a hand, after which he's rescued by Lando, who has turned against Vader. Han is frozen into a slab of carbonite and carted off by the bounty-hunter Boba Fett to decorate the palace of Jabba the Hutt, but not before he and Leia have confessed their love. Leia, Lando, Luke, and the 'droids head into space, determined to rescue Han.

Kasdan had most trouble with the relationships between Leia, Han, and Luke. Audiences had to be prepared for the revelation in Part III that Leia and Luke are brother and sister, but prevented from realizing it prematurely. Lucas also insisted on spelling out Luke's complex feelings about his father. On balance, however, Lucas felt Kasdan's first draft was sufficiently close to his conception, and in November 1978 he sent a copy to Ladd Jr with a note, 'Here's a rough idea of the film. May the Force be with us! PS: Best read listening to the *Star Wars* album.'

Within a few weeks the production was up and running, with sets being built in London, a location shoot in Norway already scheduled, and a director in charge.

Gary Kurtz had compiled a list of a hundred possible directors. He agreed with Lucas that whoever they chose must have experience in special-effects films, be prepared to adhere religiously to a script, work quickly, and deliver material on time. Above all, they needed a team player who would follow to the letter the orders relayed from Lucas at home base. Neither reckoned on the almost universal resistance among established film-makers to making the sequel to a hit. If the film worked, the first success would get all the credit. If it failed, the director would be accused of, as Spielberg put it, 'spoiling the soup.' All the bigger names on Kurtz's list turned it down.

Finally, he chose Irvin Kershner, Lucas's old tutor from USC. Kershner had made so few big-budget films, Kurtz reasoned, that he would be grateful for this chance. He had also previously directed at least one sequel, *The Return of a Man Called Horse.* True, it was a western, and derived its success from the repetition of a sequence in which adopted Indian Richard Harris is suspended by his pierced chest-muscles in a test of endurance, but a sequel was a sequel. More worrying was Kershner's background in hand-held, available-light, documentary-type shooting, not big-budget production. Also, given his maverick history, he was the last person to follow orders and stick to a script.

Most people greeted the news of Kershner's hiring with incredulity. But Lucas, always happier working with people he knew, acquiesced in Kurtz's choice. Before the crew left for Norway, he invited Kershner to San Anselmo. 'He took me into a workroom,' recalls the director, 'and on the wall were the plans for Skywalker Ranch. He said, "This is why we're making the second one. If it works, I'll build this. If it works, we'll not only build it, we'll make more *Star Wars*! If It doesn't work, it's over."' Kershner left with a sense that the whole future of Lucasfilm rested on his shoulders. The next day he started running two miles every morning, and spending the rest of the day reducing the screenplay to shot-by-shot sketches – no problem for someone who'd studied art as well as music. By the time he left for Norway, his personal storyboards comprised a volume nine inches thick.

Kasdan found working with Kershner a mixed blessing: 'He's a spiritual guy, and he's had confused moments about his career. He's made some odd choices. He also thinks he's a good writer. He's not. He's a very good director, but he never trusted that. A lot of people think *Empire*'s the best one of the trilogy. I have mixed feelings about it. But it's the most interesting visually.'

Marcia also weighed in with her suggestions. 'Marcia and I agreed a lot,' says Kasdan. 'We thought the movies could hold more character and more complexity. George thought they should be simple in another way. It was a serious philosophical difference. For me, it wasn't an emotional issue. I felt it was his movie and I was working for him.'

In April, Coppola invited Lucas to his Napa Valley estate. The seventh-grade class of the Coppolas' son Roman had persuaded Coppola to help them shoot a film called *Revenge of the Killer Grapes*, and the house was filled with girls in green tights and puffed-out grape costumes stuffed with crumpled newspapers. They mobbed Lucas for autographs. After dinner, the two directors and Michael Herr, who wrote the 1977 Vietnam classic *Dispatches*, and the commentary for *Apocalypse Now*, played Old Maid with Coppola's daughter Sofia.

This was the time for Coppola to test Lucas's ambition, expressed in the honeymoon period after *Star Wars*, that they should work together. He suggested buying up some of the strip clubs and tenements of downtown San Francisco, and restoring them to create a tourist precinct of the sort pioneered in St Louis. Lucas shied away from anything so ambitious. Their only successful collaboration would be helping their shared hero, Akira Kurosawa. His work had hit a long slump in the early seventies, exacerbated by two expensive and failed attempts to collaborate with Hollywood. He was fired from *Tora! Tora! Tora!*, a film about Pearl Harbor co-directed with an American, and his plan to shoot 'The Day Custer Died,' with Toshiro Mifune as Chief Crazy Horse, had expired in development hell. In 1971, Kurosawa attempted suicide after the wholesale dismissal of his film *Dodeska-den*. Since then, his films had been critical successes but box-office failures, a fate that seemed likely to overtake his next project, *Kagemusha: The Shadow Warrior*. An ambitious saga of medieval Japan, it would feature Tatsuya Nakadai as a thief who resembles a warlord. Recruited as a useful double to confuse the lord's enemies, he has to replace him when the warlord dies.

In 1979, Kurosawa had just received the Donatello Prize, Italy's highest film honor, for *Dersu Uzala*, about the friendship between a Siberian guide and a Japanese survey party. Since the prize included a first-class round-the-world air ticket, he took the opportunity to visit friends in California, in particular Coppola. He also wanted to check the availability of movie horses in California for *Kagemusha*. Friends arranged for him to meet Alan J. Pakula, who had just made a modern western, *Comes a Horseman*. Afterwards, Kurosawa lunched with Lucas, Charles Weber, Gary Kurtz, Irvin Kershner, Bill Norton, and Howard Kazanjian. He had seen *American Graffiti*, though not *Star Wars*, but Lucas and his friends, to his surprise, seemed to know every one of his films. Lucas explained how much of an influence he'd had on all of them. 'If I think of John Ford as my father,' mused Kurosawa, 'I guess that makes you *my* children.'

A few days later, 1500 people turned up to see Kurosawa's 1952 *Ikuru* at the Pacific Film Archive. Kurosawa spoke after the screening. Later, Coppola took them to his favorite restaurant, Alice Waters' Chez Panisse. Kurosawa's cheerfulness as he left the table wasn't entirely attributable to the food. Coppola and Lucas had promised to find him the money for *Kagemusha*, eventually put up by Alan Ladd Jr. The film, released in 1980, won the Palme d'Or at Cannes, and made a modest profit. Lucas and Coppola were credited as joint executive producers of the 'international version.'

Lucas was glad to pass the script of *Empire* to Kasdan. He had too many other things on his mind. One was *More American Graffiti*. Another was *Battlestar Galactica*.

Battlestar Galactica, backed by Universal, was the first project offered to John Dykstra's Apogee Inc. after the split with ILM. Initially a $7 million feature for television, with an option for two more, it was produced by Glen A. Larson, though he ceded Dykstra a producer credit to sweeten the deal once the studio approved it as a series for TV. Universal billed it as 'A *Wagon Train* to the Stars,' and in many respects it resembled that series, in which pioneers trundling west found a new drama each week. The opening narration of *Battlestar*, spoken by its continuing star, Lorne Greene, most famous as Pa Cartwright in the long-running western series *Bonanza*, set up the premise: 'In the seventh millennium of time, a tribe of humanoids engaged in a terrifying conflict against a race of machines. The humans lost. Now, led by their last surviving warship, the mighty *Battlestar Galactica*, a handful of survivors moves slowly across the heavens in search of their ancestral brothers, a tribe of humans known through ancient records to be located somewhere on a distant shining planet, a planet called Earth.'

Larson, not noted for his originality, first proposed such a series in the late sixties as a replacement for the expiring *Star Trek*. Then called 'Adam's Ark,' it followed a starship boldly going to other planets in search of humanoid civilizations seeded there by the 'chariots of the gods' whom, some writers of that decade speculated, might have planted man on earth. When Universal put out a call for the basis of a '*Star Wars* on TV,' Larson dusted off the project and pitched it as 'Star Worlds.'

Battlestar Galactica's characters and plot resembled *Star Wars* only peripherally, but the fact that Dykstra did the effects, and Joe Johnston and Ralph McQuarrie worked on the design, gave the series and *Star Wars* a similar look.

Although Lucas protested loudly when the series was announced, it didn't come as a surprise either to him or to Fox. The studio was still paying Dykstra's salary and those of his staff, and also the rent on the old Van Nuys premises. Shortly afterwards, they leased them to Universal. All the same, in June 1978 Fox sued Universal for copyright infringement of *Star Wars*, citing, with a show of indignation, thirty-four similarities between the two films. Universal countersued, claiming that Lucas had copied R2-D2 from the robots Huey, Dewey, and Louie in its 1973 *Silent Running*.

Larson showed Lucas the three-hour *Battlestar Galactica* pilot, but since he made no comment for the record, Larson assumed he had no major objections. Larson and Kurtz even agreed informally that the series would drop 'Star Worlds' as a title, and stay away from certain effects, notably laser pistols, which would overlap with some of *Star Wars*' top-selling toys. In an interview for *Variety*, Larson claimed Lucas was 'satisfied' with *Battlestar*. Lucas responded angrily that he was nothing of the kind. Shortly after, Lucasfilm filed its own lawsuit against Universal, though the motive was business, not intellectual property: the studio proposed to license a line of *Galactica* toys and merchandise, which could damage sales of *Star Wars* spin-offs. Later, each side filed additional suits over merchandising, breach of copyright and various violations of business and ethical codes.

In 1980, a Los Angeles Federal Court judge ruled in favor of Universal, finding that Fox had infringed its copyright on *Silent Running*, though the suits proved nothing that wasn't already widely acknowledged in movies: that each new film stood on the shoulders of those before. As Larson commented at the time, 'When it comes to who are our characters and what our story is, I would have to say that if you were trying to compare *Shane* to *Gunfight at the OK Corral*, you'd say, "Yes, they're both westerns," but I doubt if you'd find many parallels beyond that.'

The *Battlestar Galactica* TV series was a hit in its first season, and survived for seventeen episodes, to the chagrin of Lucas, who claimed he received angry mail from *Star Wars* fans who thought he had made it. Actually, he was more annoyed to see Universal and Larson exploiting the research and development he had funded at ILM during the making of *Star Wars*, and even improving on it. Dennis Muren agreed: 'Two dozen shots in *Galactica*,' he said, 'are as good as the three or four best shots in *Star Wars*.'

Also in June 1978, Eleanor Coppola had lunch at the Lucases' home. Marcia showed off what she'd done since *Star Wars*: planted flowerbeds and paved areas of the garden in brick with her own hands. She'd also gone on an orgy of antique-buying. Eleanor had shot a film about the making of *Apocalypse Now*, *Hearts of Darkness*, and asked Marcia to edit it. She refused, telling her that she was 'putting her house in order.' Coppola wrote, 'She had worked so hard for so many years without stopping, she wanted to stay home for a while.'

Lucas came down from his writing room in slippers and T-shirt, and joined them. The scene conveyed nothing of the tensions just below the surface of both marriages. Coppola was still involved with a long-term mistress, and the relationship triggered endless futile arguments, the most violent after Eleanor found that Francis had invited the other woman to see the final cut of *Apocalypse Now* before her.

As for the Lucases, after repeatedly trying to have a child, they had consulted medical experts, to discover that they could never have children together. Now they were actively discussing the idea of adoption.

In 1980, Lucas settled a long-standing debt when he pledged a third of the $14 million USC needed to build a new film school. The year before, producer Ray Stark had endowed the college with $1 million in memory of his son Peter to start a two-year graduate program in business for trainee movie executives. He also promised to raise another million from inside the industry for scholarships. The idea of USC graduating the sort of people who had barred them from making movies piqued a number of graduates, but Lucas was in the best position to do something about it. As the first payment in his grant, he put down $1.5 million for a 15,000-square-foot post-production facility with equipment for film and TV editing, sound recording, and animation. He also gave USC's radio station, KUSC, the radio rights to *Star Wars*, which resulted in a highly successful series of radio dramatizations using Mark Hamill and Anthony Daniels with a new supporting cast.

On 22 November 1981, Marcia broke ground for the new center, watched by Lucas, Spielberg, and college president James Zumberge. Construction commenced the following October, and was finished in June 1984. On 18 November 1984, it opened with a gala celebration. Awed graduates of the sixties toured the George Lucas Instructional Building, the Jack and Ann Warner Hall of Cinema, the Steven Spielberg Music Scoring Stage, the Marcia Lucas Post Production Building, the sentimentally-named Room 108 Screening Theater, and the Gary Kurtz Patio. In their speeches, Spielberg and Lucas sounded the same note as their tutors had twenty years before. It's a hard world out there. Hang on to your friends. You'll need them.

More American Graffiti remained a running sore. Between January and June 1978, Bill Norton had written and rewritten the screenplay, mostly on a card table in the middle of his Venice house, which was in the process of reconstruction. No amount of carpentry could help the script, the constituent parts of which resisted all attempts to combine them. Each time Norton tried to improvise with his characters, Kazanjian materialized like some alien invigilator to redirect him to the originals. Fast earning a reputation as one of the most unrelentingly efficient of line producers, Kazanjian was the iron hand within the velvet glove of Lucasfilm. When Lucas needed someone who 'would not be a nice guy,' Kazanjian was there, monosyllabic and unsmiling. 'He's real square,' muttered Norton. 'He's, like, from Mars.'

Gary Kurtz feels the film should never have been made. 'The script wasn't all that wonderful,' he says. 'First of all, it's one of those stories that shouldn't have a sequel, really. Everything that needed to be said about those characters was said, and the epilogues on *American Graffiti* were enough.' But once Norton delivered the final draft, both Kazanjian and Lucas were confident enough to tell him he could direct the film as well. 'George didn't want to direct it himself,' says Kurtz, 'but he wanted someone he could control.'

The first movie had been kind to most of its stars, in particular Ron Howard, who was starring in the TV sitcom *Happy Days*, reminiscent of *American Graffiti*, though the producers claimed the pilot episode had been filmed before Lucas released his film. Cindy Williams was in *Laverne and Shirley*, spun off from *Happy Days*, and Mackenzie Phillips was a regular in another sitcom, *One Day at a Time*. Because of this, however, all three were only available to film during the brief summer break. Harrison Ford also agreed to play one day, uncredited, as Bob Falfa, transformed from hot-rodder to uniformed motorcycle cop.

Norton had forty-four days to shoot the film, and an uneasy sense that it wouldn't be enough. He began with the drag-strip scenes. Lured by promises of free *Star Wars* toys, four thousand people filled the stands at the raceway. Lucas made a symbolic appearance on the first day. The thought of producing a film for Universal, whom he was suing, rankled, as did the news that Ned Tanen, now head of the studio, had pre-sold it to television for more than the $3 million it would cost to make. As usual, Old Hollywood had found a way not to lose. Once shooting began, Lucas refused to let anyone from Universal see the script or visit the set. And if they found the film he delivered too complex or unromantic for their tastes . . . well, that was their problem.

Norton immediately found himself in a logistical mire that recalled the problems of the US Army in Vietnam. Hot-rods stubbornly froze on the starting line, or blew up their engines in a burst of flame. As Terry growls when his platoon's radio packs up during a firefight, 'Nothing works over here.' Recreating 1966 San Francisco in 1978 proved almost as difficult as duplicating 1866.

Kazanjian wouldn't authorize the rental of more than three Huey helicopter gunships for the Vietnam sequences, and, no matter how imaginatively Caleb Deschanel shot them, they never approached the effect of a real airborne attack. Coppola had plenty of helicopter footage, having paid through the nose for the Philippines air force on *Apocalypse Now*. Lucas asked to use some of it, but Coppola refused. *Graffiti* would precede *Apocalypse* into the cinemas by a few days. Why should he undermine his own movie? *His* movie? Lucas filed this mentally as another offense perpetrated by the man he had once regarded as his older brother. It just proved you couldn't trust anyone.

Nevertheless, the 16mm Vietnam scenes in *More American Graffiti* come closest to Lucas's visualization of the film. Not seen since the first day of shooting, he reappeared to handle a camera, vindicating, in his own mind at least, the rightness of his conviction that Vietnam should be filmed 'up close and personal.' It's the most violent footage he ever shot. The casualty hauled into the Huey by Toad and his friend Little Joe (Bo Hopkins, another actor re-enlisted from the first film) fills the helicopter with bubbling, blood-choked screams, and Joe's own death soon after is authentically casual – the thump of a bullet, an incredulous look, and his muttering voice subsiding into silence. Norton filmed these scenes on the delta of the Sacramento River, between Stockton and Modesto, close to the original setting of *American Graffiti*, but far from Vietnam. The light is unregenerately Californian, however, and the farmland with its lazy river fringed with trees never convinces as An Loc.

The Empire Strikes Back

We don't mess around with these films. There is one thing about Lucasfilm: the intention, always, is to put all the money on the screen.

Robert Watts, line producer of *The Empire Strikes Back*

Fox wanted *The Empire Strikes Back* for summer 1980. Lucas proposed September, but the studio, superstitiously, insisted on the same Memorial Day weekend in May which had launched *Star Wars*. Its runaway success had changed Hollywood's perception of releasing patterns. 'George Lucas effectively moved the summer forward two weeks, from the middle of June to the end of May,' said Fox's head of distribution, Tom Sherak. 'The Wednesday before Memorial Day is called George Lucas Day.' The same thing would happen after James Cameron's *Titanic* in 1997. Everyone wanted their film to come out just before Christmas, in the hope of repeating that film's success.

Lucas reluctantly agreed to a May release. The new deadline, as well as the gut-churning realization that he was playing with his own money, gave the pre-production of *Empire* a special urgency. This was no time to change horses, so, despite his misgivings about the way he'd handled *Star Wars*, he re-installed Gary Kurtz as producer. Kurtz booked Elstree from March to September 1979, and hired as many of the *Star Wars* team as possible to work on the sequel. Robert Watts became line producer. Stuart Freeborn would do the masks, and John Mollo the costumes. John Barry was again production designer, though he wouldn't be around to supervise the sets. He was about to direct his first film, another piece of science fiction, *Saturn 3*, starring Kirk Douglas.

Ralph McQuarrie began visualizing the film's creatures and characters – far fewer than in *Star Wars*. There would be no cantina sequence as a pretext to parade alien diversity. The new film's creatures have no personalities. In the great tradition of low-budget sf films, they're what Leslie Stevens, producer of *The Outer Limits*, called 'the Bear,' and of which he demanded one each episode. *Empire*'s 'bears' include a monster which, when Luke lands his X-Wing in a swamp on Dagobah, devours R2-D2 after he topples into the murky water, only to spit him out as inedible. Inside the space slug, the *Millennium Falcon* is attacked by bat-like, leathery *mynocks*, which attach themselves to it with suckers. On Bespin, McQuarrie visualized a race of bald, jowly midgets called *ughnauts* who do Calrissian's dirty work, including feeding Han to the carbonite machine.

For the *wampa*, the dominant resident of Hoth, McQuarrie crossed Bigfoot with a polar bear. He saw the *tauntauns*, on which the rebels ride across the icy wastes of Hoth, as large lizards – 'a cross between a Tyrannosaurus and a camel,' according to Nick Maley, who again worked with Freeborn on the masks and make-up – but Lucas didn't like the result, so McQuarrie developed instead a hairy biped with the horns of a mountain goat and the pelt of a yak.

The most work went into creating Yoda, the Jedi master who teaches Luke the ways of the Force. Mincha-Yoda is supposedly an eight-hundred-year-old native of the planet Dagobah. Joe Johnston and Ralph McQuarrie tried numerous ideas, ranging from goblins, pixies, elves, gnomes, and dwarves, whose only shared characteristics were short stature and pointed ears, to a humanoid with a dreamy expression, bald on top but with hair hanging down to his shoulders, who wouldn't have looked out of place strolling around Haight-Ashbury.

The shorter Yoda got, the harder it became to imagine an actor playing him. Lucas also shied away from making him too obviously part of any ethnic group: 'You don't want people to say that he's German or Japanese.' Once Freeborn settled on a wizened gnome with the personality of a stooped ancient from a Kurosawa film, Lucas called in Jim Henson, the man behind *The Muppets*. Henson and Freeborn built an animatronic Yoda only twenty-six inches high, the eyes, cheeks, tongue, lips, and ears of which were operated by technicians under the false floor of the sage's tiny hutch of a home. For a year before shooting began, Lucas and Henson refined the figure, searching for a look of timeless if weary wisdom. Their eventual inspiration was the aged Albert Einstein, also a source for Spielberg's E.T.

Reassembling the *Star Wars* cast brought problems. Hamill and Fisher were under contract from the first film, but Ford wouldn't sign until Lucas promised to better define the Han Solo character. 'He wanted to be more Clark Gable-like and roguish,' says Kurtz. 'Like most actors, he was also really worried about being stereotyped.' Ford only accepted after Lucas promised him a more significant character and, more important, points in both the film and its merchandise.

Anthony Daniels and Dave Prowse both complained about their cavalier treatment during the promotion of *Star Wars*. They'd been forbidden to give interviews, and some Fox staff even insisted that both C-3PO and R2-D2 were entirely mechanical. Daniels and Lucas had a famous argument, which Lucas settled by offering him a larger credit, and points, in the new film. Daniels signed on.

Criticisms of *Star Wars'* perceived racism continued to trouble Lucas. He later claimed his early treatment stipulated that at least half the people on Bespin's Cloud City should be black, but no blacks were seen in the completed version. At the last minute, he recruited Afro-American actor Billy Dee Williams to play Lando Calrissian, Han Solo's old smuggling buddy and now boss of Cloud City. Sid Ganis, Lucasfilm's head of publicity, while agreeing that the role wasn't initially written for a black actor, insisted that this wasn't tokenism: 'We were just looking for a wonderful romantic hero.' His protestations were undercut by Williams, who told *People* magazine, 'The reason I was attracted to this role was because it wasn't written for a black person.'

Other roles were cast in Britain. Robert Watts suggested his next-door neighbor, the actor Julian Glover, for General Veers, commander of the Walker assault. One of the least likely stars created by *The Empire Strikes Back* was Jeremy Bulloch, cast as bounty-hunter Boba Fett. Bulloch, a minor actor, sandy-haired and amiable, whose main roles had been as a cheery sidekick in musicals like *Summer Holiday*, with Cliff Richard, had little expectation of becoming legendary as a result of his appearance in the film, since he had no dialogue and his face would be invisible behind a metal helmet.

The popularity of Fett was more evidence of the independent life already being taken on by *Star Wars'* characters. He would feature in a number of the many novels spun off from Lucas's film. Alan Dean Foster was already writing the first of them, *Splinter of the Mind's Eye*, his second *Star Wars* novel under the deal with Del Rey, but the first in an avalanche of books, comics and games which would explore, widen, and amplify Lucas's universe.

Kurtz decided to start building sets at Elstree in February 1979. The studios still lacked a space large enough for the sort of decor American movies now routinely demanded, so Lucasfilm and the studio management had agreed to share costs on building a new but un-soundproofed stage on the backlot that could accommodate the Dagobah scenes of *Empire*. Even before it was finished, Stanley Kubrick promised to use it for the largest set in his film of Stephen King's *The Shining*, the Colorado Lounge of the snowbound Overlook Hotel.

Shooting on the Hoth scenes would begin in Norway in March, hopefully after the worst of the winter. The unit headquartered at Finse, a village on the Oslo–Bergen railway with a population of a hundred, eighty of whom were kept busy throughout the winters clearing the line. Ominously, this was the area where Captain Robert Falcon Scott had brought his men to train for their ill-fated 1911 attempt to reach the South Pole, though most of the shooting would take place seven thousand feet higher, on the blue ice of Hardangerjokulen Glacier.

Several months ahead, Kurtz shipped in snow vehicles, and hired helicopters to ferry material and staff up the glacier to where Bruce Sharman, the production supervisor, built two camps, christened Camp Kurtz and Camp Sharman. According to the plan, Kershner, with Peter Suschitzky on camera, would spend the first week of March in Norway filming Hamill and Fisher, then travel with them to London to join Harrison Ford for interiors. The second unit, under Peter MacDonald, would keep filming in Finse for another month. *Star Wars* had been shot in eighty-two days, and Kurtz was confident he could finish *Empire* in less than a hundred. Had he known it would take 175 days, he might have quit then.

The unit took over the Finse Ski Lodge, but, even doubling up, seventy newcomers strained its facilities, particularly when bad weather kept them indoors. 'There was a blizzard most of the time the first unit was there,' recalls Kurtz. 'The weather was so unpredictable. We would be shooting near the glacier's top, and it would be relatively clear. Within fifteen minutes, the snow would close in on us. You couldn't see ten feet in either direction.'

At fifty-five, Irvin Kershner was not the ideal man to be directing a film under the freak weather conditions the crew encountered at Finse. All the jogging in the world could not have prepared him for the rigors of the Arctic winter. Cracks were also appearing in the relationship between him and Kurtz. The producer hoped for someone who, trained like himself in documentary, could think on his feet and come up with quick solutions to problems as they occurred. Instead, Kershner, aware of the importance of the project to Lucas and his plans for the ranch, appeared determined to follow the plan he'd drawn up in California. But confrontation was not Kurtz's way, and he did his best to placate Kershner and to present a united front to the crew.

Kurtz was also uneasily aware that any sign of indecisiveness would further weaken his control over the production, and his relationship with Lucas. Throughout the production of *Star Wars*, Kurtz had been the strong right arm of an often wilting and irresolute Lucas. One journalist, influenced by *The Godfather*, saw him as 'an unofficial *consigliere* – limiting access to Don Lucas, granting favors and interviews, fixing messes, pouring oil on the troubled waters. He is friend, confidant, interpreter, hatchet man. When Lucas talks, Kurtz listens.'

That trust, eroded by Lucas's increasing obsession with the ranch and his suspicion of the film industry, was already dangerously thin. These early problems with *Empire* seem merely to have confirmed the fears Lucas had from the start. As he got ready to fly to Norway for his now-traditional first-day blessing of the film, he would already have been convinced that things were going wrong with the production, and that it was up to him to save it. That he was gripped by this conviction became increasingly evident as the production wore on, making an already difficult situation worse for everyone, and, for Kurtz, impossible.

Lucas arrived in Finse to find the whole unit stranded by the weather, unable to start shooting on the high glacier. The ritual visit to rally the troops turned into a crisis-management meeting. With sets already going up in London, they had to film what they could at Finse and get out before studio costs began to mount. Scenes with the actors must have priority; once they were done, the second unit could stay behind and pick up exteriors while the cast went on to London. Harrison Ford hadn't been due to shoot in Norway, but now Lucas decided they could use the area around Finse for the scenes in which Han rescues Luke after the *wampa* attack. He rang Ford in London and ordered him on the first plane out. The following morning the star flew to Oslo, got a feeder flight to Finse, and made the rest of the trip by snowplough, arriving at midnight. By 6 a.m. the next day, he was shooting.

Superficially, the mood on the unit was amiable, but both Kurtz and Kershner recognized the steel in Lucas's manner. 'You know, this is my own money,' he told the two men, 'and we have to be careful with it – so be sure to do a good job.'

'Kersh felt really incensed by that,' says Kurtz. 'He felt it was unnecessary pressure. Kersh did his best *all* the time; it didn't matter if it was his money or Fox's money. Kersh felt it was uncalled for, especially on the first day.'

Though that winter was one of Europe's harshest in decades, the first disaster to hit the production wasn't snow but Stanley Kubrick. For more than a year, his production of *The Shining* had monopolized Elstree. He was due to leave in February, but showed no signs of wanting to finish earlier, least of all for Lucas. Kubrick resented *Star Wars*, which he regarded as inferior to his *2001: A Space Odyssey*, and was already talking to science fiction writer Brian Aldiss about a film which would outdo this upstart. It developed into 'A.I.' (for 'Artificial Intelligence'), which would occupy much of Kubrick's time over the next two decades, but would remain unmade at his death in 1999.

On 24 January 1979, fire broke out on Elstree's Stage 3, earmarked for the Dagobah swamp. Equipment parked around the stages prevented fire engines from reaching the blaze, which gutted *The Shining*'s largest set, the Colorado Lounge. The studio administration, not to mention Kurtz, hoped Kubrick would shoot his few remaining scenes elsewhere, leaving them free to rebuild the stage and install the Dagobah sets on time. They underestimated him. He insisted on the letter of his contract.

In April, he was still dragging out the last shots of *The Shining* at Elstree, to the frustration of Kurtz, who had fifty of John Barry's sets to build, and needed all of the studio's eight stages to house them. 'He was shooting the maze scenes on Stage 4,' says Kurtz. 'He was

THE EMPIRE STRIKES BACK

easily two months, maybe three months behind. And every time I saw him, I said, "Stanley, you've got to get off that stage. I have a set to build." And he said, "Just a few more days. I've just got to finish up a few things." In desperation, Kurtz moved part of the production to the much smaller Lee International, in Wembley. As a result, *Empire*'s $20 million budget had blown out to $22 million, though news that eager exhibitors had already subscribed $26 million in guarantees offered some comfort.

Kershner was showing more signs of time-consuming vacillation. 'He'd told me he's going to add more substance [to the film],' Billy Dee Williams told a journalist. 'He wants to have more than the sense of just bang-bang-shoot-'em-up.' Relations between Kurtz and Lucas also continued to deteriorate once Lucas returned to San Rafael. 'George wasn't *here*,' says Kurtz, speaking in London. '*I* was here. He was back there, working with ILM, getting the visual parts together. He came over two or three times, and the fact that it went over budget and I was pushing Kershner [made things worse]. I kept telling George, "Look, you've got to let me do this my way, because if you push him too hard, it'll just make it worse, not better. I've seen it. I've already experienced it myself. What we're getting is very good. Don't make it worse than it is."'

Lucas could be forgiven for not concentrating on the problems of *Empire*. He had others to deal with. Aware that Lucasfilm had become far too large for him to handle it on his own, he appointed a CEO. That Charles J. Weber, an investment banker in his mid-thirties, tall, bespectacled, toothy, a lookalike for Microsoft's Bill Gates, had no background in film was his greatest recommendation. 'From my perspective,' Lucas said, 'I've *given* the company to Charlie. All I ask is that he pay my overhead, including the ranch, and let me keep 10 per cent of the profits as a production fund.' In turn, Weber introduced Lucas to the intricacies of corporate life, including the trick of launching a new company for each film. That way, he would risk neither Lucasfilm's assets nor his personal fortune; only the new company would go under. The company formed to make *The Empire Strikes Back*, adopted, tongue in cheek, the term for the law protecting troubled companies from being bankrupted by creditors. It was called 'Chapter 11.'

Leaving Weber to run things, Lucas concentrated on *More American*

Graffiti. The problems of editing four narrative strands were magnified by having to handle three different time-streams as well. Split-screen proved a further maddening distraction. In all of this, Bill Norton was little help. Uninterested in editing, he sat and read magazines while relays of editors labored to make sense of the picture. Tina Hirsch did the first cut, after which Lucas took over, working with Duwayne Dunham, Lucasfilm's resident editor. He also coaxed Marcia away from her garden to unravel the split-screen sequences.

Lucas again elected to preview the film at Northpoint, but the event had nothing in common with the delirious unveiling of *Star Wars*. He was standing with Ned Tanen in the lobby when his mother and sister came out of the cinema. 'It's supposed to be funny, George,' Dorothy told him as she walked by. 'Not very funny.' His sister Wendy repeated their mother's criticism almost word for word. 'They just left him standing in the lobby, levelled,' said Tanen, with some satisfaction.

In London, shooting on *Empire* continued to be sluggish. All three stars were bored, and Ford and Fisher became more so when Hamill began working with the animatronic Yoda. Initially, Lucas wanted to set Dagobah in a real swamp. Robert Watts scouted the Florida Everglades and parts of the Caribbean, East Africa and the Yucatan, but decided that the risks of bad weather, bugs, and disease were too great. Instead, Norman Reynolds designed a set based on Ralph McQuarrie's drawings. Elstree's floors were concrete, so they couldn't simply dig them out. Instead, Reynolds re-floored the whole stage with a platform three feet high, waterproofed it, and flooded it with a further three feet of water. Set dressers festooned it with a plant called Old Man's Beard, which flourishes even without sunlight. Over the weeks of shooting, the atmosphere became noisome. The Nujol mineral oil, burned to create the authentic low-hanging fog, rendered the set even more stifling. Kershner demanded a gasmask. Soon everybody was wearing one.

Hamill, struggling to relate to a co-star with a head the size of a melon and a puppeteer's arm under its skirt, became increasingly testy, particular since his wife back in California was pregnant with their first child. Half his lines were addressed to a plastic bucket standing in for Yoda. When he did appear in the same shot as the muppet, he was uncomfortably aware of Henson, Kershner and half a dozen technicians under his feet. He found it impossible to communicate with Kershner, even when he wasn't out of sight under the floor, directing from a video screen. Kershner was often so preoccupied that Hamill had to grab him by the arm to instigate a conversation.

The Yoda scenes ended on a moment of high comedy. On the last day, as the sage urged Luke to 'feel the Force,' Miss Piggy, Henson's raucous star from *The Muppets*, erupted onto the set in a lavender gown and gloves. 'Feelings?' she squawked. 'You wanna know about feelings? Get behind this couch and I'll show ya feelings, ya little runt.' After that, she looked around and threatened to call her agent: 'I've been booked in dumps before, but nothin' like this.'

Carrie Fisher, who had left behind in New York an intense affair with songwriter Paul Simon, spent hours on the phone with him. She dissipated her frustration in binges with Ford, who had left his wife in 1978, and was ready to enjoy his freedom. 'It was like two different movies,' Fisher said. 'Mark was off on Dagobah, training to become a Jedi, and Harrison and I were getting drunk in Cloud City.' Since they had only a few hours between finishing shooting one night and starting work the next morning, they seldom slept, a fact which showed in their drawn faces, and contributed to a nervy atmosphere in their scenes. Their former closeness turned into something like loathing. Fisher later said her favorite moments of the film were those in which she felt like slapping Ford.

Tension produced crises. Fisher's mother Debbie Reynolds, ringing from Las Vegas, became convinced that criminals planned to kidnap her daughter, and demanded round-the-clock bodyguards. Accident-prone Hamill sprained his ankle and, on the day his son, Nathan, was born, wrenched his thumb in a fall from Bespin's air-shaft to the escape hatch of the *Millennium Falcon*. Furious and in pain, he accused Kurtz of saving money by not using stuntmen, ordered out of his dressing room the cast and crew who had gathered to toast his child, and disappeared for the weekend. 'Making *Empire* was nine months of torture to me,' he said later.

Kershner's ponderous direction encouraged the stars, particularly Ford, to question their lines. 'If we did just two takes,' says Kershner, 'and I'd say, "That's great," he would say, "Wait a minute, wait a minute. What's so great? Was it great for the special effects or for me?"' Star and director bickered while the crew waited in well-paid inactivity. Some arguments became so heated that Kershner stopped shooting, and told Ford he regarded him as being in breach of his contract for failing to take direction. As Ford tried to broaden his role into something more than a Flash Gordon clone, the love scenes became slower-paced and more detailed. In particular, the moment when Leia, watching Han about to be frozen in carbonite, confesses her love, went through endless refinements. Kasdan's script had her saying, 'I love you. I couldn't tell you before, but it's true,' and Han responding, 'Just remember that, 'cause I'll be back.' After Ford and Fisher were through with it, Leia simply says, 'I love you,' to which Han responds, memorably, with an offhand 'I know.'

The supporting actors felt excluded too. Almost nobody knew the whole plot of the film. Even Billy Dee Williams was only given the pages with his own dialogue. Each page of every script carried a long code-number across its center, to identify a copy should it be leaked. Since *Star Wars*, all the actors had discovered the rewards of the sf convention circuit. After years of obscurity, Dave Prowse and Peter Mayhew had found themselves in demand all over the world. Questioned at conventions about the next film, Prowse couldn't resist feeding the fans a crumb or two of fact. 'I'll always say, "Whatever happens, don't mention this to anybody,"' he insisted disingenuously, but inevitably his revelations found their way into the fan press, to the fury of Lucas, who telexed London with a list rating the cast by their tendency to run off at the mouth. Ford and Fisher scored one leak each; Prowse was the worst offender, with nine.

To trap Prowse, Kershner filmed a fake scene in which Darth Vader told Luke, 'Obi-Wan Kenobi is your father.' When this false revelation appeared in the fan press, Kershner and Kurtz took Prowse to task. On Lucas's orders, they began giving him the day's lines only when he arrived at Elstree for make-up, or, better still, just as he came on the set. Prowse believes these disputes over leaks denied him his moment of glory. He was only a little mollified when Kershner told him, 'I want you to be the thinking man's Darth Vader.'

Even then, he was kept in the dark about Luke's parentage, about which he didn't discover the truth until he saw the completed film. 'I felt ridiculous,' he said. 'I thought I was saying one thing, and here they have me saying another – worse, they have [James Earl] Jones saying it for me.' To top this, when Vader removed his helmet in *Return of the Jedi*, the face revealed wasn't Prowse's, but that of Sebastian Shaw.

The secrecy didn't stop with the cast. Through Craig Miller, a mutual friend in the marketing and publicity department of Lucasfilm, Don Glut made a pitch to write the novelization, and this time, unlike with *Star Wars*, the terms were acceptable to him. Lucasfilm staff took him to a locked trailer on the Universal lot. Inside he found the film's storyboards, Ralph McQuarrie's concept drawings, some uncaptioned stills, and a screenplay, each page numbered. They left him there, locking the door, with strict instructions that he remove nothing. When they came to let him out, he asked innocently about one still, 'Is this Yoda?' His minders looked panicky. 'Don't say the name,' they hissed. 'We're not allowed to know.'

Lucas disliked Kasdan's scene in which Luke, recovering from the *wampa* attack, babbles, 'Yoda . . . go to Yoda . . . Only hope.' He wanted Obi-Wan Kenobi to materialize as an apparition in the blizzard and order Luke to Dagobah. Out of a liking for Lucas, Guinness, after having been well dined at his favorite London restaurant, Neal's in Covent Garden, agreed to make a few brief appearances as a disembodied Kenobi, and to record some dialogue to be played as voices in Luke's mind, but refused any payment.

Unexpectedly, John Barry returned to the production. He'd started directing Martin Amis's script for *Saturn 3*, but had almost immediately fallen out with producer Stanley Donen and star Kirk Douglas. Late in May, Donen fired him, and took over directing himself. Kurtz immediately put Barry to work directing a third unit, in the hope that he could claw back some of the time lost.

On 6 June, Barry was chatting to Robert Watts in his office when he complained of a bad headache. Almost immediately, he collapsed. He was taken to hospital, where he died at two the next morning, of infectious meningitis.

The next day, Harley Cokeliss, an American director living in London, visited Elstree to go through the negative of his latest film, *That Summer*. His camera operator on that film, David Garfath, was working on the *Empire Strikes Back* second unit, so Cokeliss dropped by to say hello. 'I came on the set,' says Cokeliss, 'and there was this terrible air of sadness. I said, "What's wrong?" and they told me that John Barry had died the day before. They had a terrible amount of work, they said, and they didn't know who they were going to get for second-unit director. I said, as one does, "Well, if there's anything I can do to help." The next day, my agent got a call from Robert Watts for me to come in and meet Gary Kurtz and Irvin Kershner.' Cokeliss joined *Empire* as second-unit director. 'Gary said, "We think it'll be about four weeks." It was actually more than four months.'

The film lost another day when Kurtz halted shooting for Barry's funeral, and fell still further behind as Kershner ceased to disguise his distaste for special effects. 'He has a fixed idea of how he wants to see things done,' says Kurtz. 'I think he was a little frustrated about some of the matte shots, which were pre-set and had to be filmed in a particular way. He hadn't worked with that kind of shot before.' Kershner was more outspoken. 'It's amazing,' he said. 'I direct the actors, and then [the footage] goes to California, and then I find out what the scene is about.'

Along with Kurtz, who'd also begun directing sequences, Cokeliss inherited the scenes that Kershner didn't want to do. 'Kershner would shoot the scene, do all the key angles,' Cokeliss says. 'But anything that had a complicated effect or a blue-screen shot – in other words, anything with a window – he'd leave to the second unit.'

Cokeliss handled the film's most complicated physical effect, the freezing of Han in carbonite. 'It was thirty feet up in the air,' he says, 'because of all the mechanics involved, and they didn't want to use smoke, so they used steam. It was in the summer, and we were close to the roof, and the roof was baking hot. Steam was filling the room, so it was like being in a sauna bath. Every day the nurse would come by and give us salt tablets, as we were all sweating so much.'

To complicate scheduling even more, Kubrick returned to Elstree for retakes of *The Shining*, with all the usual difficulties of any Kubrick shoot. Cokeliss watched one such incident with amusement. 'I was on Stage 2. Stanley was on Stage 1, shooting a composite shot of the maze from *The Shining*. He had a shot of people running as if in a maze, and he had a model of the maze, and he was compositing those two shots. It was a very tricky shot, and at one point he asked the studio to shut down all movement of heavy vehicles, because he thought it would create a kind of vibration.'

As shooting lagged further behind, Lucas and Marcia arrived back in London. 'Paul [Hirsch] had put together a rough assembly, and it was pretty slow,' says Kurtz. 'George didn't like it at all.' In a fury, he attacked Kurtz, Kershner, and Hirsch, raging, 'You're ruining my movie!' Over the next two days, he recut the whole film, throwing out the early *wampa* sequence shot by Kurtz, and discarding almost all the love scenes. The result was a confused mess, going for action at every cut. 'It was awful,' says Kurtz. 'It was chopped into tiny pieces, and everything was fast.'

In the embarrassed silence which followed the screening, Hirsch persuaded Lucas to calm down and take a more considered look at the film. Lucas took over the editing. Periodically he'd emerge to 'borrow' Cokeliss's unit and film some shot missed by Kershner. Among these were one during Luke's medical treatment at the end of the film, where to smooth a transition he wanted Luke to move a piece of clothing, and another during the evacuation of Hoth, as Luke pulls on his orange flight suit over a khaki one and the medical 'droid counsels, 'Take care, sir.' Harley Cokeliss noticed none of the arrogance on the part of the crew that had marred shooting on *Star Wars*. 'I never saw technicians work so hard,' he said. Now Lucas really was 'the Guv'nor,' and deserving of their awed respect.

Off the set, Lucas was amiable, even chatting with Kubrick when they ran into one another. Lucas had just seen David Lynch's *Eraserhead*, and praised it for its timeless style: 'You couldn't tell what decade it was shot in,' he told Kubrick admiringly. Marcia invited some of the senior technicians to dinner, and started a softball team, the Sprockettes, to play in the Sunday-afternoon games in Hyde Park that provided an informal focus for the expatriate American community.

Coasting on the momentum of two hit screenplays, Lawrence Kasdan saw a chance to launch himself as a director. 'I had gone from being outside the business, and frustrated, to being in the center of the business,' he says. 'Now that I'm working for George, everyone in town is offering me writing jobs. This is something I never could have gotten before. And I didn't want them. I just wanted to direct. I was turning down everything, and finally Laddie said, "What's your problem? You won't write anything for us?" I said, "I want to write and direct," and he said, "Well, I'll make that deal." I told him the *Body Heat* idea.'

Body Heat was *Double Indemnity* and *Out of the Past* updated to the seventies, a piece of pulp cinema as gaudy as a cover of *Spicy Detective Story*, but with dialogue that spiked pillow-talk with literary allusiveness. Kasdan moved into an office at Fox and wrote the script. Other Ladd protégés on that floor of the studio included Barry Levinson and Franc Roddam. Ladd clearly understood the way Hollywood was evolving, but his sense wasn't shared by the studio's chairman, Dennis Stanfill, who had already used the disadvantageous deal on *The Empire Strikes Back* to undermine Ladd with the board. The breaking point came when Ladd proposed to award bonuses from the *Star Wars* profits to everyone in the film division. Stanfill, seeing a threat to the hierarchical studio system, forbade him. Ladd pointed out angrily that Stanfill had been more generous to his stockholders, who were wallowing in windfall dividends. As a gesture of defiance, Ladd and his deputies Gareth Wigan and Jay Kanter distributed their own $1 million bonus among the members of their team. When the board wouldn't relent, Ladd resigned over the fourth of July weekend, and took his team to Warner Brothers, where he set up The Ladd Company. Fox stock dropped $4 a share at the news.

To replace Ladd, Stanfill brought in Sherry Lansing, a one-time actress. 'She came round, she kissed us all,' says Kasdan, 'then the next day put us all on turnaround [putting the project up for sale to any producer who would pay Fox's development costs]. I brought it to Laddie. He said, "I'll make this movie, but you need to get a sponsor." I went to George and said, "Will you do this for me?" And he said, "I will do it, but I can't put my name on this movie, because it's too dirty." Then he did an extraordinary thing that I didn't even know about at the time. He went to Laddie and he said, "Look, I'll be the executive producer without credit. You pay me $250,000. But if Larry goes over budget, you can use my fee for the overages." It was an extraordinarily generous, supporting thing to do, and Laddie said OK.'

Ladd's departure from Fox left Lucas out in the cold no less than Kasdan, and at a time when he most needed the studio's support. He knew he could expect no concessions from Stanfill, which did nothing to improve his temper, or to blunt his belief that *Empire* had to be finished as quickly and as cheaply as possible. He returned to London more determined than ever to cut costs. 'It didn't help to have him around,' says Kurtz. 'George was always concerned about the money. He would always be saying, "Gotta get done, gotta get done."' Periodically he turned up on Kershner's set, Mark Hamill recalls. 'He would come and watch, but he wouldn't stand next to the camera. Kersh would say, "You want to come over here?" and George would say,

"No, no, it's your movie." And then you might see him in the background, peering around the set, sort of watching.' Kasdan came to London and visited the set too. He joined Lucas in the shadows while Kershner directed a scene. Halfway through, they looked at one another. Neither recognized a line of it.

Changes and arguments slowed the pace still further. Later, Lucas told Audie Bock, 'It was excruciating. I couldn't afford to go through that again. A movie company operates on the split-second, like a football game. If you are not there when the decision has to be made, you lose the moment. Soon those moments add up to hours, days, weeks.' For months, the British pound had been strengthening against the dollar, pushing up the costs of shooting at Elstree. Kershner claims he discussed this with Lucas, who told him, 'Keep right on going the way you're going.' After that, in Kershner's version, 'George showed some early scenes to a banker in Boston and borrowed enough money to finish the film.'

The reality was a good deal more dramatic. A week after Ladd's departure from Fox, the Bank of America called Charles Weber. Lucasfilm was inching further into the red with every payroll, and the bank threatened to stop Lucas's line of credit within a week if he didn't repay his debt, now well over $20 million. When the bank wouldn't deal, Weber renegotiated the loan with First National Bank of Boston, which upped the amount to $25 million, though only on Lucas's agreement to pay prime rate of 20 per cent. When he needed yet another $3 million, First National refused unless Fox guaranteed the loan. Humiliatingly, Lucas had to ask for Stanfill's help, which didn't come cheap. Fox demanded 15 percent of the profits of *Empire*. Weber haggled, conceding only a better deal on distribution of *Empire* and the third film of the trilogy, *Return of the Jedi*. By September, First National of Boston had been paid off in full, but the concession forced on Lucas by Fox would net the studio many more millions over the years, to his chagrin.

More American Graffiti was released in August. Ned Tanen, perversely, professed to like it better than the original, and splashed out on publicity, but it flopped spectacularly. 'The picture never opened,' he said. 'It wasn't a case of opening strong and then falling off, or not getting word of mouth, or opening small and staying small. It just didn't open at all.' Coppola fared little better with *Apocalypse Now*.

Reviews of the film ranged from respectful down to dismissive, and houses were respectable, but the film's high cost made an immediate profit impossible.

The British shooting on *Empire* wrapped on 31 August. Meredith Kurtz supervised the transformation of the Dagobah set into a picnic area. Every guest was given a hamper and invited to eat it on the artificial lawn. Lucas, his 'bad feeling' about the film more pronounced than ever, wasn't there.

Raiders of the Lost Ark

> We were going to go up there, and this was going to be
> pure cinema. We were going to do it purely for the
> artistic thing. They were artists; they weren't going to
> do this for mercenary reasons. Not for the reason of
> the opening weekend. The absolute opposite of what
> happened! John Milius

In San Rafael, Lucas devoted himself to supervising the effects
sequences of *Empire*. Kurtz stayed in England, and Howard Kazanjian
took over as line producer in California.

The ILM reborn in Marin County bore little resemblance to the
old hippie hangout in Van Nuys. The low two-story stucco buildings
hidden among trees housed a high-speed stage for shooting in ultra-
slow motion, projection rooms for both VistaVision and regular
35mm, camera stores, cutting rooms, model and matte departments,
engineering shops, and offices. The Dykstraflex system remained at
the heart of ILM; the new complex had three of them. As computers
improved, so did the electronics, but the automated camera system
remained the backbone of special effects until the arrival of computer-
generated imagery (CGI).

Everything spelled discipline. Lucas hadn't forgotten the advice of
Linwood Dunn and Cecil Love after they saw Dykstra's operation,
nor his own unhappy experience with *Empire* in London; without
proper scheduling, one *couldn't* achieve anything. Nor would the poor
security of the old ILM be replicated here. Even a Lucasfilm member
from Los Angeles couldn't enter the complex without security clear-

ance. Anyone who did get past reception found locks not only on the doors leading to the work area, but on each individual office or workroom. Fans were already ferreting through the garbage, so no piece of paper left the building without passing through the GBC 1200 Shredmaster in the hall.

To mislead snoopers, Lucas left up an old sign identifying the buildings as the Kerner Optical Company. There were no external references to ILM. Even the front door announced 'Optical Research Company.' The new logo, showing a Mandrake-like magician in top hat and tails standing in the middle of a metal cog emblazoned 'ILM,' was reserved strictly for internal use. The phone number was unlisted. One ex-employee called ILM 'cloistered. If you didn't work there, you never knew anyone who worked there, where it was or how to get in. It was like going into a convent.'

Accustomed to cluttered workshops and shoestring operations, Briton Brian Johnson, who supervised the effects of *Empire Strikes Back* with Richard Edlund, found Lucas's operation 'much like a hospital – it's clean, and everything is run at a measured pace. Very little panic goes on.' The degree of commitment also took him aback. 'It's comprised of a number of very dedicated people who have had to sacrifice quite a bit. Some of them have moved up from Los Angeles and various places, and given up whatever sort of private life they had in order to work on this film.'

For *The Empire Strikes Back*, Edlund oversaw the building of two VistaVision cameras, the first constructed since *The Ten Commandments* in 1956. (As an acknowledgment of how much showmen of an earlier era influenced and inspired them, ILM prominently displayed a poster for DeMille's film in its main office.) These so-called '*Empire* cameras,' and a special optical printer with four projector heads and a prismatic beam splitter, called The Quad, for which Edlund and his collaborators received a technical Academy Award, were typical of the advances that confirmed ILM as the world's premier special-effects house.

By contrast to *Star Wars*, Lucas elected to begin *Empire* with a major action sequence, the Walker attack on the rebels' Echo Base on Hoth, and to end with a relatively simple sword duel. Audiences impressed by the snow battle's novelty and scope wouldn't, he gambled, fidget through the slower second act, nor resent the film's overall grimness.

The snow battle, the first test of ILM's factory system, showed how effectively Lucas had absorbed the lessons of *Star Wars*. Nothing was left to chance. Each scene was meticulously planned, first through storyboards, then crudely animated storyboard images. Peter Kuran and his animation department generated 124 of these animations. Cut into the workprint, they performed the same function as the World War II dogfight clips used in *Star Wars*, blocking out the action. Christened 'Animatics,' they became another tool of serious special effects.

In early versions of the script, the Empire attacked Hoth with AT-ATs resembling modern tanks; in fact they *were* modern tanks, belonging to the Norwegian army, fitted with futuristic armor and electronics. When Lucas found them too tame, Ralph McQuarrie began playing with the idea of a crossover creation, half-creature, half-machine. He produced a concept painting showing Luke on his *tauntaun* fleeing from two Imperial Walkers encountered in a canyon, and Lucas was sold. ILM always insisted that their inspiration was a crane at the shipyard in Oakland, California, which lifted and transported containers. Endowing it with the movements of an elephant, they said, produced the lumbering Walkers, though Jon Berg's model shop built numerous versions of them and of the defenders' snowspeeders, ranging from minuscule to over three feet high.

The largest Walkers were used for the major attack, filmed over two months on a stage hundreds of yards square. Edlund decided not to use the Dykstraflex system. It might have made the action more exciting by enabling the snowspeeders to swoop realistically towards the Walkers, but he didn't want delays of the kind that had hampered the shooting of *Star Wars*. Instead, he employed stop-motion animation, in which models were moved painstakingly by hand, and photographed frame by frame – a system not fundamentally changed since *King Kong* almost half a century before. It posed its own special problems. The snow was baking soda, with microballoons, tiny spheres of glass used in plastic products, to add a realistic glint. The slightest disturbance was betrayed by a sudden wave in the material, so Berg, Phil Tippett, and their helpers surfaced from underneath the model field through trapdoors. For the ponderous collapse of the crippled Walkers, ILM's high-speed camera imposed a convincing ultra-slow motion.

The outsize negative of VistaVision and the enhanced optical quality of ILM's lenses accentuated the deficiencies of conventional special-effects techniques. The stop-action, in which each frame, photographed separately, was pin-sharp, gave a feeling of unreality to the Walker and *tauntaun* scenes. Engineers began working to add optically a more realistic blur.

More fundamentally, the travelling matte system, in which scenes were shot against a blank blue screen, then layered on one or more backgrounds, always left a blue or black halo around the image. No more than irritating on ordinary 35mm film, it became glaringly obvious in VistaVision, particularly in snow scenes, where the halo stood out sharply against the white. Technicians reduced the contrast by overexposing the layers, but at the cost of the lower images showing through. After weeks of futile experiment, ILM resigned itself to battle scenes in which the ground was faintly visible through a supposedly solid snowspeeder.

While he supervised the editing of *Empire*, Lucas was also putting together *Raiders of the Lost Ark*. He and Spielberg had agreed on the deal they wanted. This would be the contract that definitively stuck it to the studios and broke it off. In one of Lucas's high-school blue books, they spelled out their demands. They asked for $20 million. $4 million of that would go to Lucas up front as producer, and $1.5 million to Spielberg as director. After that, the producing company would divide all the revenue with the film-makers from the first dollar; no 'rolling break-even.' Lucas and Spielberg would also own part of the merchandising, video, and sequel rights. In return, they promised to make the film in eighty-five days.

In October 1979, Tom Pollock offered the deal to every studio at once, though not before leaking some details to columnist Liz Smith, who crowed, 'Hollywood will practically explode, and every executive suite in the cinema world may have to be redecorated after the screaming, scratching, clawing tantrums and furniture-throwing that will accompany its exposure.' She didn't exaggerate. One executive said it would cost $50 million just to shoot the Inca temple prologue. At Spielberg's home studio, Universal, Sidney Sheinberg and Lew Wasserman wrangled for weeks before rejecting a deal that, as one insider put it, 'went beyond their definition of how things should be.' Ted Ashley at Warners wanted to bid on the project, but Lucas, with memories of his treatment on *THX1138*, wouldn't listen until he received a personal apology. Ashley acquiesced – and Lucas rejected his offer anyway.

It was left to a relative newcomer, soft-spoken, dark-suited Michael Eisner at Paramount, to take the offer seriously. After reading twenty pages, he closed the script and told Lucas line producer Frank Marshall, 'That'll take the whole budget.'

Marshall disagreed. Eisner didn't understand any better than the rest of Old Hollywood how special effects had accelerated. He invited him to come to San Rafael. Eisner spent the day with Lucas, and left convinced of his commitment to the project, and that he could do everything he claimed. Eisner's chief bean-counter Dick Zimbert, credited as inventor of the 'rolling break,' decided *Raiders* would need to gross $60 million to break even, but for film-makers with the records of Lucas and Spielberg, that wasn't too great a risk. Eisner and Pollock negotiated. Normally a studio took 30 per cent of US rentals, 33 per cent of those in the United Kingdom, and 40 per cent from everywhere else. For *Raiders*, Paramount agreed to take an overall rate of around 20 per cent, almost exactly the cost of production, prints, and publicity. The remaining 30 per cent of income, pure profit which the studio normally creamed off for itself, would be split with the film-makers. Spielberg took his percentage from the gross, but Lucas agreed to wait until Paramount earned its 20 per cent. Both also received a further $1 million each as director and producer, and Lucasfilm an additional $1 million as the production company.

The rest was dickering. Lucas and Spielberg agreed to raise Paramount's share of rental income after the film was in profit from 40 per cent to 50 per cent. Eisner wanted sequel rights, not simply an option, and a written promise that Lucas would act as executive producer. This last became a sticking point. When Eisner pressed, Lucas said simply, 'Trust me' – a phrase he used often, but which didn't appear in the lexicon of any studio suit.

Lucas had left the Paramount office with no agreement settled, and Eisner rang Huyck and Katz for advice.

'You blew it,' they told him. 'George wants to be trusted.'

After a sleepless night, Eisner knuckled under and signed a contract agreeing to accept, essentially, whatever Lucas cared to give them. He even ceded final cut, but 'within certain specified guidelines' not spelled out to the press. To protect their investment, Paramount imposed heavy penalties if *Raiders* went over budget or was delivered late. Otherwise it was the deal Lucas and Spielberg wanted. In December 1979, Paramount agreed to finance *Raiders* and four sequels. Exceptionally, the agreement was in the form of a contract, and the contract was signed before the film began production – almost unheard of in Hollywood, where most films went forward on a 'deal memo,' leaving conditions to be haggled over and redefined as weapons in the endless war between film-makers and financiers.

The deal wasn't closed a moment too soon for Spielberg. His giant World War II farce *1941* opened on 14 December, to vituperative reviews and universal condemnation. Journalist Ben Stein gloated that 'the wonder child of Hollywood was now spoken of in sneering tones at studio commissaries as a wastrel, a man who had seen his best days before he was thirty, [someone who] could not be trusted to bring in a picture at anywhere close to the promised budget.' Spielberg confessed later, 'I thought I was immune to failure. But I couldn't come down from the power-high of making big films on large canvases. I threw everything in, and it killed the soup. *1941* was my encounter with economic reality.' Fleeing to Hawaii as Lucas had done at the time of *Star Wars* was an insufficient antidote for this kind of misery, so Spielberg suggested to Amy Irving that they spend three weeks in Japan, and get married there. An eager Irving told friends, 'I'll be pregnant by April. I can't wait to start a family,' but on the plane to Japan, a heart-to-heart between the two apparently led to the revelation that Irving had enjoyed a fling with her co-star Willie Nelson on the film she'd just finished, *Honeysuckle Rose*. Spielberg returned to Hollywood alone, and Irving moved out of his Coldwater Canyon home.

Once Kershner delivered his cut of *Empire*, Lucas got to work 'adjusting' it. Influenced by critics who had scorned the lack of adult emotions in *Star Wars*, he minimized the sequel's fantastic elements. 'Instead of doing twenty-five rubber masks,' he said, 'we'll do one really good articulate monster the way it should be done – which was Yoda.' When Kershner first saw the *wampa* sequences, he'd said, 'We can't use this. It's dreadful.' Lucas concurred, and threw them out. The *ughnauts* all but disappeared, and Lucas also dropped the Dagobah beast which devours R2-D2. Instead of building Stuart Freeborn's *Jaws*-like monster, he took a camera crew to where workmen were excavating his new swimming pool, and shot a sequence of a humped back briefly surfacing out of murky water wreathed with fog.

The impulse towards adulthood didn't survive the film's second act. Fox had changed the emphasis of its advertising to attract more women, but Lucas, worried that the love scenes between Han and Leia slowed the pace of a film already, at 124 minutes, longer than average – Star Wars had run 121 minutes – shortened them still further. The lovers now went straight from animosity to passion. Kasdan was disappointed; he'd regarded these scenes as some of his best.

John Williams again did the score, keeping the familiar march from the first film for the opening titles. After a career of modest attainment, Williams's music for the Star Wars series and Raiders of the Lost Ark would make him one of the world's most listened-to composers. In 1980 he became conductor of the Boston Pops orchestra, with C-3PO joining him on the podium at the first concert. By then, the Star Wars soundtrack had sold three million copies.

Music had become so integral to the Star Wars saga that it was difficult to imagine a scene without it. Lucas and Kershner went through the workprint of Empire with Williams, 'spotting' where music should go. 'Well,' said Lucas, 'the music should start here . . . and be here . . . and here . . . and keep going here . . .' Finally they found it easier just to nominate where they wanted silence. During the mix, Kershner deleted the more gratuitous music cues, but The Empire Strikes Back still bears the strongest resemblance of any film in the trilogy to Hollywood's adventure films of the thirties with their unrelenting background scores.

Fox cautiously decided that Empire might do about a third of its predecessor's business, but since Star Wars was on its way to making more than $200 million, they were quietly confident as they announced the opening on 21 May 1980. In Hollywood, the film premiered at Mann's Egyptian, a few blocks down Hollywood Boulevard from the Chinese. As a publicity stunt, Fox decided to run it continuously for twenty-four hours on its first day at the Egyptian. Members of the Star Wars fan club began lining up three days ahead, and the film broke first-day records at 125 cinemas across the country. Within three months, it was into profit, and by 1987 had earned $141 million domestically and $363.5 million worldwide, lifting it to number four in Variety's list of all-time box-office successes.

Knowing they'd appear drastically out of step if they slammed the film, critics lined up to praise *Empire*. 'A darker, richer and more elaborate film than the original' was a typical reaction from James Monaco's Baseline Hollywood database. The *New Yorker's* Pauline Kael said, 'There is no sense that this ebullient, youthful saga is running thin in imagination or that it has begun to depend excessively on its marvelous special effects – that it is in any danger, in short, of stiffening into mannerism or mere billion-dollar style. I'm not sure if I'm up to seven more *Star Wars* adventures (I'm pretty sure my son is) but I can hardly wait for the next one.' Michael Sragow in the *Los Angeles Herald-Examiner* even compared it, favorably, with *2001*: 'More than Kubrick's too-cool space odyssey,' he wrote, '*The Empire Strikes Back* is a sci-fi epic that would do Homer proud.' *Time* magazine gave the film the cover at last, though the face they used wasn't that of Lucas but Darth Vader, fast becoming the most interesting figure in the series. Inside, Gerald Clarke praised the film. Largely unnoticed, the magazine's 'Milestones' department noted that George Pal, producer of *Destination Moon, The War of the Worlds,* and *The Time Machine*, had died, though not before he too hailed the new force in sf film. *Star Wars*, he acknowledged, 'proved again that a special effect is as big a star as any in the world.'

Once again, Lucas and Marcia spent the release week in Hawaii, but Lucas's mind was already on *Raiders of the Lost Ark*. As soon as *Empire* vacated Borehamwood, *Raiders* moved in. Howard Kazanjian was line producer, and kept Lucas up to date on progress, day by day. The fire on *The Shining* proved unexpectedly useful. In rebuilding the stage, the studio raised the roof height, allowing more scope for *Raiders'* ambitious sets, in particular the Well of Souls.

Not all the news was so good. A forthcoming strike of the Screen Actors' Guild threatened the production. Also, the actor they wanted for Indiana Jones, Tom Selleck, had signed with CBS to play a Hawaii-based private detective in the TV series *Magnum P.I.*, and the network showed no inclination to release him. Spielberg's choice for Marion Ravenswood, Karen Allen, was a little-known actress who'd caught his eye in John Landis's *Animal House*. Her capacity to play an action heroine was unproven. As if this wasn't enough, thousands of snakes for the Well of Souls had to be imported into Britain, not always in accordance with rules on animal welfare.

*　　*　　*

Marcia had become increasingly exasperated with Lucas's empire-building. Not long before, he'd said, 'Once you've got a house and a car, what can you do with a lot of money except eat out more?' which made his subsequent dismaying profligacy all the more inexplicable. 'For someone who wants to be an experimental film-maker,' she complained, 'why are you spending this fortune on a facility to make Hollywood movies? We edited *THX* in our attic, we edited *American Graffiti* over Francis's garage. I just don't get it, George.'

She wasn't alone in noticing changes in Lucas. Shooting *Empire*, Alec Guinness had seen a different, more self-important personage emerging. 'He had a great entourage around him,' said Guinness, 'and that always rather depresses me.' Lucas's pleasure at his success had darkened into cynicism and a chronic suspicion. It's arguable that these are even evident in *Empire*. Deceptions riddle the plot, which exhibits an all-pervasive paranoia. Everything is a trap. Friends become enemies, then friends again. The villain becomes a father, a lover is transformed into a sister. Nothing is what it appears.

Lucas complained constantly of being exploited. 'Everybody wants to be my friend now,' he told Tak Fujimoto, the cameraman he often used for retakes, 'and they all want something. I don't want any more friends.' He complained to a journalist, 'People can be big pests. It's annoying having people parading in and out, or trying to eat in a restaurant and having people come up and try to sell scripts. You get harassed all the time. There are threats, letters from people whom you don't know, and you have to turn them over to the FBI. It's a unique situation that so many people have access to so much information about you as a person.' He found comfort in solitude. Parkhouse sprouted a high wooden fence, hung with signs warning 'NO SOLICITING' and 'BEWARE OF THE DOG.'

ILM already existed independently. Now Lucasfilm spun off a sound lab, Sprocket Systems, later renamed Skywalker Sound. Lucasfilm Marketing too was surging ahead. 'One day there were a dozen of us,' said Lucas, 'and the next time you looked, there were several hundred.' Most new staff had only a peripheral connection with actually making films. 'We went from two people in marketing to eighty,' Lucas said. When *Fortune* profiled him in late 1980, Lucasfilm had two hundred people on the payroll, and he confessed it worried him to keep six employees at ILM on salary between projects; by 1986, ILM alone would permanently employ 150 people.

Lucasfilm's net income would be $1.5 million a week, and Lucas would personally be worth $100 million.

Charles Weber convinced Lucas that such a lively enterprise needed a Los Angeles headquarters. None of the executives he was bringing into the firm had any desire to move to San Francisco. Spielberg also strongly urged the purchase. He still kept his office at Universal, and argued that casting, financing, and hiring technicians for *Raiders of the Lost Ark* would be impossible from San Rafael. But the real impulse was Lucas's new sense of power: 'George doesn't want the Hollywood studio types to forget who they're dealing with,' said one insider.

Spielberg thought the office ought to be near Fox and Paramount, now that they were in business with both, so Lucas bought a building on Lankershim Boulevard, opposite Universal. A two-story brick structure painted a murky green, it had housed a poultry-marketing firm. For the two years Lucas occupied it, he never erected a sign explaining who owned it, but, on the same principle as retaining the Kerner Optical board at ILM, he kept the sign in the parking lot identifying it as The Egg Co.

Paying $200,000 for the site, Lucas spent $2 million rebuilding and refurbishing it. Gary Kurtz acknowledges that the office 'looked great; lots of natural wood, a skylight and an atrium in the middle. Marcia had a lot to do with the design.' An admiring visitor noted, 'The furniture is made of cane. In the large, meticulously kept kitchen, pots of regular and decaf coffee brew constantly. The Lucasfilm lobby is conservatively plush, bookcases lined with classics – Hollywood trade paperbacks relegated to a corner rack. Throughout the building are glowing wood door panels and elegant staircases – hand-sanded, of course. The building is so slick, and so much care went into redoing it – the same kind of care George pours into his films. It's a very "crafty" experience, San Francisco style, and totally unlike Los Angeles.' Employees could expect stock options, company cars, complete with a free tank of gas every day, a health package, holiday bonuses, even free T-shirts and *Empire* cookie jars.

To Gary Kurtz and many others, The Egg Co. represented a betrayal of their early ideals. Where was the George who loathed Hollywood, who wanted only the freedom to make small, abstract, personal movies in peace? 'The sad thing about watching that process was the slow takeover by the bureaucracy,' Kurtz said. 'With that slowly came this thing about dress code, company policy, and nobody talking to the press, and a firm of PR people, and it got to be quite frustrating really. I was there longer than anybody, and had been with him for the longest period of time, and I just felt that I didn't like it.'

Charles Weber's arrival also alarmed long-timers like Charley Lippincott. 'He was somebody I did not like,' Lippincott says tersely. When Sidney Ganis and Susan Trembly from Warner Brothers were appointed over Lippincott's head to handle marketing and publicity, he saw the writing on the wall: 'I chose to get out of there. Period.' For the next eight years, licensing and merchandising would be handled by Maggie Young.

Gary Kurtz too recognized that his days with Lucasfilm were numbered. Increasingly, Lucas blamed him for the ten-week overrun of *Empire* and a budget blowout now estimated at $10 million. Kurtz says, 'The problem with *Empire*, as George saw it, was that it went over budget, it was his money, and it was my fault, because I was in charge. I have to accept that responsibility. Also, he felt a bit grated by the style, and I had picked the director. He wasn't controllable enough.'

The break came during the pre-release of *Empire*. 'Someone from publicity rang up and asked me if I'd said something-or-other in some British press piece. I said, "Yes. It was one of the official interviews we had." And they said the publicity department hadn't known about the remarks in advance. I said, "We never do that." They said, "George is unhappy." They always seemed to invoke the Great God George. I found it difficult to believe he was even concerned with this stuff. But if you were part of the machine, you could use him as a club. So I found that most uncomfortable, after all we'd gone through. The bureaucracy grew and grew. You couldn't talk to George. You had to talk to somebody's assistant. It became more Howard Hughes-like, in a way. I decided I was more interested in working on interesting films than in being tied to a machine like that.'

Kurtz bought a house in the English countryside. He also began discussing with Jim Henson an elaborate fantasy feature, the first adult Muppet movie, which would become *The Dark Crystal*.

CBS wouldn't release Tom Selleck for *Raiders of the Lost Ark*, so, with the March 1980 start-date fast approaching, Spielberg turned to his second choice, Harrison Ford. Ford had interviewed for the role, which he'd fully expected to be offered, and only found that he'd been passed over when *Variety* published the news. He retreated to his home with a surly, 'Well, they know where to find me if they change their mind.' To solace him he had his two sons, Ben and Willard, and a new girlfriend, Melissa Mathison, once Francis Coppola's babysitter. When Spielberg and Lucas came back to him, cap in hand, Ford was disinclined to be generous. He extracted seven net points as his fee, plus Spielberg's agreement to rewrite his dialogue, making Jones less the man of action and more the jock-with-a-joke which was Tom Selleck's stock in trade. As it turned out, the Screen Actors' Guild strike was postponed, so Selleck could have played Indiana Jones and fulfilled his commitments to CBS too.

The first choice to play Belloq had been Jacques Dutronc, the lanky, lantern-faced drinking pal of French pop-star Serge Gainsbourg. He wasn't available, and Spielberg was close to signing Italian actor Giancarlo Giannini when he saw the British Paul Freeman in a TV film called *Death of a Princess*. On his way back from making *The Dogs of War* in Belize, Freeman got a call to drop by The Egg Co. He found his prospective director and producer on the floor, playing with the latest electronic gadget, the Sony Walkman. Feeding them cassettes was Kathleen Kennedy, Spielberg's new assistant, recruited from *1941*. It was more like a scene from kindergarten than the movie business. But both were convinced by Freeman's brisk, tanned appearance and practiced sneer, and cast him on the spot.

On the plane to England with Spielberg, Ford insisted on going over every one of his lines in Kasdan's script, and adjusting them where he felt necessary. This eradicated the last vestiges of Han Solo from the character of Indiana. 'Solo could never look like this,' said Ford, showing him a still of Indy in professorial tweeds. 'Indy and Han wear totally different clothes; they couldn't possibly be the same person.'

Neither Spielberg nor Ford wanted the on-set wrangles that had marred *The Empire Strikes Back*. Lucas stayed in Los Angeles. So did Melissa Mathison and Spielberg's new companion, record executive Kathleen Carey. The personal problems and romantic rivalries which had impeded *Star Wars* wouldn't be allowed on this film, particularly with so much money riding on it. *Empire* was doing well, and would clearly make Lucas even more profit than had *Star Wars*, but he wouldn't see any real cash for a year or two. Meanwhile, as he admitted to *Time*, he was 'very overextended.'

★　　★　　★

Throughout the spring, Norman Reynolds had been circling the world, scouting locations and looking for vital props like the Nazi submarine. Frank Marshall remembered that while he was working with Walter Hill he'd been offered a German novel about U-boats called *Das Boot* (The Boat). A German company bought the book and assigned Wolfgang Petersen to direct it.

Reynolds rang them at Bavaria Studios and asked, 'Where are you going to get this submarine?'

'We're building it,' they told him.

'We're looking for a submarine,' Reynolds said. 'Can you send us some pictures?'

Reynolds rented the Germans' facsimile, and shipped it to the nearest submarine pens, at La Pallice, near La Rochelle on the Atlantic coast of France. Built by the Nazis, they'd survived the worst bombing the Allies could throw at them, and were now a French customs base. Reynolds faked a cave entrance to suggest the island where Belloq brings the Ark, and summoned the essential cast and crew to start shooting on 23 June 1980. The weather was atrocious, with fifteen-foot waves, and the submarine took a pounding. Later, Wolfgang Petersen would complain that Spielberg returned it, in his words, 'bent.'

Equally bent was Kasdan's screenplay, which underwent drastic revision as the production proceeded. Lucas and Spielberg decided that the emotional elements were the most expendable, and dropped them almost at once. In particular, Indy's reunion with Marion Ravenwood – now Ravenswood – in The Raven suffered drastic surgery. 'It's really weak,' says Kasdan of Spielberg's version. 'Some of the best writing I've ever done was in that scene, but all that's left is its beginning and end. Those lines actually make sense, but only when the rest of the dialogue is played out.' We never find out how Marion came to be running a bar in Nepal. 'George Lucas, though, doesn't put as much emphasis on personal development as he does on action.'

Kasdan also disliked Spielberg's sight-gag additions, though he doesn't contest their effectiveness. Toht, the Gestapo man, particularly amused Spielberg. For most people in New Hollywood, Germany meant Fritz Lang, and he was no exception. Once he had chosen giggling, goggle-eyed English actor Ronald Lacey for the role, he let his imagination run wild, dressing him in a soft black hat and overcoat like Peter Lorre in *M*. He also visualized him with an artificial arm *à la* Rotwang in *Metropolis* and Dr Strangelove in Kubrick's film. Ron

Cobb designed the apparatus and, to make it complete, incorporated a machine-gun shooting through the forefinger. Reluctantly, Spielberg dropped this as too expensive, but did assign to Lacey a gag he'd worked up for Christopher Lee as the Nazi submarine captain in *1941*. When Toht discovers Marion with Belloq at the Tanis dig, he illustrates the conventional 'We have ways of making you talk' line by producing a menacing implement of stainless steel and chains which everyone takes for an instrument of torture, until, with a twist of the wrist, it becomes a collapsible hanger for his smart leather coat. The humorless Lee couldn't get a laugh out of this, but Lacey makes it one of the best moments in the film.

Kasdan wasn't so enthusiastic about more eccentric ideas, like Sallah, Indy's Egyptian friend played by John Rhys-Davies, bursting into song after bidding farewell to him, or Marion accidentally hitting Indy on the head with a swiveling mirror, a gag out of the Three Stooges. 'Those broader comedy elements were created independently from me,' says Kasdan. 'They bothered me quite a bit, but it balances out, because some really good things in *Raiders*, such as Indy's confrontation with the Arab swordsman, the classroom scene, and the Nazi's coathanger, were also innovated by Steven.' Something that wasn't ad-libbed, though Harrison Ford later claimed to have done so, was his line, as he takes off on horseback after the fleeing Ark, 'Don't ask me. I'm making this up as I go along.' The line is Kasdan's, and appears in his earliest drafts.

'Another scene that hurt,' adds Kasdan, 'was Marion's bit with Belloq in the tent.' Mainly because he liked Paul Freeman's style, Spielberg made Belloq one of the film's most sympathetic characters. He's the one grown-up in the film; by comparison, Indiana is a boy. The Frenchman understands the significance of the Ark: 'It's a transmitter. It's a radio for talking to God.' He woos Marion and, not surprisingly, she responds. In one of the film's best scenes, he romances her in a tent on the Tanis site, producing brandy, an evening dress and even high heels.

In Kasdan's script, Marion is attracted to Belloq, and half ready to succumb; but Spielberg couldn't countenance a heroine who would willingly have sex with the villain, however suave. 'They had me write that scene four times,' complains Kasdan, 'and then they wrote an entirely new scene which they shot.' In the new version, Marion fakes drunkenness as a way of lulling Belloq into a false sense of security, despite the opening of the film having established that she can drink any man under the table.

Though Spielberg was shooting with his customary expedition, Lucas felt things could go faster. Nervously watching the budget and the schedule, as he had on *Empire*, he decided to catch up with Spielberg on the next leg of the shoot. He flew out to Tunisia, bringing Melissa Mathison and Kathleen Carey with him.

The Tunisian shoot was the usual nightmare, with temperatures as high as 130 degrees. 'It was a very open piece of work,' said Harrison Ford. 'Everyone worked very fast. It was a tough schedule; lots of movie to make. And after a couple of weeks in Tunisia, I matched Steven's enthusiasm to get out. I try not to say bad things about entire nations, but parts of Tunisia made me sick.' The sickness was dysentery, and Ford was so weak he could barely stand for some shots. 'There's one point when you think that Indiana Jones has finally met his match,' he says. 'He's up against a guy with a sword who could slice a side of beef with a single thwack. Well, I'd already done every damn useless thing in the world. I was into my fifth week of dysentery, and I was riding in at 5.30 a.m. with nothing to do but submit to wild imaginings. So I stormed Steven with the idea of just dismissing this maniac. I'd never unholstered my gun in the whole movie, so I said, "Let's just shoot the fucker." And we did. That's getting character in action.'

Melissa Mathison got dysentery too, made no better when she accompanied Ford and Spielberg on a long drive from their base at Nefta to a desert location in Sousse. In the car, however, Spielberg was able to persuade her to adapt a story he'd told her about a boy and his alien companion. When she got back to America, she started work on what became *E.T.: The Extraterrestrial*.

Lucas asked Spielberg to speed up the shoot and reduce the schedule. Specifically, he wanted the film finished in seventy-five shooting days, not eighty-five. Spielberg had four artists work out new storyboards that would cut the action to the bone. 'I've never seen a camera crew so flat out,' said Paul Freeman. 'You'd see them asleep with their faces in their lunch. Spielberg was running between shots, and shooting it like a TV film – thirty set-ups a day sometimes. The camera crew couldn't keep up. They were exhausted.' To avoid turning off the camera, Spielberg would even shout directions during the middle of shots, disconcerting actors used to more gentlemanly behavior.

But Spielberg knew he had no time to waste. 'On *Raiders*,' he confessed later, 'I learned to like instead of love. If I liked a scene after I shot it, I printed it. I didn't shoot it again seventeen times until I got one I loved.' Lucas stayed around long enough to make sure Spielberg understood the urgency. When a group of young German tourists turned up near the set, Lucas hired them as extras, then wrote a long scene featuring them as Nazi soldiers, which he himself directed the next day. 'I suspect he was giving we performers a message,' says Freeman: '"Look, acting's not so hard. Anyone can do it."' It was also a subtle hint to Spielberg. If he went over schedule, his producer was waiting in the wings.

Shooting in London was just as uncomfortable. The dressing rooms of Borehamwood were filled with large baths wriggling with snakes. Shooting the Well of Souls, Spielberg took a leaf from the book of *The Empire Strikes Back* and laid a false floor ten feet above the floor of the sound stage, strewing it with sand and snakes, both of which sifted through cracks to the cement below. (The Old Man's Beard plants from the Dagobah set of *Empire* also came in useful. Ripped out after that shoot and dumped on the studio backlot, they flourished so well that Reynolds used them to festoon the Inca temple set of the opening sequence of *Raiders*.)

Stanley Kubrick's daughter Vivian was editing her documentary about the making of *The Shining* next door to Spielberg's set, and protested to him that snakes were being killed as they fell through to the floor. Spielberg fobbed her off, so she reported the production to the Royal Society for the Prevention of Cruelty to Animals. The unit lost one precious day while inspectors wrangled with Howard Kazanjian and Robert Watts. When production recommenced, a sound stage was lined with plastic garbage bins, each containing a few snakes reclining on fresh lettuce leaves. At the door, men in white coats stood beside the open doors of ambulances, hypodermics of antivenin in their hands. Nobody was bitten, which was just as well, since the antivenin, flown in from India, was later found to be out of date and utterly useless.

Kasdan wrote an action climax to *Raiders*, with Belloq opening the Ark in a silk tent deep within the Nazis' secret island base. The resulting explosion vaporizes the tent and him, and ignites oil, which flows towards a helpless Marion, bound to a post. Indy rescues her, and they escape through the German mine workings just before the stored munitions pulverize the island. Spielberg elaborated this into a special-effects showcase set on the island's summit. The Ark contains nothing but sand. However, the grains begin to stir and swirl, and glowing, transparent female beings rise like the figures in the *Night on the Bare Mountain* sequence of *Fantasia*, heralding a burning wind that blasts through the watchers, melting their bodies like wax. Indy and Marion, bound to a post, survive because they alone don't look upon the face of the Unnameable.

ILM did the film's 110 special-effects shots, most of them for this sequence. Richard Edlund was in charge. 'We had originally planned to "materialize" the ghosts by using an animating technique,' he said, 'but when we finally started getting into it, we discovered that we weren't achieving the look that we needed – to say nothing of the time that would be needed to produce as many ghosts as finally became necessary.

'Also, the storyboards changed a little bit as we moved along, so we came up with a method of using our big tank, building armatures, and flying the "ghosts" around in water, using forward and backward motions. We had a girl who was featured in only one of the shots. We made her up and flew her around on a wire rig. I shot the plates of her in sharp focus and then rear-projected them through an inversion layer in a tank in order to achieve confusion and to break up the image, taking the sharpness away without losing the entire image. Once I had her image, I shot a skeleton to match, lining it up by projection to get the effect of a "live" ghost turning into the face of death.'

Spielberg's regular editor Michael Kahn cut *Raiders of the Lost Ark*, but Marcia took a professional interest in the result. It was she who wondered why Marion Ravenswood disappeared after her rescue. Despite Spielberg's animosity towards Karen Allen, she persuaded him to shoot a conclusion in which Indy and Marion leave the office of Military Intelligence together, while elsewhere, in Kasdan's homage to *Citizen Kane*, the Ark in its crate is wheeled off to permanent oblivion in a warehouse crowded with secrets.

For all the effort that went into its production, *Raiders* displayed an extraordinary lightness, even charm, and a sense of play. Kasdan deserved much of the credit. As *Body Heat* would prove, he had an instinctive ability to manipulate the classic characters and situations of forties cinema, updating them to a modern sensibility without losing their faint whiff of the antique.

In *1941*, Spielberg had tried to achieve the same balance, and failed – the film often looked like a pie-fight in a costume museum. But in *Raiders*, the past carries conviction. By emphasizing anachronistic details like the importance of hats, a fixture of a man's attire in the thirties, or the slowness of travel and its often bizarre artefacts, like the amphibious flying boat, or the Flying Wing in which the Nazis propose to ship the Ark to Berlin, Kasdan creates a fantasy world where the past is both living and quaint.

Spielberg was a good enough director to take the ball and run with it, and Lucas sufficiently shrewd as a producer to let him do so. Had the schedule become attenuated, as it did with *Empire*, tempting Lucas to step in and take control, much might have been different. But, under pressure, Spielberg's unique cinematic imagination came into its own. As happens rarely in cinema, each aspect of the production flowed magically into the next. *Raiders* was not exactly the film any-body set out to make, but what they created was more than any of them might have expected. There were virtues, it seemed, to making it up as you went along, though once *Raiders* was in the can, Lucas's estimation of these declined. The next *Indiana Jones* films, and indeed the remainder of his films as producer, would be marked not with lightness and improvisation, but a growing emphasis on calculation and control.

21

Fortress Lucas

LA is an aberration!
George Lucas, 1981

On 4 July 1980, Lucas marked the start of construction of Skywalker Ranch with the first of many annual cookouts. This was the high point of his dream of an alternative film industry in the woods of Northern California. Almost everyone there knew everyone else. Most had worked on a Lucas production. Some had even moved to Marin County. They drank beer and ate hotdogs in the sun as Lucas expounded his vision of a Victorian hamlet set down in this idyllic valley.

There would be the big main house for him and Marcia, a few guest houses on the other side of the lake, and facilities for simple film production. 'The original plans were for a nice small Victorian house,' says Gary Kurtz. 'George would have an office upstairs, with some assistants. But then it became: add this bit, add this bit, add this bit, add this bit . . . George reasoned that there must be a ranch office if it was going to be a working ranch with cattle and olive trees and orange groves and things, and somebody has to live there who runs it. So there would be another complex which was going to be the ranch foreman's place. Then he wanted a softball field, and the artificial lake in front of the main building which looked nice, then a cluster of working rooms behind the main house so that other writers could come up and be there for a while.'

More secure now in his standing as the avatar of a new generation of film-makers, Lucas had begun to take public stands on industry issues. With Scorsese and other directors, he formed a pressure group to protest against the sloppy manner in which Hollywood preserved films. To the studios, a film reached the end of its useful life when it was sold to TV a few years after its cinema release. Most were unconcerned if the negatives in their vaults shrank, or the dyes in the prints faded. Lucas also opposed the tendency of many TV companies to 'colorize' black-and-white films and TV episodes to make them more palatable to an audience unused to monochrome.

In 1988, he and Spielberg testified before a Senate subcommittee on the concept of intellectual property. In his testimony, Lucas raised the almost James Bond-ian specter of 'our films, records, books, and paintings being sold to a foreign entity or an egocentric gangster who would change our cultural heritage to suit his personal taste.' After this flight of fantasy, he aimed his guns at villains closer to home:

> I accuse the companies and groups who say the law [on copyright and intellectual property] is sufficient of misleading the Congress and the people for their own economic self-interest.
>
> I accuse the Motion Picture Association, for example, of seeking to protect their own narrow interest on the issue of film piracy and thereby save themselves $1 billion, without acknowledging the moral rights of the artist.
>
> I accuse the corporations that oppose the moral right of the artist of being dishonest and insensitive to America's cultural heritage and of being interested only in their quarterly bottom line, and not in the long-term interest of the nation.

The low quality of cinema sound had always depressed Lucas. Why labor on subtle mixes of sound effects and music when the average movie house's speakers reduced them to sludge? In 1980, he set up a group under Tomlinson Holman, the corporate director of Sprocket Systems, later Skywalker Sound, to investigate ways of improving it.

Most cinemas were still little more than the brick boxes they'd been in silent days. Sound usually came from speakers mounted on the walls, high above the heads of the audience, and arrived at their ears after bouncing around the auditorium. What was needed was a simple method of updating a cinema without too much expensive construction. Tom Holman found it, ingeniously, in the fabric of the building itself. If the walls could become part of the sound system, the whole cinema would become a kind of loudspeaker, with the audience inside it.

'Two things mainly distinguished this system,' says Randy Thom, who won an Oscar as one of the team which mixed *Apocalypse Now*, and who would work on a number of Lucas films. 'One was Holman's idea to mount the speakers behind the screen into a solid wall rather than having them just hanging or sitting freely by themselves. They were embedded, with the surface of the speaker flush with the wall. In theory, that gives you better low-frequency response; the wall becomes part of the speaker. The second is what they call a crossover network. All these elaborate sound systems have one. It's an electronic circuit which determines which frequencies of sound will go to which parts of the speaker system, so that you don't waste the energy of the speakers sending high frequencies to the part of the speaker only supposed to produce low frequencies.'

Holman christened his system 'THX' – a fact that was to cause an acrimony that still persists in some quarters. Randy Thom says diplomatically, 'There's some doubt in everybody's mind – maybe even in George's mind – about the exact origin of the term " THX."' Lucasfilm claims the system was named after Lucas's first feature, but Friederich 'Fritz' Koenig, who became Holman's partner after both left Lucasfilm to set up their own company, TMH, insists that 'THX' stands for 'Tom Holman's Crossover.'

'To honor the fact that Mr Holman is the sole engineer to originate all THX technologies and businesses,' says Koenig, 'Jim Kessler [head of Sprocket Systems] and George Lucas agreed that "Tom Holman's Crossover" would serve as the sole basis for the acronym THX. Mr Holman's patent 4,569,076, filed in 1983, describes a very special crossover for the first THX theater systems. After about a year of marketing as Tom Holman's Crossover, the public rationale for the name became Tom Holman's eXperiment. This was easier for sales-people to use, and was more understandable by potential customers. Any relation to Mr Lucas's first film *THX1138* is purely coincidental.

'In 1996, one year after Mr Holman and I founded TMH Corporation, Lucasfilm discontinued use of the Tom Holman's eXperiment moniker. Recently, as the THX division becomes more driven by strictly commercial interests, the THX marketing department has attempted to re-orient the public's understanding of the origin of all that is THX.'

Whatever the source of its title, THX offered the first economical method of improving cinema sound to come along in a generation.

However, it still cost anything from $15,000 to $60,000 to fit a cinema with THX sound, and exhibitors didn't exactly line up to pay. Discreetly, Lucas did his best to enthuse them. In 1982, Lucasfilm opened the first THX mixing room, and encouraged film-makers to record their films in both Dolby and THX, even if they wouldn't be shown exclusively in cinemas with THX systems.

Films thus recorded had the right to carry the distinctive THX logo at the head of each print: a conductor's hand with baton raised, the downbeat, and a burst of sound, accompanied by a plunge through a swirl of particles that recalled the *Millennium Falcon* going to light speed, with the slogan 'The Audience is Listening.'

'Jim Kessler thought up that slogan,' says Randy Thom. 'I thought it was a dumb slogan when I first saw it, but I've been in cinemas where the audience cheered when they saw it. It's a message as much to the theater owners as to the public. They spend more money on the popcorn machine than the sound system or the projectors. They save electricity by putting too little light through the projectors, and they cut corners with the sound system. So it's, "Hey, you dummies – the audience is listening, so you'd better have a good sound system in your theater."'

In 1983, Lucas would launch the THX Theater Alignment Program (TAP), a plan to modernize every cinema in the world. His inspiration was Stanley Kubrick, who had operated his private TAP system for years, monitoring projections of his films, handing out aperture plates of the correct size to every cinema screening *Barry Lyndon*, accumulating seating diagrams of cinemas in every world capital to check that they were suitable to show his work. A Lucasfilm press release called TAP 'the industry's most comprehensive quality assurance program whose services include reviewing release prints for image and soundtrack quality, distribution to theaters of technical facts about a film and proper equipment alignment, on-site equipment alignment, and a toll-free phone number and website that theater patrons can contact to report presentation problems.' Kubrick became one of TAP's first subscribers, retaining it to check on the presentation of *Full Metal Jacket*.

THX and TAP were noble initiatives, but the inertia of the film business would prove harder to overcome than anyone anticipated. When *Return of the Jedi* opened, only two cinemas in the world had THX sound, and it took two decades for the total to inch over a thousand. Visiting Australia in 1998, Lucas asked for a list of all the cinemas in the country with THX sound. There was only one. He restricted the first release of *The Phantom Empire* in 1999 to cinemas with the THX system. As a result, the most awaited film of the decade would show on only two thousand screens in the United States.

After finishing *Raiders*, Lucas was plunged back into corporate politics, a situation he loathed. Charlie Weber urged him to behave like a businessman and take risks; with interest rates low, they could borrow $50 million on the collateral of his movies and invest it. For Lucas, whose total worth, aside from the ranch, was three houses in Marin County, four in Los Angeles, a portfolio of low-earning, tax-free municipal bonds, and a few valuable paintings, mostly by Norman Rockwell, it all seemed impossibly grandiose.

In October, the business magazine *Fortune* profiled Lucas, though he might have been forgiven for thinking that the real subject was Weber. 'Weber's mandate,' said the piece, 'is to place [Lucasfilm's profits] in prosaic investments like cable-TV systems, shopping centers, and big chunks of small companies. Weber applauds the boss's idea of using all this money to build Lucasfilm into a "$250 million broad-based mini-conglomerate" with no financial dependence on film. By 1983, if all goes as planned, the corporate side of the business would throw off income exceeding $25 million a year in addition to whatever profits movies bring in – quite enough to free the film-maker in Lucas from the corrupting influence of business.'

This last phrase typified a patronizing piece which, while lauding Lucas, pictured him as fanciful and unbusinesslike. It went on, 'Lucas and Weber have already found several subjects on which to disagree, as the inevitable tension between the film-maker's vision and the imperatives of business becomes more apparent . . . Lucas wants The Egg Co. to invest in solar energy and electric cars. Weber doesn't mind losing the million or two that Lucas's product vetoes have cost him, but he and his staff still aren't ready for solar energy.'

The piece ended by describing how Lucas, while still driving his thirteen-year-old Camaro with the USC Film School parking sticker, also ran a $21,000 Ferrari Dino (bought second-hand in 1978, though this wasn't mentioned). The two cars, speculated *Fortune*, could be 'symbols perhaps of his two distinct dreams, one creative and the other financial. He is not the first gifted young man to ascend his own pyramid in Hollywood, and all those veterans he describes as "sleazy and unscrupulous" will be waiting for him to fall off, or join the club.' If Lucas hadn't already decided to get rid of Weber, this article could well have tipped the scales.

Whatever he said later, Lucas wasn't opposed in principle to investing his profits outside the film industry. A year later, he would tell the *New York Times* that he favored 'making money out of the money [from his films], by buying real estate, cable, satellite, solar energy – without buying anything we're ashamed of, like pesticides – and then the corporations will give us the money to make films.'

As the *Fortune* piece made clear, however, environmentally friendly investment didn't interest Weber. His potential targets for Lucasfilm included the bankrupt company of John DeLorean, manufacturer of the innovative gull-winged DMC-12 stainless-steel sportscar featured in the *Back to the Future* films. Lucas shied from owning an enterprise that had collapsed through flamboyant mismanagement and a cocaine scandal. On the other hand, Lucasfilm Properties did join a consortium that bought two fruit-processing plants in Modesto belonging to the Tillie Lewis company, and two warehouses; but in May 1981 the company gave up its interest to the other partners.

Once Lucas turned against Weber, he found plenty in The Egg Co. to disparage – even things he had once applauded. He told *Fortune* he preferred a small, overworked staff to a large one with time on its hands. He encouraged employees to work overtime, and boasted that a receptionist could earn $25,000 a year; but, notwithstanding his own Ferrari, he deplored the fact that car rentals cost the company $300,000 a year. From there, it was only a step to criticizing staff for demanding a resident cook to cater corporate lunches, or for attending previews and cocktail parties. Though his own contribution to The Egg Co.'s running was usually a single weekly forty-five-minute phone call to Weber, he fretted that its proximity to Hollywood was driving it to the devil. His father's Methodism had returned to haunt him, just as his grandfather's diabetes had blighted his adolescence.

But really Lucas had nobody but himself to blame for the corruption of The Egg Co. Films like *Star Wars* had seized control of a large part of the cinema from the established companies; decisions about its future had to be made somewhere, and the beach at Mauna Kea or a table at Hamburger Hamlet were no longer enough. Already the next wave of film-makers was pounding on the door, and they were

anything but naïve about business. 'Now you get out of college,' says
Robocop producer Jon Davison, 'you've got your computer science
degree. Somebody wants you to work on a monster for a special-effects
movie. You say, "What's the stock option situation? Are you gonna
go public? What's the retirement fund? What's the medical benefits?
I'd like to start at 50K a year but I don't want to stay at that salary
long . . ." You can't do this kind of film now without spending a
fortune.'

Blinded by the massive returns of films like *Star Wars*, newcomers
refused to believe that special-effects work, as well as being time-
consuming and expensive, was also mostly unprofitable. 'The effects
business is pretty shitty,' grouched ILM general manager Jim Morris
in the 1990s. 'A 2–3 per cent net after taxes means a very good year.'
Weber urged Lucas to offset ILM's low income by developing new
films, rather than simply backing iffy projects by old pals who
exploited their access to him. He wanted to expand middle management, and take producers, directors, and writers on staff. Lucas vetoed
the idea, claiming that Weber underestimated the difficulties of producing good film ideas to order. 'I keep telling Charlie that
moviemaking is a risky business that only a fool would invest in,' he
told a financial journalist. When Weber suggested that the ranch,
now costing millions in construction, also represented an unacceptable
'cash drain,' Lucas lost his temper. 'The ranch is the only thing that
counts,' he said. 'That's what everybody is working for. And if that
is getting lost in the shuffle, then something's terribly wrong here.'

Shortly after the *Fortune* article appeared, Weber's contract came
up for renewal. He visited Lucas in San Anselmo, expecting to renegotiate his salary and benefits package. Instead, Lucas, voice cracked
and trembling, told him he was closing The Egg Co. and dismissing
almost all the staff. Weber could stay, but in a position of reduced
importance. The shaken CEO left for the airport, but before he
reached it, Lucas called him back. In the interim, he'd talked to his
accountant, Richard Tong, and reviewed his decision. When Weber
returned to Parkhouse, Lucas told him he'd decided not to keep him
either. Hereafter, Lucas would run Lucasfilm himself.

At Christmas 1980 he fired almost everyone at The Egg Co., and
closed the office, which was later demolished. Thirty-four people,
almost exactly the number he had started with after *Star Wars*, were
invited to stay, but only if they moved to the San Francisco area by

the following summer. Eventually they would be expected to work from Skywalker Ranch. After an interim period as CEO and chairman, Lucas made Bob Greber, the company's former financial controller, its CEO. His remit was clear: he would do what he was told. Teamwork for Lucas had again become 'a lot of people doing what I say.'

As the physical vision of Skywalker Ranch changed, so did Lucas's concept of its function. The 'creative retreat where George and Marcia Lucas can meet, study, collaborate, write, edit, and experiment with new film-making ideas' which had convinced the Marin County Planning Department formally to approve construction on 17 September 1979, first swelled to the dimensions of a mini-Hollywood, with all Lucasfilm's enterprises concentrated inside its electrified fences, then contracted to a private museum of cinema.

Lucas spieled the virtues of the museum function in 1979. 'Suppose you want to make the best car chase-crash in history,' he suggested. 'Now, you have to rely entirely on what you happen to have seen at random, and whatever memory you have. We'll have a complete library of such sequences to study and learn from.' He also visualized such 'living institutions' as Akira Kurosawa and Orson Welles staying for days or weeks, accessible to whoever happened to be there.

But who actually *would* be there? The larger the ranch became, the smaller were the number of people qualified to spend time there. The public, of course, would be kept well away. Nor did students of cinema figure in many of Lucas's plans; clearly this was not going to be USC Marin. 'This is for Marin County film-makers only,' he told Audie Bock in 1979, 'and the ten directors who will be part of it are people who are already working for me.' He laughed. 'So, technically, of course, Francis [Coppola] can't come – but he'll have an office here. He'll continue to advise and consult for my people the way I do for him. So we're not partners any more, but we're neighbors. Good neighbors.'

As Skywalker's facilities improved, its isolation from the centers of film production would come to seem more absurd. Almost nobody used the library, bought from a Hollywood studio and moved *en bloc* to the ranch, so its staff accepted contracts to research projects for producers in Los Angeles, the very city from which its books had been removed. Skywalker Sound was recognized as one of the best recording facilities in the world, but only the richest film-makers and rock groups could afford the luxury of using it.

Who *was* the ranch for? Walter Murch quoted a conversation between Matthew Robbins and a carpenter painting one of the buildings.

'I haven't seen anything like this in years,' the workman said. 'The level of workmanship, the conception of the place . . . I don't think there's two places in California like this.'

Robbins said, 'Name one.'

The painter said, 'San Simeon.'

'The ultimate vision of the place is just Hearstian,' agreed Murch, who meant the comment as praise. But people who knew something of William Randolph Hearst's *Casa Encantada* – The Enchanted House – on the Californian hills above the Pacific, and the increasingly desperate and lonely life he lived there between the wars, surrounded by antiques, both animate and inanimate, and with only his alcoholic mistress Marion Davies for company, might have wondered why anybody should aspire to such an existence.

Increasingly, Lucas gave the impression that his ambitions for Skywalker Ranch were indeed Hearstian, and that he contemplated only one permanent tenant. 'I might go back to school,' he mused, 'and get a degree in anthropology or social psychology, which I've always liked . . . or I might just invite the professors here to be my tutors.' It was this image that seemed to give him most peace: a university with one student and a campus that went on forever.

While the ranch was being built, the Lucases stayed at San Anselmo, where his writing room at Parkhouse had accumulated some modest trophies of his success. Framed original pages from favorite comic strips like *Prince Valiant, Krazy Kat,* and *Little Nemo* decorated the walls. The bookshelves acquired a set of the *Encyclopedia Britannica*'s Great Books, like most such sets almost entirely unread. They shared space with plastic re-creations of a cheeseburger, a strawberry milkshake, and a Coke. Toys were scattered round the floor, including a spaceship, a small car and a Boba Fett figure. The toys reflected the primary new addition to the Lucases' life: an adopted baby daughter, Amanda, who arrived in 1981. Lucas immediately became the most doting of fathers. He even sold his collection of racing cars, since someone said they were inappropriate to a man with family responsibilities.

The pleasures of fatherhood weren't the only influence tempting Lucas to cut himself loose from Hollywood. In the wake of *Empire*, he found himself involved in a farcical battle not with the studios but with the Directors' Guild and the Writers' Guild – though he didn't see much difference between the two: 'The Hollywood unions have been taken over by the same lawyers and accountants who took over the studios,' he complained.

His dispute with the Writers' Guild centered on Philip Kaufman's contribution to *Raiders*. Before the film was finished, Lucas offered Kaufman part of a point for his work on the story and the character of Indiana. Kaufman accepted, then requested a screen credit as well. Lucas insisted he'd written two story outlines before Kaufman came on the project, but the Writers' Guild sided with Kaufman. They also ruled that Kaufman was entitled to a credit on all subsequent films using the Indy character. Furious, Lucas gave him equal credit for *Raiders'* original story, but on subsequent films in the series buried his name among the stuntmen, caterers and accountants at the end.

The Directors' Guild of America angered Lucas even more. Over the years, the DGA had introduced rules to protect its members from rapacious executives. To prevent a producer from taking all credit for a film, the Guild required that if any credits appeared at the start of a film, the name of the director must be among them. *Empire* opened simply with its title and the Lucasfilm emblem, but the DGA ruled that the latter constituted a credit to Lucas. When he refused to reshoot the opening credits to include Irvin Kershner's name, it fined him $250,000. Kershner said he was perfectly happy to be credited at the conclusion with everyone else, but the DGA riposted that a director under pressure from a demanding producer might well say just that.

The dispute had been bubbling behind the scenes since late in 1980, but it became public in April 1981, shortly after the Oscars were announced. *The Empire Strikes Back* got a meager three nominations, for Art Direction, Sound, and Music. Only Sound won, while Brian Johnson, Richard Edlund, Dennis Muren, and Bruce Nicholson received a Technical Achievement Award for visual effects. Martin Scorsese's audacious *Raging Bull* was rightly honored with seven nominations, but the big winner was *Ordinary People*, an old-fashioned domestic melodrama that marked the directorial debut of actor Robert Redford.

Lucas resigned not only from the DGA but from the Academy and the Writers' Guild too. He wouldn't discuss his decisions with the press, but Kershner backed him up: 'The DGA works for *me*,' he said. 'I don't work for the DGA. I think the Guild hurts itself by doing this sort of thing. As a result, Lucas is now going to get a British director for his next film, and Hollywood is losing work because of the way the DGA acted.'

Lucas, no longer a member of the two major guilds, couldn't either write or direct in the United States – but he had no inclination to do so. 'I don't have to work for a living any more,' he told Aljean Harmetz of the *New York Times*. He drove up frequently to see how work was progressing at the ranch, but most of his time was still spent at San Anselmo, usually fielding projects, still mostly from old collaborators. Harley Cokeliss tried to interest him in a film of Douglas Adams's BBC radio series *The Hitch-Hiker's Guide to the Galaxy*, but Lucas felt its humor was too verbal. John Korty proposed *Twice Upon a Time*, an animated featured in a new technique combining cut-out images with real photographic backgrounds. In April 1980, Alan Ladd Jr announced that he was backing the film, and that Lucas had joined his new Ladd Company as a consultant. The film was released in 1982, but proved too intellectual in its fantasy for the general public. Almost nobody saw it, and it all but disappeared.

Lawrence Kasdan finished directing *Body Heat*, with no interference from Lucas. 'George said to me, "This whole mentoring thing is bullshit,"' says Kasdan. 'George saw dailies; we sent him some tapes. And when Carol Littleton and I had cut the movie, he sat with us for a few hours and went through it, and had a couple of ideas that turned out to be good.'

Raiders of the Lost Ark opened on 11 June 1981, after a preview at the Cannes Film Festival. Shares in Gulf and Western, Paramount's parent company, rose 2½ points in the four days beforehand. Vincent Canby in the *New York Times* called the film 'one of the most deliriously funny, ingenious and stylish American adventure movies ever made [which] refines its tacky source materials into a movie that evokes memories of movie-going of an earlier era but that possesses its own, far more rare sensibility.' Pauline Kael complained that 'kinesthetically the film gets to you, but there's no exhilaration, and no surge of feeling at the end.' The public didn't agree. In its first month, *Raiders* made $50 million, and was soon climbing *Variety's* list of all-time box-office successes, where it hovered for the next decade.

Lucas was already at work on the third part of *Star Wars*, provisionally called 'Revenge of the Jedi.' His experiences on *The Empire Strikes Back* fundamentally affected his choices for the new film. He'd still do the studio work in Britain, but exotic locations were out. The climax would be shot as near as possible to Skywalker Ranch.

To direct it, he wanted Spielberg, who, according to Gary Kurtz, 'toyed' with the idea but, as the consummate company man, was too shrewd to defy the DGA. Nor did he have much sympathy with his friend's isolationist tendencies. The Egg Co. had delighted him. He wanted an office just like it. Universal, keen to keep him in its creative family, offered to build him one on the lot, and Spielberg began to plan the New Mexico-style hacienda which would become the headquarters of Amblin Entertaiment.

He also had his own backlog of commitments. One, 'Night Skies,' conceived as a sequel to *Close Encounters*, would become *Poltergeist*, credited to Tobe Hooper but largely controlled by Spielberg. He slightly revised *Close Encounters* into a 'Special Edition' that allowed Columbia to release the film all over again. After that, he intended to film the script Melissa Mathison had written after their Tunisian conversations, soon to be *E.T.: The Extraterrestrial.*

With Spielberg out of the picture, Lucas began looking for his antithesis – an unknown director, non-union, young, and prepared to do as he was told. Howard Kazanjian, who would again produce, began canvassing English directors, and chose Richard Marquand. In 1972, Marquand had directed *The Search for the Nile*, an ambitious six-hour dramatization with Kenneth Haigh and John Quentin as the nineteenth-century explorers Richard Burton and John Hanning Speke. Since then, he'd made one very bad feature, *The Legacy*, and was just finishing *Eye of the Needle*.

While Lucas was in London supervising the recording of John Williams's score for *Raiders*, Marquand arranged for him and Kazanjian to see the rough cut of *Eye of the Needle*, an effective thriller from Ken Follett's novel about a Nazi spy operating in wartime Britain. Astonished at his good luck, Marquand would have done anything to direct 'Revenge of the Jedi' – as Lucas well knew. It would be, a deadpan Lucas told the press, 'a very good career move' for Marquand.

Kazanjian explained that, unlike *The Empire Strikes Back*, Lucas would be on the set every day; Marquand agreed. Lucas would also edit the film, and have final cut; Marquand didn't object. Lucas also expected him to spend a few months in Marin working on the screenplay and designs; Marquand was already packing his bags.

Writing 'Revenge of the Jedi' was a thankless task for Lawrence Kasdan. From July to December 1981, he and Lucas wrote four drafts and accumulated a mountain of storyboards. Marquand sat in for two weeks. One of Kasdan's least distinguished works, the script is a Frankenstein's monster of tortuous exposition and labored exegesis. Lucas's outline set the agenda. 'He wanted more action,' says Gary Kurtz. 'He wanted to eliminate a lot of the concluding story threads. Han Solo was meant to be killed. He wanted another attack on the Death Star.'

Short cuts taken in parts 1 and 2 came back to haunt Kasdan. Who got Leia? If Luke, then Han probably had to die. Was Darth Vader really Luke's father? Then how come Obi-Wan Kenobi had told Luke that Vader killed his father? Kasdan resurrected the old Jedi for a third time to explain that Anakin Skywalker died *morally* when he became Darth Vader; telling Luke his father was dead was 'the truth – from a certain point of view.' Marquand also insisted that Yoda reappear to tell Luke, 'There is another Skywalker,' rather than Kenobi simply passing on the information that Luke and Leia are brother and sister. (This revelation was the deepest secret of 'Revenge of the Jedi.' When that section of dialogue was filmed in London, Lucas ordered the crew not to listen.)

Kasdan tried to instil some surprise into the climactic attack on the new Death Star by killing off Lando Calrissian during the attack, and destroying the *Millennium Falcon*, but after poor reactions during preview screenings, probably more at the loss of the well-loved *Falcon* than Lando's underdrawn character, both were allowed to survive. A hint of the original lingers in Han's remark as Lando leaves that it was 'like I'm not going to see her [the *Falcon*] again.' Even Harrison Ford would have preferred that Han die. 'He's got no mama, no papa, and he's got no story,' he told Lucas. 'Let's kill him and get some weight to this thing.' Lucas refused; the demise of a beloved character could alienate his audience of twelve-year-olds.

He had come to feel that *The Empire Strikes Back* was too adult for an audience which, with each film, became younger. His new fans were no older than twelve, and more involved with Yoda and Darth Vader than with the three stars, now decidedly middle-aged. Unlike *Empire*, 'Jedi' never aspired to any adult level of entertainment. From Jabba's Muppet-stuffed palace to the Disney-esque treetop victory celebrations of the *ewoks*, the film is a pre-adolescent's fantasy.

To satisfy his new fans, Lucas commissioned an entire menagerie of monsters for the palace, most of which could have come straight from *Sesame Street*. They included Salacious Crumb, a manic, ferret-like creature ('a Kowakian monkey-lizard,' according to the biography later dreamed up by the *Star Wars* mythology machine, who acts as Jabba's court jester), and a blue-faced humanoid called Bib Fortuna, 'a Twi-lek from Ryloth' with two fat tentacles emerging from the back of his head and looping round his neck. The same scene also features a blue, elephant-like bandleader, Max Rebo, lead singer Sy Snootles, sideman Droopy McCool, and miscellaneous aliens, among them three called 'Klaatu,' 'Barada,' and 'Nikto,' after the alien phrase uttered by intergalactic visitor Michael Rennie in Robert Wise's pioneering 1951 *The Day the Earth Stood Still*. Even the final battle, with the Emperor, a villain straight from one of Stan Lee's superhero comic books, cackling sepulchrally as he pours blue lightning onto a wilting Luke, belongs in a Saturday-morning cartoon show.

The speed of production never gave the modelmakers time to refine their creations. When Lucas made his Special Edition of this film, improving the creatures became his first priority. In the original, Max Rebo, visualized as having fingers on his stubby feet, is just a small blue puppet elephant, its feet and trunk visibly manipulated by wires. Stuart Freeborn's Jabba, operated from under a platform by cables, opens its eyes and mouth, but always looks like a Muppet.

Lucas announced the film's title as 'Revenge of the Jedi' well ahead of time, but shortly before release, abruptly renamed it to *Return of the Jedi*. Officially, he said he'd decided that the noble Jedi would never stoop to revenge. Another rumor implied he'd been concerned that *Star Trek II* might be subtitled 'The Revenge of Khan,' thus muddying the waters for his film (Universal chose *The Wrath of Khan* instead). More plausibly, it was suggested that the change was a marketing ploy, dreamed up well ahead of time to frustrate marketeers of illegal merchandise. If so, it had the desired effect. Many bootleggers were stuck with unsaleable items using the old name.

From the moment he outlined the trilogy, Lucas had wanted to show an entire planet inhabited by another race, but his first idea of a *wookiee* world in *Star Wars* had expired because of the potential cost. For *Jedi*, he tried again, visualizing Endor peopled by *yuzzums*, creatures with elongated legs supporting a hairy, ovoid body. Joe Johnston and Ralph McQuarrie sketched some possibilities, and Howard Kazanjian spent months finding stilt-walkers able to walk convincingly in such costumes; but Lucas, inspired, he says, by the two-year-old Amanda, shortened the legs, gave his creatures all-over fur, and called them *ewoks*. Ralph McQuarrie's concept drawings made them too troll-like, with spiky hair and flat, porcine noses, so Joe Johnston came up with a creature that was chubby, pint-sized, and cute.

Ewoks, Lucas believed, could become as popular as the teddy bear. Kenner had never made soft toys, and didn't want to start now. Lucas changed their mind, as he'd changed it with regard to guns; but their *ewok* dolls in gray, red, brown, and white fur, with cloth hats and neck-cloths distantly reminiscent of the leather bibs and capes worn in the film, never sold. Lucas didn't care. 'I wanted my daughter to have one,' he shrugged. 'That's what I care about. If nobody else wants one, that's fine with me.'

Kazanjian budgeted 'Revenge' at $35 million, all of which Lucas raised personally; not a problem when *Empire* had already made $365 million and *Star Wars* $524 million. Fox would still distribute it, but Lucas would own 100 per cent of the film after they had recouped their investment. As usual, interiors would be shot at Elstree, but all the location shooting would take place not only within the United States, but right in California.

For Endor, Lucas had to look no further than the forests on the border with Oregon, where a few groves still survived of the giant Californian redwood, over three hundred feet high and twenty feet in circumference. In the spring of 1981, while Kasdan and Marquand worked on the script, Kazanjian's crews moved into the woods around Crescent City, California, the last stop on Interstate 101 before it crossed the border into Oregon. The town had 25 percent unemployment, and local motels, restaurants, and hardware stores were glad of the work brought in by Lucas. Leasing a stretch of redwood forest overlooking the Pacific, the crews built dirt roads, cleared undergrowth, and planted seventeen thousand ferns that would grow to several feet high by the time they were needed to provide cover for the pint-sized *ewoks*. The area exemplified Lucas's contention that Northern California's film-making potential remained largely untapped.

Nervous about spies, Lucasfilm issued a cover story that they were shooting a horror film. The crew wore fake T-shirts that read '*Blue Harvest*. Horror Beyond Imagination.' On call sheets, the stars were given false names. Signs announced: 'The entire company – cast and crew alike – should be aware that the SET IS CLOSED. No visitors! No husbands, wives, children or friends . . .' If anyone enquired at the Lucasfilm press office, 'Revenge of the Jedi' was shooting in Germany.

At the same time, other crews under Kazanjian's assistant Louis Friedman were at work in the deserts of the Buttercup Valley, on the Californian side of the border with Arizona. Lucas wanted dunes as far as the eye could see, and this valley west of Yuma filled the bill, though it was also a mecca for dune-buggies, thirty-five thousand registered drivers of which lived within thirty miles. Four acres of desert were cleared of all vegetation, and two million gallons of water from a nearby canal poured onto the sand to create roads. It was harder to hide a film unit's activities in the desert than in the redwoods. A chain-link fence went up around the construction site, and Friedman posted a twenty-four-hour guard, but a news helicopter did get some pictures before it was chased off by a unit chopper bearing the 'Blue Harvest' logo.

Central to the Endor sequences were the high-speed pursuits through the redwoods by speeders, wheel-less motorbikes operated by antigravity. Since it would be too dangerous to shoot with real vehicles, ILM elected to use blue screen. For background 'plates,' Dennis Muren used the newly-developed Steadicam gyroscopically stabilized camera harness. After choosing a path and stretching a wire to keep the camera at a constant height, the operator walked slowly through the woods, filming at 1/30th normal speed – less than one frame a second. Projected at the normal twenty-four frames per second, the shots gave a dizzying effect of racing through the forest a few feet above the ground, zipping past giant trunks. The scene also used some stop-motion animation of models, which appeared more authentic now that ILM had developed 'go-motion.' Instead of each separate frame being pin-sharp, the operators moved the model fractionally while the camera shutter remained open. The result was a realistic blur.

All the principals of the first two films were back – older, richer, perhaps wiser, certainly sorer. At forty-one, Harrison Ford was beginning to feel his age. When Marion in *Raiders* remarks that he isn't the man she knew ten years ago, he tells her, 'It's not the years, honey, it's the mileage.' Now he could make the comment in real life. 'I had a great time on *Jedi*,' he told journalist Tony Crawley. 'I'm glad I did it. I'm glad I did all three of them. But, as well, I'm glad . . . (*pause*) . . . I don't . . . (*pause*) . . . have to do any more.' In a rare moment of candor, Lucas admitted: 'The reason I had to keep going on these three [films] was because I had sets gathering dust, I was paying rent, and my actors were getting older and vulnerable to accidents.'

Carrie Fisher lobbied vigorously to have the character of Leia deepened beyond the spunky tomboy of the first two films. Lucas obligingly made her both sex object and woman of action, and a tough fighter for the rest. Ford was resigned to being a cliché. 'Han Solo flies a spaceship, and shoots his mouth off,' he said, 'and that's about it. He's primarily a plot device.' He placed his hopes for screen immortality in the Indiana Jones films, and in productions like *Blade Runner* and *Witness*, which gave him characters into which he could get his teeth.

The cast all recognized that they were presiding over the death of their characters, and the series. The general reaction was relief, coupled with a certain contempt for the plot's hurried tying-up of loose ends. Even Dave Prowse, no critic, judged *Return of the Jedi* 'by far the worst of the three. Basically, it was designed to clear up the odds and ends. They killed me off. They killed Yoda off. They killed Boba Fett off, and they had all these silly little *ewoks*. I hated it.'

Center-stage of *Jedi* belonged indisputably to the *ewoks*, who would later have an independent life in two made-for-TV features, *The Ewok Adventure: Caravan of Courage*, directed by John Korty in 1984, and *Ewoks: The Battle for Endor* in 1985, and in some of the many novels spun off from the series. To play them, Richard Marquand assembled almost every short person in movies. Not since *The Wizard of Oz* had so many worked on one production. Kenny Baker escaped from inside R2-D2 to play Wicket, the first *ewok* seen by the rebels. Lucas spotted three-foot four-inch Warwick Davis, then eleven, clowning in the crowd, and marked him as a possible performer in *Willow*, a fantasy he was contemplating. Davis would eventually play the hero, Willow Ufgood.

22

Snake Surprise

I have a really bad feeling about this.

Various *Star Wars* characters, *passim*

Lucas came to London just before Christmas 1981, and was back in mid-January 1982. Normally he would have stayed for two weeks and returned to San Anselmo, but after his problems with Kershner, he hesitated to leave Marquand in total charge. He had Marcia ship him his winter clothes; he'd enlisted for the duration.

With Lucas on the set every day, filming of *Jedi* went with a semblance of smoothness. Badgering, fidgeting, criticizing, he wore down Marquand into little more than a first assistant. 'George harassed Richard Marquand into more or less doing what he wanted,' says Gary Kurtz, 'and I think the film suffered because of that.' Lucas suffered too, losing twenty-two pounds.

Shooting wrapped in June, and Lucas returned to San Anselmo, and Marcia.

While he was away, supervision at the ranch had been left to her. It was a job for which she had no patience. Plenty of people wanted her to edit films, and even to produce or direct, but since work had started on the ranch, they met only discouragement from Lucas. 'Marcia has sort of put her editorial career on hold,' he announced in the summer of 1981, 'and is now working as an interior designer. I don't really know if she'll go back to editing – and she's a good editor. Usually the offers are to go to New York or to go to Los Angeles, and that's no fun for us. It's like six months apart, and coming home at weekends maybe. But once we get our facility up here, if a director wants her to edit, it will be much easier to convince him to do it up here rather than wherever he lives. The whole reason for the ranch actually – it's just a giant facility to allow my wife to cut film in Marin County.'

The joke was lost on Marcia. Now that Lucas, supposedly, no longer wanted to make films, she'd hoped they could enjoy their wealth. She was disappointed. 'He just didn't want to have fun,' said Ronda Gomez, wife of director Howard Zieff, a family friend. 'Marcia wanted to go to Europe and see things. George wanted to stay in the hotel room and have his TV dinners.' He seemed to have no sense of the daily pleasures of life. Marcia accused him of living in the past or the future, but never in the present. Lucas agreed. 'I'm always sort of living for tomorrow,' he said, 'for better or for worse. It's just a personality quirk.'

Even now that they had Amanda, Lucas spent little time with the child. 'I see her a couple of hours a night and maybe on Sundays if I'm lucky,' he said, 'and I'm always real tired and cranky and feeling like, "Gee, I should be doing something else." I sort of speed through everything.' He acknowledged that his wife bore the brunt of his moods. 'It's been very hard on Marcia, living with somebody who is constantly in agony; uptight and worried, off in never-never land.'

Marcia found consolation where she could. Among the artisans working on the now nearly-completed main house at the ranch were six stained-glass artists, under Tom Rodriguez. Marcia and Rodriguez, ten years younger than Lucas, began an affair.

The news shocked Lucas. He'd had neither the time nor the inclination to cheat on Marcia, and the thought that she should have cheated on him staggered him. She proposed that they see a marriage therapist, but Lucas refused; psychiatrists were for people with problems, and they had none. He also rejected her suggestion of a trial separation. People within Lucasfilm were puzzled by the evident coolness between the couple. When Howard Kazanjian asked whether Marcia would help edit *Jedi*, Lucas said, 'You're gonna have to ask her.' Once she did agree to work on the film – she shares credit with Sean Barton and Duwayne Dunham – Kazanjian barely saw her, and, even when they'd worked together, Marcia and Lucas would go home separately.

Richard Walter saw the Lucases at a party at Randal Kleiser's house. 'I ended up in the corner with Marcia, chatting with her, and what she told me underscored a sense I'd always had that sexuality was not a gigantic part of George's life, that he was not really comfortable with sexuality. She just sort of blurted it out that it was extremely isolating; it was like Fortress Lucas. I'd heard this from people who worked with him at that time. They would say, "I can't stand it. He's brilliant, but it's just cold. I feel like I'm suffocating. I've got to get out of here." Marcia told me she "just couldn't stand the darkness any longer."'

Experience suggested that heavy publicity and wide reviewing, good or ill, wouldn't make the slightest difference to the box office of *Jedi*, so Fox made no particular effort to sell the film. Even the poster copy, with what one critic called 'weary nonchalance,' simply said, 'The Saga Continues.' Once again, Mann's devoted the Egyptian to a twenty-four-hour marathon opening screening, starting at one minute past midnight on the day of release. For seven days beforehand, fans slept on the sidewalk, many of the boys dressed in Luke Skywalker outfits and the girls wearing Princess Leia braids. For once, the public didn't second-guess the industry. *Jedi* broke the first-weekend record set by *E.T.*, grossing $45.3 million. It would eventually make $263 million in the US alone, $30 million more than *Empire*.

Reviews, though approving, carried a note of indifference. Pauline Kael repented of her former view that Lucas was a brilliant *pasticheur* wryly mocking science fiction, and decided instead that his decision to abandon an early commitment to a small, personal American cinema and become instead its most catchpenny showman was 'one of the least amusing ironies of cinema history.' In the *Washington Post*, Gary Arnold, while hailing the film as a crowd-pleaser, noted, '*Jedi*, directed with admirable gusto and sincerity but no discernible flair by Richard Marquand, tries to recapture the carefree, serendipitous rapture of *Star Wars* in certain respects that really can't be recaptured. The phenomenon has gone too far to avoid being self-conscious about its impact and reputation. The original may have answered a unique cultural craving in 1977, but the sequels are bound to be more and more dependent on whatever's happened in the chapters that preceded them.' Another review called it 'scraping the bottom of a very fine barrel.'

E.T., because it had been running longer, topped the year's box-office successes, but *Jedi* took sixth place, before *Star Trek II: The Wrath of Khan*, and *Poltergeist*. In an irony fast becoming typical of the new Hollywood film industry, the year's worst flop was *One from the Heart*, Coppola's ambitious musical set in a fake Las Vegas. Other disasters included Brian De Palma's *Blow Out*, and *Dragonslayer*, the failure of which further blighted the careers of Hal Barwood and Matthew Robbins.

Raiders hit $200 million gross, with no signs of flagging. At the Oscars on 29 March, Hollywood grudgingly acknowledged its success by nominating it for Best Picture, Photography, Art Direction, Sound, Original Score, Editing, and Visual Effects, as well as Best Direction; but the Hollywood community elected that year to honor the well-made, old-fashioned film, largely sharing the Oscars between *Reds*, *On Golden Pond*, and *Chariots of Fire*. *Chariots'* screenwriter Colin Welland flourished his Oscar for Best Original Screenplay and shouted, 'The British are coming!' though anybody who knew film finance realized that a revival of the British film industry depended on movies like *Raiders*, which went home with technical awards only, for Art Direction, Sound, Editing, and Visual Effects.

In March 1982, Zoetrope filed for bankruptcy, though Coppola, grandiloquent as ever, took the opportunity to announce that he, Spielberg, Scorsese, De Palma, Michael Powell, and Lucas were preparing to buy Pinewood studios outside London, the flagship of J. Arthur Rank's film-making empire, and site of the 007 Stage, the largest in Europe. Lucas immediately insisted he had nothing to do with the offer, and wasn't interested in becoming a mogul with foreign interests. The group offered $3 million, was worked up to $20 million, but dropped out when Rank demanded $30 million.

Early in June, Lucas called his staff into the office at San Rafael. As he and Marcia held hands, he informed them that they were divorcing after fifteen years of marriage. They would share custody of Amanda. On 13 June, they made the news public. Lucasfilm's head of publicity Sid Ganis reassured everyone that 'the divorce will not affect the business of the company.' News reports set Marcia's property settlement at $35 million, though some estimates placed it closer to $50 million. She and Rodriguez had already taken a house in the San Francisco suburb of Belvedere. Almost immediately she became pregnant with her first natural daughter, Amy. Ironically, Lucas's parents celebrated their fiftieth wedding anniversary in 1982. Lucas and his sisters threw a party for two hundred guests. All of them received a clockwork R2-D2 with a folded piece of paper under its arm reading '1933–1983.'

On the night of 22–23 July 1982, Steven Spielberg suffered the worst disaster of his career when a stunt went wrong on his production of *The Twilight Zone: The Movie*. As actor Vic Morrow and two Vietnamese children floundered through a shallow lake, a helicopter crashed down on them, killing all three.

Investigation revealed that the children had been hired privately and paid out of petty cash to avoid the laws on underage performers. Spielberg's line producer Frank Marshall left town for his Idaho holiday home, then flew to London, where he spent some time preparing the second *Indiana Jones* film. He was never charged with any offense, but Landis, his partner and producer of his *Twilight Zone* episode, George Folsey Jr, production manager Dan Allingham, special-effects supervisor Paul Stewart, and helicopter pilot Dorcey Wingo were indicted on charges ranging from breaching child-labor laws to manslaughter. All would be acquitted or escape with fines, and Spielberg would never even be questioned, let alone directly implicated; but this abrupt plunge into death and scandal shook him.

The *Twilight Zone* incident, coupled with the end of Lucas's marriage, had a profound effect on the next film Spielberg and Lucas did together, *Indiana Jones and the Temple of Doom*. Where *Raiders* had been playful, the new film was grim and violent. Indy had lost the last vestiges of his playboy character, and emerged as clipped, impatient, sinister.

Paramount had begun pressing Lucas about an *Indiana Jones* sequel in the summer of 1982, and Lucas told Michael Eisner the story he proposed for it. With dreams of shooting in mainland China, Lucas roughed out an opening in which Indy pursues a villain along the Great Wall on a motorbike. He also visualized a sort of *Lost World* pastiche, with a hidden valley inhabited by dinosaurs. Both ideas collapsed because of the intransigence of the Chinese authorities, still not ready to expose their country entirely to Western influences – at least not for the kind of money Paramount offered. Once Universal agreed to their terms to shoot in Shanghai on Spielberg's 1987 *Empire of the Sun*, all doors were opened.

Lucas worked up another plot, involving child slavery and a cult devoted to ritual sacrifice, and asked Kasdan to write the script. He refused. 'I didn't want to be associated with *Temple of Doom*,' Kasdan says. 'I just thought it was horrible. It's so mean. There's nothing pleasant about it. I think *Temple of Doom* represents a chaotic period in both their lives, and the movie is very ugly and mean-spirited.'

Lucas rationalized the violence of *Temple of Doom* as a response to the growing sophistication of adolescents. Saturday-morning animated series featuring Stan Lee's superheroes, live-action spin-offs of the Lee machine like *The Incredible Hulk*, and the success of *Poltergeist* and *Gremlins*, both produced by Spielberg, pointed to a growing taste for grotesquerie and the scare.

Raiders had mined the action adventures made by studios like MGM. *Indiana Jones and the Temple of Doom* raked through the cheaper *Tarzan* and *Jungle Jim* serials and features of the 1930s and forties like *Tarzan and the Leopard Woman*, *Tarzan and the Slave Girl*, and *Tarzan Escapes*. The plots never varied much. The current Tarzan, generally Johnny Weissmuller, Buster Crabbe, or some other recycled sports star, accompanied by his adopted son, simply called Boy, and occasionally by Jane, his genteel girlfriend, encountered lost cities where remote tribes, often dominated by witch-doctors or malevolent high priestesses, terrorized their neighbors with slavery or ritual sacrifice.

Once Kasdan had turned him down, Lucas called in Willard Huyck and Gloria Katz. For the opening and close, they cannibalized Kasdan's early drafts of *Raiders*. *Temple of Doom* opens with Indy in Shanghai, at the Club Obi Wan, doing business with gang boss Lao Che. A firefight breaks out during a big dance number led by American singer Willie Scott. Indy, Willie, and an eleven-year-old street kid, nicknamed Short Round, who's appointed himself Indy's bodyguard, escape the club by taking shelter behind a giant gong, used in the musical number, which absorbs the gunfire of Lao Che's gang.

At Nang Tao airfield, they board a small tri-motor plane for Siam, only to find themselves, in another Kasdan gag, stranded in the sky when the crew, henchmen of Lao Che, parachute out. Indy improvises a parachute from a rubber raft. They survive a turbulent river and reach a village where all the children have been stolen by an evil sect, which has also taken the three sacred Sankara stones that keep the land fertile. Tracking both to the palace of Pankot, they're welcomed by the thirteen-year-old Maharajah and Chattar Lal, his suave Prime Minister.

This, it emerges, is the heart of the sect. Indy comes under the baleful influence of high priest Mola Ram, and is forced to drink the blood of Kali, which turns him into a worshipper. Short Round, working in the mines, discovers that pain can break the influence of the drug, and brings Indy to his senses just as he's about to sacrifice Willie. They and the children escape by underground railway – another Kasdan idea – having meanwhile breached a giant cistern which floods the tunnels. Ejected into a crocodile-infested river, they have to make their way over a gorge on a swaying rope-bridge defended by some of Mola Ram's fanatical followers. The official synopsis of the film ended at this point, on a note echoing one of Lucas's favorite phrases: 'Can he do it? *Trust him!*'

In September 1982, Lucas handed Spielberg the first-draft screenplay. 'Steven was amazed,' said Huyck. 'He couldn't get out of it because we did it so fast.' Line producer Robert Watts and designer Elliott Scott set out around the world in search of locations for the $27 million production. Northern India appeared to provide everything they needed, including the palace at Jaipur in Rajasthan, which they had permission to use, subject to the Indian government approving the script. Shanghai was more of a problem. 'Hong Kong is just covered in skyscrapers and concrete,' says Scott, 'so we ended up in Macau.'

Once it had read the screenplay, however, the Indian government protested vigorously, particularly about the religious sequences, which showed the ruler of Pankot guilty not only of kidnapping and child slavery, but of celebrating a religion that combined the most repellent elements of Thugee with Polynesian volcano-sacrifice and South American cardiectomy. Lucas refused to change the script, so Watts abandoned the Jaipur locations and shot only in Sri Lanka, leaving the rest to be created at ILM or on the sound stages at Elstree.

Spielberg had found his Short Round, a Vietnamese boy named Ky Huy Huan, in Los Angeles. To play Willie, he chose Kate Capshaw, an ex-TV soap actress with little movie experience beyond a featured role in *Best Defense*, a comedy which Willard Huyck and Gloria Katz had written, and Huyck directed. Always slow to start with a woman – he'd waited a month before asking Amy Irving out – Spielberg was a pushover for the Texan forthrightness of Capshaw, who decided almost from their first meeting that he was the love of her life. Simply from sniffing him, she said, she experienced an animal attraction that

Richard Marquand (RIGHT) and Lucas on location in the redwoods of Northern California with the stars of *Return of the Jedi*.

Line producer Howard Kazanjian (center) with Lucas and Marquand on the set of *Return of the Jedi*. Kazanjian became Lucas's tough and trusted 'fixer,' with a reputation for icy efficiency. 'He's, like, from Mars,' according to Bill Norton (), who wrote and directed the ill-starred *More American Graffiti* (1979).

The Lost Worlds of
George Lucas

RIGHT AND BELOW Lucas
and Ron Howard on
location for *Willow* (1988).

LEFT Aubree Miller as Cindel, held hostage by the giant King Terak (Carel Struycken) in *Ewoks: The Battle for Endor*, also known as *Ewoks and the Marauders of Endor* (1983).

BELOW Stuntmen doubling as Tim Robbins and the eponymous hero in *Howard the Duck* (1986) evade the police in the film's climactic chase, filmed in the country around Modesto.

Lucas on the set of *The Young Indiana Jones Chronicles* (1992), his unsuccessful TV series.

Second thoughts. For the 'Special Edition' of 1997, Lucas reshoots the scene in *Return of the Jedi* where singers and dancers perform in the palace of Jabba the Hutt.

The burden of dreams. Lucas poses in the archive at Skywalker Ranch, which preserves the models, drawings, and props of the most popular series in the history of cinema.

made her yearn to be the mother of his children. Before work started on *Temple of Doom*, they were lovers.

The cast and crew arrived in Sri Lanka to start filming on 18 April, having delayed the shoot until after the Oscar ceremony on 11 April. *E.T.* had been up for nine awards, including Best Picture and Best Direction, but once again the Academy's voters snubbed Spielberg, giving the film only technical awards, for Music, Special Effects, and Sound Editing. Richard Attenborough won Best Director for *Gandhi*, and was embarrassed enough by the obvious injustice to give Spielberg a consoling embrace as he headed for the stage.

Harrison Ford, in less than perfect physical shape, even after working out in Hollywood with exercise guru Jake Steinfeld of 'Body By Jake Inc.,' trained two or three times a week at the ancient YMCA in Kandy. Even so, he was ill-prepared for the strains of riding an elephant. 'You ride with your legs in a hyperextended position to accommodate the girth of the animal right over its shoulders,' he recalled with distaste. 'First one leg, then the other is pulled forward, which tends to spread you apart – like being stretched on a medieval rack, I imagine. I'm not surprised the mahouts generally walk next to their animals.'

After three weeks in Sri Lanka, with the rope-bridge sequence in the can, Spielberg moved to India to grab a few shots prior to leaving for London. Amy Irving, who was also on location, playing an Indian princess in an adaptation of M.M. Kaye's novel *The Far Pavilions*, flew by light plane to meet him. 'We saw each other across the runway,' she said later, 'and by the time we came together, we knew.' That night, over a candlelit dinner, they repaired their relationship, agreed to marry immediately, and to have children. Kate Capshaw was summarily ejected from Spielberg's bed but, humiliatingly, had to keep playing in *Temple of Doom*.

'At Elstree we constructed a whole series of sets,' said Elliott Scott. 'The interior of the palace, reception halls with various rooms and corridors, an entire underground scenic railway with working cars for the Thugee mine scenes, a vast water complex meant to drive crushers and belts to carry the ore around, exterior palace shots in a courtyard on the outside lot, and, of course, the Temple of Doom set itself. At one point I think we had sixty plasterers alone at work.'

European circuses supplied elephants, and London had plenty of ethnic actors, including Roshan Seth, who played the young Maharajah's oily Prime Minister, and David Yip, who became Wu Shan, Indy's helper in the Club Obi Wan sequences. One of Stanley Kubrick's favorite actors, Philip Stone, was Captain Blumburtt, the British Raj's man in Pankot.

When the stars arrived from Sri Lanka, shooting started immediately on the mine-car sequences, which involved Ford clambering in and out of the tiny cars, and being jerked back and forth as they rocketed over a rollercoaster-like track. After a few days, he collapsed following a fall off a car. Spielberg rang Lucas, who flew out immediately. A hospital bed had been brought onto the set, and Ford rested on it between takes. 'He could barely stand up,' Lucas recalled. 'Yet he was there every day so shooting would not stop. He was in incomprehensible pain, but he was still trying to make it happen.' Lucas felt he had no alternative but to shut down the production. Ford was flown to Centinela Hospital in Los Angeles, where doctors diagnosed two ruptured discs. Surgery was deemed too risky, and for six weeks Ford remained in hospital while injections of a derivative of papaya juice ate away the damaged disc.

Once he returned, production restarted on an accelerated timetable. Some scenes which would have kept Ford in London for a few weeks longer were rescheduled for California. A 'wrap' party, for which the production manager had already booked a hall in the inner-London suburb of Camden, was hastily reconceived as a 'get-to-know-you' for the start of the main London shooting. Spielberg arrived with Amy Irving, the first anyone had known that she'd supplanted Capshaw in his affections.

Ford spent most of his last week of shooting chained to the Temple of Doom set, being whipped by Mola Ram's torturer. He and Spielberg were astonished when one morning Pat Roach, wielding the whip, was replaced by Barbra Streisand in full black-leather dominatrix gear. 'That's for *Hanover Street*,' she shouted with the first blow, referring to one of Ford's more undistinguished films, and, with the second, 'That's for making so much money out of *Star Wars*.' Carrie Fisher suddenly appeared, throwing herself across Ford's back, shouting, 'No, no, no!' Then Irvin Kershner materialized at Spielberg's side. 'Is this how you run your movies?' he asked.

★   ★   ★

Spielberg felt more at ease in California. For the scene where Ford, Willie, and Short Round ride the Himalayan rapids in their inflatable boat, he took the film to Yosemite National Park and the Toulumne River in the San Joaquin Valley. He also felt able to elaborate on some sequences. He rewrote the passenger plane as a cargo carrier, with a load of live chickens. For the Shanghai scenes, Hamilton Air Force Base doubled for the Chinese city. Costume designer Anthony Powell was inspired by a book of photographs by Henri Cartier-Bresson of China in 1937, including many of refugees fleeing the fighting. One of these contained a boy who resembled Short Round, so Powell copied his clothes, while Spielberg added his touch, a baseball cap.

'The real-life refugees were dressed in ways one could never invent,' says Powell. 'Priests wearing pith helmets and carrying tennis rackets. Chinese people wearing absolutely conventional European suits but with the most bizarre Chinese hats on their heads. Again, I showed them to Steven and we ended up putting a huge crowd of missionaries into the airport scene. If you look carefully at those missionaries, you'll see they are played by Steven Spielberg, George Lucas, Sid Ganis, and myself and others working on the movie.' The officious airport despatcher, called Weber, presumably after Lucasfilm's departed CEO, is an uncredited Dan Aykroyd.

Not all the scenes were so sunny. As Lucas refined the movie during cutting, its freakishness increased. He prevailed on Michael Kahn to cut for a faster and faster pace, emphasizing the grotesque elements. One high spot of the Pankot sequence was a dinner at which the Maharajah's guests gorged on gigantic bugs and monkey brains served in the severed heads. Lucas decided it wasn't gruesome enough, and commissioned more shots, including eyeballs swimming in a gray soup, and a python filled with wriggling live eels. 'Ah,' says a greedy gourmand as the belly is split and they spill out, 'Snake Surprise!'

23

Howard the Duck

I want to try making some films that I'm not sure will
work or not. So it goes beyond the possibility of losing
money – it goes to the point of my looking at a finished
film and saying, 'Boy, was that a mistake,' putting it on
the shelf and saying, 'Let's forget about that one!'

George Lucas interviewed by *Starlog* magazine, September 1981

Lucas justified the changes to *Temple of Doom* as a response to the new liberalism in horror films. Kids didn't flinch at violence as they had in the days when Charley Lippincott persuaded him to raise the censorship classification of *Star Wars*. Tobe Hooper's psychic thriller *Poltergeist*, produced and partly directed by Spielberg, had set new standards of acceptability for gore and the supernatural, soon to be further exploited by Joe Dante in *Gremlins*, which Spielberg also produced. When the ratings office tried to classify *Poltergeist* as 'R,' Spielberg flew to New York with MGM president Frank Rosenfelt and talked them into a 'PG' certificate. 'I don't make "R" movies,' said Spielberg irately.

Temple of Doom was an opportunity further to explore the limits of contemporary susceptibility to horror, and Lucas urged Spielberg to be audacious. The scene in which Indy, under the influence of Mola Ram, participates in the attempted sacrifice of Willie by plunging her into molten lava, and is only dissuaded when Short Round returns him to sanity by searing him with a burning torch, is overtly sadistic. Audiences were also horrified by the image of the high priest reaching into the chest of a victim and extracting a still-beating heart. The fact that there's no blood, and the flesh closes up miraculously after this piece of psychic surgery, didn't significantly diminish the element of shock. However much their children enjoyed it, this wasn't what parents had expected to see in a Lucas/Spielberg film.

As he had on *Empire*, Lucas drove the editor, in this case Spielberg's regular cutter Michael Kahn, to accelerate the pace, fearing, as before, that the audience would lose interest. Kahn's first cut assailed preview audiences like an artillery barrage. Cruelty succeeded cruelty, building up to a literally rollercoaster conclusion as Indy, Willie, and Short Round flee through the mines, pursued by maddened devotees of the sect. Spielberg persuaded Lucas to insert some breathing spaces, but even then the film remained disturbing. All Kasdan's fears about *Temple of Doom* were realized.

The film clearly reflected the dislocation taking place in the private lives of both Lucas and Spielberg. 'The divorce kind of destroyed me,' Lucas said later. 'It took me a couple of years to sort of unwind myself, and come out of it.' Spielberg agrees that the split with Marcia 'pulverized' Lucas.

Still himself trying to adjust to his revived relationship with Amy Irving, Spielberg was almost as disoriented emotionally as Lucas. Irving, competitive, ambitious, impatient of his lowbrow tastes and a circle of friends made up almost entirely of fellow male movie-makers, proved to be, for all her beauty and sexuality, as inappropriate a companion for Spielberg as she had been when they separated after *1941*. All the same, he acquiesced as she participated actively in the planning of Amblin's new headquarters on the Universal lot, persuading him that it should be designed in her favorite style, the Spanish adobe architecture of New Mexico. She also encouraged him to build them a house in the Hamptons, close to her spiritual home, New York, and to buy a Manhattan *pied-à-terre* in Trump Tower.

Spielberg has since spoken sentimentally about the Lucases and the impact of their divorce on him. 'George and Marcia, for me, were the reason you got married,' he said in 1999, 'because it was an insurance policy that marriages do work, and that working together and living together, and having understandings on many, many different planes does work. And when it didn't work, and when that marriage didn't work, I lost my faith in marriage for a long time.'

This isn't borne out by the facts. Long before the Lucases separated, Irving had complained at length and, on occasion, in print, of Spielberg's apparent unwillingness to marry her. Once they got back together, the couple plunged into conjugality with vigor. In June 1985, Irving gave birth to their first child, and they married the following November. If the Lucas divorce had any effect on Spielberg's attitude to marriage, it may have been much later, in 1991, when, having separated from Irving, he took up again with Kate Capshaw, who was no less eager to marry him than Irving had been. However, Spielberg held off his decision for some months while the lawyers for both partners worked out a pre-nuptial financial agreement which would prevent Capshaw from walking off with the kind of settlement extracted by Marcia when she left Lucas.

Once *Temple of Doom* opened in May 1984, Lucas announced he was stepping down from active management of Lucasfilm for two years. Since the departure of Charlie Weber, he had made all major corporate decisions. Now, almost overnight, he effectively retired. He would still live at Skywalker, but would take no part in running any of the divisions of Lucasfilm: 'I've put up with *Star Wars* taking over, pushing itself into first position, for too long.' Instead, he devoted himself to the raising of Amanda, and of two more children whom he later adopted as a single parent: another girl, Katie, and a son, Jett, named for Jett Rink, James Dean's character in *Giant*.

Lucas's decision was disastrous for Lucasfilm. As film historian Peter Biskind has noted, he seemed to have 'sabotaged his own business,' already weakened by repeated changes of location, periodic mass firings, and changes of corporate aims and targets. His managers at ILM and other divisions had tried to persuade him to minimize the effects of his withdrawal by giving them more autonomy, and in particular allowing some of their more talented and energetic people like David Fincher and Joe Johnston to direct films for the company. Lucas told them what he'd told Charlie Weber: there was no room in Lucasfilm for more than one film-maker. All Lucasfilm's productions over the years of Lucas's withdrawal would be made by old friends who had proved their loyalty by committing themselves to his vision of Marin County cinema.

For the moment, Fincher and Johnston stayed at ILM. Johnston designed the first project to follow *Temple of Doom* – a made-for-TV film using the *ewoks* from *Return of the Jedi*. Commissioned by ABC for their *Sunday Night Movie* spot, *Caravan of Courage*, subtitled *The Ewoks Adventure*, was pitched at the Thanksgiving-holiday market, made up largely of sub-teens. John Korty directed and photographed Bob Carrau's script, from a Lucas story that combined *Hansel and Gretel* with *Tarzan of the Apes*. Two moppets (Aubree Miller and Eric Walker), stranded on Endor when the family spaceship crashes and their parents go looking for help, are succored by the *ewoks*, led by Warwick Davis reprising his role as Wicket. Burl Ives at his most folksy narrated the story, which proved successful enough for ABC to commission *Ewoks: The Battle for Endor* the following year. Lucas again wrote the story, a dry run for *Willow*, which he was already scripting. Most of the cast from *Caravan of Courage* turn up again, but all the humans except Aubree Miller, the curly-headed blonde girl from the first film, are killed when, in an eruption from the world of fantasy, the army of giant King Terak raids the *ewok* village. Wicket helps her escape, and they hide with Wilford Brimley's gruff but loveable hermit until captured by Charal, a witch, played on autopilot by Sian Phillips. Jim and Ken Wheat wrote and directed the film, which drew 30 per cent lower ratings than *Caravan of Courage*, though it was popular enough to spin off two cartoon series, often combined as *The Ewoks and Droids Adventure Hour*, on ABC. Outside the US, both films were given perfunctory cinema releases only. The cartoon series also drew poor ratings as a new import from France, *The Smurfs*, swept the market.

In Britain, Gary Kurtz was struggling to regain his equilibrium after the collapse of his marriage and his business, and the cooling of his relationship with Lucas. Backing Walter Murch's debut film as director, *Return to Oz*, seemed to promise a partial solution to at least the last two problems. Murch remained within Lucas's inner circle, as well as being the most respected sound designer in the business, though Ben Burtt, with his flair for dramatic and fantastic effects, was fast overtaking him.

Murch and Gill Dennis's adaptation of L. Frank Baum's Oz stories shared little with MGM's *The Wizard of Oz*, which was inspired by some successful stage adaptations. 'That's where the 1939 film came from,' said Kurtz, 'the vaudeville tradition of the time; the painted backdrops and padded suits. The theatricality of the production was intentional.' Murch's vision is closer to the monochrome opening reel of the 1939 film, directed not by the credited Victor Fleming but the altogether less romantic King Vidor, which shows Dorothy stranded in a bleached, gray Kansas that reflects Baum's own grim adolescence in Aberdeen, South Dakota.

Return to Oz may be in color, but Murch's vision is black. His Dorothy, a glum, pigtailed eight-year-old Fairuza Balk, lives in the near-ruin of the Kansas homestead which her uncle and aunt haven't been able to repair since the damage of the tornado which precipitated her first trip to Oz. The crops are dead, the houses derelict. When Dorothy has persistent nightmares, Auntie Em (Piper Laurie) takes her to a black-clad quack, Dr Worley (Nicol Williamson), who, aided by the malevolent Nurse Wilson (Jean Marsh), tries to administer primitive electro-shock therapy. Saved by a bolt of lightning, Dorothy flees and, after almost being drowned in a raging river, finds herself in Oz again.

Officially the script only adapts *The Marvelous Land of Oz* and *Ozma of Oz*, but Murch also uses the robot Tik-Tok from *Tik-Tok of Oz*. A significant addition to the story, Tik-Tok – spherical, copper, and topped with a tin hat like that of a World War I soldier – operates by clockwork. Murch's painter father, a contemporary of Baum's, specialized in pictures of the interiors of machines, in particular clocks, one of which hangs on the wall of Lucas's office at Skywalker Ranch. Murch's office in the converted horse-barn next to his house in Bolinas is decorated with part of the Nome King model from the film, and the door of Dr Worley's office. As one critic remarked, '*Return to Oz* wallows in Freudian orthodoxy.'

Disney put up the $27 million budget for *Return to Oz*, and Kurtz, as with *The Dark Crystal*, retained Jim Henson to produce its creatures in puppetry and clay animation. But Murch was uncomfortable from the start. Piper Laurie praised his meticulousness, his attention to detail. 'He knew the rhythm of things,' she says, 'the pace, how fast things should move, how fast the buggy I was driving should get around the corner. That's not to say there wasn't "heart" there, it's just that, unlike most directors, he had a really magnificent, detailed understanding of the mechanics.' But, in dealing with those mechanics, Murch lagged further and further behind the timetable. Harley Cokeliss, who was close to the production, feels Murch should at least have directed a short film before embarking on such an ambitious feature, just to accustom himself to working with actors and a camera.

Murch also had the bad luck to be working for a studio in turmoil. As its stock price plunged, Disney made a belated attempt to board the speeding phenomenon of New Hollywood. It had already tried to recruit Spielberg to run the studio, but he refused when the entrenched management, mostly part of the Disney family, wouldn't cede full creative control. In 1983, Disney offered the job to Michael Eisner, who also demanded a free hand to run everything, including the theme parks. The family refused and, in a panicky move back to the apparent security of traditional management, appointed Dennis Stanfill as head of production.

Incoming administrators in Hollywood routinely ax the projects of the previous executives, and Stanfill was no exception. Claiming to be troubled by *Return to Oz*'s somber imagery, he fired the cinematographer and the first assistant director, and installed a watchdog producer. The next step was clearly to replace Murch. Lucas was in Japan promoting *Temple of Doom* when he got the news on a Wednesday morning. 'I called Disney and was told they had shut down the picture. I told them they didn't want to do that – you should never shut down a picture anyway, but if you do, you should do it on a Friday, not a Wednesday. They did continue the picture to the weekend. I flew to London and met with the Disney executive, who was already there, and told him I'd act as an executive producer myself. Things got back on track.'

Piper Laurie had been away in Scotland for two weeks, and missed the drama. 'The limo driver who picked me up and drove me to the set said, "You don't know what's been going on." When I arrived on the set, [Murch] was still working, but sitting in directors' chairs were Lucas, Coppola, and some other director for whom he had done such brilliant work [Spielberg]. They weren't even watching what he was doing, they were just chatting amongst themselves. When I found out that they flew over just to support him, I was so moved.' Jean Marsh confirms that none of the visitors took any obvious part in directing the film; but their presence, like that of Obi-Wan Kenobi and Yoda during Luke's trials, acted as a stabilizing and comforting force. *Return to Oz* wasn't shut down, and Stanfill allowed Murch to finish it in something like the form he envisaged. Its release, however, was limited, and though its reputation has risen slightly over the years, it remains an obscure footnote to the history of Marin cinema. Disney have never re-released it, and it's unavailable on home video. Murch never directed again. His monkish temperament recoiled from the brutality of the set. Coppola composed his epitaph as a director: 'He was surrounded by detractors, and he didn't have the natural political instincts to kill them before they kill you.'

Lucas also helped Paul Schrader find American backing for his film *Mishima*, based on the life of the Japanese novelist and militarist ideologue who died spectacularly in a ritual suicide in 1970 to draw attention to, as he saw it, the decline in samurai values in modern Japan. Schrader had spent years scripting the story and raising half the money in Japan. His Japanese producer, Mata Yamamoto, went to extraordinary lengths – even, according to legend, hinting he would commit suicide too if the giant Toho and Fuji companies didn't make good on their verbal promise to advance half the budget of $5 million. 'Someone at Fuji and at Toho would have had to resign and so on,' says Schrader, 'and no one wanted to be put in that embarrassing position. So apparently they came to him one night and gave him $2.5 million in cash, and said, "We did not give you this money," and still to this day they deny that they ever gave him any money, though if the film is ever released in Japan, they will own it.'

Schrader didn't threaten suicide, but he did use all his moral persuasion to raise the rest of the money in Hollywood. 'I prevailed on Lucas and Coppola, who were very flush at the time in their power and their reputation, to induce Warners to put up the other half, but I don't think anybody who invested money in that film ever expected to get it back.' Coppola liked the cool look Schrader planned for *Mishima*, with stylized recreations of moments from the novels, intercut with a black-and-white reconstruction of the day the writer and his helpers staged his formal *hara kiri*. The designer was Eiko Ishioka, famous in Japan for her TV commercials and her posters, including one for Godfrey Reggio's abstract *Koyaanisqatsi* (1983), a film Lucas admired. Coppola hired Ishioka to design a version of *Rumplestiltskin* he was directing for TV, but with a $1 million interest bill on his accumulated debt looming, he lacked the financial clout to scare up the $2.5 million Schrader needed. Instead, he prevailed on Lucas to front *Mishima* to Warner Brothers, where Terry Semel had replaced John Calley. Warners, ever hopeful that Lucas might bring one of his money-makers to them, advanced the money, but other than ILM doing the film's credits of ink seeping into paper like blood, Lucas had little to do with the film.

⋆   ⋆   ⋆

At the Academy Awards in April 1984, *Return of the Jedi* got a lone Oscar, for Special Visual Effects. On 23 May, *Indiana Jones and the Temple of Doom* opened. The film had become a *cause célèbre* even before its release. Recognizing that they were powerless to oppose the new strain of violence in Hollywood movies, the censorship board introduced a new rating, 'PG-13,' neatly covering the group which patronized Lucas's films. Foreign censors were not so lenient. In Britain, twenty-five cuts were demanded before the film could be seen by children under sixteen. But reviews like Steven Schiff's in *Vanity Fair* articulated the realization now penetrating most of show business: 'It's useless to pretend that *Indiana Jones and the Temple of Doom* isn't upsetting. And it's useless to pretend that the people it upsets most are children.'

Lucas and Spielberg agreed to impress their foot and handprints in cement in front of Mann's Chinese, along with those of R2-D2 and C-3PO, both of whom Lucas had presented to the Smithsonian Institution the previous January. Neither he nor Spielberg was looking forward to the event. Arriving ninety minutes late in a burgundy limo, they found scores of reporters waiting to ask about *Temple of Doom*. Both pressed their hands, then their feet into the wet cement, carefully wiping out the trademarks of their running shoes like seasoned merchandisers, then sped away down Hollywood Boulevard.

The failure of *Return to Oz* was disastrous for Gary Kurtz, who filed for bankruptcy in 1986. His ex-wife Meredith had returned to America from the UK, leaving him with debts of $8 million for joint business ventures. At his court hearing, he admitted he'd lost almost the whole $10 million he made from *Star Wars*.

Very occasionally, Lucas was glimpsed at rock clubs in the Bay area, and, even less often, at parties. On one such occasion, early in 1984, critic David Thomson saw him in the shadows with a girl he recognized as rock star Linda Ronstadt. 'They were both wallflowers,' Thomson recalls, noting that almost nobody else in the room seemed to know either of them. Ronstadt, one-time lead singer of the Stone Ponies, and famous for songs like 'Different Drum,' was remaking her career as a singer of standards. Her albums *What's New* (1983) and *Lush Life* (1984) featured her as a torch singer in a repertoire that Frank Sinatra had made popular. She and Lucas shared an interest in the black singer Aaron Neville, whose gigs Lucas used to catch regularly when Neville played the Bay area.

Ronstadt was an unexpectedly fast-track companion for the reclusive Lucas. She'd been the lover of, among others, California's ex-governor Jerry Brown, journalist Pete Hamill, songwriter John David Souther and, immediately before Lucas, up-and-coming comic Jim Carrey. A Ronstadt friend foretold a bumpy ride for the director: 'He will have more fun than he has ever had in his life. Then she will break his heart into thousands of pieces and go on to someone else.' She spent time at Skywalker, and Lucas at her houses in Malibu and Beverly Hills. He briefly exchanged his glasses for contact lenses, took up the guitar, even started tap-dancing lessons. Still expanding the ranch, he applied for permission to build yet another house, suggesting it could be 'a honeymoon cottage' for himself and Ronstadt. Those who knew Ronstadt responded with skepticism, and indeed the relationship was already cooling when it became public in March 1984, though it continued to tick over for another four or five years, Ronstadt coming to the ranch most days to ride the horses kept grazing in one of its paddocks.

Shortly after the break-up, Lucas began a three-year relationship with a Marin realtor, but subsequent attempts by friends to 'fix him up' ended as badly as had those at USC. An affair with as high a flier as Ronstadt had an enlivening effect on Lucas. He even flirted with the idea of launching a fourth part of *Star Wars*. In September 1984, *Cinefantastique* magazine reported that Lucas and Howard Kazanjian were scouting locations for the film, to be called 'The Old Republic' or 'The Clone Wars,' which Spielberg would direct. For the first time, Lucas wouldn't film in Britain: ILM would create not only the effects sequences, but the backgrounds as well. As for Ronstadt, the writer suggested she might provide songs. 'Sources close to Lucasfilm smiled broadly, but kept mum,' he noted.

These rumors proved to be totally unfounded, but Lucas was considering a new *Star Wars* film, though the inspiration wasn't Linda Ronstadt but John Whitney Jr, an experimental film-maker who'd developed the first viable program for computer animation. Universal had just used the system in *The Last Starfighter*, and while that film's spaceships, designed by Ron Cobb, still had the flat, graphic quality that marred earlier attempts at computer-generated imagery like Disney's *Tron*, special effects were clearly in for a shake-up. Presciently,

Whitney suggested that, in the near future, 'it will be possible to create the likeness of a human being, to generate speech electronically, and the result will evoke an emotional response. We may be able to re-create stars of the past, cast them in new roles, bring them forward into new settings if stills and old films can be used to make the likeness, the database.'

This was a crossroads in Lucasfilm's development. ILM had experimented with digital effects, making a short computer animation, *Point Reyes*, which simulated a drive down that Marin County peninsula. In 1981, Lucas had told *Time* magazine confidently, '*Revenge of the Jedi* will be the last picture we'll shoot on film,' but within the company there was disagreement on how far computers could replace actors, sets, and real locations. In 1983, ILM's computer division moved to new premises in San Rafael and divided into Lucasfilm Games, which created video games on license to Atari, and Pixar, devoted to experimenting with fully synthetic films. The remaining, and much larger, optical division, which held 75 percent of the special-effects market, continued with motion control and model animation on films like *The Goonies*, *Cocoon*, and *Back to the Future*.

The Games Division became self-supporting from its first two efforts, 'Rescue on Fractalus,' a modified flight-simulation game, with players piloting Valkyrie fighters on a rescue mission through the canyons of the planet Fractalus, and 'Ballblazer,' a sport played on a checkerboard grid. Pixar, however, would always be a drain on both the funds and the resources of Lucasfilm. Lucas decided not to make a computer-generated *Star Wars IV* film. Instead, in 1985 he sold Pixar for $10 million to Steven Jobs, co-founder with Steven Wozniak of Apple Computers.

Jobs moved the studios to Point Richmond, California, and over the next ten years invested $50 million in refining high-end computer animation. In 1997, Pixar created the first 100 per cent computer-generated feature, *Toy Story*, and developed Renderman, the graphic program behind the dinosaurs in *Jurassic Park*, seizing leadership of digital cinema. In a double humiliation for Lucas, other companies exploited ILM's breakthrough in morphing, while it was forced to buy Renderman from Pixar to keep up with the accelerating world of CGI. When Lucas started the next *Star Wars* film in 1997, it would be almost entirely computer-generated, just as he'd foretold more than a decade before.

Lucas insists he doesn't regret the loss of Pixar. 'I had Pixar for ten years,' he said. 'At that time it was primarily a hardware company that developed a lot of technology: digital printers, the first non-linear editing system we developed, high-speed graphics. I wasn't particularly interested in being in that business. I'm a movie company. But I had companies that needed those technologies, Industrial Light and Magic and Lucasfilm. A couple of guys at Pixar, Ed Catmull and John Lasseter, wanted to do computer-animated movies. There was a lot of investment that had to be made there, and I wasn't really interested in spending $50 million developing animated films. I would much rather take that $50 million and develop a game company, or a lot of other things, than push the special-effects company. It was basically a hardware company with a couple of guys whose hearts were into the animated films. So they went off, and Steve [Jobs] bought it, and after a few years Steve sold the hardware company to somebody else, and he took John and Ed and a few of those guys and said, "OK, I want to make movies, too, so let's all get together and make movies," and that's really where it started. ILM is exactly like Pixar, except we don't do animated movies. We do animated pieces in feature films. I didn't need two companies that were doing the same thing.' Among the 'animated pieces' to win acclaim for ILM and, in particular, Dennis Muren, was a scene in *Young Sherlock Holmes* where a two-dimensional knight steps down from a stained-glass window.

Haskell Wexler spent most of 1984 in Nicaragua shooting his semi-documentary *Latino*. His hero, an ex-Green Beret (Robert Beltran), is fed into the battle to help the CIA-backed Contras against the Sandinista guerrillas, but changes sides as he sees the effect of the war on local people. Lucas helped with the editing, and persuaded Cinecom to distribute the film – not very widely, since there was little enthusiasm for anything overtly political in a market which directors like Lucas and Spielberg had desensitized to such demanding material.

Ben Burtt had more luck with an hour-long animated film he made with Nelvana, the Canadian animation company which made *The Ewoks and Droids Adventure Hour*. *The Great Heep* takes its name from a huge and malevolent robot encountered by R2-D2 and C-3PO on their way to find their master, Mungo Baobab, an explorer on the planet Biltu. Joe Johnston designed the Heep. Anthony Daniels again did the voice of C-3PO, which was turning into a profitable meal ticket for him.

Jim Henson remained a name on which one could readily raise money, and Lucas backed his *Labyrinth*, a fantasy based on designs by illustrator Brian Froud, whose neo-Gothic images of lumpy gnomes and lumbering monsters had been one of the inspirations of *The Dark Crystal*. Irritated at having to babysit her younger brother (Toby Froud), Sarah (Jennifer Connelly) wishes that he'd be carried off by goblins, like the characters in the book she's reading. She recites a spell from the book, and Jareth, King of the Goblins, duly appears with his minions to take the child. Sarah pursues them into a labyrinth that takes her into Jareth's kingdom, and retrieves her brother with the help of creatures like the giant, shaggy, yeti-like Ludo.

Rock star David Bowie played Jareth in *kabuki* make-up, Japanese-style clothing, and long, pale, wispy hair; one critic called his persona 'Ziggy Stardust meets *Alice in Wonderland.*' The original idea, of a fantasy with songs to exploit the same market as *The Wizard of Oz*, was modified along the way, with some of Bowie's musical numbers cut and others curtailed. Terry Jones of the *Monty Python* comedy team, by education a scholar of medieval literature, wrote the script, from a story by Henson and Dennis Lee that recalled Lewis Carroll's *Alice* and Baum's *Oz*. *Labyrinth* did modest business in the US, where *Time* magazine hailed it as a film that 'flies worlds beyond Walt,' and it was a runaway hit in Japan.

On the ranch, Lucas settled down to a life of privacy and reflection that a Russian aristocrat of the early nineteenth century might have enjoyed. Thirty-five permanent staff catered to his needs, and kept the ranch ticking over. Marcia, who left the care of Amanda mainly to Lucas, found herself increasingly excluded from the Lucas circle. Francis and Eleanor Coppola normally invited her to their annual Christmas party, but after two years of divorce, the invitations stopped. Later, Eleanor confessed that Lucas had asked her to do so; being around Marcia made him nervous.

Much remained to be done at the ranch, but its fourteen structures effectively comprised the essentials. With money and space to play with, Lucas could indulge himself. He invited eighty-one-year-old Joseph Campbell to use Skywalker as his location for a TV series on his ideas, and insiders were summoned to a lecture by Campbell in which he analyzed the *Star Wars* films from an anthropologist's point of view. Campbell and Lucas became so friendly that Lucas described him as 'my Yoda.' 'Most of my friends are college professors,' Lucas said happily as his fantasy of the one-man university began to come true.

Lucas has always justified his inattention to Lucasfilm in the mid-eighties as a necessary result of his decision to spend more time with his growing family. 'The moment my first daughter was born, Amanda, it was just like a bolt of lightning hit me,' he said. 'From that moment on, that became my first priority. I didn't think it was going to be, because before that, making films was my first priority, and that was what I was immersed in, and that was my life. But then I realized that this *was* my life. And then within a year, I was divorced, and it *really* was my life.' But even the most affectionate father can't spend every minute of the day with his children, and the suspicion grew among his critics that, in embracing domesticity and shunning business, Lucas had taken refuge in a fantasy of childhood from a world that had become exhaustingly hostile.

In 1985, the Bass brothers of Texas took control of Disney by buying 25 per cent of the stock. Lucas advised them on the purchase, and after turning down the job as head of production, suggested Michael Eisner to run the place. Eisner immediately imported the frenetic Jeffrey Katzenberg from Paramount and put him in charge of film and TV production. Katzenberg launched a series of more adult features than Disney's traditional ouptut, starting with Paul Mazursky's revamping of Jean Renoir's 1932 *Boudu Sauvé des Eaux* as *Down and Out in Beverly Hills* with Nick Nolte and Bette Midler. He followed with Midler in *Ruthless People*, and Martin Scorsese's *The Color of Money*, a sequel to *The Hustler* with Paul Newman reprising his 1961 role as 'Fast Eddie' Felson opposite Tom Cruise.

Knowing that Spielberg and Lucas had a soft spot for Disney, Eisner invited both to think about making films for the revivified corporation. Spielberg was too concerned with major adult projects, and Lucas was preoccupied with the ranch, but both responded to the idea of doing something less time-consuming. Even before Eisner took over, each had been involved with planning rides for Disney's theme parks. At the end of 1984, Randy Bright, head of the WED Enterprises arm of the company, said, 'We have ageing assets at

Disneyland that we are going to bring brand-new life to.' One plan was for Spielberg and Lucas to collaborate on an entirely new area at Disneyland based on *Star Wars* and *Raiders of the Lost Ark*. This never eventuated, but in 1987 Disneyland opened Lucas's *Star Tours*, which adapted an earlier static ride in which visitors were injected into the human body, *à la Fantastic Voyage*. After queueing through a marshalling area in which R2-D2 and C-3PO bickered over repairs to a spaceship, the crowd for *Star Tours* filed into a vehicle mounted on gimbals and fitted with seats that sank and rose in unison on hydraulics.

Hoping to attract the youth audience which scorned rides as kid stuff, Eisner contracted with rock star Michael Jackson to make a lavish film for exclusive screening in seven-hundred-seat purpose-built 'Magic Eye' theaters at both Disneyland and Epcot, the community of the future at Disney World in Orlando, Florida. Shot on a new 70mm film developed by Eastman, which paid half the cost, it showcased a 3-D process pioneered by Disney. Smoke puffed into the theater and lasers flashed over the audience's heads to create a 'total entertainment experience.'

Lucas agreed to produce the film, but didn't want to direct it. In 1985, Coppola had just finished shooting *Peggy Sue Got Married*, so Lucas offered him the job. Disney proposed three concepts, of which Coppola chose *Captain Eo*. Jackson, as a spaceman, lands on a planet controlled by an evil witch, the Supreme Ruler. Singing and dancing through her minions, he and his group transform them into cats, and the Ruler into a beautiful woman who joins the dance as her doleful planet becomes sunny and bright.

Coppola suggested Shelley Duvall for the queen, and retained Rick Baker to create her costume. But Duvall balked at the outfit, in particular its Medusa-like mask. 'I'm not going to wear that!' she told Baker and Coppola. 'I'll have no credit. How will anybody know it's me? You could put anybody up there.' Anjelica Huston replaced her, though she too disliked Baker's designs. Coppola brought in Tom and Bari Burman, who'd worked on Richard Donner's *The Goonies* the year before. Their concept placed the Ruler, dressed like an alien dominatrix, at the heart of a web made from black rubbery tubing, an image reminiscent of H.R. Giger's monster from *Alien*.

Huston liked the idea, but when the Burmans presented their sketches to Lucas, he protested, 'This isn't what I want. I already approved Rick Baker's design.' Persuaded by Coppola, Disney commissioned a script from Rusty Lemorande, later director of action pictures like *Road House*. Vittorio Storaro shot the live-action sections; John Napier, who designed the stage musical *Cats*, created the sets; Walter Murch edited; and ILM shot the spaceships and the blue-screen work. Seventeen minutes long and costing $20 million, *Captain Eo* opened at Disneyland in 1986 with a gala party for 1400 guests. Lucas, Coppola, and Huston were there, but not the reclusive Jackson, though it was rumored he hung around on the sidelines incognito, a shrouded figure in a wheelchair. *Captain Eo* ran non-stop until 1994, when it was pulled in favor of a new show based on *Honey, I Shrunk the Kids*.

Back in 1976, Lucas had considered adapting Steve Gerber and Frank Brunner's comic character Howard the Duck to movies, with Willard Huyck and Gloria Katz. After reverting to Marvel when the studio declined to film it as a TV series, the project migrated with Frank Price, the executive who bought it in the first place, to Columbia, then back to Universal, when Price, now company president, gave a green light to producing it. Huyck and Katz were eager to work as director and producer as well as screenwriters, and Price offered to back them in a film of *Howard* if Lucas acted as their guarantor.

Huyck and Katz visualized a small film which played down the oddity of a duck hero. 'We wanted to do it in a sort of *film noir* way, as a smaller, realistic story,' Huyck said, 'but that wasn't the way Universal wanted to do it.' Price's tastes ran to the violent and gaudy, and he pressed them to see *Howard the Duck* as an action adventure filled with special effects – another *Ghostbusters*, one of his biggest hits at Columbia.

With two pages of notes from Gerber, Huyck and Katz wrote a new script in which Howard, trying to return to his own world, must defeat the Dark Overlord, an alien which takes over the body of scientist Dr Jenning (Jeffrey Jones) and transforms him into a scorpion-like monster. Other 'improvements' included some brawls between Howard and the denizens of the punk club where Bev (Lea Thompson) plays with her band, a subplot involving bumbling lab assistant Phil Blumbrutt (Tim Robbins), and an extended chase with multiple-car pile-ups, explosions, and Howard careering around the sky in a lightweight plane. Not sure whether it was comedy or drama,

Howard aimed for a relentless *Mad*-magazine facetiousness. Howard subscribes to *Playduck*, and the walls of his apartment are decorated with framed posters for *My Little Chickadee* starring Mae Nest and W.C. Fowle, and *Breeders of the Lost Stork* with a new hero, Indiana Drake, invented by 'the team that brought you *Beaks* and *Fowl Wars*.'

Huyck and Katz visited ILM to check on the feasibility of making Howard a muppet, or even animating him entirely. A few years later, Robert Zemeckis would combine live action and animation in *Who Framed Roger Rabbit*, but for the moment Lucas doubted they could bring off the effect. Jim Henson's Creature Shop proposed a variation on Yoda, operated by hidden puppeteers. It was a failure, and shortly after Lucas ended his deal with the facility, which relocated in London. Huyck and Katz elected to use a short person in a duck suit, a decision which blighted the film from the start, since the first act consisted largely of people assuming that Howard is a small person in a duck suit – exactly what he is. Seven people played Howard, depending on whether he was in a band, a brawl, or, in the film's most embarrassing moment, enduring a pass from a scantily-clad Bev; the nadir of Lea Thompson's film career.

Price demanded the film be ready to open on 1 August 1986, but shooting didn't begin until November 1985. It was complicated by Lucas's insistence that as much as possible be filmed in Marin County. The shortage of sound stages in northern California consistently bugged ILM-ers, who resorted to renting disused commercial premises, of which Marin had plenty. For large blue-screen sequences, they regularly hired the old Ford Model-A plant on the waterfront in Point Richmond. Sets for Howard's home world, Earth-normal except for two moons in the sky, were built in ex-fruit warehouses in the same town. Renters with unusable property on their hands were glad to make something on it, but this sort of improvisation merely emphasized the truth of Roger Corman's advice to Coppola when he opened Zoetrope: 'You're in the wrong city.' Lucas also put a little business the way of his old home town when he chose to shoot the flying sequences in Oakdale, a windfall for nearby Modesto, where cast and crew occupied a hundred motel rooms.

Though Lucas visited the set three or four times, he left Huyck to direct and Katz to produce – not, it proved, a very shrewd strategy, since the film went 20 per cent over budget. Almost none of the money would be returned through the box office when the film opened on 1 August. The *Philadelphia Inquirer* dubbed *Howard* 'inarguably a turkey for the ages.' *Cinefantastique* commented, 'The sheer waste of money *Howard the Duck* represents is staggering . . . The film drowns [the comic book] in misplaced, heavy-handed Hollywood glitz.' Retitling it *Howard: A New Kind of Hero* didn't help.

Lucas shrugged off the flop. 'A duck from outer space worked as a comic book,' he said. 'It didn't work as a movie. If I had to do it over, I'd do it again. Look, making movies is like a sporting event – playing the game is the best part. You put all your effort into it and sometimes you'll be successful, sometimes the public won't connect.' Nevertheless, he made it clear that, according to the *Inquirer*, 'his involvement was far less than people assumed.' Frank Price, less forbearing, took the failure as a personal defeat. Rumors were soon racing around Hollywood of a heated argument about *Howard* in the corridors of Universal's Black Tower between Price and another executive. A few weeks later, Price resigned.

24

The Height of Failure

I'm beginning to impress even myself – and I don't like
that.   George Lucas, 1985

At the beginning of 1986, Lucas officially took back control of
Lucasfilm after his two-year absence. Awaiting him was a dismaying
report by Michael Cloply in the *Wall Street Journal* that questioned
his standing as the most successful of New Hollywood's entrepreneurs.
Like the *Fortune* piece in 1980, it depicted him as an unbusinesslike
businessman, remote from the reality of profit and loss, clinging to a
dream of independence that, according to Cloply, 'has been increasingly undermined by a cult of personality that threatens to stifle creativity and excellence.'

In 1984, worldwide membership of the official *Star Wars* fan club
had peaked at 184,146. Annual sales of *Star Wars* toys, estimated in
1981 at $150 million, now stood at $50 million, with no new clients
in sight. Luke Skywalker, Chewbacca, and the *ewoks* hadn't, as Lucas
hoped, become perennials, like Mickey Mouse. Designers were
stumped by Darth Vader's emergence as the most popular *Star Wars*
character. His looming presence didn't lend itself to most products.
Dairy Time in Britain merchandised deep-purple yogurts with a Vader
motif (Bridge Farm, not to be outdone, offered Jabba the Hutt yogurt
in peach melba flavor). In Australia, Streets produced a black water-ice
with a crimson center to celebrate the heavy-breathing Darth. Stride-
Rite launched a line of shoes with a poster of Vader and the slogan
'Shoes that are out of this World.' They included baby booties, knitted
in Taiwan, with miniatures of Vader's helmet on the toes – enough

359

to mark any child for life, one would have thought, so it's just as well that, like most other *Return of the Jedi* products, they sold poorly. Today, *Jedi* merchandise is distinguished mostly by its rarity. A Canadian ceramic piggy-bank shaped like one of Jabba's Gamorrean guards is much sought-after by collectors, as is Kenner's pedal version of the Speeder bike, which never went on sale at all, but was reserved as a prize in store competitions.

Though his films continued to generate large revenues in foreign markets, on TV, and in video-cassettes, Lucas was financially over-extended, mostly because of the ranch. 'Lucas puts its cost at about $50 million,' said the *Wall Street Journal.* 'Some associates privately say the complex cost twice as much and has consumed virtually [his] entire fortune.'

Not listed in the accounting, for instance, was the cost of three neighboring properties bought by Lucas's accountant Richard Tong in his own name. When his ownership became known, Lucas claimed he'd acquired them simply to guarantee his privacy, since one, the Grady ranch, had been zoned for the construction of 130 houses.

The expanding Skywalker Ranch had become a source of conflict with Lucas's neighbors, who fiercely opposed each new incursion. Marin's County-Wide Plan aimed to confine development to an urban corridor on either side of Highway 101, and established a limit of one employee for every ten acres; about right for a farm, but useless for an enterprise like Lucasfilm. Lucas's scheme for an artistic retreat well off that road hadn't seemed to rupture the plan, but with it the camel's nose was in the tent. In September 1983, he applied to enclose 405 acres of the ranch with an electrified fence, ostensibly to keep out the deer which were ruining the trees. This was narrowly approved in October. Lucas further enraged his neighbors by buying another 927-acre ranch adjacent to his, and announcing he'd be hiring a hundred more people.

The greatest public uproar would come in 1988, when Lucas advised the county that he'd be moving ILM to the ranch, and proposed a hundred-thousand-square-yard complex to house it. If constructed, it would be the biggest building in Marin, even larger than the headquarters of Fireman's Fund insurance in Novato, the county's other large employer, and twelve times larger than San Rafael city hall. Urged by a local pressure group, the Lucas Valley Homeowners' Association, which, because almost all ILM employees would be forced to commute, feared a flood of traffic into the area, the county refused permission (though there were hints from Lucasfilm that some councillors had offered to green-light the development if Lucas handed some of his open space to the county free of charge). Lucas threatened to move ILM out of Marin, depriving the county, he estimated, of '$40 million a year in various forms of revenue from the enterprise.' He still got no permission, and the county got no land – a stand-off that would continue for a decade.

Lucas also protested at the level of property taxes levied by the county. In 1984–85, it assessed the value of the ranch at $20.8 million, and taxed him accordingly. Lucas said it was worth only $4 million. For 1985–86, they estimated $32.5 million, Lucas $8.9 million. Faced with even higher estimates for 1986–87, Lucas sued the county, alleging unfair assessment. The lawyer investigating the ranch for Marin was bemused: 'How can it be worth [only] $8.9 million, considering all that's gone into it?' To Lucas's claim that, for instance, the Skywalker Sound complex was really only a simple winery, he said, 'When I sweep away the illusion, all I see is business.'

One of Lucas's first acts in taking over Lucasfilm again was to appoint Doug Norby as president. A veteran of Silicon Valley, Norby was accustomed to 'downsizing' overextended companies. In his two years away, grouched Lucas, Lucasfilm had become fat. 'I'd go off to make movies,' he complained, 'and come back two years later and find everybody had hired an assistant.' Facing an overhead of $20 million a year, and a staff of eight hundred, Norby laid off twenty-five of the 450 people who worked at the ranch, and closed or severely reduced ten departments, including legal, publicity, personnel, marketing, and the art and photo libraries. Within a year, the payroll was down to four hundred. The survivors worked all the harder; Lucas still believed that people who were 'stretched' did better work. But by 1995, the figure was up to a thousand again.

Some problems inside the company couldn't be solved by staff cuts. If Lucas thought he'd won the definitive battle over Lucasfilm's future as a business when he fired Charles Weber, he was disappointed. The same problems returned to plague him now, but with more resilient and tenacious proponents.

Earlier in the decade, San Francisco producer Scott Ross had turned his One Pass Inc. into one of the city's most successful video production houses. In 1988, Lucas recruited him as director of operations, responsible for strategic planning and new technologies. Within nine months, the personable and aggressive Ross became general manager, and a year later vice-president, with responsibility not only for ILM but Lucasfilm Entertainment, which included Lucas Art Attractions, a think-tank of creative designers, and Skywalker Sound. Ross also inherited Edit/Droid and Sound/Droid, experimental attempts to combine sound and vision editing, whether on video or film, in a single computerized system.

Under Ross, ILM tripled in size over two years, shooting up to three hundred employees. Its effects for *Who Framed Roger Rabbit, Cocoon: The Return, Ghostbusters II,* and *The Abyss,* not to mention the company's own *Willow* and *Indiana Jones and the Last Crusade,* made it, as one admirer put it, 'the Rolls-Royce of special effects.' What had been a break-even operation became, in Ross's words, 'extremely profitable.'

Further to smooth out ILM's rollercoaster cash flow, Ross took it into the lucrative business of TV commercials. Lucasfilm Commercial Productions soon became the company's most profitable division, doing effects for between thirty and forty commercials a year. The press crowed at this apostasy. 'Throughout his career,' noted the *Philadelphia Inquirer,* 'George Lucas has scorned the crass commercialism of Hollywood. From his headquarters at Skywalker Ranch north of San Francisco, Lucas has looked south to the fleshpots of Los Angeles and, like an inflamed evangelist, decried what the Hollywood money-changers are doing to American movies. Now his company is going into the business of making commercials.'

Ross tried to persuade Lucas that the company couldn't survive simply by serving other film-makers – a difficult task, since, in his five years at the company, he only met Lucas five times. 'I was hoping that Lucasfilm would become sort of like Amblin,' said Ross, 'where you had, you know, a creative lightning-rod, Steven Spielberg – in this case George Lucas – but that Steven feels very comfortable being involved with other creators, whether it's Phil Joanou, or Bob Zemeckis, or whomever, and getting involved in different avenues of media: cartoons, television, films, etc. But George was – I don't know why, because I never really had a chance to talk to him – but what we got back, what I got back through his intermediaries was that that was not an interest that George had.' This division at the very pinnacle of the company further destabilized an already unsteady enterprise.

Instead of new technology, Lucas elected to turn back the clock and, for his first movie back in harness, make something he'd been thinking about for decades. *Willow* is Tolkien's *The Hobbit* and *Lord of the Rings* in all but name. Its three-foot tall hero, Willow Ufgood, lives in a fantasy world of witches, dragons, and creatures even smaller than himself called Brownies. Discovering an abandoned baby of that world's 'full-sized' people, the Daikini, he makes an epic journey to return her to her own lands, of which she's the lost princess and rightful heir. The usurper of her kingdom, the sorceress Bavmorda, is played by Jean Marsh from *Return to Oz*, and Willow is helped by two more Daikini, Bavmorda's tomboy daughter Sorsha (Joanne Whalley), and a wandering mercenary, Madmartigan (Val Kilmer).

Lucas provided the story, but Ron Howard, who agreed to direct it, brought in Bob Dolman, who'd written two television projects with him, and had also scripted for the TV comedy show *WKRP in Cincinnati*. A more skilled writer than Dolman, who didn't make another film until *Far and Away* (1992, also for Howard), might have found more in the complicated tale. One thinks of William Goldman's inventive, witty treatment of a similarly complex narrative in *The Princess Bride* (1987) – shot by *Willow*'s lighting cameraman Adrian Biddle, who also lit *Alien*. But Lucas as usual demanded fidelity to his ideas, and, as executive producer, was in a position to impose it.

'It was a very collaborative effort,' Howard said diplomatically. 'The three of us would throw hundreds of ideas into the hopper. When we would agree on any one thing, Bob would go off and write it, and we would hash it out all over again. Occasionally, we would go off on a wrong track, then recover. It was a very exciting creative experience.' Having already directed *Splash* and *Cocoon*, respectively about a modern mermaid and aquatic aliens who physically rejuvenate some Florida fogeys, Howard knew how difficult it could be to render fantasy credible on screen. 'They seem extremely simple. But structurally, fantasies are very complicated, very dense with detail. I probably spent more time in story conferences on *Willow* than any project I've done.'

Just as *Howard the Duck* shows no sign that Lucas either likes or understands comic books, *Willow* reveals, despite supposed years of study and intense, intimate association with Joseph Campbell, an acknowledged master of the field, a woeful ignorance of mythology. Its warmed-over clichés derive not from the *ur*-texts of legend, but from their sentimentalized nineteenth- and twentieth-century revivals. The Brownies belong in Arthur Rackham, and the transmogrification of the friendly witch Fin Balziel into possum, goat, and tiger cribs from T.H. White's *The Sword in the Stone*. When Aljean Harmetz of the *New York Times* found it 'stuffed with borrowings from the Old Testament, *Gulliver's Travels, Peter Pan, Mad Max, The Lord of the Rings, Snow White and the Seven Dwarfs, The Wizard of Oz*, and, most of all, *Star Wars*,' Lucas said defensively, 'I'm derivative – but I read where *Rambo III* is "reworking the genre."' However, since *Willow*'s sources were themselves reworkings, he was in fact copying from copies.

Though Lucas always refused to be drawn on the subject, the inclusion in *Willow* of a malevolent 'General Kael' and a two-headed dragon called 'Ebersisk,' named for TV critics Roger Ebert and Gene Siskel, suggests he saw the whole film as a personal parable. Like Willow, Lucas is a short man who, out of a sense of duty, makes a long journey with a small group of people, most of whom desert him. (It's even inviting to think of the waddling, self-important village elder Burglekutt, played by Mark Northover, as Lucas's take on Coppola.) He finds new friends, however, and triumphs even when they're transformed into pigs – the animal to which Lucas compared the directors of New Hollywood for their ability to sniff out the truffles of profit. In this interpretation, the helpless baby princess equals the cinema; Bavmorda's castle is Hollywood; Madmartigan, Sorsha, and the Brownies correspond to Alan Ladd Jr and the others who became Lucas's allies in New Hollywood. Obviously, the fairy Cherlindrea, Fin Balziel, and the Brownies are special effects.

Even with the proven Howard attached as director, Lucas found studios lukewarm toward *Willow*. $35 million was a lot of money to invest in a film with no stars, and, moreover, with a hero that only came up to their navels. At Disneyland for the opening of *Star Tours* in January 1987, Lucas made his complaints public. 'I worry about these gray-flannel types who are running the studios nowadays,' he said. 'The only thing they care about is money. I ask them, "What are you going to do with all that money?" Myself, I put all my money into my company and my ranch up north. What good is money if you don't build something with it?'

Hollywood at this time was more nervous than usual. The Directors' Guild threatened a strike which looked likely to freeze all production during the winter of 1987–88. Everywhere, studios were pushing directors to finish films quickly, or else delay them into the New Year. Inevitably, Lucas found his way back to Alan Ladd Jr, who, after the demise of The Ladd Company, had become head of the also near-defunct MGM Pictures. Ladd advanced the money for *Willow* but, to spread the risk, pre-sold the home video rights to RCA/ Columbia.

Lucas initially visualized shooting *Willow* like *Return of the Jedi*, with studio scenes in Britain and locations in northern California. Some exteriors were done around Skywalker Ranch, and on location at Burney Falls, near Mount Shasta, but after seeing the Burney Falls sequences, the first ones Howard directed on the film, Lucas worried that the setting wasn't sufficiently fantastic. During preliminary work on *Indiana Jones and the Temple of Doom*, he'd been struck by a district called Kwajein in southern China, where pinnacles of limestone jutted hundreds of feet out of the plain. The Chinese still wouldn't allow access to Western crews, so Lucas used film of the area as a background plate for a final shot of Willow's home valley, and began looking for similarly unfamiliar-looking locations for other sequences, in particular the attack on Bavmorda's castle, which he visualized as standing, like the castle in *Throne of Blood* and other Kurosawa films, on the black ash slopes of a volcano. He finally chose Tongariro Volcanic National Park in New Zealand.

Howard brought his editors Dan Hanley and Mike Hill to the production, but everyone else, cast and crew, was hired in Britain. Lucas's choice to play Willow was always Warwick Davis, whom he'd spotted as an eleven-year-old during the shooting of *Return of the Jedi*. Now eighteen, Davis had the vitality to handle the film's demanding physical action, which included horseback riding, and battle scenes choreographed by Britain's ace fight-arranger, Bill Hobbs.

In contrast to his arm's-length involvement in *Howard the Duck*, Lucas intervened at almost every stage of *Willow*. 'George Lucas is like Zorro,' joked Val Kilmer, who played Madmartigan. 'He comes and goes on the set. And he leaves his mark when he's gone!' As one critic would complain, there's a sense from the start that the incidents of *Willow* are written in stone. This realization seemed to weigh on Lucas increasingly as production went on. In January 1988 he confessed to the *New York Times*, 'It's more mythological than other works I've done, and it's in a genre that has seemed to be poison at the box office.'

Secrecy was tight, even by Lucasfilm standards. Aside from the Elstree sets being rigidly closed to the press, the company wouldn't even admit it was shooting in New Zealand. In Sydney, showbiz reporter James Oram, alerted to the Tongariro locations by 'a dwarf stuntman,' immediately flew there. 'I knew I was on the right aircraft,' said Oram, 'because there were a number of dwarfs aboard.' At the airport, he took a bus to Queenstown, a resort near the location with a population of five thousand. 'There were dwarfs on the bus – which is when I really knew I was on the right track. Some had been flying continuously for thirty-five hours – they had used a lot of imported dwarfs from Britain and Wales – so they were short-tempered dwarfs.' Before anyone in Queenstown realized he was a reporter, Oram discovered the plot of *Willow* and revealed it in his paper, the Sydney *Sunday Telegraph*, but found the public curiously underwhelmed – a bad omen for the film.

ILM prided itself on the meticulousness of its effects and the lapidary perfection of their application, but for *Willow* Lucas mandated a casual attitude to technique which often clashed with the physical realities of putting fantasy on film. The conflict would be all too visible on screen, making *Willow* look shabby and rushed; not the work of the Rolls-Royce of special effects, but of some rural garage used to chopping and channelling little deuce coupes.

'From the beginning of the show,' said Michael Gleason, one of the special-effects editors, 'George's edict was: this is not an effects picture. But when the storyboards started coming in, we all thought to ourselves, Oh, really? The real challenge editorially was just coping with the volume of film – beginning with approximately 750 background plates shot on locations all over the world. Because of that volume there was a lot of pressure to get everything right the first time. Our first count was about four hundred effects shots – which for a picture that wasn't supposed to be an effects picture was sure an awful lot of effects.' Another effects supervisor, Michael McAllister, agreed that had it been an outside project, ILM would have turned down *Willow*. 'But this was for the boss, and the boss gets to work however he wants.'

ILM's biggest challenge was the transformation of Patricia Hayes from goat to ostrich to turtle to tiger to woman in a single shot. All

Dennis Muren's inclinations were to stick to model animation and puppets, but after spending weeks making a goat's head from rubber, inflated so that it could be shrunk down onto the ostrich skull underneath, he turned to the computer department. Once the various models had been created, the interim stages were 'filled in' by computer animation. The result was the technique that came to be called 'morphing,' a contraction of 'metamorphisizing'. Scott Ross urged Lucas to patent and market its software, but the opportunity was frittered away in argument and prevarication. 'He still slaps his forehead talking about the morph phenomenon,' notes a recent profile of Ross. 'ILM missed the market opportunity, and now someone else's morphing program sells off-the-shelf for $95.'

MGM, recognizing they had a hard sell with *Willow*, gave it an unexpectedly lavish build-up. For months ahead of its release, portentous trailers passed through the cinemas. Over freeze-frame flashes from the film, a voice rumbled:

> You know what is real . . . and what is not.
> You know what is light . . . and what is dark.
> You know what makes you laugh . . . and what makes you cry.
> Now, forget all you know – or think you know.

Ladd Jr followed up at Christmas with a glossy booklet that went out to six thousand press people and exhibitors with his greetings card. Lucas also authorized the publication of the *Willow* novelization well before the film's release, a strategy that had worked with *Star Wars* and would, he hoped, do the same for this film.

The music was by James Horner, an up-and-coming composer who would hit his career climax with *Titanic*. An even more skilful *pasticheur* than John Williams, Horner, described dryly by one critic as 'a composer who is generous enough to assimilate into his own music the work of less fortunate predecessors,' borrowed liberally from Schumann's *Rhenish Symphony* for his *Willow* score. To no avail. Released on 20 May 1988, *Willow* was a dud from the start. It received Academy Award nominations for its Visual and Sound Effects, but lost out, as did most other contenders, to *Who Framed Roger Rabbit*.

The same day *Willow* started shooting, Francis Coppola turned the cameras on *Tucker*, for which Lucas acted as executive producer.

Car-maker Preston Tucker held deep significance for Coppola. Innovative, flamboyant, visionary, a little bent, Tucker was to engineering everything Coppola had hoped to be to cinema. And Tucker had also failed in almost everything he tried, just as, it seemed to Coppola, he was doomed to do himself.

Tucker erupted from the wartime boom in Californian manufacturing that launched George Lucas Sr in the office-equipment business. A tinkerer and part-time inventor, he'd worked with race-driver Harry Miller on Indianapolis 500 race-cars. During the war, he made a fortune designing and manufacturing armored vehicles for the army. It adopted his 'Tucker Turret gun,' but rejected his prototype 'combat car' as too fast to be safe. In 1945, deciding that the wartime automobile drought would make all America thirst for a new car, Tucker hired designer Alex Tremulis to create the Tucker 48 Torpedo. Designed to use as much war surplus as possible, it had a 160-horsepower Franklin helicopter engine, and incorporated most of the new ideas developed in the previous decade but shunned by a cautious Detroit: rear air-cooled engine, disk brakes, seatbelts, pop-up tail-lights, hydraulic suspension, padded dashboard, safety windows with shatterproof glass, fuel injection, and a central swivellable headlight. Its lines were sleek and futuristic.

Leasing a former B-29 plant from the government, Tucker raised capital anywhere he could, selling stock to small investors, and pre-selling the cars with flashy advertising and glitzy shows, including a gala launch that nearly turned into a riot when Tucker couldn't get the car to start; once he did, however, the look of it ravished the crowd, who broke into spontaneous applause. By 1947, fifty-one sample cars had rolled off the assembly line. Tucker priced them at a mere $1000 each, and Detroit recognized the threat. The Torpedo was too good and the price too low to let it survive, so General Motors, Chrysler, and Ford flexed their political muscle. In Coppola's version, tame politicians have Tucker indicted for minor illegalities in his stock dealings. He is cleared of all charges, but not before the paid press has smeared him and his car. The first fifty-one Tuckers become the last. Just before he died seven years later, Tucker wrote an article with a title that became his epitaph: 'My Car was too Good.' Forty-seven Tuckers survive today, and change hands at between $250,000 and half a million. The thirty-seventh is on permanent exhibition at the Smithsonian Institution.

As a boy, Coppola knew about the Tucker. His father bought stock and ordered a car, but the company went bust before it could be delivered, and Coppola Sr lost his investment. When Coppola became rich, he bought two Tuckers, the first for $50,000. Lucas also had one, and bought another during the production. To film Tucker's life had been Coppola's ambition ever since college. Sometimes he visualized it as a moody *Citizen Kane*-type biopic in the style of Orson Welles, at other times as a comedy like Frank Capra's cautionary *Mr Smith Goes to Washington*, showing an honest visionary triumphing over reaction and corruption. Most recently, he fancied it as a *kabuki*-influenced musical, designed in the style of Schrader's *Mishima*, with Jack Nicholson as Tucker, or perhaps Marlon Brando, and a plot recalling *The Music Man*, but with lyrics and music by the team that created *Fancy Free*, the original of *On the Town* – Leonard Bernstein, Betty Comden, and Adolph Green. Coppola even flew Bernstein to California for two weeks to discuss it.

Lucas liked Tucker too, but not the comedy or musical approach to his life. Cars, always for Lucas the most seductive symbol of free-dom and mobility, were not something to be co-opted in the elabor-ation of a fantasy, as Coppola had done in *One From the Heart*, setting Nastassia Kinski in a Cadillac convertible like a diamond in an engage-ment ring. 'Of all your ideas,' he told Coppola, 'that Tucker one is good, 'cause it's the story of the little guy pursuing the dream, and people can identify with that.' Later, he commented, 'Francis can get so esoteric it can be hard for an audience to relate to him. He needs someone to hold him back. With *Godfather* it was Mario Puzo; with *Tucker*, it was me.'

'Holding Francis back' meant depicting Tucker the way Lucas saw him: not as some well-built symbol of American knowhow belting his confidence to the upper circle in a fruity baritone, but as 'the little guy' – the diminutive is important – 'pursuing the dream,' working in shirtsleeves at the launch to fix an oil leak while, on the other side of the satin curtain, the Tuckerettes strut their stuff. Coppola, of course, didn't associate Tucker with Lucas even for a minute. If any-body in the film embodies 'the stinky kid,' it's Dean Stockwell in a creepy cameo as Howard Hughes, soft-spoken and haunted in the vast hangar that preserved his *Spruce Goose*, the giant sea-plane he coaxed off the water just once, to prove it could fly, then put on show in silent reproof of his detractors. Stockwell, short and nervy, isn't anyone's idea of Hughes, but it takes very little to see him as Lucas, and his enormous plywood folly as Skywalker Ranch. Even Hughes's musing about the fickleness of the audience – 'Did I change, or the cosmic sense of humor? I used to laugh when *they* did' – might have come from Lucas's lips.

Jeff Bridges played Tucker, and Joan Allen his wife Vera. Martin Landau got the plum role of Abe Karatz, Tucker's dedicated business partner whose past conviction for bank fraud precipitates the company's fall. Coppola planned to write *Tucker* himself, once he'd completed the Vietnam war drama *Gardens of Stone,* but he'd hardly finished shooting *Gardens* when his son Gio was killed in a speedboat accident. In the emotional vacuum that followed, the job of scripting *Tucker* fell to Arnold Schulman, whose intermittently glittering career began in 1959, when Frank Capra chose his play as the basis for *A Hole in the Head.* For *Tucker,* Schulman collaborated with Englishman David Seidler. Given Coppola's and Lucas's diametrically opposed visions of the character, and the continued complaints of Tucker's widow and children, who preferred that the film not mention his aristocratic mistress nor his numerous dishonesties with shareholders' money, it's a wonder that any script was written at all. Occasionally, Schulman and Seidler gave up and produced alternative versions of the same scene, leaving it for Lucas and Coppola to fight it out.

When Lucas started ringing around Hollywood looking for a backer, he found little enthusiasm for the project. Paramount had already refused Coppola, but when Lucas rang, studio boss Frank Mancuso turned him down as well; *Labyrinth* and *Howard the Duck* had tarnished the Lucas sheen. Even ex-Lucasfilm executive Sidney Ganis, now in charge of worldwide marketing for Paramount, couldn't move Mancuso, so Lucas put up the $24 million himself.

Once the film was finished, Lucas tried Paramount again, to find that Sid Ganis had persuaded Mancuso that overseas sales would make up the money *Tucker* didn't make in the domestic market. Since it was being sold on the names of its directors ('from the men who brought you *The Godfather* and *Star Wars* . . .'), both Coppola and Lucas agreed to make themselves available for press interviews. The studio also insisted on amplifying the title to *Tucker: The Man and His Dream.*

Despite all this, the film flopped. America was no longer a nation for dreamers, whether they made cars or movies. Coppola descended into his customary post-production despair and, in one of the interviews forced on him by Paramount, took the opportunity to shift part of the blame. Explaining how he got involved in *Tucker*, he said, 'I'd lost some of my confidence. I knew George has a marketing sense of what the people might want. He wanted to candy-apple it up a bit, make it like a Disney film. He was at the height of his success, and I was at the height of my failure, and I was a little insecure . . . I think it's a good movie – it's eccentric, a little wacky, like the Tucker car – but it's not the movie I would have made at the height of my power.' Stung, Lucas at first claimed Coppola had been misquoted, then fired back: 'The truth of it is, Francis and I worked on the movie together, and he made the movie he wanted to make. Who knows what it'd have been if he'd made the movie on his own? And who knows what it would have been if he'd have made it at the height of his powers – which was five or six years ago?'

It's hard not to like *Tucker*, nor to respect Lucas for having supported it, particularly as he must have been aware that it stood no chance of returning its investment. One can see why he did so. It's the kind of film he might have been making himself had he persisted with the social realism of *American Graffiti*, rather than branching off so profitably into fantasy and science fiction. Preston Tucker also resembles Lucas's old friend Allen Grant, a classic American entrepreneur whose vision outstripped his finances – a fate which Lucas now faced himself. If the film embodies a metaphor for his own troubled business history, however, it also contains the germ of a solution to those problems. *Tucker* is effectively an epitaph for Lucas's dream of Marin cinema, which he now realized had no serious chance of succeeding. Designer Dean Tavoularis had combed the county for locations, using the old Ford plant in Richmond for Tucker's factory, and a Sonoma County mansion for his home in Ypsilanti, Michigan, while the cinematography of Vittorio Storaro exploited the soft light of Northern California, giving the film a quality that would not have been possible in the desert light around Los Angeles. But that light is elegiac. It depicts Marin in the nostalgic tones of a lost world. Preston Tucker was history, and so, soon, would be Lucas's vision of an alternative cinema free of Hollywood.

25

Indiana Jones and the Last Crusade

> If I've got a smash, you can't hurt me, and if I've got a
> failure, you can't help me.
>
> Samuel Goldwyn

Willow grossed $27 million, but never looked like making the $90 million needed to turn a net profit. The Cannes Festival agreed to show it, but not as part of its competition, and Lucas came from Spain, where he'd been working on *Indiana Jones and the Last Crusade*, to share the dais at the press conference with Ron Howard, writer Bob Dolman, Val Kilmer, Joanne Whalley, Warwick Davis, and Jean Marsh. He'd been hoping that *Willow* might do as well as *E.T.*, whose later success had been signalled by a tumultuous standing ovation at Cannes in 1992, but word of the poor US reaction had already spread, and the film died.

In August, it was the turn of *Tucker*. Released on the twelfth in only a handful of theaters, it too met general indifference. During the year, Lucas, with Coppola, stood as guarantor for two more maverick productions, Godfrey Reggio's *Powaqqatsi*, the follow-up to *Koyaanisqatsi*, and the animated dinosaur film *The Land Before Time*, made by Don Bluth, who broke away from Disney to recapture the vitality and respect for craft of old hand-drawn animation. *The Land Before Time*, on which Lucas is credited as executive producer, became his only box-office success of his two-year break.

Lucas still owed Paramount two *Indiana Jones* films, but Harrison Ford was distancing himself from jock cinema. He'd held his own in the part of the manic inventor intended for Jack Nicholson in Peter Weir's *The Mosquito Coast*, and punched his weight against Sigourney

Weaver and Melanie Griffith in Mike Nichols's comedy/romance *Working Girl*, which he was just completing as Lucas and Spielberg started negotiating for the third Indy picture. Ford hadn't liked the violence of *Temple of Doom* any more than Lawrence Kasdan had. Whatever plot Lucas came up with, he wanted it to be optimistic, and to show Indy as an unabashed hero.

Lucas was now getting to the end of the stories in the 'Indy' file he'd roughed out more than a decade before. Like Spielberg, he admired *The Haunting*, Robert Wise's 1963 adaptation of Shirley Jackson's novel *The Haunting of Hill House*, and he'd imagined Indy leading a ghost hunt in some ancient mansion, like the group of psychics and sceptics assembled by investigator Richard Johnson in that film. But *Poltergeist* had exhausted Spielberg's interest in the supernatural, and he vetoed any such project.

For his part, Spielberg had been trying since 1982 to film Michael Crichton's novel *Congo*, about a tribe of savage albino gorillas guarding lost diamond-mines in the depths of Africa, and the explorers who make contact with them via a baby gorilla fitted with a computer and trained to translate. With Brian De Palma, Spielberg spent three years fighting to interest the studios, then gave up.

When Crichton heard a new Indy film was in the air, he proposed *Congo* – with a little restructuring, it would make a fine Jones adventure. Lucas didn't agree. All Indy stories, he felt, should be new. But Spielberg liked the idea well enough to discuss technicalities with Crichton. Having done so well with E.T., and seen Lucas succeed with Yoda, could the talking gorilla be animatonic? Crichton disagreed. With an alien, the audience gave you the benefit of the doubt – maybe Martians really did look like they were made out of rubber – but every kid has seen a gorilla, and would spot the slightest artificiality. Spielberg asked Frank Marshall, who was directing the second-unit African sequences of *The Color Purple*, to check out possible locations, and commissioned Chris Columbus, who had scripted *Gremlins*, to write a screenplay. Neither Spielberg nor Lucas liked the script, however, and the African idea was shelved. In 1994 Paramount filmed *Congo*. The producer/director was Frank Marshall.

Lucas was less worried about the contents of the screen story for a new Indy film than about the fact that Harrison Ford was now forty-six years old. Would sub-teens accept a hero old enough to be their father? He suggested starting the film with Indy as a boy. Bored with children after *Empire of the Sun*, Spielberg – the child of divorced parents for whom the search for the father was a career-long preoccupation – became more interested when Lucas proposed introducing Indy's father too; three Indies for the price of one. Lucas reinforced his interest in the family approach when he proposed a medieval, and specifically Arthurian, theme. The legend of the Holy Grail, the cup Christ used at the last supper, and which caught his blood on Calvary, was 'hugely powerful to Steven,' says Lawrence Kasdan. 'who sees most of his movies that way.' Menno Meyjes, scenarist of Spielberg's *The Color Purple*, went to work on an Arthurian Indy screenplay, but it didn't satisfy either Lucas or Spielberg. They switched to Jeffrey Boam, who'd written Joe Dante's *Innerspace*. Boam delivered *Indiana Jones and the Last Crusade*, in which both Spielberg and Lucas could see the shape of the future film.

'We licked it with Boam,' said Spielberg, though the licking was more an elaborate *schmooze* – Boam's first draft is dated 1985, but the film wasn't released until 1988. After all that work, the script paraphrased *Raiders of the Lost Ark*, albeit with a more mature Indy, crafted to Ford's new sensibility. No longer given to crashing tombs with the abandon of earlier times, he's glimpsed in one of his first scenes lecturing students on the need for scholarship. Cautioning that ' "X" never, ever marks the spot,' he insists, 'Seventy per cent of all archeology is done in the library. Research. Reading.' This conviction only survives until he arrives in his office, a rats' nest of dusty papers and relics of forgotten expeditions. Besieged by students, he looks around at the debris of a lifetime spent in the past, shrugs off responsibility like a wet overcoat, and escapes through the window.

Indy's father, Henry (played by Sean Connery), also an archeologist, has gone missing while on the track of a lifetime obsession, the Holy Grail, which, in Boam's invented mythology, confers eternal life on anyone who drinks from it. Indy sets out to find him, and runs into Nazis seeking the same goal, led by pretty but crooked archeologist Elsa Schneider (Alison Doody), and American businessman Donovan (Julian Glover). The search ends at Petra in Jordan, where a lone, immortal crusader stands vigil over the Grail.

The Grail's promise of eternal life turns out to be hedged around with the usual restrictions of Free Introductory Offers. The candidate must evade three booby-traps, then select the correct Grail from a few dozen on display. Donovan, choosing wrongly, suffers accelerated ageing, crumbling to dust in seconds. Indy picks the correct cup, and uses it to cure a gunshot wound that is killing his father, but learns that the revivifying effect only works within the caves: you can live forever if you live only there. Writing in the *Washington Post*, Hal Hinson disparaged these scenes: 'The final section, in which Indy must claim the Grail and save his father's life, is imbued with a turgid, pop-mystical tone. (It doesn't help that these scenes look as if they were lit with a Lava Lamp.) The sense of momentousness and wonder they strain for doesn't come across, though. And not only is there a shortage of magic, there's a shortage of sense as well.'

The logic of the story demands that one or both Joneses assume the lonely vigil of the last crusader, but Lucas realized his audience would not take kindly to being cheated of a cataclysmic climax. Elsa tries to carry the Grail out of the caves, which then collapse on her, reburying the cup, the Nazis, and the understandably weary crusader, while Indy, his father, and their friends ride away through yet another gaping hole in the plot in search of new adventures.

To be sure of thoroughly hooking the audience, *The Last Crusade* offers not one but two preliminary action sequences. The first features a teen Indy, played by Hollywood's hottest young actor, River Phoenix. His hiring became one of the best-kept of *Last Crusade*'s secrets. In the script, he's only referred to as 'Boy on Train,' and once rumors began circulating, Lucasfilm spread its own misinformation that Phoenix was playing Indy's young brother.

Henry Jones was harder to cast. Lucas considered John Houseman, but decided that at eighty-five he would be too creaky to play Harrison's sexual competitor. Once Sean Connery became available, neither Lucas nor Spielberg could resist having James Bond in their film, even though Connery was only twelve years older than Ford. Anxious to escape from a commitment to star in Terry Gilliam's *The Adventures of Baron Munchausen*, which had run into money problems, Connery welcomed the job. But big stars have big egos, and with three major names to juggle with, Boam, Spielberg and Lucas had to make some extensive revisions to the script. In particular, Connery wanted to appear at least as potent as Ford. Following *Empire of the Sun*, Spielberg had put Tom Stoppard on the payroll to assess new screenplays and occasionally rewrite them. The playwright brought his light touch to the tricky scenes in *Crusade* which reveal that father and son have shared Elsa Schneider. The film's best-remembered exchanges are his:

INDY: How did you know she was a Nazi?
HENRY: She talked in her sleep.

Indy mulls this over. Then the light dawns. Later, when the subject comes up again, Henry tries to justify his actions.

HENRY: I'm as human as the next man.
INDY: Dad, I *was* the next man.

Ford himself contributed some of the better Indy gags, including one on the zeppelin in which he and Henry flee Berlin. Rather than simply throwing overboard the Nazi sent to bring him back, Ford suggested to Spielberg that Indy disguise himself as a steward to do so. He circulates among the passengers asking for tickets. They ignore him, until, having upended the Nazi through the window, he turns and explains pointedly, 'No ticket.' Suddenly, everybody is reaching into their inside pockets.

River Phoenix deserved a major opening sequence, so Boam wrote one especially for him, set in the south-west United States in 1912. Young Indy and a group of Boy Scouts are visiting an Indian canyon village where, coincidentally, a grave-robber, identified only as 'Fedora' and dressed like the adult Indy, has just dug up the ancient Cross of Coronado. Indy, declaring righteously, 'This should be in a museum,' grabs it and sets off for town, pursued by Fedora and his men. They board a convenient circus train, a pretext for a series of encounters with savage creatures – a rhinoceros, a vat of snakes (the source of Indy's later aversion to reptiles), crocodiles, and a lion. Indy evades them all, only to be betrayed by the local sheriff. Taking back the cross, the sheriff returns it to Fedora, who passes it to his employer, an anonymous man in a white suit and a Panama hat who recalls Belloq in *Raiders*. 'You lost today, kid,' Fedora consoles him, 'but that doesn't mean you have to like it.' He gives him his stained felt hat.

The opening should have ended there, but Ford protested that his own introduction as a weary college professor in tweeds hardly did justice to his character. He also resented the space given to Phoenix, who had almost stolen *The Mosquito Coast* from under his nose, playing his son. Lucas inserted a second opening sequence in which Indy, twenty-six years later, battles more minions of the man in the white suit on the storm-drenched deck of a freighter off the Portuguese coast. At issue is the same cross, which this time Indy retrieves, leaving the ship in flames and the man in the white suit survived only by his riddled Panama.

Interiors for *Last Crusade* were shot at Elstree, but only just. With the shrinkage of American film-making in Britain, the studios had passed from hand to hand, a little more decrepit and less well-staffed with each change of ownership. Lucas viewed their decline with alarm. Now that he'd taken up the reins of Lucasfilm again, he was uncomfortably aware of how much had changed in two years. In hopes of guaranteeing the survival of one of the last complexes suitable for his kind of film-making, he tried to buy Elstree from its current owners, banking group TESE. They refused: the site, situated in the center of an area becoming increasingly residential, was ideal for a shopping mall, and the wealthy Tesco chain had already showed an interest.

Lucas appealed to the local Hertsmere Borough Council, which reassured him that they would never approve such a sale. Soon after, however, they caved in when the Brent Walker entertainment group, which had acquired the site from TESE, sold half of it to Tesco for £19 million, claiming it had to do so or go bankrupt. Most of the stages were demolished, and the huge silent stage built for *The Empire Strikes Back* was dismantled and moved to Shepperton. The council guaranteed the survival of the remaining fifteen acres and three stages, but so small a facility had no interest for Lucas, and he began looking around for alternatives – finally found, improbably, in Australia.

Indiana Jones and the Last Crusade opened on Lucas's traditional lucky day, 24 May, in 1989. Before 13 June, it had grossed $100 million, proving that the old formula still worked. After the violence and sadism of *Temple of Doom*, the tone was light, the humor effective, the characters likeable.

The rebirth of Indiana Jones attracted network TV, and ABC rose to the suggestion of an hour-long weekly series about young Indy. TV had never interested Lucas as either producer or director. He felt the production-line approach debased storytelling and cheapened technique. But his mind changed when he became frustrated with a proposed interactive project for the George Lucas Educational Foundation, his think-tank for projects aimed at the school-age audience. 'A Walk Through Early Twentieth Century History with Indiana Jones' simply wasn't large enough to encompass the amount of material Lucas wanted to include. A dramatic series in which young Indy participated in the great events of the century could, he decided, be both instructive and entertaining. ABC agreed, and commissioned a two-hour 'Movie of the Week' based on the character, followed by forty one-hour episodes of *The Young Indiana Jones Chronicles*.

ABC hoped River Phoenix would reprise his role for the series, but the young actor's career was too hot for him to commit himself to three or four years of globetrotting. Lucas cast George Hall as Indy in his nineties, who recounts tales of more than seventy years before to awed kids in the town to which he's retired. In the flashbacks, Sean Patrick Flanery played Indy between seventeen and twenty-one. Between eight and twelve, he was fourteen-year-old Corey Carrier, who brought a more world-weary quality to the role than Phoenix.

To the irritation of the Directors' and Screen Actors' Guild, Lucas produced the series in Europe, mostly using directors and writers from England, Australia, and Europe, shooting in twenty-three countries, the majority soft-currency nations like the Czech Republic, and casting in London, where the production office was located. Staying true to the initial concept of putting Indy at the heart of actual historical events, the stories involved him with real-life personalities: Lawrence of Arabia, Sigmund Freud, Pablo Picasso, Theodore Roosevelt, Arthur Conan Doyle, the Archduke Ferdinand – even Norman Rockwell, for whom Lucas invented a spell as an art student in Paris.

Insistent on the series' educational aims, Lucas named the episodes for the places where they took place. Four 1992 episodes were called *Austria, March 1917*; *Somme, Early August 1917*; *Germany, Mid-August 1916*; and *Barcelona, May 1917*. He wanted, he said, to make 'a television program for people who don't watch television, hoping I could draw them back to television' – an ambition that puzzled many, since the juvenile audience watched television relentlessly. It was just documentaries, educational programs and improving hour-long 'after-school dramas' which they shunned.

Though Lucas said soberly, 'The show is much more like *Howards End* than *Raiders of the Lost Ark*, and you don't see many movies like *Howards End* on television,' ABC screened some misleading promos showing young Indy thundering across the desert on horseback to a John Williams-type score; and while the episodes didn't really resemble James Ivory's solemn adaptation of E.M. Forster, the tone was undramatic enough and the scripts sufficiently talky for audiences to realize quickly that the series wasn't another *Raiders of the Lost Ark*. Ratings dropped following the first two episodes, and it became a wanderer in the schedule. It soon had to compete for the Saturday-night audience with CBS's popular *Dr Quinn, Medicine Woman*. Moved to Monday, it followed *Monday Night Football*, often starting long after kids were in bed.

For the second season, Lucas interspersed historical episodes with more seductively-titled two-hour specials like *Young Indiana Jones and the Mystery of the Blues*, *Young Indiana Jones and the Scandal of 1920*, and *Young Indiana Jones and the Phantom Train of Doom*. The least credible episode – directed, even less probably, by Nicolas Roeg – showed Indy in Paris in 1916 running up against the spy Mata Hari. In *Mystery of the Blues*, young Indy, working in the restaurant of gang boss 'Big Jim' Colosimo in 1920s Chicago, learns about jazz from soprano saxophonist Sidney Bechet, then teams up with old college room-mate Eliot Ness – founder of 'the Untouchables' – and reporter Ernest Hemingway to investigate Colosimo's murder. As a favor to Lucas, Harrison Ford appeared in framing incidents to top and tail this episode, but it didn't help: ABC axed the *Chronicles* after thirty-two episodes. Four programs of the last season were never aired in the US, and the series played out with made-for-cable movies expanded from those already shot: *Young Indiana Jones and the Hollywood Follies* in 1994, *Young Indiana Jones: Treasure of the Peacock's Eye*, *Young Indiana Jones: Attack of the Hawkmen* in 1995, and *Young Indiana Jones: Travels with Father* in 1996. An earlier episode, *Curse of the Jackal*, was also lengthened. Corey Carrier had grown, but Lucas shot new scenes anyway. ILM regressed him digitally to his earlier size.

Despite the ten thousand schools and teachers deluged with study guides, and the promise by Lucas of an interactive classroom learning program incorporating cassettes of the series, *Young Indiana Jones* never caught on, vindicating the contention of futurologists like John Naisbitt that popularity can't be imposed, only revealed, and that success in any overture to the mass audience depended on fulfilling a deep-felt need. As 'a vehicle for turning American kids on to the wonders of history and the thrill of exploring the world,' to quote its stated aims, *Young Indiana Jones* was a signal failure; the central failure, in fact, of Lucas's career, since it spoke to his major ambition –

to create a new mythology for a generation supposedly hungry for legends. Perversely, the public showed it had more than enough heroes for its purposes, though they preferred those they'd made themselves rather than the manufactured variety. Indy, Lucas's synthetic hero, could only approach the stature of myth by association with real cultural heroes who'd been too busy living their lives to indulge in self-mythologizing. Hemingway, Lawrence, Freud, and Bechet didn't meet Indiana Jones. He met *them*.

And yet, despite its commercial failure, *Young Indy* would help rescue Lucasfilm. Spielberg's TV series *Amazing Stories*, an attempt to update *The Twilight Zone*, had itself hemorrhaged to a standstill much like *Young Indiana Jones*, but not before it threw up a number of talents for his team, and gave him the chance to try out new ideas. *Young Indiana Jones* would do much the same for Lucas, yielding, among other people, the British producer Rick McCallum, cameraman David Tattersall and production designer Gavin Bocquet, who worked on the fourth slice of the *Star Wars* saga, and writers Jonathan Hales and Frank Darabont, the latter soon being mentioned as a possible author of later *Indiana Jones* films. McCallum, Bocquet, and Tattersall were all also brought in on the next Lucasfilm project, the long-delayed *Radioland Murders*.

Young Indiana Jones also served a more quotidian and lucrative purpose, in helping ILM perfect some of its special-effects techniques. The series was shot entirely on 16mm, but edited and mixed on video. Lucasfilm set up headquarters at Western Images in San Francisco, which used the state-of-the-art Harry system of digital compositing and editing developed by Quantel. Using Harry, Lucas staff created digital matte paintings, incorporated live action into artificial backgrounds, multiplied small groups of extras into crowds, and duplicated almost every variation of natural or artificial light. Fears that CGI would not be able to counterfeit reality were decisively dispelled. Literally nothing seemed beyond the latest generation of computers. This knowledge, and the experience gained, was almost more profitable than the series itself.

Quantel's next generation of digital editing suites, the Domino, was intended for large-screen feature films; simply by dialing up the required resolution, it could turn out TV quality, cinema quality, even images suitable for the giant-screen IMAX system. With what it had learned on *Young Indiana Jones*, ILM felt confident enough to develop its own system, which, unlike Domino, could use any software, not just Quantel's own. ILM's system, Sabre, named for the Jedi light saber, combined software from half a dozen other systems and, in theory, could create synthetic settings indistinguishable from reality, even on the large cinema screen. To test the system, Lucas needed a feature. He remembered *Radioland Murders*.

'It went through several different versions,' Gary Kurtz said of this doomed project. 'Did you ever see *The Big Clock*? Charles Laughton. It should have had some of that quality about it. Also *Who Done It?* with Abbott and Costello. That's about a murder set in a radio station. It's not exactly like *Radioland Murders* but it has some of the same elements.' *Who Done It?* is a typical Abbott and Costello vehicle, with the comics as a pair of inept soda jerks stumbling in and out of a murder mystery while live radio broadcasts go on around them. *The Big Clock* is more sinister. Meticulous magazine magnate Laughton kills his mistress, then, with the help of his sinister assistant, tries to shift the blame to two other people by manipulating the evidence, while the huge clock on top of his building ticks off the minutes to his inevitable fall.

When Willard Huyck and Gloria Katz wrote the *Radioland Murders* script in 1972, Hollywood could still accommodate parodies which only filmgoers over forty were likely to appreciate. Universal only agreed to finance the project in 1993 if Lucas modified the script for an audience accustomed to parodies like Mel Brooks's *Spaceballs*, cast it with stars known from TV, and delivered it for a rock-bottom $15 million. He took the deal, as well he might, since it amounted to the studio underwriting his research and development costs on Sabre. Jeff Reno and Ron Osborn, two writers who'd worked on *Moonlighting*, the comedy crime TV series starring Bruce Willis and Cybill Shepherd, were asked to update the Huyck and Katz script. Neither knew much about the 1930s or radio, but then, the audience wouldn't either.

Huyck and Katz's plot had been inspired by the in-fighting in the 1920s over who actually invented radio, and the competition to create national networks. The perpetrator of a series of murders at Chicago's WBN on the night it goes national with a gala evening of live broadcasting turns out to be a disgruntled engineer who feels the station's owner stole his patent. Blamed for the murders is the head of the harassed team of writers, expected to churn out new pages for the station's soaps even as members of the cast turn up dead.

The film opens with an impressive CGI shot of the transmission tower atop WBN, and extracts from real radio mystery shows like *The Lone Ranger* and *The Shadow* on the soundtrack, but once it enters the station, *Radioland Murders* becomes standard TV farce. As the writer, Lucas chose Brian Benben, star of the TV series *Dream On*, in which he played a man obsessed since birth by television who sees incidents from his life reflected in clips from old movies and TV shows. To direct, he hired British TV comic Mel Smith, whose *The Tall Guy* had been both funny and acute about the problems of an American actor (Jeff Goldblum) working in London.

Radioland Murders, which opened on 21 October 1994, has its moments. Asked how to shorten the science fiction serial, harassed producer Mary Stuart Masterson says distractedly, 'Cut the exploding asteroids and give the Venusians one-syllable grunts.' But the conflict between Benben and Masterson over his supposed infidelity with the trashy wife of the station's owner soon takes center-stage. Smith packed the cast with reliable comedians well known from TV, including Corbin Bernsen as the announcer, Michael Lerner as the investigating cop, and Christopher Lloyd as the mad Hungarian sound-effects man; but any shading is lost in the tone of manic farce, which is closer to Bugs Bunny than Jack Benny.

Richard Schickel, writing in *Time* magazine, dismissed the film as 'an all-round disaster. The flat, muddled screenplay is without period flavor; the cast is uniformly loud and tiresome; the direction ... overheated and confusing. If *Radioland Murders* is remembered at all, it will be for its extensive use of high-tech matte techniques that allowed separately filmed actors to appear in the same scene; this may account for the eerily disjointed quality of some of the dialogue.' Gary Kurtz simply called it 'terrible.'

Through the late 1980s, ILM was losing its market share and its domination of the special-effects market. Its claim of having won ten Academy Awards skirted the fact that it only shared them for some films. On *The Abyss* (1988), the ILM team under Dennis Muren created only the digitally-generated 'water creature' which extends a long, fat tentacle through the corridors of a sunken oil rig. Hoyt Yeatman of Dream Quest did the 'dry-for-wet' scenes in which rooms filled with vapor stand in for underwater, Dennis Skotak of model-makers Forward Productions, and freelance storyboard artist and designer John Bruno shared the rest.

Studios were increasingly unwilling to give all their effects work to a single company, and risk a bottleneck. 'They don't want any facility to hold them over a barrel,' said Hoyt Yeatman, 'especially with a risky or very expensive movie.' They also sensed a sameness creeping into ILM's work, a 'studio style.' Critic Michael Ling wrote in 1992, 'There's a certain computerized camera movement they keep using in their films – the way the spaceships move, the way the DeLorean flew in *Back to the Future*. It's sort of the problem you have with a marionette. You pull on its arms to simulate walking, but in real life you're *pushing* yourself forward. But the spaceships aren't internally driven, so you end up with that tugged-along marionette movement that doesn't look real.' John Lasseter came to ILM in 1983, just as *Return of the Jedi* was released. He spent three frustrating years working on films of which the effects were the most memorable element: *Star Trek III, The Neverending Story, The Ewok Adventure*. 'You'd kill yourself on effects,' he said, 'but no one remembered the films.' Lasseter moved to Pixar, where he would direct its Oscar-winning *Toy Story*.

During the making of *The Abyss*, ILM boss Scott Ross became friendly with the film's director, James Cameron, one of the first film-makers from what might be called Newer New Hollywood to make a major name. Cameron, like Robert Zemeckis, had grown up with digital special effects, and accepted them as a fact of life. Theirs was a cinema in which anything was achievable, and though they began with fantasy, they soon moved into the mainstream, taking that conviction with them. The techniques Zemeckis used in *Back to the Future* would serve him just as well in *Forrest Gump*, and the Cameron who made *Terminator* adapted himself to *Titanic* without breaking step.

Increasingly, Ross and many others inside Lucasfilm had more in common with Cameron than with Lucas. 'And so a group of us,' reminisced Ross recently, 'the key executives and the key creative people at Industrial Light and Magic, had decided that we would start another company.' In 1991, Ross quit ILM and began looking for investment capital. To Lucas, this was betrayal. The effect of his displeasure soon became evident. 'Some strange things started to happen,' says Ross circumspectly. 'Some of the folks that I was lining up for financing started to fall out for various reasons, and once that happened, a lot of the team got very, very concerned that it would leak and that they would lose their jobs at ILM and at Lucasfilm, and they became very concerned about their families and their livelihoods. And so they started one by one bowing out.'

Tom Kobayashi, who'd run Skywalker Sound since 1986, took over Ross's job at ILM. Ross became a non-person. In the company's lush official history, his name appears once. But he persisted. With $20 million from computer giant IBM, he formed Digital Domain with James Cameron and Stan Winston, responsible for the animatronic dinosaurs in *Jurassic Park* and the robot in *Terminator*. Their first film, Cameron's *True Lies* (1994), earned them an Oscar nomination, and in 1998 they won the real thing for *Titanic*, by which time they were the world's second sfx company after ILM. Meanwhile, Joe Johnston also left ILM to become a director (*The Rocketeer, Honey I Shrunk the Kids*), as did David Fincher (*Alien³, Se7en*).

In the wake of Ross's departure, Lucas reorganized his empire yet again. Doug Norby left in April 1992. Tom Kobayashi also left, to form his own company, Entertainment Digital Network. Early in 1993, Lucasfilm split into Lucasfilm Ltd and Lucas Digital Services. Lucasfilm Ltd would handle feature and TV production, distribution, toys, and licensing. Its new president was Gordon Radley, the old CEO of LucasArts Entertainment, control of which Lucas himself would now assume personally. ILM, Skywalker Sound, and LucasArts Entertainment came under Lucas Digital Services, run by a new-comer, Lindsey Parsons Jr. Described as a 'veteran producer,' Parsons, as Lindsey Parsons III, had one feature-film credit, as second assistant director on *Beyond the Poseidon Adventure* (1979). He'd worked as production manager on *SeaQuest DSV*, the underwater TV series launched by Spielberg, and directed one episode, as did Irvin Kershner – contacts that no doubt recommended him to Lucas as someone who'd toe the line. *Business Week* reported the changes without comment, though noting: 'Lucas companies have been troubled by the departure of more than a dozen key executives during the last two years.'

26

Back to the Future

Lucas the Loner Returns to '*Wars.*'

Headline in *Entertainment Weekly*, 5–11 June 1995

In 1990, the Lucas empire seemed as moribund as that depicted in *Star Wars*, which itself looked like a monument, as respected but as outdated as DeMille's *The Ten Commandments*. There were no more *Star Wars* comic books. The last *Star Wars* fiction had been a scattering of mediocre novels like *Han Solo and the Lost Legacy* and *Lando Calrissian and the Flamewind of Oseon* in the early eighties. Sales of *Star Wars* merchandise had dropped throughout the 1980s to $35 million a year, and were still falling. 'In 1985, the toys were over,' said Howard Roffman, head of mechandising for Lucasfilm. 'You couldn't even mention *Star Wars* to retailers.' In 1991, the giant Hasbro corporation bought Kenner, the major producer of *Star Wars* merchandise, and, in a flurry of house-cleaning, surrendered the license under which it had the right to manufacture *Star Wars* toys 'in perpetuity.'

Nor did there seem to be much more life in the films themselves. Special effects had shot ahead. Challenges which had once taxed the ingenuity of an entire company could be tossed off on the latest video-editing consoles, and were the common currency of TV commercials and rock clips. ILM retained its reputation for high-end work, but its slate for 1990 and 1991 consisted mainly of piecework on second-rate films, shared with its growing number of competitors.

Lucas himself remained almost incomprehensibly rich. His personal fortune, estimated at $2 billion, was bigger than that of most corporations – and, indeed, some countries. *Time* magazine regularly listed him among its top hundred people of power in new technology, the so-called Cyber Elite, but never more than a third of the way to the top. In 1997 he rated thirty-fourth, and even in 1998, after the phenomenally successful 'Special Edition' of the *Star Wars* trilogy, he still lay only thirty-first. Reasons for his low rating weren't hard to find. For someone in the volatile high-tech industries, his business profile was geriatric. Hoarding ownership, living off once fruitful but now decaying rights, indulging in quixotic changes of management, never designating a successor, immuring himself in a remote retreat where he saw almost nobody, Lucas controlled his companies as the once-innovative Hughes Tool Co. had been handled by Howard Hughes in his dotage.

The rationalizations for living in seclusion on Skywalker Ranch had long since fallen away. When Ron Magid of *American Cinematographer* magazine asked in 1997, 'Have you had a chance to work toward any of those non-linear, experimental movies that you wanted to do?' Lucas replied, 'No. The road of life leads you into many strange places, and it doesn't always go where you want to go or think you're going to go.' He hoped that in five or six years he might make such films, but for the moment his path led elsewhere. 'It's funny for some-body who started out as a very non-linear, non-character, non-story film-maker, I've become the epitome of storytelling. You know, for somebody who hated writing scripts, I've become basically a script-writer, because that's mostly what I do now.'

The craft element of film no longer interested Lucas, who had become a convert to digital movies. 'Digital in film is just like digital in writing,' he enthused. 'It makes the medium much more malleable; you can make a lot more changes. You can cut and paste and move things around, and think in a more fluid style – and I love that. We're just getting into that on a grand scale in film. I don't think I'd ever go back to analog. I haven't used an editing machine with film on sprocket holes for almost eight years. I hardly even know how to hold a piece of film anymore – I don't think I could do it. It's just too much work. It's too cumbersome, too slow, and you can't manipulate it enough. It would be like going back and scratching things on rocks!'

His enthusiasm for the new technologies was justified. The future was digital. When the actor Brandon Lee died in a gun accident while filming *The Crow* in 1993, director Alex Proyas digitally put Lee's face on another actor and finished the last few shots. Digital technol-ogy could remove the cables that supported actors during stunts, and even wipe a dribble of spit from Tom Cruise's chin in *Mission: Impossible*. In 1998, producer Paul Greenberg bought the rights to the image of George Burns a few months after the comedian's death and announced he'd shortly make *Everything's George*, a live-action film starring a virtual Burns. Many people inside the industry were convinced that, within a decade, not only would stop-animation, animatronics, matte painting, and model work disappear; there probably wouldn't be any film, sets, sound stages, or even flesh-and-blood actors. The age of the 'synthespian' was at hand.

Through the late 1980s, Lucas showed little interest in continuing his film career. He'd given up directing; now he was also ready to abandon producing. In 1982, he told Audie Bock during the shooting of *Return of the Jedi*, 'I'm only doing this because I started it and now I have to finish it. The next trilogy will be someone else's vision.' But since he jealously guarded his characters and plots, nobody came forward to pick up the *Star Wars* saga, and as the 1990s approached, the possibility of any new episodes looked increasingly remote.

Around 1990, however, Lucas experienced a rejuvenation. By the millennium, Lucasfilm would be revivified. The company would be no less centralized and subject to his whim, but its profits would have soared, and the future would look promising. Most strikingly, Lucas himself would be directing again, with both a new *Star Wars* trilogy and *Indiana Jones IV* in preparation.

What brought him back to the director's chair? Frank Darabont, one of the writers on *Young Indiana Jones* who built a career as director/writer on films like *The Shawshank Redemption*, credits *Young Indy* with the transformation. 'I think he was coming out of ten years' worth of, "OK, I've got to build this empire and make sense of it. I've got to make this machinery run." Without such guidance, companies like Lucasfilm tend to erode after a while, and it needed a steady hand on the tiller. *Young Indy* was George really hopping up on the horse, picking up the shield and sword, and saying, "We're film-makers again! We've been businessmen for too long!" This was his way of coming out of that period and sort of paving the way, I think, for the next *Star Wars* trilogy.'

Perhaps such a revival of enthusiasm did play a part. And certainly Lucas was stimulated by the new possibilities of digital movies, not the least being the relative ease with which he could direct them.

Fewer long shoots in jungle or desert, less haggling with special-effects fanatics, no more arguing with studios over release or publicity; these films could be made so cheaply that even Hollywood wouldn't complain about the cost. More likely, however, he simply wearied of fighting the system. Almost his every action had become predicated on what someone else wanted – his public, the studios, his neighbors, or the zoning authorities of Marin.

Lucas's team blew discreetly on the embers of *Star Wars*, and saw a few fingers of flame. In 1988, Lou Aronica, the new head of Bantam Spectra publishers, had proposed some new *Star Wars* novels. Lucas didn't respond for a year, then, out of the blue, asked Aronica to suggest some writers. The shortlist included Timothy Zahn, who'd been writing for a decade without cracking the big time. Lucas admitted that he never read the *Star Wars* books, but he liked Zahn's work sufficiently to anoint him as the successor of Alan Dean Foster.

In November 1989, Bantam commissioned a *Star Wars* novel from Zahn as the first in a projected trilogy. *Heir to the Empire*, published in June 1991, picked up the story of Luke Skywalker and the rebellion a few years after *Return of the Jedi*. Zahn, an admirer of *The Empire Strikes Back*, favored that film's darker tone. He showed the Empire as a powerful adversary, not easily defeated even by determined rebels: 'The heroics of your hero are measured by the strengths of your villain,' he says. In *Heir to the Empire*, the rebel attempt to reduce the remnants of the Empire is thwarted by the resourceful Admiral Thrawn, and by villains who manifest various sinister variations of the Force and Jedi teaching.

The book startled everyone by topping the *New York Times* bestseller list, almost unknown for a science fiction title, particularly by an author so little known. It remained in the list for twenty-nine weeks. The following June, Bantam published Zahn's sequel, *Dark Force Rising*, and in 1993 *The Last Command*. After that, *Star Wars* novels by Kevin J. Anderson, Barbara Hambly, Vonda McIntyre, and Michael A. Stackpole became profitable annual occurrences. Howard Roffman sold West End Games on doing a series of role-playing games using the new characters. 'It all started with the novels,' says Roffman.

Hollywood is ruled by ritual, and the rehabilitation of George Lucas took place in a time-honored fashion. Once it became clear he was ready to re-enter the community of film-makers, discreet representations were made to the Academy of Motion Picture Arts and Sciences. In 1992, it awarded Lucas its Irving Thalberg Award. Presented by the board of governors to a 'creative producer whose body of work reflects a consistently high quality of motion picture production,' the Thalberg, on which Academy members don't vote, is given periodically as a useful way of acknowledging people not widely admired by the rank-and-file, but whom the Academy feel deserve better. Ray Stark got it in 1979, Albert 'Cubby' Broccoli in 1981, and, after a long gap, it went in 1986 to Steven Spielberg, in recognition of the fact that, with films like *The Color Purple* and *Empire of the Sun*, he'd redeemed his earlier leadership of the Movie Brat generation.

Spielberg presented the award to Lucas, his 'valued colleague and great and loyal friend,' on 30 March 1992. In response, Lucas, his earlier rejection of the Academy diplomatically forgotten, acknowledged 'the thousands of talented men and women, robots and aliens and others with whom I've been lucky enough to share the creative experience [and] my teachers from kindergarten through college, and their struggle – and it was a struggle – to help me learn to grow ...' He thanked Coppola, and his two daughters (though not, oddly, his son Jett), after which Spielberg said, 'There's someone else who wants to say congratulations to you.' On a screen, the audience saw Commander Charles Bolden and the crew of the Space Shuttle *Atlantis*, then orbiting the earth. Bolden, apparently speaking live, though Spielberg had providently taped it ahead of time, said, 'We are carrying a special celebrity aboard our spaceship,' and set loose an Oscar statuette to float in zero gravity.

With the success of *Heir to the Empire*, Hasbro realized that its decision to relinquish its *Star Wars* license was, in the words of toy industry watcher James Surowiecki, 'one of the great blunders in the history of merchandising.' Galoob, smaller than Hasbro, and correspondingly hungrier, had grabbed the contract and instantly made money with its '*Star Wars* MicroMachines.' Hasbro/Kenner hurriedly reopened talks with Lucasfilm, and in 1995 released a new *Star Wars* line that became one of the year's top-selling boys' toys.

Though, by the middle of the decade, Galoob was selling $120 million-worth of *Star Wars* merchandise annually, the concession was a mixed blessing. Increasingly dependent on Lucas products, the company shifted more and more of its resources into those lines. Sales had reached $400 million a year when, in 1998, Lucas announced his intention to make three 'prequels,' and invited bids for the toy franchise. Mattel, one of the biggest players in the business, offered $1 billion for a ten-year license. Hasbro also moved to increase its $200 million-a-year share. Galoob, without the assets of its larger competitors, could only offer itself. In its winning bid, it not only agreed to pay $140 million a year in advance royalties, and a percentage of sales; Lucasfilm also acquired the option to buy 20 per cent of the company's stock at $15 a share. Paradoxically, the announcement of the deal sent Galoob stock tumbling well below that figure, though once the new trilogy hit theaters, neither the company nor Lucasfilm was likely to lose. In a shifting world, the profitability of Lucas's dreams appears as fixed and constant as the north star.

Darth Vader remained the real star of *Star Wars*. Of all the video games created by Lucas Games division, the most popular, such as 1993's *X-Wing*, revolved around the heavy-breathing heavy. He also featured centrally in the 1995 *Shadows of the Empire*, a multi-media event comprising a novel, six comic books, a 3-D interactive game, a set of Topps collecting cards, and an album of the films' music – 'a movie project without a movie,' said one writer about this idea, cooked up by Lucy Autrey Wilson, once the book-keeper at Parkhouse, now head of Lucasfilm Publishing, and Lou Aronica. Elsewhere, novelists and comic-book writers returned to the *Star Wars* lode, excavating the pasts of Boba Fett, Chewbacca, Darth Vader, and rebels like Wedge Antilles. Leia and Han married and had children, who in turn became characters in the story.

Hollywood hurried to put the first trilogy back to work. In 1993, Fox, which still owned the rights in the first film – a fact that always rankled with Lucas – reissued the three films on videodisc, and the following year, remastered and with THX sound, put out a boxed set of videocassettes which sold twenty-two million in six months. In the light of such success, Lucas began to think about a cleaned-up new version of the trilogy, a 'Special Edition.'

The 'Special Edition' of *Close Encounters of the Third Kind*, issued in 1980, three years after the first release, was a piece of cinematic sleight of hand that Lucas always envied. Pressed by Columbia to make a sequel to *Close Encounters*, Spielberg offered instead to shoot a new sequence of the alien spaceship interior, the thing audiences said they missed most, drop some scenes he didn't like, restore a few which Columbia had made him lose in editing, and reissue it as a new film. Everyone who'd enjoyed the first *Close Encounters* went again, and brought their friends.

Lucas's rivalry with Spielberg was an open secret. *Time* magazine commented, 'A Fox executive adds that Lucas has a keen sense of competition with Spielberg and is eager for the original *Star Wars* to pass *Jurassic Park* at the box office. (The score in the US is *Star Wars*, $322 million; *Jurassic Park* $357 million.)' In creating the 'Special Edition' of the *Star Wars* trilogy, Lucas had a triple aim: to beat *Jurassic Park*, to make money, and to experiment with the special effects he'd need to make the new trilogy.

He explained the sort of changes he had in mind to Paula Parisi of *Wired* magazine. 'In *The Empire Strikes Back*, there was a snow monster you didn't really see. It was just shadows and sounds; we always wanted the creature but were never able to accomplish it. Now we actually have a creature there. We have a lot of new shots in Cloud City to make it be bigger and look better. And the snow sequence was one of those state-of-the-art things at the time – doing white mattes on a white surface, which nobody had ever accomplished. Now, with digital, we can do that much better. In *Jedi*, there was a sequence in Jabba's palace that was meant to be a musical number. But it ended up just a little tiny thing with this dancer, Ula, that was maybe fifteen seconds long. Now we've turned that into about a minute and a half. There's a bigger band, and backup singers. It is what it was meant to be originally; we just didn't have the wherewithal to do it then.'

The reality turned out to be more complicated. Though Lucas added only four and a half minutes to the total running time of all three films for the 'Special Edition,' their refurbishment would take years and cost millions. Rick McCallum headed the task force, and found it a depressing responsibility. 'When I saw the first print struck off the original negative, it was gone,' he said. Fox, in its rush to pump new prints into cinemas following the first release, had made so many copies that the negative simply wore out. Worse, it turned out to have been poor-quality in the first place. In the heat of final editing, Lucas had used whatever film was available. McCallum identified four different Kodak stocks, plus a reversal stock, CRI, on which many of the last-minute effects shots were printed.

As the first step in restoration, the lab would normally have washed the negative in a sulfur bath at 104 degrees Fahrenheit, then wiped each frame by hand; but since the four different stocks each had to be washed separately, McCallum faced the frightening task of supervising the physical dissection of the *Star Wars* negative. Once this was done, they assessed the quality. Digital tinkering could restore full color to the Kodak film, but the dyes in the reversal stock were so faded that not one shot was usable. Fortunately, Lucas had saved all the individual pieces of film that made up the ruined effects shots. Finding them, however, was another matter. In repeated changes of management and premises, much documentation had been lost. McCallum's team spent months sorting through uncataloged pieces of film, optically turning them upside down and wrong-way about to match them with sequences in the completed film, like solving a jigsaw puzzle.

Other teams in the group worked on the additions. A lot of what they were doing, like the effects they'd created for *Radioland Murders,* was less restoration than research and development. 'Probably more than half the reason for doing this in the first place,' said John Knoll, the Visual Effects Supervisor, 'was to have a trial run for what's coming up,' i.e. the three 'prequels' Lucas was already writing.

The major addition to *Star Wars* was Han Solo's confrontation with Jabba the Hutt in the Mos Eisley spaceport. Lucas had shot the scene with a bulky actor in a furry jacket filling in for Jabba, but never had time to superimpose the slug-like creature, whom he'd visualized as floating on a zero-gravity sled, but whom he now wanted to squirm across the ground like a sea elephant. To complicate things, Han walks round behind the actor at one point, passing through what would have been the rear half of Jabba's body; natural enough had Jabba been on a sled, but a problem now. The team generated a CGI Jabba and, making a virtue of necessity, had Solo appear to step on his 'tail,' with a resulting yelp of pain.

Some tweaks modified lapses in character as much as in technique. In successive episodes, Han Solo matured from bombastic smuggler to sensitive lover, loyal friend, and rebel hero. The change was already evident in *The Empire Strikes Back.* Han, finding Luke freezing to death, adapts an old Amerindian/Inuit trick to save his life by gutting his *tauntaun* and placing Luke in the body cavity while he erects a shelter. The Han of *Star Wars* would have cut down his faithful steed without hesitation, but in *Empire* it conveniently drops dead at that instant. For the Special Edition, Lucas made a similar adjustment to Han's killing of Greedo in the Mos Eisley cantina. In the original, it hadn't been clear that Han shot the bounty-hunter only after being shot at himself. The revision shows Greedo's shot chipping the wall by Han's head a beat before he shoots back.

Fixing the second two films in the trilogy posed fewer problems than *Star Wars*, since the negatives were in better physical shape, and had been edited with the help of a computer, making it easier for the restorers to find the original material. For *The Empire Strikes Back*, they corrected the transparent Snowspeeders and Imperial Walkers of the Hoth sequence, and added new scenes to Bespin's Cloud City. These, and similar shots at the end of *Return of the Jedi*, showing the rejoicing in the Imperial capital of Corsucant at the fall of the Empire, were wholly synthetic: an avatar of what Lucas proposed for the new trilogy.

Lucas's triumphant return to the limelight continued everywhere. In 1995, Florida's Walt Disney World launched 'George Lucas's *Alien Encounter.*' As Richard Corliss described it in *Time* magazine, 'in this fond tribute to William Castle, sleaze showman *extraordinaire* of *13 Ghosts* and *The Tingler*, visitors enter a circular room, are strapped into seats and see a huge hideous monster writhing in a plastic tube. Then the alien escapes – and the lights go out. Heavy footsteps approach, and your seat gets a violent rattle. You feel the creature's breath and reptilian tongue on the back of your neck. An icky liquid drenches you; is it someone's exploding guts or your own fear-sweat? The experience is divinely cheesy: 3-D radio, aiming only to scare you nuts. And it works; the crowd happily screams along.'

At the same time, interest revived in another *Indiana Jones* film when Harrison Ford made it known he was prepared to star in it. After a few films as a serious actor, he had found a niche as war technologist Tom Ryan in the movies of Tom Clancy's novels *Patriot Games* and *Clear and Present Danger*, and as a runaway doctor in *The Fugitive*. Audiences evidently wanted to see Ford running for his life more than they wanted him sensitive and thoughtful, and *Indy IV* was resuscitated, with Steven Spielberg to direct a script by Jeffrey Boam.

★　　★　　★

On 31 January 1997, Fox released the *Star Wars* 'Special Edition' in 2100 theaters across the US. At the ranch, there was an office pool on what it would earn on its first weekend. Lucas guessed $10 million. It actually took $36.2 million. 'I am flabbergasted,' Lucas told the *New York Times*. 'It's a twenty-year-old movie. I just did not expect this to happen.' The film set a record for a January and February opening, and became the first in history to break $400 million in US domestic box-office, easily reclaiming its title as the highest-grossing film of all time. *The Empire Strikes Back* Special Edition premiered on 21 February, and also set new records, as did *Return of the Jedi* on 14 March. A few diehards who complained at the loss of the first series' casual 'starvation' quality were drowned out in a wave of approval. Against all expectations, the audience was equally divided between those under twenty-five and those above. Lucas had reintroduced the films to an audience not even born when they were made.

In May, the Directors' Guild (to which Lucas had quietly been reinstated) presented a twentieth-anniversary screening of *Star Wars*. It was a festive occasion, with a huge party attended by almost everyone from the original cast, except Ford and Alec Guinness, who were filming. Lucas, 'deep in his Howard Hughes mode,' according to Harley Cokeliss, was driven down, alone, from Marin in his limo, and appeared at the preliminary presentation to answer a few questions, but left before the party, again alone.

As early as 1983, Lucas knew what the first three *Star Wars* 'prequels' would be like. He told *Time* magazine that they 'will be altogether different in look and tone from the existing trilogy . . . They will be more melodramatic, showing the political intrigue and Machiavellian plotting that led to the downfall of the once-noble Republic. They will have only enough outward action to keep the plot moving. Obi-Wan Kenobi . . . and Darth Vader will be seen as younger men, while Luke Skywalker may make a brief appearance as a baby in Episode III.'

In 1995, Rick McCallum, who would be line producer on the first of the new *Star Wars* series, began doling out limited information. 'George is still meeting with our artists once a week to discuss new ideas,' he said. 'We're expecting our production designer, Gavin Bocquet, to start soon . . . Gavin will initially work on some preliminary ideas for a couple of months, and then he'll take a break until we're ready to go into pre-production.'

Bocquet and cameraman David Tattersall came out of *Young Indiana Jones*. 'We're only interested in people who can park their egos long enough to work for a single individual dream,' said McCallum. 'That's why I want the people who were with us on *Young Indy*. They worked on the longest location shoot in the history of film or television. They are the ones who suffered to make *Young Indy* a great project. Being away from home so long created great hardships in their lives, yet they never complained – they did it all for the series. But nothing they ever suffered on *Young Indy* will come close to the experience they will have on the new *Star Wars* films!'

McCallum began casting early in 1995. The main characters would be Qui-Gon Jinn, a Jedi knight, and his young apprentice Obi-Wan Kenobi. Lucas visualized the Jedi in this period as 'the guardians of peace and justice in the galaxy, sort of like the old marshals out west. And there are thousands of them.' On Tatooine, Jinn and Kenobi encounter eight-year-old Anakin Skywalker, a boy slave who has a powerful affinity for the Force. When Queen Amidala of the planet Naboo, later to marry Anakin and produce Luke and Leia, calls on the Jedi to protect her from the ships of the sinister migratory 'Trade Federation' which have blockaded her world in a dispute over customs duty and taxes, Jinn and Kenobi are thrown into conflict with the Empire. Working behind the scenes to undermine the galactic order is Darth Sidious, last of the Sith, a group of evil knights, and his apprentice Darth Maul, distinctive for his seven-foot-long double light saber.

Supporting players include Jinn's friend Jar-Jar Binks, a *gungan* who looks like a cross between a lizard and a horse; the later-to-be Emperor Palpatine, here an ambitous senator; *jawas*; and of course R2-D2 and C-3PO, part of a strong robot contingent. We see C-3PO being built, and watch legions of his counterparts used as shock troops.

By mid-1996, the cast was known. Liam Neeson would play Qui-Gon Jinn. Kenobi would be Ewan McGregor, young Scots star of the slice-of-life drug drama *Trainspotting* (and, by coincidence, nephew of *Star Wars*' Wedge Antilles, Dennis Lawson). Natalie Portman would be Queen Amidala, and martial-arts performer Ray Park took the part of Darth Maul. Jake Lloyd was cast as Anakin Skywalker, and Pernilla August, ex-wife of Bille August, one of the directors on *Young Indy*, as his mother, Shmi. Ian McDiarmid would reprise his role as Palpatine. Terence Stamp would play Darth Sidious.

Without Elstree, McCallum was hard put to find studio space sufficiently large for his purposes. He settled on the Leavesden Studios at Watford, outside London, which had been a car factory. Lucas shot his interiors there through winter 1996–97, and in August was in Tunisia, creating the town of Mos Espa, where most of the Tatooine action takes place. After considerable searching, his scouts rediscovered some of the original *Star Wars* locations, plus a few, like the high-rise Berber granaries, that he hadn't had the time to use in the first film, but could employ now.

Pressure was taken off both the English and the Tunisian shooting by the fact that not only the special effects, but many sets, and even characters, would be generated on computer. Lucas estimated the total budget of each film at between $60 million and $70 million – little more than a conventional drama like *The Bridges of Madison County*. Had he shot them on real sets, he said, and with old-fashioned special effects, they'd have cost twice that. 'This first film will be a big experiment,' he admitted, 'because we're taking a lot of the ideas I've learned from doing the *Young Indy* TV series and moving it to this larger level to see what happens. Some of it is going to work; some of it's not. The reason I'm directing the first one is so I can learn how to do it myself. We're going out there in a whole different style of film-making.'

He originally intended to shoot everything digitally, but scaling the videotape up to wide screen posed unforeseen visual problems. The production switched to film, and in April 1998 Lucasfilm's Gordon Radley told *Variety* that Part I would cost close to $115 million once they 'get their arms around the digital work.' Rick McCallum foresaw 'up to 1500 shots' of visual effects.

The effect of those shots became apparent when Lucasfilm released the first trailer in December 1998 with the film *Meet Joe Black*. Thousands of fans paid full price just to see the three-minute teaser, not bothering to stay for the feature. Snatches of ground-level races between souped-up versions of the landspeeder, armies of C-3PO-like robots, huge CGI cities, shadowy creatures emerging from alien swamps, and a younger, perkier Yoda reassured the public that they were going to be treated to the mixture as before, but with more potent ingredients. The film was now subtitled *The Phantom Menace*.

★   ★   ★

Once curiosity was satisfied about the look and story of *The Phantom Menace*, speculation turned to *Indiana Jones IV*, the theme of which fired some of the most inventive running fantasies of the Internet, now overflowing with websites dedicated to every Lucas enterprise, past and future.

Rick McCallum dispelled some doubts in late 1998. 'We're waiting for a script from our new writer, Jeffrey Boam . . . Once we receive the script, and if it works and everybody is happy with it, then it is a question of getting everybody together to make it happen.' The idea, he said, came from Lucas. 'It's an idea that George had about two years ago that just kept gnawing at him. He ultimately presented the idea to Harrison and Steven, and they loved it.' An Indy website commented: 'The most recent (speculative) titles have been *Indiana Jones and the Garden of Life*, *Raiders of the Fallen Empire*, and *Indiana Jones and the Lost Continent*. According to the latest report, "Paramount and DreamWorks SKG will be co-funding this number like they did for *Deep Impact* to help save on the expenses of the large budget. The Area 51 story [about a legendary facility for studying alien visitations] has been dropped in favor of the new one that follows the lines of the lost city of Atlantis. Due out for a summer 2000 release, it was written by Jeffrey Boam . . . George Lucas is executive producer and Rick McCallum is a producer as well. Music will be by the god of music Mr John Williams. Spielberg will be directing as long as Harrison Ford decides that it is a good script."'

In February 1999, Lucas quietly brought to an end the dream of a Marin County cinema. Fought to a standstill by the zoning authorities, he put in a bid to take over part of the Presidio, San Francisco's once-busy army base at the foot of the Golden Gate bridge, now a 1500-acre park and museum. 'George Lucas says he has outgrown bucolic Marin County,' said a newspaper report. 'Lucas will keep his Marin ranches as headquarters for his movie company Lucasfilm Ltd and maintain up to six hundred employees there. However, Lucasfilm President Gordon Radley says there is no room in Marin County for a campus that would bring together Lucas's special-effects, sound and software subsidiaries now scattered across Marin's San Rafael in leased offices and warehouses. "We've been looking for some place to get our businesses back in a common campus," said Radley. "It makes good business sense and builds morale."'

Lucas proposed taking over twenty-three acres of buildings on the Presidio which had once housed Letterman Military Hospital and a research laboratory. According to Radley, he would build 'offices and a state-of-the-art digital center and production facility in the Presidio for four subsidiaries: Industrial Light and Magic . . . the THX Group . . . LucasArts Entertainment Co., which makes computer games; and Lucas Learning Ltd, which makes educational software. "We're entering a brave new world of entertainment," Radley said. "We don't want to remake an MGM-type studio. We want a digital center for this new technology."'

The plan faced considerable opposition, not just from environmentalists who preferred the area as a park, but from three other companies, including the Marriott hotel chain, who had their own schemes. Lucas was sanguine about his chances. If not the Presidio, then some other site would eventually permit him to collect his enterprises under a single roof. Clearly, however, he no longer expected that roof to be on Skywalker Ranch.

The search for sites led Lucas even further afield. In Sydney, Australia, Fox, now 50 per cent owned by Australian-born media entrepreneur Rupert Murdoch, had refurbished the exhibition halls of the old Sydney Showground as a film studio. With its equable climate, a currency softer than those of the US and Europe, and a pool of low-cost labor and acting talent, Australia had been a convenient, if remote, location for American films from the silent days, and the Showground site with its six large sound stages was a temptation too good to miss. Eager to keep the under-used facility busy, Fox and co-owners Lend Lease Corp. offered advantageous terms. In November 1998, Lucas visited Sydney, ostensibly to address its Film Producers' Association, but actually to announce the deal Rick McCallum had been negotiating for a year. Live action for the next two *Star Wars* prequels, now budgeted at $120 million each, would be shot in Sydney.

'This is one of the most competitive screen-making capitals in the world,' McCallum told the press, having been stung by suggestions that Lucasfilm was exploiting Australia's soft dollar. 'It's not about the exchange rate; it is about the talent that we can get.' In press statements, Lucas claimed that shooting the first three *Star Wars* films at Elstree had boosted British production. 'I could go anywhere in the world and shoot, and we could use any warehouse for a studio,' he said. 'In the end it is the talent that is here. I go where the talent is.' Pressed to say exactly what talent he expected to find in the relatively basic Australian industry which wasn't more readily available in San Rafael, he shifted his ground. 'We are very keen to help bring in [to Australia] and update some of the more esoteric crafts that are necessary for large stage productions and to expand that part of the industry.' Locals were skeptical. Lucas would let Australians do his special effects? Numerous American producers had made extravagant offers over the last half-century about enlivening the Australian film industry, but all they'd left behind in the empty sound stages were promises and paper cups.

Not many movies were more eagerly awaited than *The Phantom Menace*. Janet Maslin, writing in the *New York Times*, called it 'pathologically anticipated' – by opponents as well as enthusiasts. Few critics doubted they would loathe the film, long before any had seen more than a few minutes of it. Lucas made a detached response almost impossible by emphasizing in almost every interview and preview that his audience was children, and the child in everyone. To appreciate its 130 action-filled minutes, he implied, you needed to be eleven years old, or feel as if you were. The perception of *Menace* as a kiddie pic was driven home when, slouching out of a New York preview which had been attended by all the security and secrecy of a top-line rock concert – journalists even had their hand stamped with luminous dye to deter gatecrashers – hardened hacks surrounded an eleven-year-old boy who'd been at the screening, and quizzed him for his opinion.

Inevitably, the kid loved it. *All* kids loved it. They spilled out of the first shows on Saturday morning to shout at friends waiting in line, 'Don't listen to the critics. It's great!' The *New York Times*'s Janet Maslin was one of the few writers in the national media to find the film generally agreeable, if marred by racism in the attachment of Caribbean or Jewish characteristics to some of the electronic characters.

The rest of the critical community formed a chorus of negativity. 'A disappointment. A big one,' said David Ansen in *Newsweek*. In the *Los Angeles Times*, Kenneth Turan called it 'a considerable letdown,' and Todd McCarthy in *Variety* judged it 'easily consumable eye candy, but it contains no nutrients for the heart and mind.' Anthony Lane's relentless *New Yorker* notice rated it 'childishly unknowing and rotten with cynicism.' Many found the film's talkiness indicative of an unwonted solemnity on the part of Lucas, as if he had begun to *believe* in all this nonsense. Some took the time to demolish the concept of a galactic empire which lies at the heart of the *Star Wars* films, pointing out that even when Frank Herbert and Isaac Asimov, sources for most of Lucas's concepts, explored the idea, it was with tongue in cheek.

By common consent, the characters in *Phantom Menace* spent far too much time talking politics and not enough establishing human relationships. The friendships that lay at the heart of the first three films, insofar as those films had a heart, were absent here. As if determined to show that the *Star Wars* back-story really makes sense, Lucas labored to dignify first-draft ideas by cementing them into a rickety quasi-historical framework. The 'Trade Federation,' which *is* the 'phantom menace' of the film, a heterogeneous group of grotesques drawn from a score of races, and apparently without a planet or a society of its own, is the Chrome Barons of the early drafts of *Star Wars* writ large – or, if you prefer, the exploitative and rapacious forces of Old Hollywood, thinly disguised – but, either way, a throwback to the Lucas of the seventies. Mace Windu, the first name he invented for the series, present from Lucas's earliest treatment, turns up in the person of Samuel L. Jackson, only to disappear just as abruptly. Lucas even raises a corner of the curtain on his future use of the Force and of its rival good and evil elements, Ashlar and Bogon, by having young Anakin born of a virgin, establishing him as a potential Christ figure who will, however, evolve into that black embodiment of evil, Darth Vader. Who will become his matching opposite number and the symbol of good? To find out, we will have to wait for Part II of the *Star Wars* saga, promised for just after the millennium, and the third and last by 2005.

Lucasfilm's president Gordon Radley was as ready with a response to the skepticism about *Phantom Menace* as the critics had been with their attacks. 'The wonderful thing about movies is, it's a people's medium,' he said. 'The only critic that counts is the individual moviegoer.' Disconcertingly, however, individual moviegoers didn't clutch *The Phantom Menace* to their bosom as Fox and Lucas had hoped. In its first five days, it took $102.7 million at 2500 screens – an undoubted success, but far from the mega-hit its makers hoped for. The $61.8 million it earned over the 1999 Memorial Day weekend was significantly less than *The Lost World*'s $72.2 million, and the week after, analysts were already estimating its take would fall well short of *Titanic*'s. Not only had Lucas failed to beat his old rival Spielberg; he'd been outpaced by the upstart James Cameron.

Not that either Fox or Lucasfilm was hurting. The *Hollywood Reporter* remarked cynically that this was 'the first film that will make money even if nobody buys a ticket to see it.' Just as Chicago meat-packers used to boast they sold every part of the slaughtered pig except the squeal, every fragment of *Phantom Menace* had a spin-off, and a corresponding price tag. The TriCon Group, owners of Pizza Hut, Taco Bell, and Kentucky Fried Chicken, alone paid $2 billion for the right to merchandise *Phantom Menace* food. There would be posters, books, comics, T-shirts, and cheap plastic figures in quantity, as with earlier films; but Lucasfilm were determined this time to tap into the newly rich sub-teen market, and the doting parents who funded it. Toys were larger, more numerous, more sophisticated technically, and therefore more expensive than anything created for the first trilogy. Factories in China worked around the clock to make the trio of mechanized moneyboxes in the forms of Qui-Gon Jinn, Darth Maul, and Obi-Wan Kenobi. Driven by tiny motors and a computer chip, the figures fought one another – an incentive to spend £120 to buy all three, and re-create the film's climactic battle. According to the *New York Times*, Fox expected to make $100 million from releasing the film, but Lucas's personal profit, almost entirely from its merchandising, would top $2 billion.

In this frenzy of commerce, the virtues of *The Phantom Menace* tended to be forgotten. On the level at which it set out to succeed, the film is a triumph. Every scene vindicates Lucas's belief in the supremacy of computer-generated film over that which depends on fallible human performers and artists. So smoothly have ILM's technicians integrated the live actors that one forgets, when Liam Neeson rumbles, 'Calm yourself, my blue friend,' that he's talking to an imaginary creature. Though Lucas placed Queen Amidala in an authentic Italian palace, we soon lose track of the difference between real eighteenth-century architecture and the film's invented underwater city, or the imperial bombast of Coruscant, just as we sometimes wonder if the doll-like Natalie Portman, dwarfed by yet another heavy, bead-crusted costume, her pale face surmounted by a gigantic head-dress and spotted with three ritual dots of colour, one on each cheek and a third on her lower lip, isn't an electronic puppet like the jabbering Jar Jar Binks.

It could hardly be better done, but the doubts linger as to whether it is worth doing at all. Clearly, the next step, whatever claims Lucas may make about the essential presence of live actors, will be to replace the principals with 'synthespians,' subjugating human reactions totally to the needs of the digital laboratory. Neeson for one felt his irrelevance, since, after *Phantom Menace*, he announced his retirement from films. The torch has passed to Ewan McGregor, following in the footsteps of Alec Guinness, and Jake Lloyd, who will grow to fill the black jackboots of Darth Vader. Part of the generation that grew up with *Star Wars*, McGregor and Lloyd don't share the discomfort older actors felt for the degrading of their significance. Even contemplating his new price tag of $8 million a film, McGregor is still the six-year-old boy thrilled to be taken to a *Star Wars* preview to see his uncle Denis Lawson play Wedge. 'I fell in love with Princess Leia,' he says. 'I wanted to be Han Solo. I knew the old guy was the wizard character – at six, I absolutely got it. I remember standing in my shorts and red socks outside school waiting to be picked up and taken for this treat, and all my mates being really jealous.'

McGregor is right to remind us that *Phantom Menace* remains a small boy's movie; and the small boy is George Walton Lucas II. *He* is the eleven-year-old at the heart of this film. The boy who read comic books in Modesto and dreamed that the colored imaged might come to life had achieved his ambition at last. The backyard environments he built now encompass a universe. The garage haunted house has swelled to the dimensions of space itself, and its monsters are vividly real. The excitement he felt flooring the pedal of his Bianchini, and which he evoked only fitfully in *American Graffiti* and *More American Graffiti*, swells in this film to inflate the pod race on Tatooine into an intergalactic version of the chariot race in *Ben Hur*, with drivers from a dozen cultures being wiped by Anakin Skywalker, the brilliant boy in a rustbucket. Little Georgie Lucas, the Stinky Kid with the big ears, had showed them all.

With his moves away from Marin and in the furthest corners of the world, Lucas signalled that he meant to put his mark on the twenty-first century as indelibly as he had signed the last quarter of the twentieth.

Thanks to him and a small group of like-minded media artists, American popular culture had been immeasurably enriched in technique, widened in scope, but cheapened in content. In the sixties, English novelist Kingsley Amis, speaking of the explosion of new universities with more elastic admission standards, remarked tersely, 'More means worse,' a truism which Lucas, it seems, was born to embody. In his hands, cinema became synonymous in sensibility and style with the comic book, the hamburger, the soda. *Star Wars* is Diet Coke cinema. Fizzy, sweet, refreshing, colorful, but without calories, vitamins or food value; less a drink than the idea of one.

Jean Renoir said that every artist has only one story. If that is true, then what is Lucas's? It's a question he's always been unwilling to answer. If pressed, he disclaims any personal vision, referring back always to the body of myth, the thirty-two basic plot situations enumerated by Joseph Campbell in *The Hero with a Thousand Faces*, or the accumulation of racial memory evoked by Carl Gustav Jung. 'I took off from the folk side of things,' he told the *New York Times*, looking back on *Star Wars* from the perspective of a quarter-century, 'and tried to stay with universal themes apart from violence and sex, which are the only other two universal themes that seem to work around the world. My films aren't that violent or sexy. Instead, I'm dealing with the need for humans to have friendships, to be compassionate, to band together to help each other and to join together against what is negative.' Except it was precisely that aspect of earlier *Star Wars* adventures that critics found lacking in *The Phantom Menace*.

Perhaps what Lucas really believes in is the *idea* of story. He seems convinced that narrative, even innocent of content, is worthwhile in itself. And while he may have no new tale to tell, his skill in recounting old ones is undoubted. The *Star Wars* cycle, for all its lack of originality, is stirring. It reaffirms the best in us, celebrating heroism, dignifying our worthier emotions by crowding every alien creature and technological creation under the often leaky umbrella of human nature. We may cringe at the clichés, feel embarrassment at the way, despite ourselves, we thrill to the heroics or become wet-eyed at the sentimentality, but we will be in the minority. Lucas, like Sam Goldwyn 'one of the lucky ones whose great hearts, shallow and commonplace as bedpans, beat in instinctive tune with the great heart of the public, who laugh as it likes to laugh, weep the sweet and easy tears that it likes to weep,' speaks not to the jaded, fastidious, or analytical, but to those to whom hearing an old story well retold remains the greatest and most enduring of pleasures.

For that audience, *Star Wars* embodies the eternal. The cinema becomes a dusty corner of a crowded souk. A storyteller in a greasy turban squats comfortably in the shade. His listeners crowd in, cross-legged, leaning forward, attentive. With a glance of satisfaction, he settles his back against the sun-warmed wall, closes his eyes and murmurs that most seductive of all phrases – 'Once upon a time . . .'

That corner of the world falls quiet. An ancient mystery is about to be re-enacted. The audience is listening.

NOTES

CHAPTER ONE : The Emperor of the West

All quotes from Gary Kurtz, John Milius, and Harley Cokeliss are from interviews conducted by the author in London and Beverly Hills in 1998.

Many details of the building and design of Skywalker Ranch from *George Lucas: The Creative Impulse* by Charles Champlin. Lucas's modest early plans for Skywalker Ranch are detailed in numerous newspaper and magazine reports, among them 'Lucas to Build Film Center' in *Boxoffice*, 29 January 1979, 'George Lucas Severs Last Hollywood Bonds' by Aljean Harmetz in the *New York Times*, 30 July 1981, 'Lucas and his $50 million (or so) Retreat' in *San Francisco Sun*, 5 June 1983, 'Lucas Strikes Back with his Secret Film Empire' in London *Observer*, 20 July 1986, 'Lucas Wants a Fence' in *Variety*, 21 September 1983, 'A Long Time Ago, on a Ranch Far Far Away . . .' in *LA Herald Examiner*, 28 January 1986. Some details of the interior of the Main House in the eighties from 'Meanwhile, Back at Skywalker Ranch,' *New York Times*, 21 May 1989. Reports on the success of Lucas's various enterprises appeared in the *Star Wars* tenth anniversary issue of *Variety*, 3 June 1987, along with a '*Star Wars* Chronology'. Articles include '*Star Wars* All-Time Boxoffice Force,' 'Fantasy Meets Film under ILM Wands,' and 'Merchandise Aimed at Long Haul Pulled in $410 Mil in Britain.' 'My little films' and 'The last thing we want' from 'Inside George Lucas,' *Modesto Bee*, 1 June 1980. 'A creative retreat' from *San Francisco Chronicle*, 11 September 1979. 'Chairman of the bored' from *Los Angeles Times*, 27 January 1984. 'We would pay not to be on the T-shirts' from conversation between the author and Jean Marsh, London, 1998. Lucas's speech at the opening of the USC Film School from *New York Times*, 25 November 1981. Marvin Davis embracing Lucas described by Julia Phillips in *You'll Never Eat Lunch in this Town Again* (Random House, New York, 1991).

CHAPTER TWO : Modesto

Many details of Lucas's family life supplied by Ed Bearden of Modesto. Additional research was undertaken in the files of the *Modesto Bee*.

Much background on Wolfman Jack from www.stinky.com/wolfman. Lucas on the Van Nuys Club Night from 'The Stinky Kid Hits the Big Time' by Stephen Farber, *Film Quarterly*, Spring 1974. Harrison Ford on watching

Lucas direct from BBC TV *Omnibus* documentary on Lucas, 1996. 'Lucas testifies' from *A Biographical Dictionary of Film: Revised and Enlarged Edition* (André Deutsch, London, 1994). Lindsay Anderson on Sam Goldwyn from *Sequence* 13. Details of George Lucas Sr's life and background, including details of conversations with L.M. Morris, from various reports in the *Modesto Bee*, including 'George Lucas Sr Story Rivals Son's Film Saga,' 30 January 1976, 'Business Leader G.W. Lucas Dies,' 19 December 1991, 'Inside George Lucas,' 1 June 1980. 'Dorothy B. Lucas Dead at 75,' 12 March 1989. 'He was one of those people' quoted in *Skywalking*. 'Nobody knows where we originally came from' from *Los Angeles Herald Examiner*, 21 May 1980.

CHAPTER THREE : An American Boy

William Manchester quoted from *The Glory and the Dream* (Little, Brown, New York, 1974). Quotes from John Plummer from BBC TV *Omnibus*. Some additional details of Lucas's childhood from *Skywalking*. Janet Montgomery Deckard on doll house from 'Inside George Lucas.' Lucas on making environments with Melvin Cellini and publishing *Daily Bugle* from 'Newspaper for Juniors is Published by Two Boys,' *Modesto Bee*, 18 August 1955. 'He was his mother's pet' from *Time* magazine, 21 May 1983. 'Like a pair of aborigines' from *Newsweek*, 31 May 1971. 'Movies had extremely little effect' from 'Young Directors, New Films' in *American Film Institute Report*, Winter 1973.

CHAPTER FOUR : Cars

Quotes from Charley Lippincott and Randy Thom from interviews with author, Los Angeles and Sausalito, 1998.

'I love things that are fast' from 'An Empire of his Own' by Patrick Goldstein, *Los Angeles Times Magazine*, 2 January 1997. Quotes from John Plummer *passim* on Lucas's resemblance to Terry, their efforts to enrol in USC etc., from BBC TV *Omnibus*. Gloria Katz and Willard Huyck on USC film school from the same source. Lucas on growing up from *Skywalking*. Details of Lucas's school days from Leslie Kay Swigart and 'Lucas' Downey Classmates Applaud *Graffiti*,' *Modesto Bee*, 17 February 1974. Quotes from Marty Reiss, Ted Tedesco and other members of the Faros *passim* from 'Weekend of Nostalgia Revs up Some Memories. Yeas, Nays from Guys on the Drag' and 'Faros Recall when Car was King,' *Modesto Bee*, 8 June 1991. 'I was a hell-raiser. My father thought I was going to be an automobile mechanic' from interview with Joanne Williams, *San Francisco Herald-Examiner*, 21 May 1980.

CHAPTER FIVE : Where Were You in '62?

'Youth Survives Crash. DHS Student is Injured' from *Modesto Bee*, 13 June 1962. Disputed claims about circumstances of accident from *From Star Wars to Indiana Jones: The Best of the Lucasfilm Archives*. Material on Wolfman Jack from obituary in *Los Angeles Times*, 2 July 1995, profiles in *People* magazine, 15 August 1977, and *Los Angeles Times Calendar*, 3 December 1972.

CHAPTER SIX : USC

Unless otherwise indicated, all quotes are from conversations with John Milius, Don Glut, Randy Epstein, Charley Lippincott, and Richard Walker in Los Angeles, 1998, and Gary Kurtz in London, 1998.

'A citadel of privilege' from 'The Man Behind the Mask' by Teresa Carpenter in *Esquire*, November 1994. Irvin Kershner interviewed by Craig Miller for *Bantha Tracks 5, Newsletter of the Official Star Wars Fan Club*, 15 August–5 September 1979. Lucas quote on soundtracks from 'Retouching Evil' by Michael Sragow, *San Francisco Weekly*, 9 September 1998.

CHAPTER SEVEN : Electronic Labyrinth

Quotes from Bill Warren from interview in Los Angeles, 1998, and later conversations. Gary Kurtz, John Milius, Richard Walter, and Charley Lippincott quoted from interviews with the author, Los Angeles and London, 1998.

Marcia Lucas on meeting Lucas from *Easy Riders, Raging Bulls*. Some other details from *Skywalking*. Julia Phillips on Marcia as editor from *You'll Never Eat Lunch in this Town Again*. Frank Herbert on resemblances between *Star Wars* and *Dune* from 'Should Sci-fi Author Sue? Writer of *Dune* Says *Star Wars* Used Elements of Novel Without Permission' in *Eugene* (Oregon) *Register-Guard*, 1 December 1977. Audie Bock on Toshiro Mifune from *Japanese Film Directors* (Kodansha, San Francisco, 1978). Dave Johnson and Willard Huyck on Lucas and his navy crew from *Skywalking*. Walter Murch quoted in BBC TV *Omnibus*.

CHAPTER EIGHT : Big Boy Now

Much material on Francis Ford Coppola from *On the Edge: The Life and Times of Francis Coppola* by Michael Goodwin and Naomi Wise (Morrow, New York, 1989). 'Stinky kid' quote from 'The Stinky Kid Hits the Big Time' by Stephen Farber, *Film Quarterly*, Spring 1974. Walter Murch on *The Rain People* from *On the Edge*. 'I got a little angry about that' from *Easy Riders, Raging Bulls*. John Milius quoted from interview with author, Los Angeles, 1998. 'George was like a younger brother' from *On the Edge*.

CHAPTER NINE : The March Up-Country

Quotes from John Milius, Gary Kurtz, and Richard Walter from interviews with the author, Los Angeles and London, 1998.

Coppola on going to San Francisco from 'Two Who Made the Revolution' by David Osborne, *San Francisco* magazine, March 1982. Joan Didion on Hollywood after *Easy Rider* from *The White Album* (Simon & Schuster, New York, 1979). Coppola on Laterna and many details of setting up American Zoetrope from *On the Edge*. 'Rotary cam photography' from '30 Minutes with the Godfather of Digital Cinema' by Don Shay, *Cinefex*, May 1966. 'At the studios they don't understand scripts' and 'Everyone calls it science fiction' from 'The Movie Business is Alive and Well and Living in San Francisco' by Louise Sweeney, *Show* magazine, April 1970. Robert Duvall on working on *THX1138* from *Robert Duvall: Hollywood Maverick* by Judith Slawson (St Martin's Press, New York, 1985). Murch on mixing *THX* from BBC TV *Omnibus* and 'Retouching Evil' by Michael Sragow.

CHAPTER TEN : *American Graffiti*

Quotes from John Milius, Richard Walter, Charley Lippincott, and Gary Kurtz from interviews with author, Los Angeles and London, 1998.

Lucas on source of name from '*Graffiti* Reflects its Director's Youth' by Paul Gardner, *New York Times*, 19 September 1973. Some details on Coppola and the circumstances of American Zoetrope's relationship to Warners from *On the Edge* and *Easy Riders, Raging Bulls*. Many technical details of shooting *American Graffiti* from 'The Filming of *American Graffiti*' by Larry Sturhahn, *Filmmakers' Newsletter*, March 1974. 'Written in to add a love story angle' from 'The Writing is on the Wall for George Lucas' by David Rensin, *Crawdaddy* magazine, November 1973. 'I was agonizing' from interview with Audie Bock, *Take One* magazine, May 1979. PBS film on Lucas reviewed in 'Documentary Looks at Film-Maker Lucas' in *Los Angeles Times*, 13 April 1971. The *Variety* review appeared in the issue of 15 April 1971. Dorothy Lucas on life in Modesto from 'Lucas' Downey Classmates Applaud *Graffiti*,' *Modesto Bee*, 17 February 1974. Tanen quote from 'The New Hollywood Hotshots' by Jim Watters, *Life* magazine, April 1979. Lucas on seeing *Duel* from *Hollywood Reporter*, 10 March 1994. Lucas on Coppola producing *American Graffiti* from Audie Bock interview, *Take One*. Roos on casting *Graffiti* from various places, including 'The Fugitive Star' by David Halberstam in *Vanity Fair*, July 1993, *Harrison Ford: Imperfect Hero* and 'Production Notes,' an addendum to the published screenplay (Ballantine, New York, 1973). Many details and quotes on the shooting of *American Graffiti* from *Harrison Ford: Imperfect Hero*. Quotes from Ron Howard *passim* from BBC TV *Omnibus*. Lucas on 'ugly' lighting from *New York Times*, 7 October 1973. Ford on donuts from BBC TV *Omnibus*.

CHAPTER ELEVEN : The Road to the Stars

Quotes from Richard Walter, Gary Kurtz, and John Milius from interviews with the author, Los Angeles and London, 1998.

Details of cutting *American Graffiti* from BBC TV *Omnibus*, *Easy Riders, Raging Bulls*. Details of Murch recording the *Graffiti* track from 'Retouching Evil.' 'Francis really stood up to Ned' from *Easy Riders, Raging Bulls*. Lucas on 'cutting off your child's fingers' from *Skywalking* and many other sources. Lucas and Murch on parallels between *Apocalypse Now* and *Star Wars* from BBC TV *Omnibus*. *Modesto Bee* review of *American Graffiti* by Fred Herman in issue of 13 September 1973. Lucas on local reviews from 'The Nine Lives of R2-D2,' *LA Reader*, 7 March 1980.

CHAPTER TWELVE : I am a White Room

Quotes from Gary Kurtz and Charley Lippincott from interviews with the author, London, 1998.

Some details of Lucas's home life and working methods from *Skywalking*. Lucas on the origin of *Star Wars* characters from various sources, including *Skywalking* and BBC TV *Omnibus*. Herbert on *Dune* parallels from 'Should Sci-fi Author Sue?' John Morrow in letter to the author. 'George became frightened' from BBC TV *Omnibus*. Account of conversation between Marcia and Lucas, and Lucas on Marcia in *Easy Riders, Raging Bulls*.

CHAPTER THIRTEEN : For Sale: Universe, Once Used

Quotes from Charley Lippincott, Jon Davison, and Gary Kurtz from interviews with the author, Los Angeles and London, 1998.

Michael Minor's letter appeared in the *Hollywood Reporter*, 16 June 1977. 'The Dream Factory Woke up' in *Life* magazine, March 1970. Peter Kuran interviewed by Paul Mandell in *Fantastic Films* magazine, July 1980, and in *Cinefantastique*, May 1985. James Surowiecki on *Star Wars* toys from 'Toy Story: A *Star Wars* Tale for Your Holiday Enjoyment,' *Slate* magazine, 25 December 1989. Details on reaction of Danforth, Trumbull, and Dykstra to the *Star Wars* project from various websites, with additional information from Bill Warren. Some details of the setting up of ILM from *Industrial LightMagic: Into the Digital Realm*. 'He rang me once' from BBC TV *Omnibus*. Robert Watts quoted in interview by Jessie Horsting, *Fantastic Films*, 1984. Alsup on Borehamwood in *Skywalking*. Details of casting *Star Wars* are drawn from numerous sources, including David Halberstam's 'The Fugitive Star' and *Harrison Ford: Imperfect Hero*. Willard Huyck and Mark Hamill spoke about the casting in BBC TV *Omnibus*. Paul LeMat is quoted in *Empire* magazine, February 1999.

CHAPTER FOURTEEN : 'Put Some More Light on the Dog'

Quotes from Charley Lippincott and Gary Kurtz from interviews with the author, Los Angeles and London, 1998.

Many quotes about the conception, casting, and shooting of *Star Wars*, including interviews with Diane Crittenden, John Dykstra, Richard Edlund, Jim Nelson, and others, were first collected by Lee Rosenthal for 'The Empire Talks Back' in *Details* magazine, February 1987. Ralph McQuarrie on the design of Darth Vader *passim* from *Star Wars: From Concept to Screen to Collectible*. 'This was promoted as a low-budget movie' from *George Lucas: The Creative Impulse*. Champlin comparison with westerns and later description of the 'used future' concept from 'Futurist Film's Tricks to Treat the Eyes: Used Future Present and Accounted For,' *LA Times Calendar*, 20 June 1975. Dave Prowse on costume of Darth Vader from 'The Man Without a Face,' *Modesto Bee*, 22 May 1980. Anthony Daniels on his casting, including 'hated what I was doing,' from *People* magazine, 3 February 1997. Gloria Katz on the attitude of the *Star Wars* crew from BBC TV *Omnibus*. Scene in the garbage compactor described in 'From *American Graffiti* to Outer Space' by Donald Goddard, *New York Times*, 12 September 1976. Dave Prowse on relationship between Ford and Fisher from *Harrison Ford: Imperfect Hero*. 'How about a big cooking scene?' from *Starlog 71*, June 1983. Mark Hamill's 'They decided to nail me to the wall' from *US* magazine, 22 July 1980.

CHAPTER FIFTEEN : Saving *Star Wars*

All quotes from Charley Lippincott, Don Glut, Gary Kurtz, and Bill Warren from interviews with the author, Los Angeles, 1998.

'One of the worst periods of my life' from interview with Mitch Tuchman and Anne Thompson, *Film Comment*, July/August 1981. Scorsese on Lucas's reaction to *New York New York* and other quotes *passim* from *Scorsese on Scorsese*. Quotes from Nick Maley *passim* from his website cinesecrets.com. Mark Hamill on his injuries from *People* magazine, 18 July 1977. Alan Dean Foster from *Overstreet's Fan Magazine*, January 1996. Dave Prowse quoted in *Harrison Ford: Imperfect Hero*. Ben Burtt on the sound recording of the laser gun from *Details*. Numerous facts about the shooting of *Star Wars* from the invaluable double issue of *Cinefantastique*, Vol. 6 No. 4/Vol. 7 No. 1, 1978, including quotes from John Dykstra, Richard Edlund, Dennis Muren, Ken Ralston, Dave Prowse, Carrie Fisher, John Stears, Rick Baker, Phil Tippett, Ben Burtt, Ralph McQuarrie, and Gary Kurtz. The previews of *Star Wars* have been variously described, seldom with any agreement on details. This account was compiled from a number of sources, including interviews with Gloria Katz and Willard Huyck in BBC TV's *Omnibus*, *Easy Riders, Raging Bulls*, and *Scorsese on Scorsese*. Lucas on the readability or otherwise of the opening crawl from *Easy Riders, Raging Bulls*. Charley Lippincott quoted from '*Star Wars* All-Time Boxoffice Force,' *Variety*, 3 June

1987. John Williams on Lucas's briefing from *George Lucas: The Creative Impulse*. Quotes on recording the score from interview with David Thomas, *Total Film*, September 1997.

CHAPTER SIXTEEN : Twerp Cinema

All quotes from Charley Lippincott and Jon Davison from interviews with the author, Los Angeles, 1998.

Gareth Wigan quoted in *Empire Building: The Remarkable Real Life Story of Star Wars*. Atmosphere of editing room described by Eleanor Coppola in *Notes* and Carrie Fisher in 'An Empire of his Own' by Patrick Goldstein. Alan Dean Foster from *Overstreet's Fan Magazine*. Fluctuations in Fox stock and other effects of *Star Wars*' success detailed in 'The *Star Wars* Explosion,' *Time* magazine, 27 June 1977. Gareth Wigan and Adam Beckett quoted in *Empire Building*. Richard Corliss in *New Times*, 24 June 1977. John Williams on Joseph Campbell from *Total Film*, September 1997. Lucas's suit for copyright infringement against commercials for Reagan's 'Star Wars Initiative' reported in *Wall Street Journal*, 13 November 1985, and *Los Angeles Herald-Examiner*, 13 November 1985. Lucas on profits of *Star Wars* and Marcia Lucas quote from *Easy Riders, Raging Bulls*.

CHAPTER SEVENTEEN : Leaving Los Angeles

Quotes from John Milius, Charley Lippincott, Lawrence Kasdan, Don Glut, and Gary Kurtz from interviews with the author, Los Angeles and London, 1998.

Hamill on problems of stardom from *US* magazine, 22 July 1980 and others *passim People* magazine, 31 August 1981. Harrison Ford accounts of post-*Star Wars* fame from *Easy Riders, Raging Bulls*, and *Harrison Ford: Imperfect Hero*. 'Where are the guns?' from *Star Wars: From Concept to Screen to Collectible*. Lucas on slapstick comedy from 'The Stinky Kid Hits the Big Time' by Stephen Farber, *Film Quarterly*, Spring 1974. 'You should make a film about that' from *Easy Riders, Raging Bulls*. Other details of the relationship between Lucas and Coppola from *On the Edge*. William Flanagan on *Close Encounters* in *New York* magazine, 31 October 1977. Coppola on Lucas's Oscar wins from Eleanor Coppola in *Notes*.

CHAPTER EIGHTEEN : Writing *Raiders*

Quotes from Lawrence Kasdan and Gary Kurtz from interviews with the author, Los Angeles and London, 1998.

Some additional quotes from Kasdan, including account of first version of *Raiders of the Lost Ark*, from 'Dialogue with Lawrence Kasdan,' *American*

Film magazine, July 1982, and interview with James H. Burns, *Starlog* magazine, September 1981. Details of Kurosawa's Californian visit from report by Audie Bock in *Take One* magazine, March 1979. Glen A. Larson on *Battlestar Galactica* in *Science Fantasy Film Classics* magazine, October 1978. Other material from article in *Future* 6, November 1978. Lucas's application to build Skywalker Ranch detailed in various news reports, including 'Lucas Marin Film Center is in Orbit,' *San Francisco Chronicle*, 11 September 1979. Norton on Kazanjian from *Los Angeles Times*, 1 August 1979. Additional information on the filming of *More American Graffiti* from *Los Angeles Times* article on Norton, 1 August 1979, and 'Sixties Slapstick,' a joint interview with Norton and Charles Martin Smith, *Films and Filming* magazine, October 1979.

CHAPTER NINETEEN : *The Empire Strikes Back*

Quotes from Lawrence Kasdan, Harley Cokeliss, Don Glut, and Gary Kurtz from interviews with the author, Los Angeles and London, 1998.

'George Lucas effectively moved the summer' from '*Star Wars* is Ten, and Lucas Reflects,' *New York Times*, 21 May 1987. Nick Maley from www.cinesecrets. 'You don't want people to say that he's German or Japanese' from interview with Gene Siskel, *New York Daily News*, 22 May 1983. Lucas briefing Kershner is described in various places, including 'An Empire of his Own' by Patrick Goldstein. Quotes from Billy Dee Williams *passim* from interview with Bob Woods for *Starlog* magazine, June 1980, and *People* magazine, 7 July 1980. Some details of Norway shooting from interview with special-effects co-supervisor Brian Johnson by David Hutchison, *Starlog*, June 1980. Others from 'Of Ice Planets, Bog Planets and Cities in the Sky' by Don Shay in *Cinefex* 2, August 1980. Kurtz as Lucas's *consiglieri* from 'George Lucas Goes Far Out' by Stephen Zito, *American Film* magazine, April 1977. Ford on working with Irvin Kershner, and tension between Fisher and Ford from *Harrison Ford: Imperfect Hero*. Howard Kazanjian profiled by Richard Combs in *Monthly Film Bulletin*, June 1983. Premiere of *More American Graffiti* from *Easy Riders, Raging Bulls*. Dave Prowse quoted in 'The Man Without a Face,' *Modesto Bee*, 22 May 1980. 'It was excruciating' from 'Last of the *Star Wars* Dramas' by Audie Bock, *Modesto Bee*, 18 August 1982.

CHAPTER TWENTY : *Raiders of the Lost Ark*

Quotes from Gary Kurtz, Charley Lippincott, Lawrence Kasdan, and John Milius from interviews with the author, London and Los Angeles, 1998. Some comments by Kasdan are from interview with James H. Burns in *Starlog*.

'Cloistered' said by Scott Ross and quoted by Patrick Goldstein in 'An Empire of his Own.' Brian Johnson quoted from interview with David Hutchison, *Starlog*, June 1980. Negotiations between Lucas and Michael Eisner detailed in 'Par Floating Lucasfilm's *Ark*' in *Variety*, 30 November 1979, and 'Paramount in Deal for *Lost Ark* and Four Sequels,' *Variety*, 5 December 1979. Ben Stein on Spielberg's failure in 'A Deal to Remember,' *New West* magazine, August 1981. 'I thought I was immune to failure' from *Time* magazine, 31 May 1982. 'Instead of having twenty-five rubber masks' from 'George Lucas Wants to Play Guitar' by Paul Scanlon, *Rolling Stone*, 21 July–4 August 1983. Marcia's complaints to Lucas detailed in *Easy Riders, Raging Bulls*. 'People can be big pests' from interview with Joanne Williams, *San Francisco Herald-Examiner*, 21 May 1980. Description of The Egg Company premises from *In Cinema*, July 1980. Harrison Ford on his Indiana Jones persona and shooting in Tunisia from interview with Michael Sragow, *Rolling Stone*, September 1981. Lucas on 'making money out of money' from 'Two who Made the Revolution' by David Osborne. Sale of Tillie Lewis factories reported in *Modesto Bee*, 7 May 1981.

CHAPTER TWENTY-ONE : Fortress Lucas

Quotes from Gary Kurtz, Randy Thom, Jon Davison, Richard Walter, Lawrence Kasdan, and John Milius from interviews with the author, Los Angeles, Sausalito, and London, 1998.

'LA is an aberration' from interview in *Starlog* magazine, September 1981. Lucas's statement on intellectual copyright quoted in *Washington Post*, 1 March 1988. Fritz Koening quoted from TMH website (www.tmhlabs.com). Lucasfilm's official position on THX and TAP dealt with in detail in the 'Tenth Anniversary Issue' of *Hollywood Reporter*, June 1993. Other material from the official Lucasfilm website (www.lucasfilm.com). Profile of Lucas and Weber in 'The Empire Pays Off' by Stratford P. Sherman, *Fortune* magazine, 6 October 1980. Zoning permission for Sykwalker Ranch reported in *San Francisco Chronicle*, 11 September 1979. Lucas on function of Skywalker Ranch in interview with Audie Bock, *Take One*, May 1979. Workmen on craftsmanship at ranch reported in 'Two who Made the Revolution' by David Osborne. Resignation from DGA detailed in 'George Lucas Cuts H'wood Ties; Directors Guild "Protects" Members Against their own Preferences' in *Variety*, 8 April 1981. 'I don't have to work for a living' from interview with Aljean Harmetz, reprinted in *Rolling Breaks and Other Movie Business* (Knopf, New York, 1983). Many details of shooting on *Return of the Jedi* from 'Jedi Journal,' *Cinefex 13*, July 1983. Lucas on Marquand from interview with Mitch Tuchman and Anne Thompson, *Republic Scene*, December 1981. Marquand on working with Lucas from interview in *Science Fiction Filmmaking in the 1980s* (McFarland, Jefferson, NC, 1995). Lucas on ewok toys, *San Francisco Star*, 28 June 1983. 'I'm glad I did *Jedi*,' Harrison Ford to Tony Crawley, Deauville, 1982, in *Starburst 53*.

CHAPTER TWENTY-TWO : Snake Surprise

Quotes from Richard Walter and Lawrence Kasdan from interviews with the author, Los Angeles, 1998.

Lucas on Marcia's career in interview with Mitch Tuchman and Anne Thompson, *Film Comment*, July/August 1981. Ronda Gomez quoted in *Easy Riders, Raging Bulls*. Marcia Lucas also profiled in *Playgirl*, April 1976. 'I'm always sort of living for tomorrow' in *Rolling Stone*, 12 June 1980. 'I see her a couple of hours every night' and 'It's been very hard on Marcia' from 'George Lucas Wants to Play Guitar' by Paul Scanlon, *Rolling Stone*. Lucas's announcement of divorce was covered in 'Lucas, Wife Split,' *Variety*, 22 June 1983, and the *Modesto Bee*, 'The Lucases Plan "Amicable" Divorce,' 16 June 1983. Details of Harrison Ford's injury on *Temple of Doom*, Lucas's tributes to his courage, etc., quoted in *Harrison Ford: Imperfect Hero*. Details of Spielberg's reunion with Amy Irving from *McCalls*, June 1985, *Ladies Home Journal*, March 1989, *US*, 3 October 1988, *People* magazine, 27 March 1988 and 7 August 1989, and *Los Angeles Times*, 17 April 1984.

CHAPTER TWENTY-THREE : *Howard the Duck*

'The divorce kind of destroyed me' and Spielberg's claim of its impact on him from *60 Minutes*, CBS TV, April 1999. 'Sabotaged his business' from *Easy Riders, Raging Bulls*. Quotes from Piper Laurie, Lucas, and Coppola on Disney's attempt to close down *Return to Oz* from 'Retouching Evil' by Michael Sragow. Other details from author's conversations with Jean Marsh and Harley Cokeliss, London, 1998. Schrader on *Mishima* from *Schrader on Schrader*. Steven Schiff on *Temple of Doom* in *Vanity Fair*, September 1984. Lucas's relationship with Linda Ronstadt reported in *People* magazine, 26 March 1984. Possible production of 'The Clone Wars' noted in *Cinefantastique*, September 1984. John Whitney on synthetic film in *Industrial LightMagic: Into the Digital Realm*. Lucas on Pixar in '30 Minutes With the Grandfather of Digital Cinema,' by Don Shay, *Cinefex*, May 1996. Lucas on Joseph Campbell and 'most of my friends are college professors' from *New York Times*, 20 October 1994. Details of problems over *Captain Eo* from *Cinefantastique*, January 1987. Willard Huyck on *Howard the Duck* from the same issue. Location shooting in Modesto area covered in *Modesto Bee*, 27 March 1986. Similarities to *E.T.* noted in *People* magazine, 24 February 1986. 'A turkey for the ages' and Lucas's comments from *Philadelphia Inquirer*, 1 February 1987. *Cinefantastique* review in issue of January 1987.

CHAPTER TWENTY-FOUR : The Height of Failure

'George Lucas Moves to Produce TV Shows, Movies in Volume' by Michael Cieply, *Wall Street Journal*, 22 January 1986. Lucas's attempts to enlarge

Skywalker Ranch and resulting conflict with the Marin County authorities detailed by Susan Braudy in *Los Angeles Times Calendar*, 15 May 1988, and 'Bureaucracy Brings Lucas Down to Earth,' *Modesto Bee*, 3 April 1988. Some details of Scott Ross's experience with Lucasfilm from 'Digital Deal' by Matt Rothman, *Wired* magazine, July–August 1993. Interview with Ross by Mark London Phillips, 'Building a Domain,' *Los Angeles Times*, 10 July 1998. Ron Howard on *Willow* from film's production notes. Aljean Harmetz's comments from 'A Pained Lucas Ponders Attacks on *Willow*' in *New York Times*, 9 June 1988. 'I worry about those gray-flannel types' from 'George Lucas: Hollywood Won't do my New Film' by Bob Thomas, *Trentonian*, 28 January 1987. 'George Lucas is like Zorro' from film's production notes. Michael Gleason on special effects for *Willow* in *Cinefex 35*, August 1988. 'Reworking the genre' from 'A Pained Lucas Ponders Attacks on *Willow*.' Description of Cannes press conference by Michael Cieply from *Modesto Bee*, 27 May 1988, reprinted from *Los Angeles Times*. The long-term significance of morphing discussed in 'They put the ILM in Film,' *Time* magazine, 13 April 1992. Lucas on *Tucker passim* from 'Coppola and Lucas: Motor Mouths' in *Time Out*, 2 November 1988, and 'The Road Warrior,' *American Film*, June 1988. Coppola's 'I lost some of my confidence' and Lucas's response in 'George Lucas. Hot-Rodding Down the Street of Dreams' by Michael Sragow, *Los Angeles Herald-Examiner*, 10 August 1988.

CHAPTER TWENTY-FIVE : *Indiana Jones and the Last Crusade*

Quotes from Gary Kurtz from interview with the author, London, 1998.

Lawrence Kasdan on the Grail motif from 'Kasdan on Kasdan' in *Projections 3* (Faber, London, 1994). Hal Hinson in 'Indiana's Hooey Grail: The Last, Limp Spielberg Installment,' *Washington Post*, 24 March 1989. Details of negotiations for sale of Elstree from 'Lucas: Interested in Elstree at Right Price,' *Variety*, 8 July 1988, 'Lucas May Try to Buy Elstree,' *New York Times*, 8 July 1988, 'Lucas Blasts Elstree Closure; Leads Charge to Save Studios,' *Hollywood Reporter*, 8 July 1988. Lucas on commercial prospects for *The Young Indiana Jones Chronicles* in 'Lucas Won't Fight TV's Rating Wars,' *USA Today*, 16 September 1992. Coverage of *Young Indiana Jones Chronicles*' opening program includes 'Lucas: *Young Indiana* Doesn't Follow Formulas' and review by Miles Beller in *Hollywood Reporter*, 4 March 1992. Also Lucas's 'Indiana Jones and Me' in *TV Guide*, 19 February 1992. Poor reactions and resulting scaling-back reported in 'ABC Gives *Indiana* a Third Try,' *Los Angeles Times Calendar*, 9 March 1993. Background to production of *Radioland Murders* from *Los Angeles Times Calendar*, 20 June 1993, Richard Schickel review of *Radioland Murders* in *Time* magazine, 24 October 1994. Hoyt Yeatman on ILM in *New York Newsday*, 21 February 1992. Scott Ross from interview with Rob Letterman and Shahril Ibrahim (www2.cinenet.net). Corporate changes in the wake of Scott Ross's departure covered in 'Lucas Empire Splitting in 2,' *Variety*, 10 August 1992.

CHAPTER TWENTY-SIX : Back to the Future

Howard Roffman quoted in *The Unauthorized Star Wars Compendium*. Lucas 'Cyber Elite' listing, *Time* magazine, 15 September 1997. The sag in Lucasfilm's fortunes described in 'George Lucas Moves to Produce TV Shows, Movies in Volume' by Michael Cieply, *Wall Street Journal*. Lucas quotes *passim* from interview with Ron Magid in *American Cinematographer*, February 1997. Lucas to Audie Bock in *Modesto Bee*, 18 August 1982. Frank Darabont on *Young Indiana Jones* from *The Unauthorized Star Wars Compendium*. James Surowiecki in 'Toy Story: A *Star Wars* Tale for Your Holiday Enjoyment' in *Slate*. Negotiations on merchandise for new *Star Wars* films from numerous sources, including *Star Wars: From Concept to Screen to Collectible*. Rivalry between Lucas and Spielberg mentioned in Audie Bock interview, *Take One*. Lucas on restoration of *Star Wars* trilogy in interview with Kevin Kelly and Paula Parisi, *Wired* magazine, February 1997. Rick McCallum and John Knoll on restoration in *American Cinematographer*, February 1997. Lucas on digital production in 'Digital Studios: It's the Economy, Stupid,' *New York Times*, 25 December 1995, 'Computers: George Lucas and the Tech Revolution in Filmmaking' in *Los Angeles Times*, 4 June 1995, and 'Digital Yoda' in *Los Angeles Times*, 11 June 1995. First estimates of budgets from 'The Lucas Wars,' *Time* magazine, 30 September 1996. Harley Cokeliss quoted from interview with the author, London, 1998. Reports on the deal to make *Phantom Menace* include 'Lucas Cuts Deal with Fox for next *Star Wars*' in *Los Angeles Times*, 3 April 1998. Report on Lucas's decision to relocate ILM in San Francisco from '*Star Wars* Creator Plans Empire's Move' by Mary Curtius, *Los Angeles Times*, 8 February 1999. Rick McCallum on opportunities for film production in Australia from 'Movie-Making Grows in Australia' by Rohan Sullivan, Associated Press Online, 13 January 1999.

FILMOGRAPHY

1965
Look at Life
Also scripted, edited, and photographed.

Freiheit
Also scripted, edited, and photographed.

1966
Herbie
Co-directed with Paul Golding

1:42:08: A Man and his Car
Also photographed and scripted.

1967
The Emperor
Also scripted, edited, and photographed.

THX 1138:4EB (later retitled *THX1138 4EB: Electronic Labyrinth*)
Also scripted and edited.

6/18/67
Also scripted, photographed, and edited.

anyone lived in a pretty (how) town
Co-directed and co-scripted with Paul Golding, from a poem by e.e. cummings.

1968
filmmaker: a film diary
Also scripted, edited, and photographed.

FEATURES

THX1138 (Released 11 March 1971)

An American Zoetrope Production. A Warner Brothers release. Executive producer Lawrence Sturhahn. Director George Lucas. Screenplay by George Lucas and Walter Murch, based on a story by George Lucas. Edited by George Lucas. Art direction by Michael Haller. Photography by Dave Meyers and Albert Kihn. Music by Lalo Schifrin. Sound by Walter Murch, Louis Yates, Jim Manson.

Featuring: Robert Duvall, Donald Pleasence, Don Pedro Colley, Maggie McOmie, Ian Wolfe.

American Graffiti (Released 1 August 1973)

A Lucasfilm Ltd/Coppola Company Production. A Universal Pictures release. Producer Francis Ford Coppola. Director George Lucas. Screenplay by George Lucas, Gloria Katz, and Willard Huyck. Edited by Verna Fields and Marcia Lucas. Art direction by Denis Clark. Visual Consultant Haskell Wexler. Directors of Photography Ron Eveslage and Jan D'Alquen. Sound montage and rerecording by Walter Murch. Costume design by Agnes Guerard Rodgers.

Featuring: Richard Dreyfuss, Ron Howard, Paul LeMat, Charlie Martin Smith, Cindy Williams, Candy Clark, McKenzie Phillips, Wolfman Jack, Harrison Ford, Bo Hopkins, Manuel Padilla, Jr., Bo Gentry.

Star Wars (Released 25 May 1977)

A Lucasfilm Ltd Production. A Twentieth Century-Fox release. Executive producer George Lucas. Producer Gary Kurtz. Written and directed by George Lucas. Edited by Paul Hirsch, Marcia Lucas, and Richard Chew. Production design by John Barry. Photography by Gilbert Taylor, B.S.C. Music by John Williams. Special dialogue and sound effects by Ben Burtt. Special Photographic Effects Supervisor John Dykstra. Costume design by John Mollo.

Featuring: Mark Hamill, Harrison Ford, Carrie Fisher, Alec Guinness, Anthony Daniels, Peter Mayhew, Kenny Baker, Peter Cushing, David Prowse.

More American Graffiti (Released 3 August 1979)

A Lucasfilm Ltd Production. A Universal Pictures release. Executive producer George Lucas. Producer Howard Kazanjian. Written and directed by B. W. L. Norton, based on characters created by George Lucas, Gloria Katz, and Willard Huyck. Edited by Tina Hirsch. Art direction by Ray Storey. Director of Photography Caleb Deschanel. Costume design by Agnes Rodgers.

Featuring: Candy Clark, Bo Hopkins, Ron Howard, Cindy Williams, Paul LeMat, McKenzie Phillips, Charlie Martin Smith.

The Empire Strikes Back (Released 21 May 1980)

A Lucasfilm Ltd Production. A Twentieth Century-Fox release. Executive producer George Lucas. Producer Gary Kurtz. Director Irvin Kershner.

Screenplay by Leigh Brackett and Lawrence Kasdan, from a story by George Lucas. Edited by Paul Hirsch, A.C.E. Production design by Norman Reynolds. Director of Photography Peter Suschitzsky, B.S.C. Music by John Williams. Sound design by Ben Burtt. Special visual effects by Brian Johnson and Richard Edlung, A.S.C. Costume design by John Mollo.

Featuring: Mark Hamill, Harrison Ford, Carrie Fisher, Billy Dee Williams, Alec Guinness, Anthony Daniels, Kenny Baker, Peter Mayhew, Frank Oz, David Prowse.

Raiders of the Lost Ark (Released 12 June 1981)

A Lucasfilm Ltd Production. A Paramount Pictures release. Executive producers George Lucas and Howard Kazanjian. Producer Frank Marshall. Director Steven Spielberg. Screenplay by Lawrence Kasdan, from a story by George Lucas and Philip Kaufman. Edited by Michael Kahn, A.C.E. Production design by Norman Reynolds. Director of Photography Douglas Slocombe. Music by John Williams. Sound design by Ben Burtt. Visual Efects Supervisor Richard Edlund, A.S.C. Costume design by Deborah Nadoolman.

Featuring: Harrison Ford, Karen Allen, John Rhys-Davies, Denholm Elliott, Paul Freeman, Ronald Lacey.

Twice Upon a Time (Released August 1982) Animation

A Kirty Films and Lucasfilm Ltd Presentation. A Ladd Company Production. A Warner Brothers release. Executive producer George Lucas. Producer Bill Couturie. Produced and directed by John Korty and Charles Swenson. Screenplay by John Korty, Charles Swenson, Suella Kennedy, Bill Couturie. Story by John Korty, Bill Couturie, Suella Kennedy. Edited by Jennifer Gallagher. Art direction by Harley Jessup. Music by Dawn Atkinson and Ken Melville. Sound design by Walt Kraemer.

Featuring the voices of Marshall Efron, Hamilton Camp, Paul Frees, Judith Kahan Kampmann, James Cranna, Julie Payne.

Return of the Jedi (Released 25 May 1983)

A Lucasfilm Ltd Production. A Twentieth Century-Fox release. Executive producer George Lucas. Producer Howard Kazanjian. Director Richard Marquand. Screenplay by Lawrence Kasdan and George Lucas, from a story by George Lucas. Edited by Sean Barton, Marcia Lucas, and Duwayne Dunham. Production design by Norman Reynolds. Director of Photography Alan Hume, B.S.C. Music by John Williams. Sound design by Ben Burtt. Visual effects by Richard Edlund, A.S.C., Dennis Muren, Ken Ralston. Costume design by Aggie Guerard Rodgers and Nilo Rodis-Jamero.

Featuring: Harrison Ford, Mark Hamill, Carrie Fisher, Billy Dee Williams, Anthony Daniels, Peter Mayhew, Alec Guinness, James Earl Jones, Sebastian Shaw, Ian McDiarmid, Frank Oz, David Prowse.

Indiana Jones and the Temple of Doom (Released 23 May 1984)

A Lucasfilm Ltd Production. A Paramount Pictures release. Executive producers George Lucas and Frank Marshall. Producer Robert Watts. Director Steven Spielberg. Screenplay by Willard Huyck and Gloria Katz, based on a story by George Lucas. Edited by Michael Kahn, A.C.E. Production design by Elliott Scott. Director of Photography Douglas Slocombe. Music by John Williams. Sound design by Ben Burtt. Visual Effects Supervisor Dennis Muren. Costume design by Anthony Powell.

Featuring: Harrison Ford, Kate Capshaw, Ke Huy Quan, Philip Stone, Amrish Puri, Roshan Seth.

Mishima (Released September 1985)

A Francis Ford Coppola and George Lucas Presentation. A Zoetrope Studios/Filmlink Intl (Tokyo)/Lucasfilm Ltd Production. A Warner Brothers release. Executive producers George Lucas and Francis Coppola. Director Paul Schrader. Screenplay by Paul and Leonard Schrader. Edited by Michael Chandler. Production design by Eiko Ishioka. Director of Photography John Bailey. Music by Philip Glass. Sound design by Leslie Shatz. Costume design by Etsuko Yagyu.

Featuring: Ken Ogala, Ken Sawada, Yasosuke Bando, Masayuki Shionoya, Toshi Yuki Nagashima.

Latino (Released February 1986)

A Lucasfilm Ltd Presentation. A Cinecom International release. Producer Benjamin Berg. Director Haskell Wexler. Screenplay by Haskell Wexler. Edited by Robert Dalva. Director of Photography Tome Sigel. Music by Diane Louie.

Featuring: Robert Beltran, Annette Cardona, Tony Plana.

Labyrinth (Released 27 June 1986)

A Henson Associates and Lucasfilm Ltd Presentation. A Tri-Star release. Executive producer George Lucas. Producer Eric Rattray. Director Jim Henson. Screenplay by Terry Jones, from a story by Dennis Less and Jim Henson. Edited by John Grover. Production design by Elliott Scott. Conceptual design by Brian Froud. Director of Photography Alex Thomson, B.S.C. Score composed by Trevor Jones. Songs composed and performed by David Bowie. Special Effects Supervisor George Gibbs. Costume design by Brian Froud and Ellis Flyte.

Featuring: David Bowie, Jennifer Connelly, Toby Froud.

Howard the Duck (Released 1 August 1986)

A Lucasfilm Ltd Production. A Universal Pictures release. Executive producer George Lucas. Producer Gloria Katz. Director Willard Huyck. Screenplay by Willard Huyck and Gloria Katz, based on the Marvel Comics character created by Steve Gerber. Edited by Michael Chandler and Sidney Wolinsky. Director of Photography Richard H. Kline, A.S.C. Production design by Peter Jamison. Music by John Barry. Sound design by Randy Thom. Visual Effects Supervisor Michael J. McAllister. Costume Designer Joe Thompkins.

Featuring: Lea Thompson, Jeffrey Jones, Tim Robbins, Ed Gale, Chip Zien.

Captain Eo (Released at Disneyland 13 September 1986)

A George Lucas Presentation. Executive producer George Lucas. Producer Rusty Lemorande. Director Francis Ford Coppola. Screenplay by George Lucas. Art direction by Geoffrey Kirkland. Cinematography Consultant Vittorio Storaro. Choreography by Jeffrey Homaday. Music by Michael Jackson. Theater and Costume Consultant John Napier.

Featuring: Michael Jackson, Anjelica Huston.

Willow (Released 20 May 1988)

A Lucasfilm Ltd Production in association with Imagine Entertainment. An MGM-UA release. Executive producer George Lucas. Producer Nigel Wooll. Director Ron Howard. Screenplay by Bob Dolman, from a story by George Lucas. Edited by Daniel Hanley and Michael Hill. Production design by Allan Cameron. Director of Photography Adrian Biddle, B.S.C. Music by James Horner. Sound design by Ben Burtt. Visual effects by Industrial Light and Magic (Dennis Muren, Michael J. McAllister, Phil Tippett). Costume design by Barbara Lane.

Featuring: Val Kilmer, Warwick Davis, Joanne Whalley, Jean Marsh, Patricia Hayes, Billy Barty, Pat Roach, Gavan O'Herlihy.

Tucker: The Man and his Dream (Released 12 August 1988)

A Lucasfilm Ltd/Zoetrope Studios Production. A Paramount Pictures release. Executive producer George Lucas. Producers Fred Roos and Fred Fuchs. Director Francis Ford Coppola. Screenplay by Arnold Schulman and David Seidler. Edited by Priscilla Nedd. Production design by Dean Tavoularis. Cinematography by Vittorio Storaro, A.I.C. Music by Joe Jackson. Sound design by Richard Beggs. Costume design by Milena Canonero.

Featuring: Jeff Bridges, Martin Landau, Joan Allen, Frederic Forrest, Mako, Dean Stockwell.

Indiana Jones and the Last Crusade (Released 24 May 1989)

A Lucasfilm Ltd Production. A Paramount Pictures release. Executive producers George Lucas and Frank Marshall. Producer Robert Watts. Director Steven Spielberg. Screenplay by Jeff Boam, from a story by George Lucas and Menno Meyjes. Edited by Michael Kahn, A.C.E. Production design by Eliot Scott. Director of Photography Douglas Slocombe. Music by John Williams. Sound design by Ben Burtt. Visual Effects Supervisor Michael J. McAllister. Costume design by Anthony Powell.

Featuring: Harrison Ford, Sean Connery, Denholm Elliott, Alison Doody, John Rhys-Davies, Julian Glover.

The Phantom Menace (Released 19 May 1999)

A Lucasfilm Ltd Production. A Twentieth Century-Fox release. Executive producer George Lucas. Producer Rick McCallum. Director George Lucas. Screenplay by George Lucas. Edited by Ben Burtt and Paul Martin Smith. Production design by Gavin Bocquet. Director of Photography David Tattersall. Music by John Williams. Sound design by Ben Burtt. Senior Visual Effects Supervisor Dennis Muren. Special Effects Supervisors Peter Hutchinson, John Knoll, Scott Squires.

Featuring: Liam Neeson, Ewan McGregor, Natalie Portman, Jake Lloyd, Pernilla August, Ian McDiarmid, Terence Stamp, Ray Park, Samuel L. Jackson, Warwick Davis, Kenny Baker, Anthony Daniels.

TELEVISION FILMS

The Star Wars Holiday Special (First broadcast on CBS 17 November 1978)

A Smith-Hemion production for CBS, in association with Lucasfilm Ltd. Produced by Dwight Hemion. Animated section by Nelvana Films. Directed by David Acumba. Original story (uncredited) by George Lucas. Script by Lenny Ripps.

Featuring: Harrison Ford, Mark Hamill, Carrie Fisher, Peter Mayhew, Bea Arthur, Diahann Carroll, Harvey Korman, Art Carney.

The Ewok Adventure: Caravan of Courage (First broadcast on ABC 25 November 1984)

A Lucasfilm Ltd and Korty Films Production. Executive producer George Lucas. Producer Thomas G. Smith. Director John Korty. Screenplay by Bob Carrau, from a story by George Lucas. Edited by John Nutt. Production design by Joe Johnston. Director of Photography John Korty. Music by Peter Bernstein. Sound design by Randy Thom. Visual Effects Supervisor Michael Pangrazio. Costume design by Cathleen Edwards and Michael Becker.

Featuring: Eric Walker, Warwick Davis, Fionnula Flanagan, Aubree Miller.

Ewoks and Droids Adventure Hour (*Ewoks and Droids: The Adventure of R2-D2 and C-3PO*. Animation. First-season initial broadcast on ABC 12 September 1985)

A Nelvana Production in association with Lucasfilm Ltd. Executive producer Miki Herman. Supervising Editor Rob Kirkpatrick. Music by Taj Mahal (Ewoks) and Stewart Copeland (Droids).

Featuring the voices of Jim Henshaw and Cree Summer Francks (Ewoks), and Anthony Daniels (Droids).

Ewoks: The Battle for Endor (First broadcast on ABC 24 November 1985)

A Lucasfilm Ltd Production. Executive producer George Lucas. Producer Thomas G. Smith. Written and directed by Jim and Ken Wheat, based on a story by George Lucas. Edited by Eric Jenkins. Production design by Joe Johnston and Harley Jessup. Director of Photography Isidore Mankofsky, A.S.C. Music by Peter Bernstein. Sound design by Randy Thom. Visual Effects Supervisor Michael J. McAllister. Costume Supervisor Michael Becker.

Featuring: Wilford Brimley, Aubree Miller, Warwick Davis, Sian Phillips.

The Great Heep (First broadcast on ABC 7 June 1986)

A Nelvana Production for Lucasfilm Ltd, based on characters created by George Lucas. Executive producer Miki Herman. Director Clive Smith. Screenplay by Ben Burtt. Production design by Joe Johnston. Music by Patricia Cullen and Patrick Gleeson, with songs by Stewart Copeland and Derek Holt. Sound design by Ben Burtt.

Featuring: Anthony Daniels, Long John Baldry, Winston Rekert, Graeme Campbell.

Ewoks (Animation. Second-season initial broadcast on ABC 1 November 1986)

A Lucasfilm Ltd Production in association with Nelvana. Executive producers Cliff Ruby and Elana Lesser. Story Editor Paul Dini. Production design by Kirk Henderson. Music by Patrick Gleeson.

Featuring the voices of James Cranna, Sue Murphy, Denny Delk, Jeanne Reynolds.

Maniac Mansion (First broadcast on the Family Channel 14 September 1990)

Produced by Atlantis Films Ltd in association with the Family Channel and YTV/Canada, Inc. and Lucasfilm Ltd Television. Based on the original computer game by Lucasfilm Games. Executive producers Peter Sussman,

Eugene Levy, and Barry Jossen. Series created by Michael Short, Eugene Levy, David Flaherty, and John Hemphill. Developed for television by Cliff Ruby, Elana Lesser, and Bob Carrau. Production design by Stephen Roleff. Director of Photography Ray Braunstein. Music by Louis Natale.

Featuring: Joe Flaherty, Deb Faker, Cathleen Robertson, George Buza, Mary Charlotte Wilcox, John Hemphill.

The Young Indiana Jones Chronicles (First broadcast on ABC 4 March 1992)

A Lucasfilm Ltd Production. Executive producer George Lucas. Produced by Rick McCallum. Directed by Jim O'Brien, Carl Schultz, René Manzor, Bille August, Nicolas Roeg, Simon Wincer, Terry Jones, Gavin Millar, Vic Armstrong, and Deepa Mehta. Screenplays by Jonathan Hales, Rosemary Anne Sisson, Reg Gadney, Jonathan Hensleigh, Matthew Jacobs, Carrie Fisher, Frank Darabont, and Gavin Scott, from a story by George Lucas. Edited by Edgar Burcksen, Louise Rubacky, and Ben Burtt. Production design by Gavin Bocquet. Directors of Photography David Tattersall, Oliver Stapleton, Miguel Icaza Solana, Jorgen Persson, and Giles Nuttgens. Music by Laurence Rosenthal and Joel McNeely. Costume design by Charlotte Holdich.

Featuring: Sean Patrick Flanery, Corey Carrier, Margaret Tyzack, Ruth De Sosa, Lloyd Owen, George Hall, Ronny Coutteure.

NON-LUCASFILM PRODUCTIONS

Kagemusha (The Shadow Warrior) (Released October 1980)

A Twentieth Century-Fox release. A film by Akira Kurosawa. Executive producers of the international version George Lucas and Francis Coppola.

Body Heat (Released August 1981)

A Warner Brothers release. A Ladd Company Presentation. Written and directed by Lawrence Kasdan. Executive producer (uncredited) George Lucas.

Return to Oz (Released June 1985)

A Buena Vista release. Directed and co-written by Walter Murch. Credit at end: 'Special Thanks to Robert Watts and George Lucas.'

Powaqqatsi (Released April 1988)

A Cannon Group release. A Francis Coppola and George Lucas Presentation. A film by Godfrey Reggio.

The Land Before Time (Released November 1988) Animated feature

A Universal Pictures release. A Don Bluth production. Executive producers Steven Spielberg and George Lucas. Script by Stu Krieger, from a story by Judy Freudberg and Tony Geiss.

BIBLIOGRAPHY

Biskind, Peter, *Easy Riders, Raging Bulls: How the Sex-Drugs-and Rock'n'Roll Generation Saved Hollywood*, Simon & Schuster, 1998

Bova, Ben, *THX1138* (novelization of the screenplay by George Lucas and Walter Murch), Warners, New York, 1971

Champlin, Charles, *George Lucas: The Creative Impulse*, Virgin, New York, 1992

Coppola, Eleanor, *Notes*, Simon & Schuster, New York, 1979

Cowie, Peter, *Coppola*, André Deutsch, London, 1989

Edwards, Ted, *The Unauthorized Star Wars Companion*, Little, Brown, New York, 1999

Glut, Don, *The Empire Strikes Back* (based on a story by George Lucas), Warners, New York, 1995

Goodwin, Michael, and Wise, Naomi, *On the Edge: The Life and Times of Francis Coppola*, William Morrow, New York, 1989

Jackson, Kevin (editor), *Schrader on Schrader and Other Writings*, Faber, London, 1990

Jacobs, Diane, *Hollywood Renaissance*, Delta, New York, 1980

Jenkins, Garry, *Empire Building: The Remarkable Real Life Story of Star Wars*, Simon & Schuster, New York, 1997

Jenkins, Garry, *Harrison Ford: Imperfect Hero*, Simon & Schuster, London, 1997

Kahn, James, *Return of the Jedi* (based on a screenplay by Lawrence Kasdan and George Lucas, and a story by Lucas), Little, Brown, New York, 1996

Lucas, George, with Huyck, Willard, and Katz, Gloria, *American Graffiti: The Screenplay*, Ballantine, New York, 1973

Lucas, George, and others, *Star Wars: The Scripts*, Boxtree, London, 1995

Lucas, George (actually Foster, Alan Dean), *Star Wars* (a novelization), Warner, London, 1995

McQuarrie, Ralph, and Anderson, Kevin J., *The Illustrated Star Wars Universe*, Bantam, New York, 1997

Madsen, Axel, *The New Hollywood: American Movies in the '70s*, Thomas E. Crowell, New York, 1975

Mangels, Andy, *Star Wars: The Essential Guide to Characters*, Ballantine, New York, 1995

Minahan, John, *The Complete American Graffiti* (novelized from the

screenplays of William Huyck, Gloria Katz, George Lucas, and
B.W.L. Norton), MCA, London, 1979

Pollock, Dale, *Skywalking: The Life and Films of George Lucas*, Harmony,
New York, 1983

Slavicsek, Bill, *A Guide to the Star Wars Universe*, Boxtree, London, 1995

Stansweet, Stephen J., *Star Wars: From Concept to Screen to Collectible*,
Chronicle, San Francisco, 1999

Thompson, David, and Christie, Ian (editors), *Scorsese on Scorsese*, Faber,
London, 1989

Titelman, Carol (editor), *The Art of Star Wars: Episode IV, A New Hope*,
Ballantine, New York, 1997 (In the same series, Ballantine also
published *The Art of Star Wars: Episode V, The Empire Strikes Back*,
edited by Deborah Call, with text by Vic Bullock and Valerie
Hoffman, with Mark Cotta Vaz, and *The Art of Star Wars: Episode VI,
Return of the Jedi*, no editor indicated)

Vaz, Mark Cotta, with Hata, Shinji, *From Star Wars to Indiana Jones: The
Best of the Lucasfilm Archives*, Chronicle, San Francisco, 1994

Vaz, Mark Cotta, with Duignan, Patricia Rose, *Industrial Light+Magic: Into
the Digital Realm*, Ballantine, New York, 1996

INDEX